"ENGAGING."
—*The New York Times Book Review*

Forget IBM. The real history of computers begins here.
HACKERS
Heroes of the Computer Revolution

"A WELL-WRITTEN, INTERESTING ACCOUNT OF AN IMPORTANT PIECE OF CURRENT HISTORY . . . This reviewer enjoyed the book immensely."—*Choice*

"FUN TO READ . . . Numerous fascinating mini-biographies of the many individuals who by now are near legendary in computer and business circles—Steve Wozniak, Ken Williams, John Draper (Captain Crunch)."—*Library Journal*

"LIVELY, ENTERTAINING."—*Publishers Weekly*

"NOT A BOOK FOR BUFFS ONLY . . . Good solid character-sketching . . . becomes an interesting exercise in technological history and cultural change."—*Kirkus Reviews*

"A TOUR DE FORCE OF STORYTELLING. It'll hook you from the first page."—*Whole Earth Software Review*

"A REALLY INTRIGUING STORY. Levy has managed to convey the true hacker personality."—*Stephen Wozniak, designer of the Apple Computer*

Also by Steven Levy

Artificial Life: How Computers Are Transforming Our Understanding of Evolution and the Future of Life.

Insanely Great: The Life and Times of Macintosh, the Computer That Changed Everything

HACKERS
Heroes of the Computer Revolution

STEVEN LEVY

D e l t a
Trade Paperbacks

To Teresa

A Delta Book
Published by
Dell Publishing
a division of
Bantam Doubleday Dell Publishing Group, Inc.
1540 Broadway
New York, New York 10036

ISBN: 0-385-31210-5

Manufactured in the United States of America

Published simultaneously in Canada

February 1994

10 9 8 7 6 5 4 3 2 1

RRH

CONTENTS

PREFACE

I was first drawn to writing about hackers—those computer programmers and designers who regard computing as the most important thing in the world—because they were such fascinating people. Though some in the field used the term "hacker" as a form of derision, implying that hackers were either nerdy social outcasts or "unprofessional" programmers who wrote dirty, "nonstandard" computer code, I found them quite different. Beneath their often unimposing exteriors, they were adventurers, visionaries, risk-takers, artists . . . and the ones who most clearly saw why the computer was a truly revolutionary tool. Among themselves, they knew how far one could go by immersion into the deep concentration of the hacking mind-set: one could go infinitely far. I came to understand why true hackers consider the term an appellation of honor rather than a pejorative.

As I talked to these digital explorers, ranging from those who tamed multimillion-dollar machines in the 1950s to contemporary young wizards who mastered computers in their suburban bedrooms, I found a common element, a common philosophy which seemed tied to the elegantly flowing logic of the computer itself. It was a philosophy of sharing, openness, decentralization, and getting your hands on machines at any cost—to improve the machines, and to improve the world. This Hacker Ethic is their gift to us: something with value even to those of us with no interest at all in computers.

It is an ethic seldom codified, but embodied instead in the behavior of hackers themselves. I would like to introduce you to these people who not only saw but *lived* the magic in the computer, and worked to liberate the magic so it could benefit us all. The people include the true hackers of the MIT artificial intelligence lab in the fifties and sixties; the populist, less sequestered hardware hackers in California in the seventies; and the young game hackers who made their mark in the personal computer age of the eighties.

This is in no way a formal history of the computer era, or of the particular arenas I focus upon. Indeed, many of the people you will meet here are not the most famous names (certainly not the most wealthy) in the annals of computing. Instead, these are the backroom geniuses who understood the machine at its most profound levels, and presented us with a new kind of life-style and a new kind of hero.

Hackers like Richard Greenblatt, Bill Gosper, Lee Felsenstein, and John Harris are the spirit and soul of computing itself. I believe their story—their vision, their intimacy with the machine itself, their experiences inside their peculiar world, and their sometimes dramatic, sometimes absurd "interfaces" with the outside world—is the *real* story of the computer revolution.

WHO'S WHO
The Wizards and their Machines

Bob Albrecht Founder of People's Computer Company who took visceral pleasure in exposing youngsters to computers.

Altair 8800 The pioneering microcomputer that galvanized hardware hackers. Building this kit made you learn hacking. Then you tried to figure out what to *do* with it.

Apple II Steve Wozniak's friendly, flaky, good-looking computer, wildly successful and the spark and soul of a thriving industry.

Atari 800 This home computer gave great graphics to game hackers like John Harris, though the company that made it was loath to tell you how it worked.

Bob and Carolyn Box World-record-holding gold prospectors turned software stars, working for Sierra On-Line.

Doug Carlston Corporate lawyer who chucked it all to form the Brøderbund software company.

Bob Davis Left job in liquor store to become bestselling author of Sierra On-Line computer game "Ulysses and the Golden Fleece." Success was his downfall.

Peter Deutsch Bad in sports, brilliant at math, Peter was still in short pants when he stumbled on the TX-0 at MIT—and hacked it along with the masters.

Steve Dompier Homebrew member who first made Altair sing, and later wrote the "Target" game on the Sol which entranced Tom Snyder.

John Draper The notorious "Captain Crunch" who fearlessly explored phone systems, got jailed, later hacked microcomputers. Cigarettes made him violent.

Mark Duchaineau The young Dungeonmaster who copy-protected On-Line's disks at his whim.

Chris Espinosa Fourteen-year-old follower of Steve Wozniak and early Apple employee.

Lee Felsenstein Former "military editor" of *Berkeley Barb*, and hero of an imaginary science-fiction novel, he designed computers with "junkyard" approach and was central figure in Bay Area hardware hacking in the seventies.

Ed Fredkin Gentle founder of Information International, thought himself world's greatest programmer until he met Stew Nelson. Father figure to hackers.

Gordon French Silver-haired hardware hacker whose garage held not cars but his homebrewed Chicken Hawk computer, then held the first Homebrew Computer Club meeting.

Richard Garriott Astronaut's son who, as Lord British, created the Ultima world on computer disks.

Bill Gates Cocky wizard, Harvard dropout who wrote Altair BASIC, and complained when hackers copied it.

Bill Gosper Horowitz of computer keyboards, master math and LIFE hacker at MIT AI lab, guru of the Hacker Ethic and student of Chinese restaurant menus.

Richard Greenblatt Single-minded, unkempt, prolific, and canonical MIT hacker who went into night phase so often that he zorched his academic career. The hacker's hacker.

John Harris The young Atari 800 game hacker who became Sierra On-Line's star programmer, but yearned for female companionship.

IBM PC IBM's entry into the personal computer market which amazingly included a bit of the Hacker Ethic, and took over.

IBM 704 IBM was The Enemy, and this was its machine, the Hulking Giant computer in MIT's Building 26. Later modified into the IBM 709, then the IBM 7090. Batch-processed and intolerable.

Jerry Jewell Vietnam vet turned programmer who founded Sirius Software.

Steven Jobs Visionary, beaded, non-hacking youngster who took Wozniak's Apple II, made lots of deals, and formed a company that would make a billion dollars.

Tom Knight At sixteen, an MIT hacker who would name the Incompatible Time-sharing System. Later, a Greenblatt nemesis over the LISP machine schism.

Alan Kotok The chubby MIT student from Jersey who worked under the rail layout at TMRC, learned the phone system at Western Electric, and became a legendary TX-0 and PDP-1 hacker.

Efrem Lipkin Hacker-activist from New York who loved machines but hated their uses. Co-founded Community Memory; friend of Felsenstein.

LISP Machine The ultimate hacker computer, invented mostly by Greenblatt and subject of a bitter dispute at MIT.

"Uncle" John McCarthy Absent-minded but brilliant MIT (later Stanford) professor who helped pioneer computer chess, artificial intelligence, LISP.

Bob Marsh Berkeley-ite and Homebrewer who shared garage with Felsenstein and founded Processor Technology, which made the Sol computer.

Roger Melen Homebrewer who co-founded Cromemco company to make circuit boards for Altair. His "Dazzler" played LIFE program on his kitchen table.

Louis Merton Pseudonym for the AI chess hacker whose tendency to go catatonic brought the hacker community together.

Jude Milhon Met Lee Felsenstein through a classified ad in the *Berkeley Barb,* and became more than a friend—a member of the Community Memory collective.

Marvin Minsky Playful and brilliant MIT prof who headed AI lab and allowed the hackers to run free.

Fred Moore Vagabond pacifist who hated money, loved technology, and co-founded Homebrew Club.

Stewart Nelson Buck-toothed, diminutive, but fiery AI lab hacker who connected the PDP-1 computer to hack the phone system. Later co-founded Systems Concepts company.

Ted Nelson Self-described "innovator" and noted curmudgeon who self-published the influential *Computer Lib* book.

Russell Noftsker Harried administrator of MIT AI lab in late sixties; later president of Symbolics company.

Adam Osborne Bangkok-born publisher-turned-computer-manufacturer who considered himself a philosopher. Founded Osborne Computer Company to make "adequate" machines.

PDP-1 Digital Equipment's first minicomputer, and in 1961 an interactive godsend to the MIT hackers and a slap in the face to IBM fascism.

PDP-6 Designed in part by Kotok, this mainframe computer was cornerstone of AI lab, with its gorgeous instruction set and sixteen sexy registers.

Tom Pittman The religious Homebrew hacker who lost his wife but kept the faith with his Tiny BASIC.

Ed Roberts Enigmatic founder of MITS company who shook the world with his Altair computer. He wanted to help people build mental pyramids.

Steve (Slug) Russell McCarthy's "coolie," who hacked the Spacewar program, first videogame, on the PDP-1. Never made a dime from it.

Peter Samson MIT hacker, one of the first, who loved systems, trains, TX-0, music, parliamentary procedure, pranks, and hacking.

Bob Saunders Jolly, balding TMRC hacker who married early, hacked till late at night eating "lemon gunkies," and mastered the "CBS strategy" on Spacewar.

Warren Schwader Big blond hacker from rural Wisconsin who went from the assembly line to software stardom but couldn't reconcile the shift with his devotion to Jehovah's Witnesses.

David Silver Left school at fourteen to be mascot of AI lab; maker of illicit keys and builder of a tiny robot that did the impossible.

Dan Sokol Long-haired prankster who reveled in revealing technological secrets at Homebrew Club. Helped "liberate" Altair BASIC program on paper tape.

Sol Computer Lee Felsenstein's terminal-and-computer, built in two frantic months, almost the computer that turned things around. Almost wasn't enough.

Les Solomon Editor of *Popular Eletronics,* the puller of strings who set the computer revolution into motion.

Marty Spergel The Junk Man, the Homebrew member who supplied circuits and cables and could make you a deal for anything.

Richard Stallman The Last of the Hackers, who vowed to defend the principles of hackerism to the bitter end. Remained at MIT until there was no one to eat Chinese food with.

Jeff Stephenson Thirty-year-old martial arts veteran and hacker who was astounded that joining Sierra On-Line meant enrolling in Summer Camp.

Jay Sullivan Maddeningly calm wizard-level programmer at Informatics who impressed Ken Williams by knowing the meaning of the word "any."

Dick Sunderland Chalk-complexioned MBA who believed that firm managerial bureaucracy was a worthy goal, but as president of Sierra On-Line found that hackers didn't think that way.

Gerry Sussman Young MIT hacker branded "loser" because he smoked a pipe and "munged" his programs; later became "winner" by algorithmic magic.

Margot Tommervik With her husband Al, long-haired Margot parlayed her game show winnings into a magazine that deified the Apple Computer.

Tom Swift Terminal Lee Felsenstein's legendary, never-to-be-built computer terminal which would give the user ultimate leave to get his hands on the world.

TX-0 Filled a small room, but in the late fifties this $3 million machine was world's first personal computer—for the community of MIT hackers that formed around it.

Jim Warren Portly purveyor of "techno-gossip" at Homebrew, he was first editor of hippie-styled *Dr. Dobbs Journal,* later started the lucrative Computer Faire.

Randy Wigginton Fifteen-year-old member of Steve Wozniak's kiddie corps, he helped Woz trundle the Apple II to Homebrew. Still in high school when he became Apple's first software employee.

Ken Williams Arrogant and brilliant young programmer who saw the writing on the CRT and started Sierra On-Line to make a killing and improve society by selling games for the Apple computer.

Roberta Williams Ken Williams' timid wife who rediscovered her own creativity by writing "Mystery House," the first of her many bestselling computer games.

Stephen "Woz" Wozniak Openhearted, technologically daring hardware hacker from San Jose suburbs, Woz built the Apple Computer for the pleasure of himself and friends.

PART ONE

TRUE HACKERS

CAMBRIDGE:
The Fifties and Sixties

1

THE TECH MODEL
RAILROAD CLUB

JUST why Peter Samson was wandering around in Building 26 in the middle of the night is a matter that he would find difficult to explain. Some things are not spoken. If you were like the people whom Peter Samson was coming to know and befriend in this, his freshman year at the Massachusetts Institute of Technology in the winter of 1958–59, no explanation would be required. Wandering around the labyrinth of laboratories and storerooms, searching for the secrets of telephone switching in machine rooms, tracing paths of wires or relays in subterranean steam tunnels . . . for some, it was common behavior, and there was no need to justify the impulse, when confronted with a closed door with an unbearably intriguing noise behind it, to open the door uninvited. And then, if there was no one to physically bar access to whatever was making that intriguing noise, to touch the machine, start flicking switches and noting responses, and eventually to loosen a screw, unhook a template, jiggle some diodes and tweak a few connections. Peter Samson and his friends had grown up with a specific relationship to the world, wherein things had meaning only if you found out how they worked. And how would you go about that if not by getting your hands on them?

It was in the basement of Building 26 that Samson and his friends discovered the EAM room. Building 26 was a long glass-and-steel structure, one of MIT's newer buildings, contrasting with the venerable pillared structures that fronted the Institute on Massachusetts Avenue. In the basement of this building void of personality, the EAM room. Electronic Accounting Machinery. A room that housed machines which ran like computers.

Not many people in 1959 had even seen a computer, let alone touched one. Samson, a wiry, curly-haired redhead with a way of extending his vowels so that it would seem he was racing through lists of possible meanings of statements in mid-word, had viewed computers on his visits to MIT from his hometown of Lowell, Massachusetts, less than thirty miles from campus. This made him a "Cambridge urchin," one of dozens of science-crazy high schoolers in the region who were drawn, as if by gravitational pull, to the Cambridge campus. He had even tried to rig up his own computer with discarded parts of old pinball machines: they were the best source of logic elements he could find.

Logic elements: the term seems to encapsulate what drew Peter Samson, son of a mill machinery repairman, to electronics. The subject made sense. When you grow up with an insatiable curiosity as to how things work, the delight you find upon discovering something as elegant as circuit logic, where all connections have to complete their loops, is profoundly thrilling. Peter Samson, who early on appreciated the mathematical simplicity of these things, could recall seeing a television show on Boston's public TV channel, WGBH, which gave a rudimentary introduction to programming a computer in its own language. It fired his imagination: to Peter Samson, a computer was surely like Aladdin's lamp—rub it, and it would do your bidding. So he tried to learn more about the field, built machines of his own, entered science project competitions and contests, and went to the place that people of his ilk aspired to: MIT. The repository of the very brightest of those weird high school kids with owl-like glasses and underdeveloped pectorals who dazzled math teachers and flunked PE, who dreamed not of scoring on prom night, but of getting to the finals of the General Electric Science Fair competition. MIT, where he would wander the hallways at two o'clock in the morning, looking for something interesting, and where he would indeed discover something that would help draw him deeply into a new form of creative process, and a new life-style, and would put him into the forefront of a society envisioned only by a few science-fiction writers of mild disrepute. He would discover a computer that he could play with.

The EAM room which Samson had chanced on was loaded with large keypunch machines the size of squat file cabinets. No one was protecting them: the room was staffed only by day, when a select group who had attained official clearance were privileged enough to submit long manila cards to operators who would then use these machines to punch holes in them according to what data the privileged ones wanted entered on the cards. A hole in the card would represent some instruction to the computer, telling it to put a piece of data somewhere, or perform a function on a piece of data, or move a piece of data from one place to another. An entire stack of these cards made one computer program, a program being a series of instructions which yield some expected result, just as the instructions in a recipe, when precisely followed, lead to a cake. Those cards would be taken to yet another operator upstairs who would feed the cards into a "reader" that would note where the holes were and dispatch this information to the IBM 704 computer on the first floor of Building 26. The Hulking Giant.

The IBM 704 cost several million dollars, took up an entire room, needed constant attention from a cadre of professional machine operators, and required special air-conditioning so that the glowing vacuum tubes inside it would not heat up to data-destroying temperatures. When the air-conditioning broke down—a fairly common occurrence—a loud gong would sound, and three engineers would spring from a nearby office to frantically take covers off the machine so its innards wouldn't melt. All these people in charge of punching cards, feeding them into readers, and pressing buttons and switches on the machine were what was commonly called a Priesthood, and those privileged enough to submit data to those most holy priests were the official acolytes. It was an almost ritualistic exchange.

Acolyte: Oh machine, would you accept my offer of information so you may run my program and perhaps give me a computation?

Priest (on behalf of the machine): We will try. We promise nothing.

As a general rule, even these most privileged of acolytes were not allowed direct access to the machine itself, and they would not be able to see for hours, sometimes for days, the results of the machine's ingestion of their "batch" of cards.

This was something Samson knew, and of course it frustrated the hell out of Samson, who wanted to get at the damn machine. For this was what life was all about.

What Samson did not know, and was delighted to discover, was that the EAM room also had a particular keypunch machine called the 407. Not only could it punch cards, but it could also read cards, sort them, and print them on listings. No one seemed to be guarding these machines, which were computers, sort of. Of course, using them would be no picnic: one needed to actually wire up what was called a plug board, a two-inch-by-two-inch plastic square with a mass of holes in it. If you put hundreds of wires through the holes in a certain order, you would get something that looked like a rat's nest but would fit into this electromechanical machine and alter its personality. It could do what you wanted it to do.

So, without any authorization whatsoever, that is what Peter Samson set out to do, along with a few friends of his from an MIT organization with a special interest in model railroading. It was a casual, unthinking step into a science-fiction future, but that was typical of the way that an odd subculture was pulling itself up by its bootstraps and growing to underground prominence—to become a culture that would be the impolite, unsanctioned soul of computerdom. It was among the first computer hacker escapades of the Tech Model Railroad Club, or TMRC.

•

Peter Samson had been a member of the Tech Model Railroad Club since his first week at MIT in the fall of 1958. The first event that entering MIT freshmen attended was a traditional welcoming lecture, the same one that had been given for as long as anyone at MIT could remember. *Look at the person to your left . . . look at the person to your right . . . one of you three will not graduate from the Institute.* The intended effect of the speech was to create that horrid feeling in the back of the collective freshman throat that signaled unprecedented dread. All their lives, these freshmen had been almost exempt from academic pressure. The exemption had been earned by virtue of brilliance. Now each of them had a person to the right and a person to the left who was just as smart. Maybe even smarter.

But to certain students this was no challenge at all. To these youngsters, classmates were perceived in a sort of friendly haze: maybe they would be of assistance in the consuming quest to find out how things worked, and then to master them. There were enough obstacles to learning already—why bother with stupid things like brown-nosing teachers and striving for grades? To students like Peter Samson, the quest meant more than the degree.

Sometime after the lecture came Freshman Midway. All the

campus organizations—special-interest groups, fraternities, and such—set up booths in a large gymnasium to try to recruit new members. The group that snagged Peter was the Tech Model Railroad Club. Its members, bright-eyed and crew-cutted upperclassmen who spoke with the spasmodic cadences of people who want words out of the way in a hurry, boasted a spectacular display of HO gauge trains they had in a permanent clubroom in Building 20. Peter Samson had long been fascinated by trains, especially subways. So he went along on the walking tour to the building, a shingle-clad temporary structure built during World War II. The hallways were cavernous, and even though the clubroom was on the second floor it had the dank, dimly lit feel of a basement.

The clubroom was dominated by the huge train layout. It just about filled the room, and if you stood in the little control area called "the notch" you could see a little town, a little industrial area, a tiny working trolley line, a papier-mâché mountain, and of course a lot of trains and tracks. The trains were meticulously crafted to resemble their full-scale counterparts, and they chugged along the twists and turns of track with picture-book perfection.

And then Peter Samson looked underneath the chest-high boards which held the layout. It took his breath away. Underneath this layout was a more massive matrix of wires and relays and crossbar switches than Peter Samson had ever dreamed existed. There were neat regimental lines of switches, and achingly regular rows of dull bronze relays, and a long, rambling tangle of red, blue, and yellow wires—twisting and twirling like a rainbow-colored explosion of Einstein's hair. It was an incredibly complicated system, and Peter Samson vowed to find out how it worked.

The Tech Model Railroad Club awarded its members a key to the clubroom after they logged forty hours of work on the layout. Freshman Midway had been on a Friday. By Monday, Peter Samson had his key.

•

There were two factions of TMRC. Some members loved the idea of spending their time building and painting replicas of certain trains with historical and emotional value, or creating realistic scenery for the layout. This was the knife-and-paintbrush contingent, and it subscribed to railroad magazines and booked the club for trips on aging train lines. The other faction centered on the Signals and Power Subcommittee of the club, and it cared far more about what went on under the layout. This was The System, which worked something like a collaboration between Rube Goldberg and Wernher von Braun, and it was constantly being improved, revamped, perfected, and sometimes "gronked"—in club jargon, screwed up. S&P people were obsessed with the way The System worked, its increasing complexities, how any change you made would affect other parts, and how you could put those relationships between the parts to optimal use.

Many of the parts for The System had been donated by the Western Electric College Gift Plan, directly from the phone company. The club's faculty advisor was also in charge of the campus phone system, and had seen to it that sophisticated phone equipment was available for the model railroaders. Using that equipment as a starting point, the Railroaders had devised a scheme which enabled several people to control trains at once, even if the trains were at different parts of the same track. Using dials appropriated from telephones, the TMRC "engineers" could specify which block of track they wanted control of, and run a train from there. This was done by using several types of phone company relays, including crossbar executors and step switches which let you actually hear the power being transferred from one block to another by an otherworldly chunka-chunka-chunka sound.

It was the S&P group who devised this fiendishly ingenious scheme, and it was the S&P group who harbored the kind of restless curiosity which led them to root around campus buildings in search of ways to get their hands on computers. They were lifelong disciples of a Hands-On Imperative. Head of S&P was an upperclassman named Bob Saunders, with ruddy, bulbous features, an infectious laugh, and a talent for switch gear. As a child in Chicago, he had built a high-frequency transformer for a high school project; it was his six-foot-high version of a Tesla coil, something devised by an engineer in the 1800s which was supposed to send out furious waves of electrical power. Saunders said his coil project managed to blow out television reception for blocks around. Another person who gravitated to S&P was Alan Kotok, a plump, chinless, thick-spectacled New Jerseyite in Samson's class. Kotok's family could recall him, at age three, prying a plug out of a wall with a screwdriver and causing a hissing shower of sparks to erupt. When he was six, he was building and wiring lamps. In high school he had once gone on a tour of the Mobil Research Lab in nearby Haddonfield, and saw his first computer—the exhilaration of that experience helped him decide to enter MIT. In his freshman year, he earned a reputation as one of TMRC's most capable S&P people.

The S&P people were the ones who spent Saturdays going to Eli Heffron's junkyard in Somerville scrounging for parts, who would spend hours on their backs resting on little rolling chairs they called "bunkies" to get underneath tight spots in the switching system, who would work through the night making the wholly unauthorized connection between the TMRC phone and the East Campus. Technology was their playground.

The core members hung out at the club for hours; constantly improving The System, arguing about what could be done next, developing a jargon of their own that seemed incomprehensible to outsiders who might chance on these teen-aged fanatics, with their checked short-sleeve shirts, pencils in their pockets, chino pants, and, always, a bottle of Coca-Cola by their side. (TMRC purchased its own Coke machine for the then forbidding sum of $165; at a tariff of five cents a bottle, the outlay was replaced in three months; to facilitate sales, Saunders built a change machine for Coke buyers that was still in use a decade later.) When a piece of equipment wasn't working, it was "losing"; when a piece of equipment was ruined, it was "munged" (Mash Until No Good); the two desks in the corner of the room were not called the office, but the "orifice"; one who insisted on studying for courses was a "tool"; garbage was called "cruft"; and a project undertaken or a product built not solely to fulfill some constructive goal, but with some wild pleasure taken in mere involvement, was called a "hack."

This latter term may have been suggested by ancient MIT lingo —the word "hack" had long been used to describe the elaborate college pranks that MIT students would regularly devise, such as covering the dome that overlooked the campus with reflecting foil. But as the TMRC people used the word, there was serious respect implied. While someone might call a clever connection between relays a "mere hack," it would be understood that, to qualify as a hack, the feat must be imbued with innovation, style, and technical virtuosity. Even though one might self-deprecatingly say he was "hacking away at The System" (much as an axe-wielder hacks at logs), the artistry with which one hacked was recognized to be considerable.

The most productive people working on Signals and Power called themselves "hackers" with great pride. Within the confines of the clubroom in Building 20, and of the "Tool Room" (where some study and many techno bull sessions took place), they had unilaterally endowed themselves with the heroic attributes of Icelandic legend. This is how Peter Samson saw himself and his friends in a Sandburg-esque poem in the club newsletter:

Switch Thrower for the World,
Fuze Tester, Maker of Routes,
Player with the Railroads and the System's Advance Chop-
          per;
Grungy, hairy, sprawling,
Machine of the Point-Function Line-o-lite:
They tell me you are wicked and I believe them; for I have
          seen your painted light bulbs under the lucite
          luring the system coolies . . .
Under the tower, dust all over the place, hacking with bifur-
          cated springs . . .
Hacking even as an ignorant freshman acts who has never lost
          occupancy and has dropped out
Hacking the M-Boards, for under its locks are the switches,
          and under its control the advance around the
          layout,
                      Hacking!
Hacking the grungy, hairy, sprawling hacks of youth; un-
          cabled, frying diodes, proud to be Switch-
          thrower, Fuze-tester, Maker of Routes, Player
          with Railroads, and Advance Chopper to the
          System.

Whenever they could, Samson and the others would slip off to the EAM room with their plug boards, trying to use the machine to keep track of the switches underneath the layout. Just as important, they were seeing what the electromechanical counter could do, taking it to its limit.

That spring of 1959, a new course was offered at MIT. It was the first course in programming a computer that freshmen could take. The teacher was a distant man with a wild shock of hair and an equally unruly beard—John McCarthy. A master mathematician, McCarthy was a classically absent-minded professor; stories abounded about his habit of suddenly answering a question hours, sometimes even days after it was first posed to him. He would approach you in the hallway, and with no salutation would begin speaking in his robotically precise diction, as if the pause in conversation had been only a fraction of a second, and not a week. Most likely, his belated response would be brilliant.

McCarthy was one of a very few people working in an entirely new form of scientific inquiry with computers. The volatile and controversial nature of his field of study was obvious from the very arrogance of the name that McCarthy had bestowed upon it: Artificial Intelligence. This man actually thought that computers could be *smart*. Even at such a science-intensive place as MIT, most people considered the thought ridiculous: they considered computers to be useful, if somewhat absurdly expensive, tools for number-crunching huge calculations and for devising missile defense systems (as MIT's largest computer, the Whirlwind, had done for the early-warning SAGE system), but scoffed at the thought that computers themselves could actually be a scientific field of study. Computer Science did not officially exist at MIT in the late fifties, and McCarthy and his fellow computer specialists worked in the Electrical Engineering Department, which offered the course, No. 641, that Kotok, Samson, and a few other TRMC members took that spring.

McCarthy had started a mammoth program on the IBM 704—the Hulking Giant—that would give it the extraordinary ability to play chess. To critics of the budding field of Artificial Intelligence, this was just one example of the boneheaded optimism of people like John McCarthy. But McCarthy had a certain vision of what computers could do, and playing chess was only the beginning.

All fascinating stuff, but not the vision that was driving Kotok and Samson and the others. They wanted to learn how to *work* the damn machines, and while this new programming language called LISP that McCarthy was talking about in 641 was interesting, it was not nearly as interesting as the act of programming, or that fantastic moment when you got your printout back from the Priesthood—word from the source itself!—and could then spend hours poring over the results of the program, what had gone wrong with it, how it could be improved. The TMRC hackers were devising ways to get into closer contact with the IBM 704, which soon was upgraded to a newer model called the 709. By hanging out at the computation center in the wee hours of the morning, and by getting to know the Priesthood, and by bowing and scraping the requisite number of times, people like Kotok were eventually allowed to push a few buttons on the machine, and watch the lights as it worked.

There were secrets to those IBM machines that had been pains-

takingly learned by some of the older people at MIT with access to
the 704 and friends among the Priesthood. Amazingly, a few of
these programmers, grad students working with McCarthy, had
even written a program that utilized one of the rows of tiny lights:
the lights would be lit in such an order that it looked like a little
ball was being passed from right to left: if an operator hit a switch
at just the right time, the motion of the lights could be reversed—
Computer Ping-Pong! This obviously was the kind of thing that
you'd show off to impress your peers, who would then take a look
at the actual program you had written and see how it was done.

To top the program, someone else might try to do the same thing
with fewer instructions—a worthy endeavor, since there was so
little room in the small "memory" of the computers of those days
that not many instructions could fit into them. John McCarthy had
once noticed how his graduate students who loitered around the
704 would work over their computer programs to get the most out
of the fewest instructions, and get the program compressed so that
fewer cards would need to be fed to the machine. Shaving off an
instruction or two was almost an obsession with them. McCarthy
compared these students to ski bums. They got the same kind of
primal thrill from "maximizing code" as fanatic skiers got from
swooshing frantically down a hill. So the practice of taking a computer program and trying to cut off instructions without affecting
the outcome came to be called "program bumming," and you
would often hear people mumbling things like "Maybe I can bum a
few instructions out and get the octal correction card loader down
to three cards instead of four."

McCarthy in 1959 was turning his interest from chess to a new
way of talking to the computer, the whole new "language" called
LISP. Alan Kotok and his friends were more than eager to take
over the chess project. Working on the batch-processed IBM, they
embarked on the gargantuan project of teaching the 704, and later
the 709, and even after that its replacement the 7090, how to play
the game of kings. Eventually Kotok's group became the largest
users of computer time in the entire MIT computation center.

Still, working with the IBM machine was frustrating. There was
nothing worse than the long wait between the time you handed in
your cards and the time your results were handed back to you. If
you had misplaced as much as one letter in one instruction, the
program would crash, and you would have to start the whole process over again. It went hand in hand with the stifling proliferation
of goddamn *rules* that permeated the atmosphere of the computa-

tion center. Most of the rules were designed to keep crazy young computer fans like Samson and Kotok and Saunders physically distant from the machine itself. The most rigid rule of all was that no one should be able to actually touch or tamper with the machine itself. This, of course, was what those Signals and Power people were dying to do more than anything else in the world, and the restrictions drove them mad.

One priest—a low-level sub-priest, really—on the late-night shift was particularly nasty in enforcing this rule, so Samson devised a suitable revenge. While poking around at Eli's electronic junk shop one day, he chanced upon an electrical board precisely like the kind of board holding the clunky vacuum tubes which resided inside the IBM. One night, sometime before 4 A.M., this particular sub-priest stepped out for a minute; when he returned, Samson told him that the machine wasn't working, but they'd found the trouble —and held up the totally smashed module from the old 704 he'd gotten at Eli's.

The sub-priest could hardly get the words out. "W-where did you get that?"

Samson, who had wide green eyes that could easily look maniacal, slowly pointed to an open place on the machine rack where, of course, no board had ever been, but the space still looked sadly bare.

The sub-priest gasped. He made faces that indicated his bowels were about to give out. He whimpered exhortations to the deity. Visions, no doubt, of a million-dollar deduction from his paycheck began flashing before him. Only after his supervisor, a high priest with some understanding of the mentality of these young wiseguys from the Model Railroad Club, came and explained the situation did he calm down.

He was not the last administrator to feel the wrath of a hacker thwarted in the quest for access.

•

One day a former TMRC member who was now on the MIT faculty paid a visit to the clubroom. His name was Jack Dennis. When he had been an undergraduate in the early 1950s, he had worked furiously underneath the layout. Dennis lately had been working a computer which MIT had just received from Lincoln Lab, a military development laboratory affiliated with the Institute. The computer was called the TX-0, and it was one of the first transistor-run computers in the world. Lincoln Lab had used it specifically to test a giant computer called the TX-2, which had a memory so complex that only with this specially built little brother could its ills be capably diagnosed. Now that its original job was over, the three-million-dollar TX-0 had been shipped over to the Institute on "long-term loan," and apparently no one at Lincoln Lab had marked a calendar with a return date. Dennis asked the S&P people at TMRC whether they would like to see it.

Hey you nuns! Would you like to meet the Pope?

The TX-0 was in Building 26, in the second-floor Research Laboratory of Electronics (RLE), directly above the first-floor Computation Center which housed the hulking IBM 704. The RLE lab resembled the control room of an antique spaceship. The TX-0, or Tixo, as it was sometimes called, was for its time a midget machine, since it was one of the first computers to use finger-size transistors instead of hand-size vacuum tubes. Still, it took up much of the room, along with its fifteen tons of supporting air-conditioning equipment. The TX-0's workings were mounted on several tall, thin chassis, like rugged metal bookshelves, with tangled wires and neat little rows of tiny, bottle-like containers in which the transistors were inserted. Another rack had a solid metal front speckled with grim-looking gauges. Facing the racks was an L-shaped console, the control panel of this H. G. Wells spaceship, with a blue countertop for your elbows and papers. On the short arm of the L stood a Flexowriter, which resembled a typewriter converted for tank warfare, its bottom anchored in a military gray housing. Above the top were the control panels, boxlike protrusions painted an institutional yellow. On the sides of the boxes which faced the user were a few gauges, several lines of quarter-inch blinking lights, a matrix of steel toggle switches the size of large grains of rice, and, best of all, an actual cathode ray tube display, round and smoke-gray.

The TMRC people were awed. *This machine did not use cards.* The user would first punch in a program onto a long, thin paper tape with a Flexowriter (there were a few extra Flexowriters in an adjoining room), then sit at the console, feed in the program by running the tape through a reader, and be able to sit there while the program ran. If something went wrong with the program, you knew immediately, and you could diagnose the problem by using some of the switches, or checking out which of the lights were blinking or lit. The computer even had an audio output: while the program ran, a speaker underneath the console would make a sort of music, like a poorly tuned electric organ whose notes would vibrate with a fuzzy, ethereal din. The chords on this "organ" would change, depending on what data the machine was reading at any given microsecond; after you were familiar with the tones, you could actually *hear* what part of your program the computer was working on. You would have to discern this, though, over the clacking of the Flexowriter, which could make you think you were in the middle of a machine-gun battle.

Even more amazing was that, because of these "interactive" capabilities, and also because users seemed to be allowed blocks of time to use the TX-0 all by themselves, you could even modify a program *while sitting at the computer.* A miracle!

There was no way in hell that Kotok, Saunders, Samson, and the others were going to be kept away from that machine. Fortunately, there didn't seem to be the kind of bureaucracy surrounding the TX-0 that there was around the IBM 704. No cadre of officious priests. The technician in charge was a canny white-haired Scotsman named John McKenzie. While he made sure that graduate students and those working on funded projects—Officially Sanctioned Users—maintained access to the machine, McKenzie tolerated the crew of TMRC madmen who began to hang out in the RLE lab, where the TX-0 stood.

Samson, Kotok, Saunders, and a freshman named Bob Wagner soon figured out that the best time of all to hang out in Building 26 was at night, when no person in his right mind would have signed up for an hour-long session on the piece of paper posted every Friday beside the air conditioner in the RLE lab. The TX-0 as a rule was kept running twenty-four hours a day—computers back then were too expensive for their time to be wasted by leaving them idle through the night, and besides, it was a hairy procedure to get the thing up and running once it was turned off. So the TMRC hackers, who soon were referring to themselves as TX-0 hackers, changed their life-style to accommodate the computer. They laid claim to what blocks of time they could, and would "vulture time" with nocturnal visits to the lab on the off chance that someone who was scheduled for a 3 A.M. session might not show up.

"Oh!" Samson would say delightedly, a minute or so after someone failed to show up at the time designated in the logbook. "Make sure it doesn't go to waste!"

It never seemed to, because the hackers were there almost all the time. If they weren't in the RLE lab waiting for an opening to occur, they were in the classroom next to the TMRC clubroom, the Tool Room, playing a "hangman"-style word game that Samson had devised called "Come Next Door," waiting for a call from someone who was near the TX-0, monitoring it to see if someone had not shown up for a session. The hackers recruited a network of informers to give advance notice of potential openings at the computer—if a research project was not ready with its program in time, or a professor was sick, the word would be passed to TMRC and the hackers would appear at the TX-0, breathless and ready to jam into the space behind the console.

Though Jack Dennis was theoretically in charge of the operation, Dennis was teaching courses at the time, and preferred to spend the rest of his time actually writing code for the machine. Dennis played the role of benevolent godfather to the hackers: he would give them a brief hands-on introduction to the machine, point them in certain directions, be amused at their wild programming ventures. He had little taste for administration, though, and was just as happy to let John McKenzie run things. McKenzie early on recognized that the interactive nature of the TX-0 was inspiring a new form of computer programming, and the hackers were its pioneers. So he did not lay down too many edicts.

The atmosphere was loose enough in 1959 to accommodate the strays—science-mad people whose curiosity burned like a hunger, who like Peter Samson would be exploring the uncharted maze of laboratories at MIT. The noise of the air-conditioning, the audio output, and the drill-hammer Flexowriter would lure these wanderers, who'd poke their heads into the lab like kittens peering into baskets of yarn.

One of those wanderers was an outsider named Peter Deutsch. Even before discovering the TX-0, Deutsch had developed a fascination for computers. It began one day when he picked up a manual that someone had discarded, a manual for an obscure form of computer language for doing calculations. Something about the orderliness of the computer instructions appealed to him: he would later describe the feeling as the same kind of eerily transcendent recognition that an artist experiences when he discovers the medium that is absolutely right for him. *This is where I belong.* Deutsch tried writing a small program, and, signing up for time under the name of one of the priests, ran it on a computer. Within weeks, he had attained a striking proficiency in programming. He was only twelve years old.

He was a shy kid, strong in math and unsure of most everything else. He was uncomfortably overweight, deficient in sports, but an intellectual star performer. His father was a professor at MIT, and Peter used that as his entree to explore the labs.

It was inevitable that he would be drawn to the TX-0. He first wandered into the small "Kluge Room" (a "kluge" is a piece of inelegantly constructed equipment that seems to defy logic by working properly), where three off-line Flexowriters were available for punching programs onto paper tape which would later be fed into the TX-0. Someone was busy punching in a tape. Peter watched for a while, then began bombarding the poor soul with questions about that weird-looking little computer in the next room. Then Peter went up to the TX-0 itself, examined it closely, noting how it differed from other computers: it was smaller, had a CRT display, and other neat toys. He decided right then to act as if he had a perfect right to be there. He got hold of a manual and soon was startling people by spouting actual make-sense computer talk, and eventually was allowed to sign up for night and weekend sessions, and to write his own programs.

McKenzie worried that someone might accuse him of running some sort of summer camp, with this short-pants little kid, barely tall enough to stick his head over the TX-0's console, staring at the code that an Officially Sanctioned User, perhaps some self-important graduate student, would be hammering into the Flexowriter, and saying in his squeaky, preadolescent voice something like "Your problem is that this credit is wrong over here . . . you need this other instruction over there," and the self-important grad student would go crazy—*who is this little worm?*—and start screaming at him to go out and play somewhere. Invariably, though, Peter Deutsch's comments would turn out to be correct. Deutsch would also brazenly announce that he was going to write better programs than the ones currently available, and he would go and do it.

Samson, Kotok, and the other hackers accepted Peter Deutsch: by virtue of his computer knowledge he was worthy of equal treatment. Deutsch was not such a favorite with the Officially Sanctioned Users, especially when he sat behind them ready to spring into action when they made a mistake on the Flexowriter.

These Officially Sanctioned Users appeared at the TX-0 with the regularity of commuters. The programs they ran were statistical analyses, cross correlations, simulations of an interior of the nucleus of a cell. Applications. That was fine for Users, but it was sort of a waste in the minds of the hackers. What hackers had in mind was getting behind the console of the TX-0 much in the same way as getting in behind the throttle of a plane. Or, as Peter Samson, a classical music fan, put it, computing with the TX-0 was like playing a musical instrument: an absurdly expensive musical instrument upon which you could improvise, compose, and, like the beatniks in Harvard Square a mile away, wail like a banshee with total creative abandon.

One thing that enabled them to do this was the programming system devised by Jack Dennis and another professor, Tom Stockman. When the TX-0 arrived at MIT, it had been stripped down since its days at Lincoln Lab: the memory had been reduced considerably, to 4,096 "words" of eighteen bits each. (A "bit" is a *bi*nary digi*t*, either a one or zero. These binary numbers are the only thing computers understand. A series of binary numbers is called a "word.") And the TX-0 had almost no software. So Jack Dennis, even before he introduced the TMRC people to the TX-0, had been writing "systems programs"—the software to help users utilize the machine.

The first thing Dennis worked on was an assembler. This was something that translated assembly language—which used three-letter symbolic abbreviations that represented instructions to the machine—into machine language, which consisted of the binary numbers 0 and 1. The TX-0 had a rather limited assembly language: since its design allowed only two bits of each eighteen-bit word to be used for instructions to the computer, only four instructions could be used (each possible two-bit variation—00, 01, 10, and 11—represented an instruction). Everything the computer did could be broken down to the execution of one of those four instructions: it took one instruction to add two numbers, but a series of perhaps twenty instructions to multiply two numbers. Staring at a long list of computer commands written as binary numbers—for example, 10011001100001—could make you into a babbling mental case in a matter of minutes. But the same command in assembly language might look like this: ADD Y. After loading the computer with the assembler that Dennis wrote, you could write programs in this simpler symbolic form, and wait smugly while the computer did the translation into binary for you. Then you'd feed that binary "object" code back into the computer. The value of this was incalculable: it enabled programmers to write in something that *looked* like code, rather than an endless, dizzying series of ones and zeros.

The other program that Dennis worked on with Stockman was something even newer—a debugger. The TX-0 came with a debugging program called UT-3, which enabled you to talk to the computer while it was running by typing commands directly into the Flexowriter. But it had terrible problems—for one thing, it only accepted typed-in code that used the octal numeric system. "Octal" is a base-eight number system (as opposed to binary, which is base two, and Arabic—ours—which is base ten), and it is a difficult system to use. So Dennis and Stockman decided to write something better than UT-3 which would enable users to use the symbolic, easier-to-work-with assembly language. This came to be called FLIT, and it allowed users to actually find program bugs during a session, fix them, and keep the program running. (Dennis would explain that "FLIT" stood for *F*lexowriter *I*nterrogation *T*ape, but clearly the name's real origin was the insect spray with that brand name.) FLIT was a quantum leap forward, since it liberated programmers to actually do original composing on the machine—just like musicians composing on their musical instruments. With the use of the debugger, which took up one third of the 4,096 words of the TX-0's memory, hackers were free to create a new, more daring style of programming.

And what did these hacker programs *do?* Well, sometimes, it didn't matter much at all what they did. Peter Samson hacked the night away on a program that would instantly convert Arabic numbers to Roman numerals, and Jack Dennis, after admiring the skill with which Samson had accomplished this feat, said, "My God, why would anyone want to do such a thing?" But Dennis knew why. There was ample justification in the feeling of power and accomplishment Samson got when he fed in the paper tape, monitored the lights and switches, and saw what were once plain old blackboard Arabic numbers coming back as the numerals the Romans had hacked with.

In fact it was Jack Dennis who suggested to Samson that there were considerable uses for the TX-0's ability to send noise to the audio speaker. While there were no built-in controls for pitch, amplitude, or tone character, there was a way to control the speaker —sounds would be emitted depending on the state of the fourteenth bit in the eighteen-bit words the TX-0 had in its accumulator in a given microsecond. The sound was on or off depending on whether bit fourteen was a one or zero. So Samson set about writing programs that varied the binary numbers in that slot in different ways to produce different pitches.

At that time, only a few people in the country had been experimenting with using a computer to output any kind of music, and the methods they had been using required massive computations before the machine would so much as utter a note. Samson, who reacted with impatience to those who warned he was attempting the impossible, wanted a computer playing music right away. So he learned to control that one bit in the accumulator so adeptly that he could command it with the authority of Charlie Parker on the saxophone. In a later version of this music compiler, Samson rigged it so that if you made an error in your programming syntax, the Flexowriter would switch to a red ribbon and print "To err is human to forgive divine."

When outsiders heard the melodies of Johann Sebastian Bach in a single-voice, monophonic square wave, no harmony, they were universally unfazed. Big deal! Three million dollars for this giant hunk of machinery, and why shouldn't it do at least as much as a five-dollar toy piano? It was no use to explain to these outsiders that Peter Samson had virtually bypassed the process by which music had been made for eons. Music had always been made by directly creating vibrations that were sound. What happened in Samson's program was that a load of numbers, bits of information fed into a computer, comprised a code in which the music resided. You could spend hours staring at the code, and not be able to divine where the music was. It only became music while millions of blindingly brief exchanges of data were taking place in the accumulator sitting in one of the metal, wire, and silicon racks that comprised the TX-0. Samson had asked the computer, which had no apparent knowledge of how to use a voice, to lift itself in song—and the TX-0 had complied.

So it was that a computer program was not only metaphorically a musical composition—it was *literally* a musical composition! It looked like—and was—the same kind of program which yielded complex arithmetical computations and statistical analyses. These digits that Samson had jammed into the computer were a universal language which could produce *anything*—a Bach fugue or an anti-aircraft system.

Samson did not say any of this to the outsiders who were unimpressed by his feat. Nor did the hackers themselves discuss this—it is not even clear that they analyzed the phenomenon in such cosmic terms. Peter Samson did it, and his colleagues appreciated it, because it was obviously a neat hack. That was justification enough.

To hackers like Bob Saunders—balding, plump, and merry disciple of the TX-0, president of TMRC's S&P group, student of systems—it was a perfect existence. Saunders had grown up in the suburbs of Chicago, and for as long as he could remember the workings of electricity and telephone circuitry had fascinated him. Before beginning MIT, Saunders had landed a dream summer job, working for the phone company installing central office equipment. He would spend eight blissful hours with soldering iron and pliers in hand, working in the bowels of various systems, an idyll broken by lunch hours spent in deep study of phone company manuals. It was the phone company equipment underneath the TMRC layout that had convinced Saunders to become active in the Model Railroad Club.

Saunders, being an upperclassman, had come to the TX-0 later in his college career than Kotok and Samson: he had used the breathing space to actually lay the foundation for a social life, which included courtship of and eventual marriage to Marge French, who had done some non-hacking computer work for a research project. Still, the TX-0 was the center of his college career, and he shared the common hacker experience of seeing his grades suffer from missed classes. It didn't bother him much, because he knew that his real education was occurring in Room 240 of Building 26, behind the Tixo console. Years later he would describe himself and the others as "an elite group. Other people were off studying, spending their days up on four-floor buildings making obnoxious vapors or off in the physics lab throwing particles at things or whatever it is they do. And we were simply not paying attention to what other folks were doing because we had no interest in it. They were studying what they were studying and we were studying what we were studying. And the fact that much of it was not on the officially approved curriculum was by and large immaterial."

The hackers came out at night. It was the only way to take full advantage of the crucial "off-hours" of the TX-0. During the day, Saunders would usually manage to make an appearance in a class or two. Then some time spent performing "basic maintenance"— things like eating and going to the bathroom. He might see Marge for a while. But eventually he would filter over to Building 26. He would go over some of the programs of the night before, printed on the nine-and-a-half-inch-wide paper that the Flexowriter used. He would annotate and modify the listing to update the code to whatever he considered the next stage of operation. Maybe then he would move over to the Model Railroad Club, and he'd swap his program with someone, checking simultaneously for good ideas and potential bugs. Then back to Building 26, to the Kluge Room next to the TX-0, to find an off-line Flexowriter on which to update his code. All the while he'd be checking to see if someone had canceled a one-hour session on the machine; his own session was scheduled at something like two or three in the morning. He'd wait in the Kluge Room, or play some bridge back at the Railroad Club, until the time came.

Sitting at the console, facing the metal racks that held the computer's transistors, each transistor representing a location that either held or did not hold a bit of memory, Saunders would set up the Flexowriter, which would greet him with the word "WAL-RUS." This was something Samson had hacked, in honor of Lewis Carroll's poem with the line "The time has come, the Walrus said . . ." Saunders might chuckle at that as he went into the drawer for the paper tape which held the assembler program and fed that into the tape reader. Now the computer would be ready to assemble his program, so he'd take the Flexowriter tape he'd been working on and send that into the computer. He'd watch the lights go on as the computer switched his code from "source" (the symbolic assembly language) to "object" code (binary), which the computer would punch out into another paper tape. Since that tape was in the object code that the TX-0 understood, he'd feed it in, hoping that the program would run magnificently.

There would most probably be a few fellow hackers kibitzing behind him, laughing and joking and drinking Cokes and eating some junk food they'd extracted from the machine downstairs. Saunders preferred the lemon jelly wedges that the others called "lemon gunkies." But at four in the morning, anything tasted good. They would all watch as the program began to run, the lights going on, the whine from the speaker humming in high or low register depending on what was in Bit 14 in the accumulator, and the first thing he'd see on the CRT display after the program had been assembled and run was that the program had crashed. So he'd reach into the drawer for the tape with the FLIT debugger and feed *that* into the computer. The computer would then be a debugging machine, and he'd send the program back in. Now he could start trying to find out where things had gone wrong, and maybe if he was lucky he'd find out, and change things by putting in some commands by flicking some of the switches on the console in precise order, or hammering in some code on the Flexowriter. Once things got running—and it was always incredibly satisfying when something worked, when he'd made that roomful of transistors and wires and metal and electricity all meld together to create a precise output that he'd devised—he'd try to add the next advance to it. When the hour was over—someone already itching to get on the machine after him—Saunders would be ready to spend the next few hours figuring out what the heck had made the program go belly-up.

The peak hour itself was tremendously intense, but during the hours before, and even during the hours afterward, a hacker attained a state of pure concentration. When you programmed a computer, you had to be aware of where all the thousands of bits of information were going from one instruction to the next, and be able to predict—and exploit—the effect of all that movement. When you had all that information glued to your cerebral being, it was almost as if your own mind had merged into the environment of the computer. Sometimes it took hours to build up to the point where your thoughts could contain that total picture, and when you did get to that point, it was such a shame to waste it that you tried to sustain it by marathon bursts, alternatively working on the computer or poring over the code that you wrote on one of the off-line Flexowriters in the Kluge Room. You would sustain that concentration by "wrapping around" to the next day.

Inevitably, that frame of mind spilled over to what random shards of existence the hackers had outside of computing. The knife-and-paintbrush contingent at TMRC were not pleased at all by the infiltration of Tixo-mania into the club: they saw it as a sort of Trojan horse for a switch in the club focus, from railroading to computing. And if you attended one of the club meetings held every Tuesday at five-fifteen, you could see the concern: the hackers would exploit every possible thread of parliamentary procedure to create a meeting as convoluted as the programs they were hacking on the TX-0. Motions were made to make motions to make motions, and objections ruled out of order as if they were so many computer errors. A note in the minutes of the meeting on November 24, 1959, suggests that "we frown on certain members who would do the club a lot more good by doing more S&P-ing and less reading *Robert's Rules of Order*." Samson was one of the worst offenders, and at one point an exasperated TMRC member made a motion "to purchase a cork for Samson's oral diarrhea."

Hacking parliamentary procedure was one thing, but the logical mind-frame required for programming spilled over into more commonplace activities. You could ask a hacker a question and sense his mental accumulator processing bits until he came up with a precise answer to the question you asked. Marge Saunders would drive to the Safeway every Saturday morning in the Volkswagen and upon her return ask her husband, "Would you like to help me bring in the groceries?" Bob Saunders would reply, "No." Stunned, Marge would drag in the groceries herself. After the same thing occurred a few times, she exploded, hurling curses at him and demanding to know why he said no to her question.

"That's a stupid question to ask," he said. "Of course I won't *like* to help you bring in the groceries. If you ask me if I'll help you bring them in, that's another matter."

It was as if Marge had submitted a program into the TX-0, and the program, as programs do when the syntax is improper, had crashed. It was not until she debugged her question that Bob Saunders would allow it to run successfully on his own mental computer.

2

THE HACKER ETHIC

SOMETHING new was coalescing around the TX-0: a new way of life, with a philosophy, an ethic, and a dream.

There was no one moment when it started to dawn on the TX-0 hackers that by devoting their technical abilities to computing with a devotion rarely seen outside of monasteries they were the vanguard of a daring symbiosis between man and machine. With a fervor like that of young hot-rodders fixated on souping up engines, they came to take their almost unique surroundings for granted. Even as the elements of a culture were forming, as legends began to accrue, as their mastery of programming started to surpass any previous recorded levels of skill, the dozen or so hackers were reluctant to acknowledge that their tiny society, on intimate terms with the TX-0, had been slowly and implicitly piecing together a body of concepts, beliefs, and mores.

The precepts of this revolutionary Hacker Ethic were not so much debated and discussed as silently agreed upon. No manifestos were issued. No missionaries tried to gather converts. The computer did the converting, and those who seemed to follow the Hacker Ethic most faithfully were people like Samson, Saunders, and Kotok, whose lives before MIT seemed to be mere preludes to that moment when they fulfilled themselves behind the console of the TX-0. Later there would come hackers who took the implicit Ethic even more seriously than the TX-0 hackers did, hackers like the legendary Greenblatt or Gosper, though it would be some years yet before the tenets of hackerism would be explicitly delineated.

Still, even in the days of the TX-0, the planks of the platform were in place. The Hacker Ethic:

Access to computers—and anything which might teach you something about the way the world works—should be unlimited and total. Always yield to the Hands-On Imperative!

Hackers believe that essential lessons can be learned about the systems—about the world—from taking things apart, seeing how they work, and using this knowledge to create new and even more interesting things. They resent any person, physical barrier, or law that tries to keep them from doing this.

This is especially true when a hacker wants to fix something that (from his point of view) is broken or needs improvement. Imperfect systems infuriate hackers, whose primal instinct is to debug them. This is one reason why hackers generally hate driving cars—the system of randomly programmed red lights and oddly laid out one-way streets causes delays which are so goddamned *unnecessary* that the impulse is to rearrange signs, open up traffic-light control boxes . . . redesign the entire system.

In a perfect hacker world, anyone pissed off enough to open up a control box near a traffic light and take it apart to make it work better should be perfectly welcome to make the attempt. Rules which prevent you from taking matters like that into your own hands are too ridiculous to even consider abiding by. This attitude helped the Model Railroad Club start, on an extremely informal basis, something called the Midnight Requisitioning Committee. When TMRC needed a set of diodes, or some extra relays, to build some new feature into The System, a few S&P people would wait until dark and find their way into the places where those things were kept. None of the hackers, who were as a rule scrupulously honest in other matters, seemed to equate this with "stealing." A willful blindness.

All information should be free.

If you don't have access to the information you need to improve things, how can you fix them? A free exchange of information, particularly when the information was in the form of a computer program, allowed for greater overall creativity. When you were working on a machine like the TX-0, which came with almost no software, everyone would furiously write systems programs to make programming easier—Tools to Make Tools, kept in the drawer by the console for easy access by anyone using the machine. This prevented the dread, time-wasting ritual of reinventing the wheel: instead of everybody writing his own version of the same program, the best version would be available to everyone, and everyone would be free to delve into the code and improve on *that*. A world studded with feature-full programs, bummed to the minimum, debugged to perfection.

The belief, sometimes taken unconditionally, that information should be free was a direct tribute to the way a splendid computer, or computer program, works—the binary bits moving in the most straightforward, logical path necessary to do their complex job. What was a computer but something which benefited from a free flow of information? If, say, the accumulator found itself unable to get information from the input/output (i/o) devices like the tape reader or the switches, the whole system would collapse. In the hacker viewpoint, any system could benefit from that easy flow of information.

Mistrust Authority—Promote Decentralization.

The best way to promote this free exchange of information is to have an open system, something which presents no boundaries between a hacker and a piece of information or an item of equipment that he needs in his quest for knowledge, improvement, and time on-line. The last thing you need is a bureaucracy. Bureaucracies, whether corporate, government, or university, are flawed systems, dangerous in that they cannot accommodate the exploratory impulse of true hackers. Bureaucrats hide behind arbitrary rules (as opposed to the logical algorithms by which machines and computer programs operate): they invoke those rules to consolidate power, and perceive the constructive impulse of hackers as a threat.

The epitome of the bureaucratic world was to be found at a very large company called International Business Machines—IBM. The reason its computers were batch-processed Hulking Giants was only partially because of vacuum tube technology. The real reason was that IBM was a clumsy, hulking company which did not understand the hacking impulse. If IBM had its way (so the TMRC hackers thought), the world would be batch-processed, laid out on those annoying little punch cards, and only the most privileged of priests would be permitted to actually interact with the computer.

All you had to do was look at someone in the IBM world, and note the button-down white shirt, the neatly pinned black tie, the hair carefully held in place, and the tray of punch cards in hand. You could wander into the Computation Center, where the 704, the 709, and later the 7090 were stored—the best IBM had to offer —and see the stifling orderliness, down to the roped-off areas beyond which non-authorized people could not venture. And you could compare that to the extremely informal atmosphere around the TX-0, where grungy clothes were the norm and almost anyone could wander in.

Now, IBM had done and would continue to do many things to advance computing. By its sheer size and mighty influence, it had made computers a permanent part of life in America. To many people, the words IBM and computer were virtually synonymous. IBM's machines were reliable workhorses, worthy of the trust that businessmen and scientists invested in them. This was due in part to IBM's conservative approach: it would not make the most technologically advanced machines, but would rely on proven concepts and careful, aggressive marketing. As IBM's dominance of the computer field was established, the company became an empire unto itself, secretive and smug.

What really drove the hackers crazy was the attitude of the IBM priests and sub-priests, who seemed to think that IBM had the only "real" computers, and the rest were all trash. You couldn't talk to those people—they were beyond convincing. They were batch-processed people, and it showed not only in their preference of machines, but in their idea about the way a computation center, and a world, should be run. Those people could never understand the obvious superiority of a decentralized system, with no one giving orders: a system where people could follow their interests, and if along the way they discovered a flaw in the system, they could embark on ambitious surgery. No need to get a requisition form. Just a need to get something done.

This antibureaucratic bent coincided neatly with the personalities of many of the hackers, who since childhood had grown accustomed to building science projects while the rest of their classmates were banging their heads together and learning social skills on the field of sport. These young adults who were once outcasts found the computer a fantastic equalizer, experiencing a feeling, according to Peter Samson, "like you opened the door and walked through this grand new universe . . ." Once they passed through that door and sat behind the console of a million-dollar computer, hackers had power. So it was natural to distrust any force which might try to limit the extent of that power.

Hackers should be judged by their hacking, not bogus criteria such as degrees, age, race, or position.

The ready acceptance of twelve-year-old Peter Deutsch in the TX-0 community (though not by non-hacker graduate students) was a good example. Likewise, people who trotted in with seemingly impressive credentials were not taken seriously until they proved themselves at the console of a computer. This meritocratic trait was not necessarily rooted in the inherent goodness of hacker hearts—it was mainly that hackers cared less about someone's superficial characteristics than they did about his potential to advance the general state of hacking, to create new programs to admire, to talk about that new feature in the system.

You can create art and beauty on a computer.

Samson's music program was an example. But to hackers, the art of the program did not reside in the pleasing sounds emanating from the on-line speaker. The code of the program held a beauty of its own. (Samson, though, was particularly obscure in refusing to add comments to his source code explaining what he was doing at a given time. One well-distributed program Samson wrote went on for hundreds of assembly language instructions, with only one comment beside an instruction which contained the number 1750. The comment was RIPJSB, and people racked their brains about its meaning until someone figured out that 1750 was the year Bach died, and that Samson had written an abbreviation for Rest In Peace Johann Sebastian Bach.)

A certain esthetic of programming style had emerged. Because of the limited memory space of the TX-0 (a handicap that extended to all computers of that era), hackers came to deeply appreciate innovative techniques which allowed programs to do complicated tasks with very few instructions. The shorter a program was, the more space you had left for other programs, and the faster a program ran. Sometimes when you didn't need speed or space much, and you weren't thinking about art and beauty, you'd hack together an ugly program, attacking the problem with "brute force" methods. "Well, we can do this by adding twenty numbers," Samson might say to himself, "and it's quicker to write instructions to do that than to think out a loop in the beginning and the end to do the same job in seven or eight instructions." But the latter program might be admired by fellow hackers, and some programs were bummed to the fewest lines so artfully that the author's peers would look at it and almost melt with awe.

Sometimes program bumming became competitive, a macho contest to prove oneself so much in command of the system that one could recognize elegant shortcuts to shave off an instruction or two, or, better yet, rethink the whole problem and devise a new algorithm which would save a whole block of instructions. (An algorithm is a specific procedure which one can apply to solve a complex computer problem; it is sort of a mathematical skeleton key.) This could most emphatically be done by approaching the problem from an offbeat angle that no one had ever thought of before but that in retrospect made total sense. There was definitely an artistic impulse residing in those who could utilize this genius-from-Mars technique—a black-magic, visionary quality which enabled them to discard the stale outlook of the best minds on earth and come up with a totally unexpected new algorithm.

This happened with the decimal print routine program. This was a subroutine—a program within a program that you could sometimes integrate into many different programs—to translate binary numbers that the computer gave you into regular decimal numbers. In Saunders' words, this problem became the "pawn's ass of programming—if you could write a decimal print routine which worked you knew enough about the computer to call yourself a programmer of sorts." And if you wrote a *great* decimal print routine, you might be able to call yourself a hacker. More than a competition, the ultimate bumming of the decimal print routine became a sort of hacker Holy Grail.

Various versions of decimal print routines had been around for some months. If you were being deliberately stupid about it, or if you were a genuine moron—an out-and-out "loser"—it might take you a hundred instructions to get the computer to convert machine language to decimal. But any hacker worth his salt could do it in less, and finally, by taking the best of the programs, bumming an instruction here and there, the routine was diminished to about fifty instructions.

After that, things got serious. People would work for hours, seeking a way to do the same thing in fewer lines of code. It became more than a competition; it was a quest. For all the effort expended, no one seemed to be able to crack the fifty-line barrier. The question arose whether it was even possible to do it in less. Was there a point beyond which a program could not be bummed?

Among the people puzzling with this dilemma was a fellow named Jensen, a tall, silent hacker from Maine who would sit quietly in the Kluge Room and scribble on printouts with the calm demeanor of a backwoodsman whittling. Jensen was always looking for ways to compress his programs in time and space—his code was a completely bizarre sequence of intermingled Boolean and arithmetic functions, often causing several different computations to occur in different sections of the same eighteen-bit "word." Amazing things, magical stunts.

Before Jensen, there had been general agreement that the only logical algorithm for a decimal print routine would have the machine repeatedly subtracting, using a table of the powers of ten to keep the numbers in proper digital columns. Jensen somehow figured that a powers-of-ten table wasn't necessary; he came up with an algorithm that was able to convert the digits in a reverse order but, by some digital sleight of hand, print them out in the proper order. There was a complex mathematical justification to it that was clear to the other hackers only when they saw Jensen's program posted on a bulletin board, his way of telling them that he had taken the decimal print routine to its limit. *Forty-six instructions.* People would stare at the code and their jaws would drop. Marge Saunders remembers the hackers being unusually quiet for days afterward.

"We knew that was the end of it," Bob Saunders later said. "That was Nirvana."

Computers can change your life for the better.

This belief was subtly manifest. Rarely would a hacker try to impose a view of the myriad advantages of the computer way of knowledge to an outsider. Yet this premise dominated the everyday behavior of the TX-0 hackers, as well as the generations of hackers that came after them.

Surely the computer had changed *their* lives, enriched their lives, given their lives focus, made their lives adventurous. It had made them masters of a certain slice of fate. Peter Samson later said, "We did it twenty-five to thirty percent for the sake of doing it because it was something we could do and do well, and sixty percent for the

sake of having something which was in its metaphorical way alive,
our offspring, which would do things on its own when we were
finished. That's the great thing about programming, the magical
appeal it has . . . Once you fix a behavioral problem [a computer
or program] has, it's fixed forever, and it is exactly an image of
what you meant."

Like Aladdin's lamp, you could get it to do your bidding.

Surely everyone could benefit from experiencing this power.
Surely everyone could benefit from a world based on the Hacker
Ethic. This was the implicit belief of the hackers, and the hackers
irreverently extended the conventional point of view of what computers could and should do—leading the world to a new way of
looking and interacting with computers.

This was not easily done. Even at such an advanced institution
as MIT, some professors considered a manic affinity for computers
as frivolous, even demented. TMRC hacker Bob Wagner once had
to explain to an engineering professor what a computer *was*. Wagner experienced this clash of computer versus anti-computer even
more vividly when he took a Numerical Analysis class in which the
professor required each student to do homework using rattling,
clunky electromechanical calculators. Kotok was in the same class,
and both of them were appalled at the prospect of working with
those lo-tech machines. "Why should we," they asked, "when
we've got this computer?"

So Wagner began working on a computer program that would
emulate the behavior of a calculator. The idea was outrageous. To
some, it was a misappropriation of valuable machine time. According to the standard thinking on computers, their time was so precious that one should only attempt things which took maximum
advantage of the computer, things that otherwise would take
roomfuls of mathematicians days of mindless calculating. Hackers
felt otherwise: anything that seemed interesting or fun was fodder
for computing—and using interactive computers, with no one
looking over your shoulder and demanding clearance for your specific project, you could act on that belief. After two or three
months of tangling with intricacies of floating-point arithmetic
(necessary to allow the program to know where to place the decimal point) on a machine that had no simple method to perform
elementary multiplication, Wagner had written three thousand
lines of code that did the job. He had made a ridiculously expensive computer perform the function of a calculator that cost a
thousand times less. To honor this irony, he called the program

Expensive Desk Calculator, and proudly did the homework for his class on it.

His grade—zero. "You used a computer!" the professor told him. "This *can't* be right."

Wagner didn't even bother to explain. How could he convey to his teacher that the computer was making realities out of what were once incredible possibilities? Or that another hacker had even written a program called Expensive Typewriter that converted the TX-0 to something you could write text on, could process your writing in strings of characters and print it out on the Flexowriter —could you imagine a professor accepting a classwork report *written by the computer?* How could that professor—how could, in fact, anyone who hadn't been immersed in this uncharted man-machine universe—understand how Wagner and his fellow hackers were routinely using the computer to simulate, according to Wagner, "strange situations which one could scarcely envision otherwise"? The professor would learn in time, as would everyone, that the world opened up by the computer was a limitless one.

If anyone needed further proof, you could cite the project that Kotok was working on in the Computation Center, the chess program that bearded AI professor "Uncle" John McCarthy, as he was becoming known to his hacker students, had begun on the IBM 704. Even though Kotok and the several other hackers helping him on the program had only contempt for the IBM batch-processing mentality that pervaded the machine and the people around it, they had managed to scrounge some late-night time to use it interactively, and had been engaging in an informal battle with the systems programmers on the 704 to see which group would be known as the biggest consumer of computer time. The lead would bounce back and forth, and the white-shirt-and-black-tie 704 people were impressed enough to actually let Kotok and his group touch the buttons and switches on the 704: rare sensual contact with a vaunted IBM beast.

Kotok's role in bringing the chess program to life was indicative of what was to become the hacker role in Artificial Intelligence: a Heavy Head like McCarthy or like his colleague Marvin Minsky would begin a project or wonder aloud whether something might be possible, and the hackers, if it interested them, would set about doing it.

The chess program had been started using FORTRAN, one of the early computer languages. Computer languages look more like English than assembly language, are easier to write with, and do more things with fewer instructions; however, each time an instruction is given in a computer language like FORTRAN, the computer must first translate that command into its own binary language. A program called a compiler does this, and the compiler takes up time to do its job, as well as occupying valuable space within the computer. In effect, using a computer language puts you an extra step away from direct contact with the computer, and hackers generally preferred assembly or, as they called it, "machine" language to less elegant, "higher-level" languages like FORTRAN.

Kotok, though, recognized that because of the huge amounts of numbers that would have to be crunched in a chess program, part of the program would have to be done in FORTRAN, and part in assembly. They hacked it part by part, with "move generators," basic data structures, and all kinds of innovative algorithms for strategy. After feeding the machine the rules for moving each piece, they gave it some parameters by which to evaluate its position, consider various moves, and make the move which would advance it to the most advantageous situation. Kotok kept at it for years, the program growing as MIT kept upgrading its IBM computers, and one memorable night a few hackers gathered to see the program make some of its first moves in a real game. Its opener was quite respectable, but after eight or so exchanges there was real trouble, with the computer about to be checkmated. Everybody wondered how the computer would react. It took a while (everyone knew that during those pauses the computer was actually "thinking," if your idea of thinking included mechanically considering various moves, evaluating them, rejecting most, and using a predefined set of parameters to ultimately make a choice). Finally, the computer moved a pawn two squares forward—illegally jumping over another piece. A bug! But a clever one—it got the computer out of check. Maybe the program was figuring out some new algorithm with which to conquer chess.

At other universities, professors were making public proclamations that computers would never be able to beat a human being in chess. Hackers knew better. They would be the ones who would guide computers to greater heights than anyone expected. And the hackers, by fruitful, meaningful association with the computer, would be foremost among the beneficiaries.

But they would not be the only beneficiaries. Everyone could gain something by the use of thinking computers in an intellectually automated world. And wouldn't everyone benefit even more by approaching the world with the same inquisitive intensity, skepticism toward bureaucracy, openness to creativity, unselfishness in sharing accomplishments, urge to make improvements, and desire to build as those who followed the Hacker Ethic? By accepting others on the same unprejudiced basis by which computers accepted anyone who entered code into a Flexowriter? Wouldn't we benefit if we learned from computers the means of creating a perfect system, and set about emulating that perfection in a human system? If *everyone* could interact with computers with the same innocent, productive, creative impulse that hackers did, the Hacker Ethic might spread through society like a benevolent ripple, and computers would indeed change the world for the better.

In the monastic confines of the Massachusetts Institute of Technology, people had the freedom to live out this dream—the hacker dream. No one dared suggest that the dream might spread. Instead, people set about building, right there at MIT, a hacker Xanadu the likes of which might never be duplicated.

3

SPACEWAR

IN the summer of 1961, Alan Kotok and the other TMRC hackers learned that a new company was soon to deliver to MIT, absolutely free, the next step in computing, a machine that took the interactive principles of the TX-0 several steps further. A machine that might be even better for hackers than the TX-0 was.

The PDP-1. It would change computing forever. It would make the still hazy hacker dream come a little closer to reality.

Alan Kotok had distinguished himself as a true wizard on the TX-0, so much so that he, along with Saunders, Samson, Wagner, and a few others, had been hired by Jack Dennis to be the Systems Programming Group of the TX-0. The pay would be a munificent $1.60 an hour. For a few of the hackers, the job was one more excuse not to go to classes—some hackers, like Samson, would never graduate, and be too busy hacking to really regret the loss. Kotok, though, was able not only to manage his classes, but to establish himself as a "canonical" hacker. Around the TX-0 and TMRC, he was acquiring legendary status. One hacker who was just arriving at MIT that year remembers Kotok giving newcomers a demonstration of how the TX-0 worked: "I got the impression he was hyperthyroid or something," recalled Bill Gosper, who would become a canonical hacker himself, "because he spoke very slowly and he was chubby and his eyes were half-closed. That was completely and utterly the wrong impression. [Around the TX-0] Kotok had infinite moral authority. He had written the chess program. He understood hardware." (This last was not an inconsiderable compliment—"understanding hardware" was akin to fathoming the Tao of physical nature.)

The summer that the word came out about the PDP-1, Kotok was working for Western Electric, kind of a dream job, since of all possible systems the phone system was admired most of all. The Model Railroad Club would often go on tours of phone company exchanges, much in the way that people with an interest in painting might tour a museum. Kotok found it interesting that at the phone company, which had gotten so big in its decades of development, only a few of the engineers had a broad knowledge of the interrelations within that system. Nevertheless, the engineers could readily provide detail on specific functions of the system, like crossbar switching and step-relays; Kotok and the others would hound these experts for information, and the flattered engineers, probably having no idea that these ultra-polite college kids would actually *use* the information, would readily comply.

Kotok made it a point to attend those tours, to read all the technical material he could get his hands on, and to see what he could get by dialing different numbers on the complex and little-understood MIT phone system. It was basic exploration, just like exploring the digital back alleys of the TX-0. During that previous winter of 1960–61, the TMRC hackers had engaged in an elaborate "telephone network fingerprinting," charting all the places you could reach by MIT's system of tie lines. Though not connected to general telephone lines, the system could take you to Lincoln Lab, and from there to defense contractors all over the country. It was a matter of mapping and testing. You would start with one access code, add different digits to it, see who might answer, ask whoever answered where they were, then add digits to that number to piggyback to the next place. Sometimes you could even reach outside lines in the suburbs, courtesy of the unsuspecting phone company. And, as Kotok would later admit, "If there was some design flaw in the phone system such that one could get calls that weren't intended to get through, I wasn't above doing that, but that was their problem, not mine."

Still, the motive was exploration, not fraud, and it was considered bad form to profit illegally from these weird connections. Sometimes outsiders could not comprehend this. Samson's roommates in the Burton Hall dorm, for instance, were non-hackers who thought it was all right to exploit system bugs without the holy justification of system exploration. After they pressured Samson for days, he finally gave in and handed them a twenty-digit number that he said would access an exotic location. "You can dial this from the hall phone," he told them, "but I don't want to be around." As they anxiously began dialing, Samson went to a downstairs phone, which rang just as he reached it. "This is the Pentagon," he boomed in his most official voice. "What is your security clearance, please?" From the phone upstairs, Samson heard terrified gasps, and the click of a phone being hung up.

Network fingerprinting was obviously a pursuit limited to hackers, whose desire to know the system overruled any fear of getting nailed.

But as much as phone company esoterica fascinated Kotok, the prospect of the PDP-1 took precedence. Perhaps he sensed that nothing, even phone hacking, would be the same afterward. The people who designed and marketed this new machine were not your ordinary computer company button-downs. The company was a brand-new firm called Digital Equipment Corporation (DEC), and some of the TX-0 users knew that DEC's first products were special interfaces made specifically for that TX-0. It was exciting enough that some of DEC's founders had a view of computing that differed from the gray-flannel, batch-processed IBM mentality; it was positively breathtaking that the DEC people seemed to have looked at the freewheeling, interactive, improvisational, hands-on-über-alles style of the TX-0 community, and designed a computer that would reinforce that kind of behavior. The PDP-1 (the initials were short for Programmed Data Processor, a term considered less threatening than "computer," which had all kinds of hulking-giant connotations) would become known as the first minicomputer, designed not for huge number-crunching tasks but for scientific inquiry, mathematical formulation . . . and hacking. It would be so compact that the whole setup was no larger than three refrigerators—it wouldn't require as much air-conditioning, and you could even turn it on without a whole crew of sub-priests being needed to sequence several power supplies in the right order or start the time-base generator, among other exacting tasks. The retail price of the computer was an astoundingly low $120,000—cheap enough so people might stop complaining about how precious every second of computer time was. But the machine, which was the second PDP-1 manufactured (the first one was sold to the nearby scientific firm of Bolt Beranek and Newman, or BBN), cost MIT nothing: it was donated by DEC to the RLE lab.

So it was clear that hackers would have even more time on it than they did on the TX-0.

The PDP-1 would be delivered with a simple collection of systems software which the hackers considered completely inadequate. The TX-0 hackers had become accustomed to the most advanced interactive software anywhere, a dazzling set of systems programs, written by hackers themselves and implicitly tailored to their relentless demands for control of the machine. Young Peter Deutsch, the twelve-year-old who had discovered the TX-0, had made good on his promise to write a spiffier assembler, and Bob Saunders had worked up a smaller, faster version of the FLIT debugger called Micro-FLIT. These programs had benefited from an expanded instruction set: one day, after considerable planning and designing by Saunders and Jack Dennis, the TX-0 had been turned off, and a covey of engineers exposed its innards and began hard-wiring new instructions into the machine. This formidable task expanded the assembly language by several instructions. When the pliers and screwdrivers were put away and the computer carefully turned on, everyone madly set about revamping programs and bumming old programs using the new instructions.

The PDP-1's instruction set, Kotok learned, was not too different from that of the expanded TX-0, so Kotok naturally began writing systems software for the PDP-1 that very summer, using all the spare time he could manage. Figuring that everyone would jump in and begin writing as soon as the machine got there, he worked on a translation of the Micro-FLIT debugger so that writing the software for the "One" would be easier. Samson promptly named Kotok's debugger "DDT," and the name would stick, though the program itself would be modified countless times by hackers who wanted to add features or bum instructions out of it.

Kotok was not the only one preparing for the arrival of the PDP-1. Like a motley collection of expectant parents, other hackers were busily weaving software booties and blankets for the new baby coming into the family, so this heralded heir to the computing throne would be welcome as soon as it was delivered in late September.

The hackers helped bring the PDP-1 into its new home, the Kluge Room next door to the TX-0. It was a beauty: sitting behind a console half as long as the Tixo's, you'd look at one compact panel of toggle switches and lights; next to that was the display screen, encased in a bright blue, six-sided, quasi-deco housing; behind it were the tall cabinets, the size of a refrigerator and three times as deep, with the wires, boards, switches, and transistors—entry to that, of course, was forbidden. There was a Flexowriter connected for on-line input (people complained about the noise so much that the Flexowriter was eventually replaced by a modified IBM typewriter which didn't work nearly so well) and a high-speed paper-tape reader, also for input. All in all, a downright heavenly toy.

Jack Dennis liked some of the software written by BBN for the prototype PDP-1, particularly the assembler. Kotok, though, felt like retching when he saw that assembler run—the mode of operation didn't seem to fit the on-the-fly style he liked—so he and a few others told Dennis that they wanted to write their own. "That's a bad idea," said Dennis, who wanted an assembler up and running right away, and figured that it would take weeks for the hackers to do it.

Kotok and the others were adamant. This was a program that they'd be living with. It had to be just perfect. (Of course no program ever is, but that never stopped a hacker.)

"I'll tell you what," said Kotok, this twenty-year-old Buddha-shaped wizard, to the skeptical yet sympathetic Jack Dennis. "If we write this program over the weekend and have it working, would you pay us for the time?"

The pay scale at that time was such that the total would be something under five hundred dollars. "That sounds like a fair deal," said Dennis.

Kotok, Samson, Saunders, Wagner, and a couple of others began on a Friday night late in September. They figured they would work from the TX-0 assembler that Dennis had written the original of and that twelve-year-old Peter Deutsch, among others, had revamped. They wouldn't change inputs or outputs, and they wouldn't redesign algorithms; each hacker would take a section of the TX-0 program and convert it to PDP-1 code. And they wouldn't sleep. Six hackers worked around two hundred and fifty man-hours that weekend, writing code, debugging, and washing down take-out Chinese food with massive quantities of Coca-Cola shipped over from the TMRC clubroom. It was a programming orgy, and when Jack Dennis came in that Monday he was astonished to find an assembler loaded into the PDP-1, which as a demonstration was assembling its own code into binary.

By sheer dint of hacking, the TX-0—no, the *PDP-1*—hackers had turned out a program in a weekend that it would have taken the computer industry weeks, maybe even months to pull off. It was a project that would probably not be undertaken by the computer industry without a long and tedious process of requisitions, studies, meetings, and executive vacillating, most likely with considerable compromise along the way. It might never have been done at all. The project was a triumph for the Hacker Ethic.

The hackers were given even more access to this new machine than they had managed to get on the TX-0, and almost all of them switched their operations to the Kluge Room. A few stubbornly stuck to the Tixo, and to the PDP-1 hackers this was grounds for some mild ridicule. To rub it in, the PDP-1 hackers developed a little demonstration based on the mnemonics of the instruction set of this bold new machine, which included such exotic instructions as DAC (Deposit Accumulator), LIO (Load Input-Output), DPY (Deplay), and JMP. The PDP-1 group would stand in a line and shout in unison:

> LAC,
> DAC,
> DIPPY DAP,
> LIO,
> DIO,
> JUMP!

When they chanted that last word—"Jump!"—they would all jump to the right. What was lacking in choreography was more than compensated for by enthusiasm: they were supercharged by the beauty of the machine, by the beauty of computers.

The same kind of enthusiasm was obvious in the even more spontaneous programming occurring on the PDP-1, ranging from serious systems programs, to programs to control a primitive robot arm, to whimsical hacks. One of the latter took advantage of a hacked-up connection between the PDP-1 and the TX-0—a wire through which information could pass, one bit at a time, between the two machines. According to Samson, the hackers called in the venerable AI pioneer John McCarthy to sit by the PDP-1. "Professor McCarthy, look at our new chess program!" And then they called another professor to sit by the TX-0. "Here's the chess program! Type in your move!" After McCarthy typed his first move, and it appeared on the Flexowriter on the TX-0, the hackers told the other professor that he had just witnessed the TX-0's opening move. "Now make yours!" After a few moves, McCarthy noticed that the computer was outputting the moves one letter at a time, sometimes with a suspicious pause between them. So McCarthy followed the wire to his flesh-and-blood opponent. The hackers rocked with mirth. But it would not be long before they would come up with programs for computers—no joke—to actually play tournament chess.

The PDP-1 beckoned the hackers to program without limit. Samson was casually hacking things like the Mayan calendar (which worked on a base-twenty number system) and working overtime on a version of his TX-0 music program that took advantage of the PDP-1's extended audio capabilities to create music in three voices—three-part Bach fugues, melodies interacting . . . computer music erupting from the old Kluge Room! The people at DEC had heard about Samson's program and asked him to complete it on the PDP-1, so Samson eventually worked it so that someone could type a musical score into the machine by a simple translation of notes into letters and digits, and the computer would respond with a three-voice organ sonata. Another group coded up Gilbert and Sullivan operettas.

Samson proudly presented the music compiler to DEC to distribute to anyone who wanted it. He was proud that other people would be using his program. The team that worked on the new assembler felt likewise. For instance, they were pleased to have paper tape bearing the program in the drawer so anyone using the machine could access it, try to improve it, bum a few instructions from it, or add a feature to it. They felt honored when DEC asked for the program so it could offer it to other PDP-1 owners. The question of royalties never came up. To Samson and the others, using the computer was such a joy that they would have paid to do it. The fact that they were getting paid the princely sum of $1.60 an hour to work on the computer was a bonus. As for royalties, wasn't software more like a gift to the world, something that was reward in itself? The idea was to make a computer more usable, to make it more exciting to users, to make computers so interesting that people would be tempted to play with them, explore them, and eventually hack on them. When you wrote a fine program you were building a community, not churning out a product.

Anyway, people shouldn't have to pay for software—information should be free!

•

The TMRC hackers were not the only ones who had been devising plans for the new PDP-1. During that summer of 1961, a plan for the most elaborate hack yet—a virtual showcase of what could come out of a rigorous application of the Hacker Ethic—was being devised. The scene of these discussions was a tenement building on Higham Street in Cambridge, and the original perpetrators were three itinerant programmers in their mid-twenties who'd been hanging around various computation centers for years. Two of the three lived in the tenement, so in honor of the pompous proclamations emanating from nearby Harvard University the trio mockingly referred to the building as the Higham Institute.

One of the Fellows of this bogus institution was Steve Russell, nicknamed, for unknown reasons, Slug. He had that breathless-chipmunk speech pattern so common among hackers, along with thick glasses, modest height, and a fanatic taste for computers, bad movies, and pulp science fiction. All three interests were shared by the resident attendees at those bull sessions on Higham Street.

Russell had long been a "coolie" (to use a TMRC term) of Uncle John McCarthy. McCarthy had been trying to design and implement a higher-level language that might be sufficient for artificial intelligence work. He thought he had found it in LISP. The language was named for its method of List Processing; by simple yet powerful commands, LISP could do many things with few lines of code; it could also perform powerful recursions—references to things within itself—which would allow programs written in that language to actually "learn" from what happened as the program ran. The problem with LISP at that time was that it took up an awful amount of space on a computer, ran very slowly, and generated voluminous amounts of extra code as the programs ran, so much so that it needed its own "garbage collection" program to periodically clean out the computer memory.

Russell was helping Uncle John write a LISP interpreter for the Hulking Giant IBM 704. It was, in his words, "a horrible engineering job," mostly due to the batch-processing tedium of the 704.

Compared to that machine, the PDP-1 looked like the Promised Land to Slug Russell. More accessible than the TX-0, and no batch-processing! Although it didn't seem big enough to do LISP, it had other marvelous capabilities, some of which were objects of discussion of the Higham Institute. What particularly intrigued Russell and his friends was the prospect of making up some kind of elaborate "display hack" on the PDP-1, using the CRT screen. After considerable midnight discourse, the three-man Higham Institute put itself on record as insisting that the most effective demonstration of the computer's magic would be a visually striking game.

There had been several attempts to do this kind of thing on the TX-0. One of them was a hack called Mouse in the Maze—the user first constructed a maze with the light pen, and a blip on the screen representing a mouse would tentatively poke its way through the maze in search of another set of blips in the shape of cheese wedges. There was also a "VIP version" of the game, in which the mouse would seek martini glasses. After it got to the glass, it would seek another, until it ran out of energy, too drunk to continue. When you flicked the switches to run the mouse through the maze a second time, though, the mouse would "remember" the path to the glasses, and like an experienced barfly would unhesitatingly scurry toward the booze. That was as far as display hacks would go on the TX-0.

But already on the PDP-1, which had a screen that was easier to program than the TX-0's, there had been some significant display hacks. The most admired effort was created by one of the twin gurus of artificial intelligence at MIT, Marvin Minsky. (The other one was, of course, McCarthy.) Minsky was more outgoing than his fellow AI guru, and more willing to get into the hacker mode of activity. He was a man with very big ideas about the future of computing—he really believed that one day machines would be able to think, and he would often create a big stir by publicly calling human brains "meat machines," implying that machines not made of meat would do as well some day. An elfish man with twinkling eyes behind thick glasses, a starkly bald head, and an omnipresent turtleneck sweater, Minsky would say this with his usual dry style, geared simultaneously to maximize provocation and to leave just a hint that it was all some cosmic goof—*of course machines can't think, heh-heh*. Marvin was the real thing; the PDP-1 hackers would often sit in on his course, Intro to AI 6.544, because not only was Minsky a good theoretician, but he knew his stuff. By the early 1960s, Minsky was beginning to organize what would come to be the world's first laboratory in artificial intelligence; and he knew that, to do what he wanted, he would need programming geniuses as his foot soldiers—so he encouraged hackerism in any way he could.

One of Minsky's contributions to the growing canon of interesting hacks was a display program on the PDP-1 called the Circle Algorithm. It was discovered by mistake, actually—while trying to bum an instruction out of a short program to make straight lines into curves or spirals, Minsky inadvertently mistook a "Y" character for a "Y prime," and instead of the display squiggling into inchoate spirals as expected, it drew a circle: an incredible discovery, which was later found to have profound mathematical implications. Hacking further, Minsky used the Circle Algorithm as a stepping-off point for a more elaborate display in which three particles influenced each other and made fascinating, swirling patterns on the screen, self-generating roses with varying numbers of leaves. "The forces particles exerted on others were totally outlandish," Bob Wagner later recalled. "You were simulating a violation of natural law!" Minsky called the hack a "Tri-Pos: Three-Position Display" program, but the hackers affectionately renamed it the Minskytron.

Slug Russell was inspired by this. At the Higham Institute sessions some months back, he and his friends had discussed the criteria for the ultimate display hack. Since they had been fans of trashy science fiction, particularly the space opera novels of E. E. "Doc" Smith, they somehow decided that the PDP-1 would be a perfect machine to make a combination grade-B movie and $120,000 toy. A game in which two people could face each other in an outer-space showdown. A Higham Institute Study Group on Space Warfare was duly organized, and its conclusion strongly implied that Slug Russell should be the author of this historic hack.

But months later, Russell hadn't even started. He would watch the Minskytron make patterns, he'd flip switches to see new patterns develop, and every so often he'd flip more switches when the program got wedged into inactivity. He was fascinated, but thought the hack too abstract and mathematical. "This demo is a crock," he finally decided—only thirty-two or so instructions, and it didn't really *do* anything.

Slug Russell knew that his war-in-outer-space game *would* do something. In its own kitschy, sci-fi terms, it would be absorbing the way no previous hack had ever been. The thing that got Slug into computers in the first place was the feeling of power you got from running the damn things. You can tell the computer what to do, and it fights with you, but it finally does what you tell it to. Of course it will reflect your own stupidity, and often what you tell it to do will result in something distasteful. But eventually, after tortures and tribulations, it will do *exactly* what you want. The feeling you get then is unlike any other feeling in the world. It can make you a junkie. It made Slug Russell a junkie, and he could see that it had done the same thing to the hackers who haunted the Kluge

Room until dawn. It was that feeling that did it, and Slug Russell guessed the feeling was power.

Slug got sort of a similar, though less intense, feeling from Doc Smith's novels. He let his imagination construct the thrill of roaring across space in a white rocket ship . . . and wondered if that same excitement could be captured while sitting behind the console of the PDP-1. *That* would be the Spacewar he dreamed about. Once again he vowed to do it.

Later.

Slug was not as driven as some of the other hackers. Sometimes he needed a push. After he made the mistake of opening up his big mouth about this program he was going to write, the PDP-1 hackers, always eager to see another hack added to the growing pile of paper tapes in the drawer, urged him to *do* it. After mumbling excuses for a while, he said he would, but he'd first have to figure out how to write the elaborate sine-cosine routines necessary to plot the ships' motion.

Kotok knew that hurdle could be easily solved. Kotok at that point had been getting fairly cozy with the people at DEC, several miles away at Maynard. DEC was informal, as computer manufacturers went, and did not regard MIT hackers as the grungy, frivolous computer-joyriders that IBM might have taken them for. For instance, one day when a piece of equipment was broken, Kotok called up Maynard and told DEC about it; they said, Come up and get a replacement. By the time Kotok got up there, it was well after five and the place was closed. But the night watchman let him go in, find the desk of the engineer he'd been talking to, and root through the desk until he found the part. Informal, the way hackers like it. So it was no problem for Kotok to go up to Maynard one day, where he was positive someone would have a routine for sine and cosine that would run on the PDP-1. Sure enough, someone had it, and since information was free, Kotok took it back to Building 26.

"Here you are, Russell," Kotok said, paper tapes in hand. "Now what's your excuse?"

At that point, Russell had no excuse. So he spent his off-hours writing this fantasy PDP-1 game the likes of which no one had seen before. Soon he was spending his "on" hours working on the game. He began in early December, and when Christmas came he was still hacking. When the calendar wrapped around to 1962, he was still hacking. By that time, Russell could produce a dot on the screen which you could manipulate: by flicking some of the tiny toggle switches on the control panel you could make the dots accelerate and change direction.

He then set about making the shapes of the two rocket ships: both were classic cartoon rockets, pointed at the top and blessed with a set of fins at the bottom. To distinguish them from each other, he made one chubby and cigar-shaped, with a bulge in the middle, while the second he shaped like a thin tube. Russell used the sine and cosine routines to figure out how to move those shapes in different directions. Then he wrote a subroutine to shoot a "torpedo" (a dot) from the rocket nose with a switch on the computer. The computer would scan the position of the torpedo and the enemy ship; if both occupied the same area, the program would call up a subroutine that replaced the unhappy ship with a random splatter of dots representing an explosion. (That process was called "collision detection.")

All of this was actually a significant conceptual step toward more sophisticated "real-time" programming, where what happens on a computer matches the frame of reference in which human beings are actually working. In another sense, Russell was emulating the on-line, interactive debugging style that the hackers were championing—the freedom to see what instruction your program stopped dead on, and to use switches or the Flexowriter to jimmy in a different instruction, all while the program was running along with the DDT debugger. The game Spacewar, a computer program itself, helped show how all games—and maybe everything else—worked like computer programs. When you went a bit astray, you modified your parameters and fixed it. You put in new instructions. The same principle applied to target shooting, chess strategy, and MIT course work. Computer programming was not merely a technical pursuit, but an approach to the problems of living.

In the later stages of programming, Saunders helped Slug Russell out, and they hacked a few intense six-to-eight-hour sessions. Sometime in February, Russell unveiled the basic game. There were the two ships, each with thirty-one torpedoes. There were a few random dots on the screen representing stars in this celestial battlefield. You could maneuver the ships by flicking four switches on the console of the PDP-1, representing Clockwise turn, Counterclockwise turn, Accelerate, and Fire torpedo.

Slug Russell knew that by showing a rough version of the game, and dropping a paper tape with the program into the box with the PDP-1 system programs, he was welcoming unsolicited improvements. Spacewar was no ordinary computer simulation—you could actually *be* a rocket-ship pilot. It was Doc Smith come to life. But the same power that Russell had drawn on to make his program—the power that the PDP-1 lent a programmer to create his own little universe—was also available to other hackers, who naturally felt free to improve Slug Russell's universe. They did so instantly.

The nature of the improvements might be summed up by the general hacker reaction to the original routine Slug Russell used for his torpedoes. Knowing that military weapons in real life aren't always perfect, Russell figured that he'd make the torpedoes realistic. Instead of having them go in a straight line until they ran out of steam and exploded, he put in some random variations in the direction and velocity. Instead of appreciating this verisimilitude, the hackers denounced it. They loved smooth-running systems and reliable tools, so the fact that they would be stuck with something that *didn't work right* drove them crazy. Russell later figured out that "weapons or tools that aren't very trustworthy are held in very low esteem—people really like to be able to trust their tools and weapons. That was very clear in that case."

But of course that could be easily fixed. The advantage that a world created by a computer program had over the real world was that you could fix a dire problem like faulty torpedoes just by changing a few instructions. That was why so many people found it easy to lose themselves in hackerism in the first place! So the torpedoes were fixed, and people spent hours in outer-space dueling. And even more hours trying to make the Spacewar world a better one.

Peter Samson, for instance, loved the idea of Spacewar, but could not abide the randomly generated dots that passed themselves off as the sky. Real space had stars in specific places. "We'll have the real thing," Samson vowed. He obtained a thick atlas of the universe, and set about entering data into a routine he wrote that would generate the actual constellations visible to someone standing on the equator on a clear night. All stars down to the fifth magnitude were represented; Samson duplicated their relative brightness by controlling how often the computer lit the dot on the screen which represented the star. He also rigged the program so that, as the game progressed, the sky would majestically scroll—at any one time the screen exposed 45 percent of the sky. Besides adding verisimilitude, this "Expensive Planetarium" program also gave rocket fighters a mappable background from which to gauge position. The game could truly be called, as Samson said, Shootout-at-El-Cassiopeia.

Another programmer named Dan Edwards was dissatisfied with the unanchored movement of the two dueling ships. It made the game merely a test of motor skills. He figured that adding a gravity factor would give the game a strategic component. So he programmed a central star—a sun—in the middle of the screen; you could use the sun's gravitational pull to give you speed as you circled it, but if you weren't careful and got too close, you'd be drawn into the sun. Which was certain death.

Before all the strategic implications of this variation could be employed, Shag Garetz, one of the Higham Institute trio, contributed a wild-card type of feature. He had read in Doc Smith's novels how space hot-rodders could suck themselves out of one galaxy and into another by virtue of a "hyper-spatial tube," which would throw you into "that highly enigmatic Nth space." So he added a "hyperspace" capability to the game, allowing a player to avoid a dire situation by pushing a panic button that would zip him to this hyperspace. You were allowed to go into hyperspace three times in the course of a game; the drawback was that you never knew where you might come out. Sometimes you'd reappear right next to the sun, just in time to see your ship hopelessly pulled to an untimely demise on the sun's surface. In tribute to Marvin Minsky's original hack, Garetz programmed the hyperspace feature so that a ship entering hyperspace would leave a "warp-induced photonic stress emission signature"—a leftover smear of light in a shape that often formed in the aftermath of a Minskytron display.

The variations were endless. By switching a few parameters you could turn the game into "hydraulic spacewar," in which torpedoes flow out in ejaculatory streams instead of one by one. Or, as the night grew later and people became locked into interstellar mode, someone might shout, "Let's turn on the Winds of Space!" and someone would hack up a warping factor which would force players to make adjustments every time they moved. Though any improvement a hacker wished to make would be welcome, it was extremely bad form to make some weird change in the game unannounced. The effective social pressures which enforced the Hacker Ethic—which urged hands-on for improvement, not damage—prevented any instance of that kind of mischief. Anyway, the hackers were already engaged in a mind-boggling tweak of the system—they were using an expensive computer to play the world's most glorified game!

Spacewar was played a hell of a lot. For some, it was addictive. Though no one could officially sign up the PDP-1 for a Spacewar session, the machine's every free moment that spring seemed to have some version of the game running. Bottles of Coke in hand (and sometimes with money on the line), the hackers would run marathon tournaments. Russell eventually wrote a subroutine that would keep score, displaying in octal (everyone could sight-read that base-eight number system by then) the total of games won. For a while, the main drawback seemed to be that working the switches on the console of the PDP-1 was uncomfortable—everybody was getting sore elbows from keeping their arms at that particular angle. So one day Kotok and Saunders went over to the TMRC clubroom and found parts for what would become the first computer joysticks. Constructed totally with parts lying around the clubroom and thrown together in an hour of inspired construction, the control boxes were made of wood, with Masonite tops. They had switches for rotation and thrust, as well as a button for hyperspace. All controls were, of course, silent, so that you could surreptitiously circle around your opponent or duck into Nth space, should you care to.

While some hackers lost interest in Spacewar once the fury of the programming phase had died down, others developed a killer instinct for devising strategies to mow down opponents. Most games were won and lost in the first few seconds. Wagner became adept at the "lie in wait" strategy, in which you stayed silent while gravity whipped you around the sun, then straightened out and began blasting torps at your opponent. Then there was a variation called the "CBS Opening," where you angled to shoot and *then* whipped around the star: the strategy got its name because when both Spacewar gladiators tried it, they would leave a pattern on the screen that bore a remarkable resemblance to the CBS eye. Saunders, who took his Spacewar seriously, used a modified CBS strategy to maintain dominance through the tournaments—there was a time when he couldn't be beaten. However, after twenty minutes of protecting your place in the king-of-the-hill-structured contest, even a master Spacewarrior would get a bit blurry-eyed and slower on the draw, and most everybody got a chance to play Spacewar more than was probably sensible. Peter Samson, second only to Saunders in Spacewarring, realized this one night when he went home to Lowell. As he stepped out of the train, he stared upward into the crisp, clear sky. A meteor flew overhead. *Where's the spaceship?* Samson thought as he instantly swiveled back and grabbed the air for a control box that wasn't there.

In May 1962, at the annual MIT Open House, the hackers fed

the paper tape with twenty-seven pages worth of PDP-1 assembly language code into the machine, set up an extra display screen—actually a giant oscilloscope—and ran Spacewar all day to a public that drifted in and could not believe what they saw. The sight of it —a science-fiction game written by students and controlled by a computer—was so much on the verge of fantasy that no one dared predict that an entire genre of entertainment would eventually be spawned from it.

It wasn't till years later, when Slug Russell was at Stanford University, that he realized that the game was anything but a hacker aberration. After working late one night, Russell and some friends went to a local bar which had some pinball machines. They played until closing time; then, instead of going home, Russell and his coworkers went back to their computer, and the first thing his friends did was run Spacewar. Suddenly it struck Steve Russell: "These people just stopped playing a pinball machine and went to play Spacewar—by gosh, it *is* a pinball machine." The most advanced, imaginative, expensive pinball machine the world had seen.

Like the hackers' assemblers and the music program, Spacewar was not sold. Like any other program, it was placed in the drawer for anyone to access, look at, and rewrite as they saw fit. The group effort that stage by stage had improved the program could have stood for an argument for the Hacker Ethic: an urge to get inside the workings of the thing and make it better had led to measurable improvement. And of course it was all a huge amount of fun. It was no wonder that other PDP-1 owners began to hear about it, and the paper tapes holding Spacewar were freely distributed. At one point the thought crossed Slug Russell's mind that maybe someone *should* be making money from this, but by then there were already dozens of copies circulating. DEC was delighted to get a copy, and the engineers there used it as a final diagnostic program on PDP-1s before they rolled them out the door. Then, without wiping the computer memory clean, they'd shut the machine off. The DEC sales force knew this, and often, when machines were delivered to new customers, the salesman would turn on the power, check to make sure no smoke was pouring out the back, and hit the "VY" location where Spacewar resided. And if the machine had been carefully packed and shipped, the heavy star would be in the center, and the cigar-shaped rocket and the tube-shaped rocket would be ready for cosmic battle. A maiden flight for a magic machine.

•

Spacewar, as it turned out, was the lasting legacy of the pioneers of MIT hacking. In the next couple of years many of the TX-0 and PDP-1 joyriders departed the Institute. Saunders would take a job in industry at Santa Monica (where he would later write a Spacewar for the PDP-7 he used at work). Bob Wagner went off to the Rand Corporation. Peter Deutsch went to Berkeley, to begin his freshman year of college. Kotok took a part-time job which developed into an important designing position at DEC (though he managed to hang around TMRC and the PDP-1 for years afterward). In a development which was to have considerable impact on spreading MIT-style hackerism outside of Cambridge, John McCarthy left the Institute to begin a new artificial intelligence lab on the West Coast, at Stanford University. Slug Russell, ever McCarthy's LISP-writing coolie, tagged along.

But new faces and some heightened activity in the field of computing were to insure that the hacker culture at MIT would not only continue, but thrive and develop more than ever. The new faces belonged to breathtakingly daring hackers destined for word-of-mouth, living-legend fame. But the developments which would allow these people to take their place in living the hacker dream were already under way—initiated by people whose names would become known by more conventional means: scholarly papers, academic awards, and, in some cases, notoriety in the scientific community.

These people were the planners. Among them were scientists who occasionally engaged in hacking—Jack Dennis, McCarthy, Minsky—but who were ultimately more absorbed by the goals of computing than addicted to the computing process. They saw computers as a means to a better life for the human race, but did not necessarily think that working on a computer would be the key element in making that life better.

Some of the planners envisioned a day when artificially intelligent computers would relieve man's mental burdens, much as industrial machinery had already partially lifted his physical yoke. McCarthy and Minsky were the vanguard of this school of thought, and both had participated in a 1956 Dartmouth conference that established a foundation for research in this field. McCarthy's work in the higher-level language LISP was directed toward this end, and was sufficiently intriguing to rouse hackers like Slug Russell, Peter Deutsch, Peter Samson, and others into working with LISP. Minsky seemed interested in artificial intelligence with a more theoretical basis: a gleeful, bald-headed Johnny Appleseed in the field, he would spread his seeds, each one a thought capable of blooming into a veritable apple tree of useful AI techniques and projects.

The planners were also extremely concerned about getting the power of computers into the hands of more researchers, scientists, statisticians, and students. Some planners worked on making computers easier to use; John Kemeny of Dartmouth showed how this could be done by writing an easier-to-use computer language called BASIC—programs written in BASIC ran much slower than assembly language and took up more memory space, but did not require the almost monastic commitment that machine language demanded. MIT planners concentrated on extending actual computer access to more people. There were all sorts of justifications for this, not the least being the projected scale of economy—one that was glaringly preferable to the then current system, in which even seconds of computer time were valuable commodities (though you would not know it around the Spacewar-playing PDP-1). If more people used computers, more expert programmers and theoreticians would emerge, and the science of computing—yes, these aggressive planners were calling it a science—could only benefit by that new talent. But there was something else involved in this. It was something any hacker could understand—the belief that computing, in and of itself, was positive. John McCarthy illustrated that belief when he said that the natural state of man was to be online to a computer all the time. "What the user wants is a computer that he can have continuously at his beck and call for long periods of time."

The man of the future. Hands on a keyboard, eyes on a CRT, in touch with the body of information and thought that the world had been storing since history began. It would all be accessible to Computational Man.

None of this would occur with the batch-processed IBM 704. Nor would it occur with the TX-0 and PDP-1, with their weekly log sheets completely filled in within hours of being posted on the wall. No, in order to do this, you'd have to have several people use the computer at once. (The thought of each person having his or her own computer was something only a hacker would think worthwhile.) This multi-user concept was called time-sharing, and in 1960 the heaviest of the MIT planners began the Long-Range Computer Study Group. Among the members were people who had watched the rise of the MIT hacker with amusement and assent, people like Jack Dennis, Marvin Minsky, and Uncle John McCarthy. They knew how important it was for people to actually get their hands on those things. To them, it was not a question of whether to time-share or not—it was a question of how to do it.

Computer manufacturers, particularly IBM, were not enthusiastic. It was clear that MIT would have to go about it pretty much on its own. (The research firm of Bolt Beranek and Newman was also working on time-sharing.) Eventually two projects began at MIT: one was Jack Dennis' largely solo effort to write a time-sharing system for the PDP-1. The other was undertaken by a professor named F. J. Corbató, who would seek some help from the reluctant goliath, IBM, to write a system for the 7090.

The Department of Defense, especially through its Advanced Research Projects Agency (ARPA), had been supporting computers since the war, mindful of their eventual applications toward military use. So by the early sixties, MIT had obtained a long-range grant for its time-sharing project, which would be named Project MAC (the initials stood for two things: Multiple Access Computing, and Machine Aided Cognition). Uncle Sam would cough up three million dollars a year. Dennis would be in charge. Marvin Minsky would also be a large presence, particularly in using the one-third share of the money that would go not for time-sharing development, but for the still ephemeral field of artificial intelligence. Minsky was delighted, since the million dollars was ten times his previous budget for AI, and he realized that a good part of the remaining two thirds would see its way into AI activities as well. It was a chance to set up an ideal facility, where people could plan for the realization of the hacker dream with sophisticated machines, shielded from the bureaucratic lunacy of the outside world. Meanwhile, the hacker dream would be lived day by day by devoted students of the machine.

The planners knew that they'd need special people to staff this lab. Marvin Minsky and Jack Dennis knew that the enthusiasm of brilliant hackers was essential to bring about their Big Ideas. As Minsky later said of his lab: "In this environment there were several things going on. There were the most abstract theories of artificial intelligence that people were working on and some of [the hackers] were concerned with those, most weren't. But there was the question of how do you make the programs that do these things and how do you get them to work."

Minsky was quite happy to resolve that question by leaving it to the hackers, the people to whom "computers were the most interesting thing in the world." The kind of people who, for a lark, would hack up something even wilder than Spacewar and then, instead of playing it all night (as sometimes was happening in the Kluge Room), would hack some more. Instead of space simulations, the hackers who did the scut work at Project MAC would be tackling larger systems—robotic arms, vision projects, mathematical conundrums, and labyrinthine time-sharing systems that boggled the imagination. Fortunately, the classes that entered MIT in the early sixties were to provide some of the most devoted and brilliant hackers who ever sat at a console. And none of them so fully fit the title "hacker" as Richard Greenblatt.

4

GREENBLATT
AND GOSPER

Ricky Greenblatt was a hacker waiting to happen. Years later, when he was known throughout the nation's computer centers as the archetypal hacker, when the tales of his single-minded concentration were almost as prolific as the millions of lines of assembly language code he'd hacked, someone would ask him how it all started. He'd twist back in his chair, looking not as rumpled as he did back as an undergraduate, when he was cherub-faced and dark-haired and painfully awkward of speech; the question, he figured, came down to whether hackers were born or made, and out came one of the notorious non sequiturs which came to be known as Blatt-isms: "If hackers are born, then they're going to get made, and if they're made into it, they were born."

But Greenblatt would admit that he was a born hacker.

Not that his first encounter with the PDP-1 had changed his life. He was interested, all right. It had been freshman rush week at MIT, and Ricky Greenblatt had some time on his hands before tackling his courses, ready for academic glory. He visited the places that interested him most: the campus radio station WTBS (MIT's was perhaps the only college radio station in the country with a surfeit of student audio engineers and a shortage of disc jockeys), the Tech Model Railroad Club, and the Kluge Room in Building 26 which held the PDP-1.

Some hackers were playing Spacewar.

It was the general rule to play the game with all the room lights turned off, so the people crowded around the console would have their faces eerily illuminated by this display of spaceships and heavy stars. Rapt faces lit by the glow of the computer. Ricky Greenblatt was impressed. He watched the cosmic clashes for a while, then went next door to look over the TX-0, with its racks of tubes and transistors, its fancy power supplies, its lights and switches. His high school math club back in Columbia, Missouri, had visited the state university's batch-processed computer, and he'd seen a giant card-sorting machine at a local insurance company. But nothing like this. Still, despite being impressed with the radio station, the Model Railroad Club, and especially the computers, he set about making dean's list.

This scholastic virtue could not last. Greenblatt, even more than your normal MIT student, was a willing conscript of the Hands-On Imperative. His life had been changed irrevocably the day in 1954 that his father, visiting the son he hadn't lived with since an early divorce, took him to the Memorial Student Union at the University of Missouri, not far from Ricky's house in Columbia. Ricky Greenblatt took to the place immediately. It wasn't merely because of the comfortable lounge, the television set, the soft-drink bar . . . It was because of the students, who were more of an intellectual match for nine-year-old Ricky Greenblatt than were his classmates. He would go there to play chess, and he usually had no problem beating the college students. He was a very good chess player.

One of his chess victims was a UM engineering student on the GI bill. His name was Lester, and Lester's gift to this nine-year-old prodigy was a hands-on introduction to the world of electronics. A world where there were no ambiguities. Logic prevailed. You had a degree of control over things. You could build things according to your own plan. To a nine-year-old whose intelligence might have made him uncomfortable with his chronological peers, a child affected by a marital split which was typical of a world of human relations beyond his control, electronics was the perfect escape.

Lester and Ricky worked on ham radio projects. They tore apart old television sets. Before finishing college, Lester introduced Ricky to a Mr. Houghton, who ran a local radio shop, and that became a second home to the youngster through high school. With a high school friend, Greenblatt built a gamut of hairy projects. Amplifiers, modulators, all sorts of evil-looking vacuum tube contraptions. An oscilloscope. Ham radios. A television camera. A television camera! It seemed like a good idea, so they built it. And of course when it came time to choose a college, Richard Greenblatt picked MIT. He entered in the fall of 1962.

The course work was rigid during his first term, but Greenblatt was handling it without much problem. He had developed a relationship with a few campus computers. He had gotten lucky, landing the elective course called EE 641—Introduction to Computer Programming—and he would often go down to the punch-card machines at EAM to make programs for the Hulking Giant 7090. Also, his roommate, Mike Beeler, had been taking a course in something called Nomography. The students taking the class had hands-on access to an IBM 1620—set in yet another enclave of those misguided priests whose minds had been clouded with the ignorant fog that came from the IBM sales force. Greenblatt would often accompany Beeler to the 1620, where you would punch up your card deck, and stand in line. When your turn came, you'd dump your cards in the reader and get an instant printout from a plotter-printer. "It was sort of a fun, evening thing to do," Beeler would later recall. "We'd do it the way others might watch a sports game, or go out and have a beer." It was limited but gratifying. It made Greenblatt want more.

Around Christmas time, he finally felt comfortable enough to hang out at the Model Railroad Club. There, around such people as Peter Samson, it was natural to fall into hacker mode. (Computers had various states called "modes," and hackers often used that phrase to describe conditions in real life.) Samson had been working on a big timetable program for the TMRC operating sessions on the giant layout; because of the number crunching required, Samson had done it in FORTRAN on the 7090. Greenblatt decided to write the first FORTRAN for the PDP-1. Just why he decided to do this is something he could never explain, and chances are no one asked. It was common, if you wanted to do a task on a machine and the machine didn't have the software to do it, to write the proper software so you *could* do it. This was an impulse that Greenblatt would later elevate to an art form.

He did it, too. Wrote a program that would enable you to write in FORTRAN, taking what you wrote and compiling the code into machine language, as well as transforming the computer's machine language responses back into FORTRAN. Greenblatt did his FORTRAN compiler largely in his room, since he had trouble getting enough access to the PDP-1 to work on-line. Besides that, he got involved in working on a new system of relays underneath the layout at TMRC. It seems that the plaster in the room (which was always pretty grungy anyway, because custodial people were officially barred entry) kept falling, and some of it would get on the contacts of the system that Jack Dennis had masterminded in the mid-fifties. Also, there was something new called a wire-spring relay which looked better than the old kind. So Greenblatt spent a good deal of time that spring doing that. Along with PDP-1 hacking.

It is funny how things happen. You begin working conscientiously as a student, you make the dean's list, and then you discover something which puts classes into their proper perspective: they are totally irrelevant to the matter at hand. The matter at hand was hacking, and it seemed obvious—at least, so obvious that no one around TMRC or the PDP-1 seemed to think it even a useful topic of discourse—that hacking was a pursuit so satisfying that you could make a life of it. While a computer is very complex, it is not nearly as complex as the various comings and goings and interrelationships of the human zoo; but, unlike formal or informal study of the social sciences, hacking gave you not only an understanding of the system but an addictive control as well, along with the illusion that total control was just a few features away. Naturally, you go about building those aspects of the system that seem most necessary to work within the system in the proper way. Just as naturally, working in this improved system lets you know of more things that need to be done. Then someone like Marvin Minsky might happen along and say, "Here is a robot arm. I am leaving this robot arm by the machine." Immediately, nothing in the world is as essential as making the proper interface between the machine and the robot arm, and putting the robot arm under your control, and figuring a way to create a system where the robot arm knows what the hell it is doing. Then you can see your offspring come to life. How can something as contrived as an engineering class compare to that? Chances are that your engineering professor has never done anything half as interesting as the problems you are solving every day on the PDP-1. Who's right?

By Greenblatt's sophomore year, the computer scene around the PDP-1 was changing considerably. Though a few more of the original TX-0 hackers had departed, there was new talent arriving, and the new, ambitious setup, funded by the benevolent Department of Defense, nicely accommodated their hacking. A second PDP-1 had arrived; its home was the new, nine-story rectangular building on Main Street—a building of mind-numbing dullness, with no protuberances, and sill-less windows that looked painted onto its off-white surface. The building was called Tech Square, and among the MIT and corporate clients moving in was Project MAC. The ninth floor of this building, where the computers were, would be home to a generation of hackers, and none would spend as much time there as Greenblatt.

Greenblatt was getting paid (sub-minimum wages) for hacking as a student employee, as were several hackers who worked on the system or were starting to develop some of the large programs that would do artificial intelligence. They started to notice that this awkwardly polite sophomore was a potential PDP-1 superstar.

He was turning out an incredible amount of code, hacking as much as he could, or sitting with a stack of printouts, marking them up. He'd shuttle between the PDP-1 and TMRC, with his head fantastically wired with the structures of the program he was working on, or the system of relays he'd hacked under the TMRC layout. To hold that concentration for a long period of time, he lived, as did several of his peers, the thirty-hour day. It was conducive to intense hacking, since you had an extended block of waking hours to get going on a program, and, once you were really rolling, little annoyances like sleep need not bother you. The idea was to burn away for thirty hours, reach total exhaustion, then go home and collapse for twelve hours. An alternative would be to collapse right there in the lab. A minor drawback of this sort of schedule was that it put you at odds with the routines which everyone else in the world used to do things like keep appointments, eat, and go to classes. Hackers could accommodate this—one would commonly ask questions like "What phase is Greenblatt in?" and someone who had seen him recently would say, "I think he's in a night phase now, and should be in around nine or so." Professors did not adjust to those phases so easily, and Greenblatt "zorched" his classes.

He was placed on academic probation, and his mother came to Massachusetts to confer with the dean. There was some explaining to do. "His mom was concerned," his roommate Beeler would later say. "Her idea was that he was here to get a degree. But the things he was doing on the computer were completely state-of-the-art—no one was doing them yet. He saw additional things to be done. It was very difficult to get excited about classes." To Greenblatt, it wasn't *really* important that he was in danger of flunking out of college. Hacking was paramount: it was what he did best and what made him happiest.

His worst moment came when he was so "out of phase" that he slept past a final exam. It only hastened his exit from the student body of MIT. Flunking out probably wouldn't have made any difference at all in his life had it not been for a rule that you couldn't be a student employee when you were an exiled student. So Greenblatt went looking for work, fully intending to get a daytime programming job that would allow him to spend his nights at the place he wanted to spend his time—the ninth floor at Tech Square. Hacking. And that is exactly what he did.

•

There was an equally impressive hacker who had mastered the PDP-1 in a different manner. More verbal than Greenblatt, he was better able to articulate his vision of how the computer had changed his life, and how it might change all our lives. This student was named Bill Gosper. He had begun MIT a year before Greenblatt, but had been somewhat slower at becoming a habitué of the PDP-1. Gosper was thin, with birdlike features covered by thick spectacles and an unruly head of kinky brown hair. But even a brief meeting with Gosper was enough to convince you that here was someone whose brilliance put things like physical appearance into their properly trivial perspective. He was a math genius. It was actually the idea of hacking the world of mathematics, rather than hacking systems, that attracted Gosper to the computer, and he was to serve as a long-time foil to Greenblatt and the other systems-oriented people in the society of brilliant foot soldiers now forming around brand-new Project MAC.

Gosper was from Pennsauken, New Jersey, across the river from Philadelphia, and his pre-MIT experience with computers, like Greenblatt's, was limited to watching Hulking Giants operate from behind a pane of glass. He could vividly recall seeing the Univac at Philadelphia's Franklin Institute churn out pictures of Benjamin Franklin on its line printer. Gosper had no idea what was going on, but it looked like great fun.

He tasted that fun himself for the first time in his second MIT semester. He'd taken a course from Uncle John McCarthy—open only to freshmen who'd gotten disgustingly high grade point averages the previous term. The course began with FORTRAN, went on to IBM machine language, and wound up on the PDP-1. The problems were non-trivial, things like tracing rays through optical systems with the 709, or working routines with a new floating-point interpreter for the PDP-1.

The challenge of programming appealed to Gosper. Especially on the PDP-1, which after the torture of IBM batch-processing could work on you like intoxicating elixir. Or having sex for the first time. Years later, Gosper still spoke with excitement of "the rush of having this live keyboard under you and having this machine respond in milliseconds to what you were doing . . ."

Still, Gosper was timid about continuing on the PDP-1 after the course was over. He was involved with the math department, where people kept telling him that he would be wise to stay away from computers—they would turn him into a clerk. The unofficial slogan of the math department, Gosper found, was "There's no such thing as Computer Science—it's witchcraft!" Well then, Gosper would be a witch! He signed up for Minsky's course in artificial intelligence. The work was again on the PDP-1, and this time Gosper got drawn into hacking itself. Somewhere in that term, he wrote a program to plot functions on the screen, his first real project, and one of the subroutines contained a program bum so elegant that he dared show it to Alan Kotok. Kotok by then had attained, thought Gosper, "godlike status," not only from his exploits on the PDP-1 and TMRC, but from the well-known fact that his work at DEC included a prime role in the design of a new computer, a much-enhanced version of the PDP-1. Gosper was rapturous when Kotok not only looked over his hack, but thought it clever enough to show to someone else. *Kotok actually thought I'd done something neat!* Gosper hunkered down for more hacking.

His big project in that course was an attempt to "solve" the game Peg Solitaire (or HI-Q), where you have a board in the shape of a plus sign with thirty-three holes in it. Every hole but one is filled by a peg: you jump pegs over each other, removing the ones you jump over. The idea is to finish with one peg in the center. When Gosper and two classmates proposed to Minsky that they solve the problem on the PDP-1, Minsky doubted they could do it, but welcomed the try. Gosper and his friends not only solved it— "We demolished it," he'd later say. They hacked a program that would enable the PDP-1 to solve the game in an hour and a half.

Gosper admired the way the computer solved HI-Q because its approach was "counterintuitive." He had a profound respect for programs which used techniques that on the surface seemed improbable, but in fact took advantage of the situation's deep mathematical truth. The counterintuitive solution sprang from understanding the magical connections between things in the vast mandala of numerical relationships on which hacking ultimately was based. Discovering those relationships—making new mathematics on the computer—was to be Gosper's quest; and as he began hanging out more around the PDP-1 and TMRC, he made himself indispensable as the chief "math hacker"—not so much interested in systems programs, but able to come up with astoundingly clear (non-intuitive!) algorithms which might help a systems hacker knock a few instructions off a subroutine, or crack a mental logjam on getting a program running.

•

Gosper and Greenblatt represented two kinds of hacking around TMRC and the PDP-1: Greenblatt focused on pragmatic systems building, and Gosper on mathematical exploration. Each respected the other's forte, and both would participate in projects, often collaborative ones, that exploited their best abilities. More than that, both were major contributors to the still nascent culture that was beginning to flower in its fullest form on the ninth floor of Tech Square. For various reasons, it would be in this technological hothouse that the culture would grow most lushly, taking the Hacker Ethic to its extreme.

The action would shift among several scenes. The Kluge Room, with the PDP-1 now operating with the time-sharing system which Jack Dennis had worked for a year to write, was still an option for some late-night hacking, and especially Spacewarring. But more and more, the true hackers would prefer the Project MAC computer. It stood among other machines on the harshly lit, sterilely furnished ninth floor of Tech Square, where one could escape from the hum of the air conditioners running the various computers only by ducking into one of several tiny offices. Finally, there was TMRC, with its never-empty Coke machine and Saunders' change box and the Tool Room next door, where people would sit at all hours of the night and argue what to an outsider would be bafflingly arcane points.

These arguments were the lifeblood of the hacker community. Sometimes people would literally scream at each other, insisting on a certain kind of coding scheme for an assembler, or a specific type of interface, or a particular feature in a computer language. These differences would have hackers banging on the blackboard, or throwing chalk across the room. It wasn't so much a battle of egos as it was an attempt to figure out what The Right Thing was. The term had special meaning to the hackers. The Right Thing implied that to any problem, whether a programming dilemma, a hardware interface mismatch, or a question of software architecture, a solution existed that was just . . . it. The perfect algorithm. You'd have hacked right into the sweet spot, and anyone with half a brain would see that the straight line between two points had been drawn, and there was no sense trying to top it. "The Right Thing," Gosper would later explain, "very specifically meant the unique, correct, elegant solution . . . the thing that satisfied all the constraints at the same time, which everyone seemed to believe existed for most problems."

Gosper and Greenblatt both had strong opinions, but usually Greenblatt would tire of corrosive human interfacing, and wander away to actually *implement* something. Elegant or not. In his thinking, *things had to be done.* And if no one else would be hacking them, he would. He would sit down with paper and pencil, or maybe at the console of the PDP-1, and scream out his code. Greenblatt's programs were robust, meaning that their foundation was firm, with built-in error checks to prevent the whole thing from bombing as a result of a single mistake. By the time Greenblatt was through with a program, it was thoroughly debugged. Gosper thought that Greenblatt loved finding and fixing bugs more than anybody he'd ever met, and suspected he sometimes wrote buggy code just so he could fix it.

Gosper had a more public style of hacking. He liked to work with an audience, and often novice hackers would pull up a chair behind him at the console to watch him write his clever hacks, which were often loaded with terse little mathematical points of interest. He was at his best at display hacks, where an unusual algorithm would evoke a steadily unpredictable series of CRT pyrotechnics. Gosper would act as tour guide as he progressed, sometimes emphasizing that even typing mistakes could present an interesting numerical phenomenon. He maintained a continual fascination with the way a computer could spit back something unexpected, and he would treat the utterances of the machine with infinite respect. Sometimes the most seemingly random event could lure him off into a fascinating tangent on the implications of this quadratic surd or that transcendental function. Certain subroutine wizardry in a Gosper program would occasionally evolve into a scholarly memo, like the one that begins:

On the theory that continued fractions are underused, probably because of their unfamiliarity, I offer the following propaganda session on the relative merits of continued fractions versus other numerical representations.

The arguments in the Tool Room were no mere college bull sessions. Kotok would often be there, and it was at those sessions that significant decisions were made concerning the computer he was designing for DEC, the PDP-6. Even in its design stage, this PDP-6 was considered the absolute Right Thing around TMRC. Kotok would sometimes drive Gosper back to South Jersey for holiday breaks, talking as he drove about how this new computer would have *sixteen independent registers.* (A register, or accumulator, is a place within a computer where actual computation occurs. Sixteen of them would give a machine a heretofore unheard-of versatility.) Gosper would gasp. *That'll be,* he thought, *the greatest computer in the history of the world!*

When DEC actually built the PDP-6, and gave the first proto-type to Project MAC, everyone could see that, while the computer had all the necessary sops for commercial users, it was at heart a hacker's machine. Both Kotok and his boss, Gordon Bell, recalling their TX-0 days, used the PDP-6 to demolish the limitations that had bothered them on that machine. Also, Kotok had listened closely to the suggestions of TMRC people, notably Peter Samson, who took credit for the sixteen registers. The instruction set had everything you needed, and the overall architecture was symmetrically sound. The sixteen registers could be accessed three different ways each, and you could do it in combinations, to get a lot done by using a single instruction. The PDP-6 also used a "stack," which allowed you to mix and match your subroutines, programs, and activities with ease. To hackers, the introduction of the PDP-6 and its achingly beautiful instruction set meant they had a power-ful new vocabulary with which to express sentiments that previously could be conveyed only in the most awkward terms.

Minsky set the hackers to work writing new systems software for the PDP-6, a beautiful sea-blue machine with three large cabinets, a more streamlined control panel than the One, rows of shiny cantilevered switches, and a winking matrix of lights. Soon they were into the psychology of this new machine as deeply as they had been on the PDP-1. But you could go further on the Six. One day in the Tool Room at TMRC the hackers were playing around with different ways to do decimal print routines, little programs to get the computer to print out in Arabic numbers. Someone got the idea of trying some of the flashy new instructions on the PDP-6, the ones that utilized the stack. Hardly anyone had integrated these new instructions into his code; but as the program got put on the blackboard using one instruction called Push-J, to everyone's amazement the entire decimal print routine, which normally would be a page worth of code, came out only six instructions long. After that, everyone around TMRC agreed that Push-J had certainly been The Right Thing to put into the PDP-6.

The Tool Room discussions and arguments would often be carried over to dinner, and the cuisine of choice was almost always Chinese food. It was cheap, plentiful, and—best of all—available late at night. (A poor second choice was the nearby greasy spoon on Cambridge's Main Street, a maroon-paneled former railroad car named the F&T Diner, but called by hackers "The Red Death.") On most Saturday evenings, or spontaneously on weeknights after ten o'clock, a group of hackers would head out, sometimes in Greenblatt's blue 1954 Chevy convertible, to Boston's Chinatown.

Chinese food was a system, too, and the hacker curiosity was applied to that system as assiduously as to a new LISP compiler. Samson had been an aficionado from his first experience on a TMRC outing to Joy Fong's on Central Square, and by the early sixties he had actually learned enough Chinese characters to read menus and order obscure dishes. Gosper took to the cuisine with even greater vigor; he would prowl Chinatown looking for restaurants open after midnight, and one night he found a tiny little cellar place run by a small family. It was fairly dull food, but he noticed some Chinese people eating fantastic-looking dishes. So he figured he'd take Samson back there.

They went back loaded with Chinese dictionaries, and demanded a Chinese menu. The chef, a Mr. Wong, reluctantly complied, and Gosper, Samson, and the others pored over the menu as if it were an instruction set for a new machine. Samson supplied the translations, which were positively revelatory. What was called "Beef with Tomato" on the English menu had a literal meaning of Barbarian Eggplant Cowpork. "Wonton" had a Chinese equivalent of Cloud Gulp. There were unbelievable things to discover in this system! So after deciding the most interesting things to order ("Hibiscus Wing? Better order that, find out what that's about"), they called over Mr. Wong, and he jabbered frantically in Chinese disapproval of their selections. It turned out he was reluctant to serve them the food Chinese-style, thinking that Americans couldn't take it. Mr. Wong had mistaken them for typically timid Americans—but these were explorers! They had been inside the machine, and lived to tell the tale (they would tell it in assembly language). Mr. Wong gave in. Out came the best Chinese meal that any of the hackers had eaten to date.

So expert were the TMRC people at hacking Chinese food that they could eventually go the restauranteurs one better. On a hacker excursion one April Fools' Day, Gosper had a craving for a little-known dish called Bitter Melon. It was a wart-dotted form of green pepper, with an intense quinine taste that evoked nausea in all but those who'd painfully acquired the taste. For reasons best known to himself, Gosper decided to have it with sweet-and-sour sauce, and he wrote down the order in Chinese. The owner's daughter came out giggling. "I'm afraid you made a mistake—my father says that this says 'Sweet-and-Sour Bitter Melon.' " Gosper took this as a challenge. Besides, he was offended that the daughter couldn't even read Chinese—that went against the logic of an efficient Chinese Restaurant System, a logic Gosper had come to respect. So, even though he knew his order was a preposterous request, he acted indignant, telling the daughter, "Of course it says Sweet-and-Sour Bitter Melon—we Americans *always* order Sweet-and-Sour Bitter Melon the first of April." Finally, the owner himself came out. "You can't eat!" he shouted. "No taste! No taste!" The hackers stuck to the request, and the owner slunk back to the kitchen.

Sweet-and-Sour Bitter Melon turned out to be every bit as hideous as the owner promised. The sauce at that place was wickedly potent, so much so that if you inhaled while you put some in your mouth you'd choke. Combined with the ordinarily vile bitter melon, it created a chemical that seemed to squeak on your teeth, and no amount of tea or Coca-Cola could dilute that taste. To almost any other group of people, the experience would have been a nightmare. But to the hackers it was all part of the system. It made no human sense, but had its logic. It was The Right Thing; therefore every year on April Fools' Day they returned to the restaurant and insisted that their appetizer be Sweet-and-Sour Bitter Melon.

It was during those meals that the hackers were most social. Chinese restaurants offered hackers a fascinating culinary system and a physically predictable environment. To make it even more comfortable, Gosper, one of several hackers who despised smoke in the air and disdained those who smoked, brought along a tiny, battery-powered fan. The fan was something kluged up by a teenage hacker who hung around the AI lab—it looked like a mean little bomb, and had been built using a cooling fan from a junked computer. Gosper would put it on the table to gently blow smoke back into offenders' faces. On one occasion at the Lucky Garden in Cambridge, a brutish jock at a nearby table became outraged when the little fan redirected the smoke from his date's cigarette back to their table. He looked at these grungy MIT types with their little fan and demanded the hackers turn the thing off. "OK, if she stops smoking," they said, and at that point the jock charged the table, knocking dishes around, spilling tea all over, and even sticking his chopsticks into the blades of the fan. The hackers, who considered physical combat one of the more idiotic human interfaces, watched in astonishment. The incident ended as soon as the jock noticed a policeman sitting across the restaurant.

That was an exception to what were usually convivial gatherings. The talk revolved around various hacking issues. Often, people would have their printouts with them and during lulls in conversation would bury their noses in the reams of assembly code. On occasion, the hackers would even discuss some events in the "real world," but the Hacker Ethic would be identifiable in the terms of the discussion. It would come down to some flaw in a system. Or an interesting event would be considered in light of a hacker's natural curiosity about the way things work.

A common subject was the hideous reign of IBM, the disgustingly naked emperor of the computer kingdom. Greenblatt might go on a "flame"—an extended and agitated riff—about the zillions of dollars being wasted on IBM computers. Greenblatt would go home on vacation and see that the science department at the University of Missouri, which allegedly didn't have any money, was spending four million dollars a year on the care and feeding of an IBM Hulking Giant that wasn't nearly as nifty as the PDP-6. And speaking of grossly overrated stuff, what about that IBM timesharing system at MIT, with that IBM 7094 right there on the ninth floor? Talk about waste!

This could go on for a whole meal. It is telling, though, to note the things that the hackers did not talk about. They did not spend much time discussing the social and political implications of computers in society (except maybe to mention how utterly wrong and naïve the popular conception of computers was). They did not talk sports. They generally kept their own emotional and personal lives —as far as they had any—to themselves. And for a group of healthy college-age males, there was remarkably little discussion of a topic which commonly obsesses groups of that composition. Females.

Though some hackers led somewhat active social lives, the key figures in TMRC-PDP hacking had locked themselves into what would be called "bachelor mode." It was easy to fall into—for one thing, many of the hackers were loners to begin with, socially uncomfortable. It was the predictability and controllability of a computer system—as opposed to the hopelessly random problems in a human relationship—which made hacking particularly attractive. But an even weightier factor was the hackers' impression that computing was much more *important* than getting involved in a romantic relationship. It was a question of priorities.

Hacking had replaced sex in their lives.

"The people were just so interested in computers and that kind of stuff that they just really didn't have time [for women]," Kotok would later reflect. "And as they got older, everyone sort of had the view that one day some woman would come along and sort of plunk you over the head and say, *you!*" That was more or less what happened to Kotok, though not until his late thirties. Meanwhile, hackers acted as if sex didn't exist. They wouldn't notice some gorgeous woman at the table next to them in the Chinese restaurant, because "the concept of gorgeous woman wasn't in the vocabulary," hacker David Silver later explained. When a woman did come into the life of a serious hacker, there might be some discussion—"What's happened to so-and-so . . . the guy's just completely falling apart . . ." But generally that kind of thing was not so much disdained as it was shrugged off. You couldn't dwell on those who might have fallen by the wayside, because you were involved in the most important thing in the world—hacking. Not only an obsession and a lusty pleasure, hacking was a mission. You would hack, and you would live by the Hacker Ethic, and you knew that horribly inefficient and wasteful things like women burned too many cycles, occupied too much memory space. "Women, even today, are considered grossly unpredictable," one PDP-6 hacker noted, almost two decades later. "How can a hacker tolerate such an imperfect being?"

Maybe it would have been different if there had been more women around TMRC and the ninth floor—the few that did hang around paired off with hackers. (*"They* found *us,"* one hacker would later note.) There were not too many of these women, since outsiders, male or female, were often put off by the group: the hackers talked strangely, they had bizarre hours, they ate weird food, and they spent all their time thinking about computers.

And they formed an exclusively male culture. The sad fact was that there never was a star-quality female hacker. No one knows why. There were women *programmers* and some of them were good, but none seemed to take hacking as a holy calling the way Greenblatt, Gosper, and the others did. Even the substantial cultural bias against women getting into serious computing does not explain the utter lack of female hackers. "Cultural things are strong, but not *that* strong," Gosper would later conclude, attributing the phenomenon to genetic, or "hardware," differences.

In any case, only rarely were women in attendance at the Chinese restaurant excursions or the sessions at the Tool Room next door to TMRC. So naturally, one did not have to look one's best. Greenblatt, perhaps, took this to an extreme. He worked on several mammoth projects in the mid-sixties, and would often get so wrapped up in them that his personal habits became a matter of some concern to his fellow hackers.

After he dropped out of school, Greenblatt had taken a job at a firm called Charles Adams Associates, which was in the process of buying and setting up a PDP-1. Greenblatt would work at their offices near Boston's "Technology Highway" outside the city during the day and drive thirty miles back to MIT after work for some all-night hacking. Originally he moved from the dorms to the Cambridge YMCA, but they booted him out because he wouldn't keep his room clean. After his stint at Adams, he got rehired at the AI Lab, and though he had a stable living situation—as a boarder in a Belmont house owned by a retired dentist and his wife—he would often sleep on a cot on the ninth floor. Cleanliness was apparently a low priority, since tales abounded of his noticeable grunginess. (Later Greenblatt would insist that he was no worse than some of the others.) Some hackers recall that one of the things Greenblatt's hacking precluded was regular bathing, and the result was a powerful odor. The joke around the AI lab was that there was a new scientific olfactory measure called a milliblatt. One or two milliblatts was extremely powerful, and one full blatt was just about inconceivable. To decrease the milliblatts, the story goes, hackers maneuvered Greenblatt to a place in the hallway of Building 20 where there was an emergency shower for cases of accidental exposure to chemicals, and let it rip.

Gosper would sometimes tweak Greenblatt for his personal habits, and was particularly bothered at Greenblatt's habit of rubbing his hands together, which resulted in little pieces of dirt falling out. Gosper called these blattlies. When Greenblatt worked on Gosper's desk and left blattlies behind, Gosper would make a point of washing the area with ammonia. Gosper would also sometimes kid Greenblatt about his awkward speech patterns, his frequent coughing, his poor spelling, his mumbling—even though many of Greenblatt's expressions became integrated into the specific vernacular which all the hackers used to some degree. For instance, it was probably Greenblatt who popularized the practice of doubling words for emphasis—like the times he'd get revved up explaining something to Gosper, Kotok, and Samson, and the words would get tangled up, and he'd sigh, saying, "Oh, *lose*-y *lose*-y" and begin over. Gosper and the others would laugh—but, like the way a family will take on a baby's speech patterns and cute malapropisms, the community adopted many Greenblattisms.

Despite these odd personal traits, the hackers held Greenblatt in awe. He was the way he was because of conscious priorities: he was a hacker, not a socialite, and there was nothing more useful than hacking. It so consumed him that he sometimes would go six months without finding time to pick up his MIT paycheck. "If he randomly sat around and tried to articulate what he was thinking and doing all the time, he wouldn't have gotten anything *done,*" Gosper would later say. "If he worried how to spell things, he wouldn't have gotten anything written. He did what he was good at. He was a complete pragmatist. What people thought, be damned. If anyone thought he was stupid or nerdly, that was their problem. Some people did, and they were wrong."

Gosper could appreciate Greenblatt's single-mindedness because his own insistence on graduating (which he did in 1965) had led him to trouble. It was not that his final year at MIT was an academic disaster, because he managed to fulfill the graduation requirements by a slim margin. The problem was a pact he had made with the United States Navy. Before he entered MIT, he'd taken a civil service exam and placed high enough to be included in an exclusive student engineering development program. He worked summers for the Navy, which paid half his tuition and required him to work there for three years after graduation. When Gosper signed up, there had been an escape clause that allowed you to postpone your commitment if you went to graduate school; and if you could get a corporation to pay off the Navy's three-thousand-dollar investment after that, you'd no longer be obligated. But during Gosper's senior year the graduate school loophole closed. Only a buy-out would save him, and he didn't have the money.

The prospect of going into the Navy was hideous. During his summer employment stints he had been exposed to a pathetic system that was antithetical to the Hacker Ethic. Programmers were kept in a room totally separated from the machine; sometimes, as a reward for years of service, they would let a particularly obedient worker venture into the computer room and actually see his program run. (One woman, the story goes, was allowed this privilege, and the sight of the lights flashing and disks whirring caused her to faint.) In addition, Gosper's Navy boss was a man who could not understand why the logarithm of the sums in a given equation was not the sum of the logarithms. There was no way in hell Bill Gosper was going to work under a man who did not know why the logarithm of the sum was not the sum of the logarithms.

Then there was Gosper's perception that the Navy was in bed with Univac. He considered the Univac machine a grotesque parody of a computer, a Hulking Giant. The Navy had to know it was a basically phony computer, he figured, but used it anyway—it was a classic example of the inevitably warped outcome of Outside World bureaucracy. Living with that machine would be immersion in hell. Gosper used computers to seek things that no one had ever found before, and it was essential that the computer he used be optimal in every way. The PDP-6 was the best thing he had found so far, and he was determined not to leave it, especially for a dog like the Univac. "If I see a machine has some incredibly stupid thing wrong with it, some error in its design or whatever, it just irritates the hell out of me," Gosper would later explain. "Whereas the PDP-6 always seemed like an infinitely perfectible machine. If there was something wrong, you would change it. In some sense, we lived inside the damn machine. It was part of our environment. There was almost a society in there . . . I couldn't imagine being without a PDP-6."

Gosper was determined to find the money to pay back the Navy, and to earn it while working for a company with a PDP-6. He fulfilled these rigid criteria by landing a job with the firm that Greenblatt had worked for that past year, Charles Adams. The fact that the Adams company never quite got their PDP-6 working right (Greenblatt insists that he did his part of the preparation adequately) did not seem to upset Gosper: what freaked him was the fact that Charles Adams scrapped the project and bought a carbon copy of the same Hulking Giant Univac that the Navy had.

But by that time more funding for Project MAC had come through, and Bill Gosper found his way onto the payroll. He hardly had to change his habits, since during his whole stint at Addams he had been working on the PDP-6 on the ninth floor every night.

•

Greenblatt by then was in full hacking swing. One of the first projects he worked with on the PDP-6 was a LISP compiler, to allow the machine to run the latest and most nifty version of John McCarthy's artificial intelligence language. Young Peter Deutsch had written a LISP for the PDP-1, but it was not too effective, since the One had less memory; and LISP, which works with symbols and not numbers easily translated to binary, consumes an incredible amount of memory.

Some people, notably Gosper, thought that LISP would be a waste of time on the PDP-6 as well. Gosper was always concerned with what he considered the atrocious lack of computer power in those days, and later would marvel at how ignorant they all were in the AI lab, trying impossible tasks and blaming their failures not on the piddling machines they had, but on themselves. In his senior year, Gosper had been put to work by Minsky on a display that would test whether a certain visual phenomenon was binocular or monocular. Gosper did manage to come close with a clever, cloverleaf shape which at least *displayed* the phenomenon, but generally was banging his head against the wall trying to make the machine do more than it could do. One of the tasks that Gosper considered impossible was a useful LISP on a PDP-6—it might be nice as a symbol evaluator, but not to *do* anything. He considered it one of Minsky's follies that Greenblatt and the others had been tricked into implementing.

But Greenblatt saw more. Though he realized that LISP on the PDP-6 would be to some extent a hack, not fully pragmatic, he did see the need to move toward it. It was a powerful language that would help the field of artificial intelligence move forward: it was the language by which computers would do extremely difficult tasks, by which they could actually learn. Greenblatt was just starting then to have a certain vision of the future, an inkling of a technical implementation of the hacker dream. So he and some others—even Kotok came down from DEC—began implementing LISP on the PDP-6. They filled the blackboards of TMRC with layers and layers of code, and finally got it going on the machine.

The crucial sections were written by Greenblatt and another hacker. Two or three people on a project were considered The Right Thing—far fewer than IBM's so-called "human wave" style of throwing dozens of programmers at a problem and winding up with junk. And it was better to rely on two or three people than on a single crusader—so that when one person was at the end of his thirty-hour phase, someone else could come in and keep hacking. Kind of a tag team project.

With PDP-6 MacLISP (named for Project MAC), the hackers began integrating that computer language into their programs, and even into their conversation. The LISP convention of using the letter "p" as a predicate, for instance, was the inspiration for a common hacker style of asking a question. When someone said "Food-P?" any hacker knew he was being asked if he wanted to get something to eat. The LISP terms "T" and "nil" came to stand, respectively, for "yes" and "no." LISP's acceptance did not diminish the hacker love for assembly language, particularly the elegant PDP-6 instruction set. But as Greenblatt and even Gosper later realized, LISP was a powerful system builder that fit neatly into the hands-on Hacker Ethic.

DEC had shown an interest in MacLISP, and Kotok arranged for Greenblatt and the others to go to Maynard late at night to work on the program, type in their code, and debug it. It was all part of the easy arrangement between MIT and DEC, and no one questioned it. The Right Thing to do was to make sure that any good program got the fullest exposure possible, because *information was free* and the world would only be improved by its accelerated flow.

After working on MacLISP, Greenblatt was perhaps the most authoritative of the systems hackers on the PDP-6. The new administrator of the AI lab, a young man from the Southwest named Russell Noftsker, had hired Greenblatt mainly to maintain and improve the organic creation that is a computer operating system. But Greenblatt's vision did not stop at systems; he was intensely drawn by the concepts of artificial intelligence. He decided to use the system to actually *do* something in that realm, and, since he had been a chess player all his life, it was only logical that he work on a chess program that would go far beyond Kotok's effort and beyond the other AI chess projects that had been attempted at various labs around the country.

Like any good hacker, no sooner did he decide to do something than he began work on it. No one asked him for a proposal. He didn't bother to notify his superiors. Minsky did not have to ponder the relative virtues of the project. There were no channels to go through because in the mid-sixties, in those early days of the AI lab, the hackers themselves were the channels. It was the Hacker Ethic put to work, and Greenblatt made the most of it.

He'd seen a game played by the Kotok program and thought it was crap. Basically, those guys did not know how to play chess: swayed by the romance of a computer making moves, they had somehow forgotten the idea that the name of the game was to take the other guy's pieces. Greenblatt's program used sophisticated artificial intelligence techniques to try and figure out moves in accordance with certain criteria that he considered good chess. Working with a couple of other hackers, Greenblatt went on a coding blitz. He'd manage to get four hours of PDP-6 time a day, and he'd keep writing off-line when he wasn't on the machine. He got the program actually playing chess in one week. The program was debugged, given features, and generally juiced up over the next few months. (Greenblatt was eventually offered an MIT degree if he would write a thesis about his chess program; he never got around to it.)

Circulating around MIT around 1965 was a notorious Rand Corporation memo called "Alchemy and Artificial Intelligence." Its author, an academic named Herbert Dreyfus, lambasted the field and its practitioners. To hackers, his criticism was particularly noxious, since the computer was their implicit model of behavior, at least in their theories of information, fairness, and action. Dreyfus focused on the computer's ridiculously limited structure (compared to the structure of the human brain). His coup de grace was the blunt assertion that no computer program would be able to play a good enough game of chess to beat a ten-year-old.

After Greenblatt finished his chess program, called MacHack, MIT invited Dreyfus to play the PDP-6. The hackers gathered round to watch the computer surrogate of Richard Greenblatt play this cocky, thin, red-headed, bespectacled anti-computer opponent. Artificial intelligence pioneer Herbert Simon, who watched the match, later was quoted as saying that it was

. . . a real cliffhanger. It's two woodpushers . . . fighting each other . . . Dreyfus was being beaten fairly badly and then he found a move which could've captured the opponent's queen. And the only way the opponent could get out of this was to keep Dreyfus in check with his own queen until he could fork the queen and king and exchange them. And the program proceeded to do exactly that. As soon as it had done that, Dreyfus' game fell to pieces, and then it checkmated him right in the middle of the board.

Peter Samson later recalled the scene immediately following Dreyfus' loss: the defeated critic looked around at the assembled MIT professors and hackers, including a victorious Greenblatt, with a look of puzzlement. Why weren't they cheering, applauding, rubbing it in? Because *they knew*. Dreyfus was part of that Real World which couldn't possibly comprehend the amazing nature of computers, or what it was like working with computers so closely that a PDP-6 could actually become your environment. This was something which Dreyfus would never know. Even Minsky, who never really immersed himself in the thirty-hour-day, seven-day-week assembly-language baptistery, had not experienced what the hackers had. The hackers, the Greenblatts and the Gospers, were secure in having been there, knowing what it was like, and going back there—producing, finding things out, making their world different and better. As for convincing skeptics, bringing the outside world into the secret, proselytizing for the Hacker Ethic—all that was not nearly as interesting as living it.

5

THE MIDNIGHT COMPUTER
WIRING SOCIETY

GREENBLATT was hacker of systems and visionary of application; Gosper was metaphysical explorer and handyman of the esoteric. Together they were two legs of a techno-cultural triangle which would serve as the Hacker Ethic's foundation in its rise to cultural supremacy at MIT in the coming years. The third leg of the triangle arrived in the fall of 1963, and his name was Stewart Nelson.

Not long after his arrival, Stew Nelson displayed his curiosity and ability to get into uncharted electronic realms, traits which indicated his potential to become a master magician in service to the Hacker Ethic. As was the custom, Nelson had come a week early for Freshman Rush. He was a short kid, generally taciturn, with curly hair, darting brown eyes, and a large overbite which gave him the restlessly curious look of a small rodent. Indeed, Stewart Nelson was sniffing out sophisticated electronics equipment that he could play on, and it did not take him long to find what he wanted at MIT.

It began at WTBS, the campus radio station. Bob Clements, a student worker at the station who would later do some PDP-6 hacking, was showing a group of freshmen the control rooms when he opened a door that opened to the complex machinery—and found Stew Nelson, "a weaselly little kid," he later remembered, "who had his fingers on the guts of our phone lines and our East Campus radio transmitter."

Eventually, he found his way to the PDP-1 in the Kluge Room. The machine got Stewart Nelson very excited. He saw this friendly computer which you could put your hands on, and with a confidence that came from what Greenblatt might call born hackerism he got to work. He noticed immediately how the One's outside speaker was hooked to the computer, and how Peter Samson's music program could control that speaker. So one night, very late, when John McKenzie and the people tending the TX-0 next door were asleep in their homes, Stewart Nelson set about learning to program the PDP-1, and it did not take him long to teach the PDP-1 some new tricks. He had programmed some appropriate tones to come out of the speaker and into the open receiver of the campus phone that sat in the Kluge Room. These tones made the phone system come to attention, so to speak, and dance. Dance, phone lines, dance!

And the signals did dance. They danced from one place on the MIT tie-line system to the next and then to the Haystack Observatory (connected to MIT's system), where they danced to an open line—and, thus liberated, danced out into the world. There was no stopping them, because the particular tones which Stew Nelson had generated on the PDP-1 were the exact tones which the phone company used to send its internal calls around the world, and Stew Nelson knew that they would enable him to go all around the marvelous system which was the phone company—without paying a penny.

This analog alchemist, the new hacker king, was showing a deeply impressed group of PDP-1 programmers how a solitary college freshman could wrest control of the nearly hundred-year-old phone system, using it not for profit but for sheer joyriding exploration. Word spread of these exploits, and Nelson began to achieve heroic status around TMRC and the Kluge Room; soon some of the more squeamish PDP-1 people were doing some hand-wringing about whether he had gone too far. Greenblatt did not think so, nor did any true hacker: people had done that sort of thing around TMRC for years; and if Nelson took things a step beyond, that was a positive outgrowth of the Hacker Ethic. But when John McKenzie heard of it he ordered Nelson to stop, probably realizing that there was not much he could do to slow Stew Nelson's eternal quest for systems knowledge. "How can you stop talent like that?" he later reflected. As it turned out, things were going to go much further before Stewart Nelson was through. In some ways, they would never stop.

Nelson's freshman pyrotechnics were not so startling in light of his life before MIT. Born in the Bronx, Nelson was the son of a physicist-turned-engineer who had done some pioneering work on color TV design. Stewart's own interest in electronics, though, needed no parental urging. It was as natural as walking, and by the time he was five he was building crystal radios. At eight, he was working on dual-relay burglar alarms. He had little interest, socially or educationally, in school, but gravitated to the electronics shop, where he'd engage in relentless experimentation. It wasn't long before the other kids' mothers would ban their children from playing with Stewart—they were afraid that their progeny would be fried by a dose of electricity. These were inevitable dangers of fooling around with powerful vacuum tube circuits and state-of-the-art transistors powered by 110-volt electrical lines. Stew on occasion would get shocks so severe that he'd be painfully jolted. He would later tell stories of his equipment flying halfway across the room and exploding into smithereens. After one particularly searing shock, he swore off playing with electricity. But after about two days he was back at it, a young loner working on fantastic projects.

Stew loved the telephone. His family had moved to Haddonfield, New Jersey, and he soon found out that by clicking the switches on which the receiver rests, you could actually dial a number. Someone on the other end will be saying, "Hello . . . yes? *Hello?*" and you realize that this is not just a random piece of equipment, but something hooked to a system that you can endlessly explore. Stewart Nelson was soon building things that few of his neighbors in the mid-1950s had seen, like automatic dialers and gadgets that could connect to several phone lines, receiving a call on one line and automatically calling out on the other. He learned to handle telephone equipment with the deftness with which an artist wields his tools; witnesses would later report how Nelson, when confronted with a phone, would immediately dismantle it, first removing the filter which prevents the caller from hearing the dialing signals, and then making a few adjustments so that the phone would dial significantly faster. Essentially, he was reprogramming the telephone, unilaterally debugging Western Electric equipment.

Stew's father died when he was fourteen, and his mother moved them up to Poughkeepsie, New York. He struck a deal with his high school teachers wherein he would fix their radios and televisions in exchange for not having to go to class. Instead, he spent time at a small radio station starting up nearby—Nelson "pretty much put it together," he later explained, connecting the elements, tuning the transmitter, finding sources of noise and hums in the system. When the radio station was running, he was the main engineer, and sometimes he would even be the disc jockey. Every glitch in the system was a new adventure, a new invitation to explore, to try something new, to see what might happen. To Stewart Nelson, wanting to find out what might happen was the ultimate justification, stronger than self-defense or temporary insanity.

With that attitude, he fit in comfortably at the Tech Model Railroad Club and the PDP-1. There had already been avid interest in "phone hacking" around the club; with Nelson around, that interest could really flower. Besides being a technical genius, Nelson would attack problems with bird-dog perseverance. "He approached problems by taking action," Donald Eastlake, a hacker in Nelson's class, later recalled. "He was very persistent. If you try a few times and give up, you'll never get there. But if you keep at it . . . There's a lot of problems in the world which can really be solved by applying two or three times the persistence that other people will."

Nelson was displaying an extension of the Hacker Ethic—if we all acted on our drive to discover, we'd discover more, produce more, be in control of more. Naturally, the phone system was his initial object of exploration at MIT. First the PDP-1 and later the PDP-6 were ideal tools to use in these excursions. But even as Nelson set off on these electronic journeys, he adhered to the unofficial hacker morality. You could call anywhere, try anything, experiment endlessly, but you should not do it for financial gain. Nelson disapproved of those MIT students who built "blue boxes" —hardware devices to make illegal calls—for the purpose of ripping off the phone company. Nelson and the hackers believed that they were *helping* the phone company. They would get hold of priority phone company lines to various locations around the country and test them. If they didn't work, they would report it to the appropriate repair service.

To do this, of course, you had to successfully impersonate technical employees of the Bell Telephone System, but the hackers became quite accomplished at that, especially after reading such contraband books as the classic *Principles of Electricity and Electronics Applied to Telephone and Telegraph Work*, or *Notes on Distant Dialing*, or recent issues of the *Bell System Technical Journal*.

Armed with this information, you could travel around the world, saying to an operator, "I'm calling from the test board in Hackensack and I'd like you to switch me through to Rome. We're trying to test the circuit." She would "write up the number," which would lead you to another number, and soon you would be asking a phone operator in Italy what the weather was like there. Or you'd use the PDP-1 in Blue Box Mode, letting it route and reroute your calls until you were connected to a certain phone number in England where callers would hear a children's bedtime story, a number inaccessible from this country except by blue box.

In the mid-sixties, the phone company was establishing its system of toll-free area-code-800 numbers. Naturally, the hackers knew about this. With scientific precision, they would attempt to chart these undocumented realms: excursions to 800-land could send you to bizarre places, from the Virgin Islands to New York. Eventually someone from the phone company gave a call to the line near the computer, asking what were these four hundred or so calls to places that, as far as the phone company was concerned, did not exist. The unlucky Cambridge branch of the phone company had coped with MIT before, and would again—at one point, they burst into the ninth floor at Tech Square, and demanded that the hackers show them the blue box. When the hackers pointed to the PDP-6, the frustrated officials threatened to take the whole machine, until the hackers unhooked the phone interface and handed it over.

Though Nelson's initial interest in the PDP-1 was its phone hacking potential, he became more versatile with it, and was eventually programming all sorts of things. The more he programmed, the better he got, and the better he got, the more he wanted to program. He would sit by the console of the machine while some graduate student would fumble with a program, and he'd sort of peck around the grad student's back, which would only make the graduate student fumble more, and finally he would burst out, "If I solve that problem for you, will you let me have the computer?" The grad student, who probably had been trying to crack the problem for weeks, would agree, not really believing this quirky fellow could solve it, but Nelson would already be pushing him away, sitting down at the console, bringing up the "TECO" editing program, and pounding in code at a blinding rate. In five minutes, he'd be done, leaping up to print it on the Model 33 teletype near the machine, and in a rush of motion he'd rip the paper off the line printer, run back to the machine, pull off the tape with the grad student's program, and send him off. Then he'd do his own hacking.

He knew no bounds. He used both the PDP-1 in the Kluge Room and the newer machine at Project MAC. When others used the PDP-1 and its limited instruction set, they might have grumbled at having to use several instructions for a simple operation, and then figured out the subroutines to do the programs. Nelson could bum code with the best of them, but he wanted more instructions actually on the machine. Putting an instruction on the computer itself—*in hardware*—is a rather tricky operation. When the TX-0 was given its new instructions, it had to be shut down for a while until official priests, trained to the level of Pope, almost, performed the necessary brain surgery. This seemed only logical—who would expect a university to allow underclassmen to tamper with the delicate parts of a fantastically expensive computer?

No one. In fact, Dan Edwards, one of Minsky's graduate students who had done some hacking on Spacewar, had set himself up as protector of the hardware. According to Gosper, Edwards had declared that "Anyone who does as much as change a ribbon in the typewriter is going to get permanently barred from this place!" But hackers did not care what the university allowed or didn't allow. What Dan Edwards thought was of even less concern: his position of authority, like that of most bureaucrats, was deemed an accident.

Nelson thought that adding an "add to memory" instruction would improve the machine. It would take *months,* perhaps, to go through channels to do it, and if he did it himself he would learn something about the way the world worked. So one night Stewart Nelson spontaneously convened the Midnight Computer Wiring Society. This was an entirely ad hoc organization which would, when the flow of history required it, circumvent the regulations of the Massachusetts Institute of Technology against unauthorized tampering with expensive computers. The MCWS, which that night consisted of Nelson, a student worker, and several interested bystanders, opened up the cabinet and proceeded to rewire the PDP-1. Nelson fused a couple of diodes between the "add" line and the "store" line outputs of the instruction decoder, and had himself a new op-code, which presumably supported all the previous instructions. He then proceeded to reassemble the machine to an apparent pristine state.

The machine was taken through its paces by the hackers that night, and worked fine. But the next day an Officially Sanctioned

User named Margaret Hamilton showed up on the ninth floor to work on something called a Vortex Model for a weather-simulation project she was working on. Margaret Hamilton was just beginning a programming career which would see her eventually in charge of on-board computers on the Apollo moon shot, and the Vortex program at that time was a very big program for her. She was well aware of the hackers' playfulness around the ninth floor, and she was moderately friendly with some of them, even though they would eventually blend into one collective personality in her memory: one unkempt, though polite, young male whose love for the computer had made him lose all reason.

The assembler that Margaret Hamilton used with her Vortex program was not the hacker-written MIDAS assembler, but the DEC-supplied DECAL system that the hackers considered absolutely horrid. So of course Nelson and the MCWS, when testing the machine the previous night, had not used the DECAL assembler. They had never even considered the possibility that the DECAL assembler accessed the instruction code in a different manner than MIDAS, a manner that was affected to a greater degree by the slight forward voltage drop created by the addition of two diodes between the add line and the store line. Margaret Hamilton, of course, was unaware that the PDP-1 had undergone surgery the previous night. So she did not immediately know the reason why her Vortex program, after she fed it in with the DECAL assembler . . . broke. Stopped working. Died. Mysteriously, a perfectly good program had bombed. Though programs often did that for various reasons, this time Margaret Hamilton complained about it, and someone looked into why, and someone else fingered the Midnight Computer Wiring Society. So there were repercussions. Reprimands.

That was not the end of the Midnight Computer Wiring Society. Edwards and his ilk could not stay up all night to watch the machines. Besides, Minsky and the others in charge of Project MAC knew that the hackers' nocturnal activities were turning into a hands-on postgraduate course on logic design and hardware skills. Partially because Nelson and the others got good enough so disasters like the Great Margaret Hamilton Program Clobber were less likely to occur, the official AI lab ban against hardware tampering gradually faded away to the status of one of those antiquated laws that nobody bothers to take off the books, like a statute forbidding you from publicly beating a horse on Sunday. Eventually the Midnight Computer Wiring Society felt free enough to change instructions, make new hardware connections, and even rig the computer to the room lights on the ninth floor, so that when you fired up the TECO text-editing program, the lights automatically dimmed so that you could read the CRT display more easily.

This last hack had an unexpected consequence. The TECO editor rang a bell on the teletype to signal when the user made an error. This normally was no problem, but on certain days the machine got flaky, and was extremely sensitive to power line variations—like those generated by the bell on the teletype. Those times, when someone made a mistake with TECO, the bell would ring, and the machine would be thrown into randomness. The computer would be out of control; it would type spastically, ringing the bell, and most unsettling, *turning the room lights on and off*. The computer had run amok! Science-fiction Armageddon!

The hackers considered this extremely humorous.

The people in charge of the lab, particularly Marvin Minsky, were very understanding about these things. Marvin, as the hackers called him (they invariably called each other by last name), knew that the Hacker Ethic was what kept the lab productive, and he was not going to tamper with one of the crucial components of hackerism. On the other hand, there was Stew Nelson, constantly at odds with the rules, a hot potato who got hotter when he was eventually caught red-handed at phone hacking. Something had to be done. So Minsky called up his good friend Ed Fredkin, and told him he had this problem with an incredibly brilliant nineteen-year-old who had a penchant for getting into sophisticated mischief. Could Fredkin hire him?

•

Besides being a close friend of Marvin Minsky and the founder of Information International Incorporated (Triple-I), Ed Fredkin considered himself the greatest programmer in the world.

A dark-haired man with warm brown eyes behind glasses that rested on a nose with a slight intellectual hook, Fredkin had never finished college. He'd learned computers in the Air Force in 1956, as one of the first men working on the SAGE computer air defense system, then reputed to be the most complicated system known to man. Fredkin and nineteen others began an intensive course in the budding field of computation—memory drums, logic, communications, and programming. Fredkin later recalled, in his soothing, story-teller voice, "After a week, everyone dropped out but me."

Ed Fredkin did not fall into computers head-over-heels as had

Kotok, Samson, Greenblatt, or Gosper—in some ways he was a very measured man, too much an intellectual polyglot to fixate solely on computers. But he was intensely curious about them, so after leaving the service he took a job at MIT-affiliated Lincoln Lab, where he soon earned the reputation of top program bummer around. He could consistently come up with original algorithms, some of which became well known as standard programming protocols. He also was one of the first to see the significance of the PDP-1—he knew about it before the prototype was built, and ordered the very first one. He was talked out of the purchase by Bolt Beranek and Newman, who instead hired him to program the machine and write an assembler. Fredkin did so and modestly considered it a masterpiece of programming. Besides systems work, Fredkin engaged in the kind of math hacking that would later be Bill Gosper's forte, and he did some early theorizing on automatons. But not being a pure hacker—he had business instincts and a family to support—he left BBN to start his own company, Information International, which would perform all sorts of digital troubleshooting and special computer consultations. The company was eventually based in Los Angeles, but for a long time it had facilities in Tech Square, two floors below the PDP-6.

Fredkin was delighted with the hacker community at Tech Square; they had taken hackerism beyond its previous state, found only part-time in the few places in the world (such as MIT, DEC, the Army, BBN) where computers were accessible to people for whom computing was an end in itself. Around MIT, hackerism was full-time. Fredkin came to love the hackers—he could speak their language and admire their work. Sometimes he would accompany them on their Chinatown excursions, and on those occasions the discussions could get quite freewheeling. Many of the hackers were avid science-fiction fans (note the origins of Spacewar), but Fredkin was able to link the wonders of Heinlein and Asimov to the work that the hackers were doing—making computers into powerful systems and building a software groundwork for artificial intelligence. Fredkin had a talent for sparking their imaginations, as he did when he mused that one day people would have tiny robots on their heads which would snip off hair when it reached the precise length for the desired coiffure. (Fredkin would cause a national ruckus when he repeated this prediction on a television talk show.)

As much as Fredkin admired the hackers, though, he still thought he was the best programmer. While the Hacker Ethic encouraged group effort for general improvement, every hacker wanted to be recognized as a wizard, and fast programs and blazing code-crafting efforts would be eagerly displayed and discussed. It was a heady ego boost to be at the top of the hacking hill, where Fredkin considered himself. Hacking, to Fredkin, was above all a pride in craftsmanship.

"I had never run into anyone who could outcode me, in any sense," Fredkin later recalled. "But it was really clear that Nelson could." Nelson was genius-level in his computer knowledge, innovative in approach, fantastically intense in attacking problems, and capable of superhuman concentration. Fredkin did hire the young hacker on Minsky's recommendation, and it did not take Fredkin long to realize that even in a place where exceptional programming was commonplace, Nelson was something special, a one-man human wave of programmers. Of course, since Triple-I was in Tech Square, Nelson was also able to hang out around the AI lab on the ninth floor and do the work of several programmers up there as well. But that was no cause for complaint; when Fredkin needed him, Nelson could almost always come up with magic.

There was a programming project in particular, a task on the DEC PDP-7, that Fredkin wanted Nelson to work on, but for some reason Nelson couldn't get motivated. Fredkin's company also needed at the same time a design for an interface between a certain computer and a disk drive for data storage. Fredkin considered the latter a six man-month project, and wanted the other task done first. Nelson promised him that he'd get some results during the weekend. That next Monday, Nelson came in with a giant piece of paper almost completely covered with tiny scrawlings, long lines connecting one block of scribblings to another, and evidence of frantic erasing and write-overs. It was not the PDP-7 program Fredkin had asked for, but the entire disk-drive interface. Nelson had tried it as a constructive escape from the assigned task. Fredkin's company built the piece of equipment straight from that piece of paper, and it worked.

Fredkin was delighted, but he still wanted the PDP-7 problem done, too. So he said, "Nelson, you and I are going to sit down and program this together. You write this routine, and I'll write that." Since they did not have a PDP-7 around, they sat down at tables to write their pre-debugged assembly code. They began hacking away. Maybe it was about then that Ed Fredkin realized, once and for all, that he was not the best programmer in the world. Nelson was racing along as if it were just a matter of how fast he could get his scribbles on paper. Fredkin was finally overcome with curiosity and looked at Nelson's program. He couldn't believe it. It was bizarre. Totally non-obvious, a crazy quilt of interlacing subroutines. And it was clear that it would work. "Stew," Fredkin burst out, "why on earth are you writing it this way?" Nelson explained that he had once written something similar on the PDP-6, and instead of *thinking* about it he was merely transliterating the previous routines, from memory, into PDP-7 code. A perfect example of the way Nelson's mind worked. He had his own behavior down to the point where he could bum mental instructions, and minimize the work he did.

It was clearly an approach that was better suited to working with machines than it was to human interaction. Nelson was extremely shy, and Fredkin probably acted like a father figure to the young hacker. He would later recall being startled one day when Nelson marched into his office and said, "Guess what? I'm getting married!"

Fredkin would have judged that Nelson did not know how to go about asking a female for a date, let alone tender a proposal of marriage. "Fantastic!" he said. "Who's the lucky girl?"

"Oh, I don't know," said Nelson. "I just decided it would be a good thing to do."

Fifteen years later, Nelson was still in Bachelor Mode.

While women might not have been much of a presence in his life, Nelson did have the companionship of fellow hackers. He moved into a house with Gosper and two others. Although this "Hacker House" was in nearby Belmont, then shifted to Brighton, Nelson resisted buying a car. He couldn't stand driving. "It takes too much processing to deal with the road," he would later explain. He would take public transportation, or get a ride from another hacker, or even take a cab. Once he got to Tech Square, he was good for hours: Nelson was among those hackers who had settled on the twenty-eight-hour-day, six-day-week routine. He didn't worry about classes—he figured that he could get whatever job he wanted whether he had a degree or not, so he never did rematriculate.

Nelson was completely a creature of the Hacker Ethic, and the influence of his behavior was a contributing factor to the cultural and scientific growth of the AI lab. If Minsky needed someone to point out why a certain subroutine was not working, he would go to Nelson. Meanwhile, Nelson would be all over the place. Working for Fredkin, doing systems work with Greenblatt, display hacking with Gosper, and creating all sorts of strange things. He hacked a weird connection between the Triple-I computer on the seventh floor and the PDP-6 on the ninth which sent signals between an oscilloscope on one line and a TV camera on another. He pulled off all sorts of new phone hacks. And, again more by example than by organizing, he was a leader in the hallowed black art of lock hacking.

•

"Lock hacking" was the skillful solution of physical locks, whether on doors, file cabinets, or safes. To some extent, the practice was an MIT tradition, especially around TMRC. But once it was combined with the Hacker Ethic, lock hacking became more of a crusade than an idle game, though the playful challenge of overcoming artificial obstacles contributed to lock hacking's popularity.

To a hacker, a closed door is an insult, and a locked door is an outrage. Just as information should be clearly and elegantly transported within a computer, and just as software should be freely disseminated, hackers believed people should be allowed access to files or tools which might promote the hacker quest to find out and improve the way the world works. When a hacker needed something to help him create, explore, or fix, he did not bother with such ridiculous concepts as property rights.

Say you are working on the PDP-6 one night, and it goes down. You check its innards and discover that it needs a part. Or you may need a tool to install a part. Then you discover that what you need —a disk, a tape, a screwdriver, a soldering iron, a spare IC (integrated circuit)—is locked up somewhere. A million dollars' worth of hardware wasted and idle, because the hardware wizard who knows how to fix it can't get at the seventy-five-cent IC, or the oscilloscope kept in a safe. So the hackers would manage to get the keys to these lockers and these safes. So they could get hold of the parts, keep the computers working, carefully replace what they'd taken, and go back to work.

As a hacker named David Silver later put it, it was "ultra-highly-clever warfare . . . there were administrators who would have high-security locks and have vaults where they would store the keys, and have sign-out cards to issue keys. And they felt secure, like they were locking everything up and controlling things and preventing information from flowing the wrong way and things from being stolen. Then there was another side of the world where people felt everything should be available to everybody, and these hackers had pounds and pounds and pounds of keys that would get them into every conceivable place. The people who did this were very ethical and honest and they weren't using this power to steal or injure. It was kind of a game, partly out of necessity, and partly out of ego and fun . . . At the absolute height of it, if you were in the right inside circle, you could get the combination to any safe and you'd get access to anything."

The basic acquisition of every lock hacker was a master key. The proper master key would unlock the doors of a building, or a floor of a building. Even better than a master key was a grand-master key, sort of a master master-key; one of those babies could open perhaps two thirds of the doors on campus. Just like phone hacking, lock hacking required persistence and patience. So the hackers would go on late-night excursions, unscrewing and removing locks on doors. Then they would carefully dismantle the locks. Most locks could be opened by several different key combinations; so the hackers would take apart several locks in the same hallway to ascertain which combination they accepted in common. Then they would go about trying to make a key shaped in that particular combination.

It might be that the master key had to be made from special "blanks"—unavailable to the general public. (This is often the case with high-security master keys, such as those used in defense work). This did not stop the hackers, because several of them had taken correspondence courses to qualify for locksmith certification; they were officially allowed to buy those restricted blank keys. Some keys were so high-security that even licensed locksmiths could not buy blanks for them; to duplicate those, the hackers would make midnight calls to the machine shop—a corner work space on the ninth floor where a skilled metal craftsman named Bill Bennett worked by day on such material as robot arms. Working from scratch, several hackers made their own blanks in the machine shop.

The master key was more than a means to an end; it was a symbol of the hacker love of free access. At one point, the TMRC hackers even considered sending an MIT master key to every incoming freshman as a recruitment enticement. The master key was a magic sword to wave away evil. Evil, of course, was a locked door. Even if no tools were behind locked doors, the locks symbolized the power of bureaucracy, a power that would eventually be used to prevent full implementation of the Hacker Ethic. Bureaucracies were always threatened by people who wanted to know how things worked. Bureaucrats knew their survival depended on keeping people in ignorance, by using artificial means—like locks —to keep people under control. So when an administrator upped the ante in this war by installing a new lock, or purchasing a Class Two safe (government-certified for classified material), the hackers would immediately work to crack the lock, open the safe. In the latter case, they went to a super-ultra-techno surplus yard in Taunton, found a similar Class Two safe, took it back to the ninth floor, and opened it up with acetylene torches to find out how the locks and tumblers worked.

With all this lock hacking, the AI lab was an administrator's nightmare. Russ Noftsker knew; he was the administrator. He had arrived at Tech Square in 1965 with an engineering degree from the University of Mexico, an interest in artificial intelligence, and a friend who worked at Project MAC. He met Minsky, whose prime grad student–administrator, Dan Edwards, had just left the lab. Minsky, notoriously uninterested in administration, needed someone to handle the paperwork of the AI lab, which was eventually to split from Project MAC into a separate entity with its own government funding. So Marvin hired Noftsker, who in turn officially hired Greenblatt, Nelson, and Gosper as full-time hackers. Somehow, Noftsker had to keep this electronic circus in line with the values and policy of the Institute.

Noftsker, a compactly built blond with pursed features and blue eyes which could alternatively look dreamy or troubled, was no stranger to weird technological exploits: when he was in school, he had hacked explosives with a friend. They worked for a high-tech company and took their salaries in primacord (a highly combustible material) or dynamite, and set off explosions in caves to see how many spiders they could blow out, or see how much primacord it took to split a sixty-five-gallon drum in half. Noftsker's friend once was melting thirty pounds of TNT late one night in his mother's oven when it caught fire—the oven and refrigerator actually melted, and the boy was in the awkward position of having to go to the next-door neighbors' and say, "Excuse me, uh, I think it would be a good idea if you kind of, uh, moved down the *street* a little ways . . ." Noftsker knew he'd been lucky to survive those days; yet, according to Gosper, Noftsker later would cook up a plan for clearing snow from his sidewalk with primacord, until his wife put a stop to the idea. Noftsker also shared the hacker aversion to cigarette smoke, and would sometimes express his displeasure by shooting a jet of pure oxygen from a canister he kept for that purpose; the astonished smoker would find his or her cigarette bursting into a fierce orange blur. Obviously, Noftsker understood the concept of technological extremism to maintain a convivial environment.

On the other hand, Noftsker was in *charge,* dammit, and part of his job was keeping people out of locked areas and keeping confidential information private. He would bluster, he would threaten, he would upgrade locks and order safes, but he knew that ultimately he could not prevail by force. Naïve as the thought was in the Real World, hackers believed that property rights were nonexistent. As far as the ninth floor was concerned, that was indeed the case. The hackers could get into anything, as Noftsker graphically saw one day when a new safe with a twenty-four-hour pick-proof lock arrived and someone inadvertently closed the safe and spun the dial before Noftsker got the combination from the manufacturer. One of the hackers who was a registered locksmith volunteered to help out, and had the safe open in twenty minutes.

So what was Noftsker to do?

"Erecting barriers [would raise] the level of the challenge," Noftsker would later explain. "So the trick was to sort of have an unspoken agreement—that 'This line, imaginary as it may be, is off limits'—to give the people who felt they had to have some privacy and security the sense that they really had some privacy and security. And if someone violated those limits, *the violation would be tolerated as long as no one knew about it.* Therefore if you gained something by crawling over the wall to get into my office, you had to never say anything about it."

Unilateral disarmament. Give the hackers free rein to go where they wanted in their explorations, take what they wanted to aid them in their electronic meanderings and computer-science jam sessions . . . as long as they didn't go around boasting how the bureaucratic emperor had no clothes. That way, Noftsker and the administration he represented could maintain some dignity while the hackers could pretend the administration did not exist. They went wherever they wanted, entering offices by traveling in the crawl space created by the low-hanging artificial ceiling, removing a ceiling tile, and dropping into their destinations—commandos with pencil-pals in their shirt pockets. One hacker hurt his back one night when the ceiling collapsed and he fell into Minsky's office. But more often, the only evidence Noftsker would find was the occasional footprint on his wall. And, of course, sometimes he would enter his locked office and discover a hacker dozing on the sofa.

Some people, though, never could tolerate the Hacker Ethic. Apparently, one of these was the machine shop craftsman Bill Bennett. Though he was a TMRC member, he was by no means a hacker: his allegiance was not to the Signals & Power faction, but to what Gosper called the "Let's-Build-Precise-Little-Miniature-Physical-Devices Subculture." He was a good old boy from Marietta, Georgia, and had a near-religious respect for his tools. His homeland tradition thought of tools as sanctified objects, things you nurture and preserve and ultimately hand over to your grandchildren. "I'm a fanatic," he would later explain. "A tool should be in its right place, cleaned and ready to use." So he not only locked up all his tools but would forbid the hackers to even enter his work space, which he cordoned off by setting up a rope fence and painting stripes on the floor.

Bennett could not prevent the inevitable result of drawing a line and telling hackers they could not cross. He would come in and see his tools had been used, and would complain to Minsky. He would threaten to quit; Noftsker recalls him threatening to booby-trap his area. He would especially demand that Minsky take vengeance on Nelson, whom he apparently saw as the worst offender. Minsky or Noftsker might go through the motions of reprimanding Nelson, but privately they considered the drama rather amusing. Eventually Noftsker would come up with the idea of giving each hacker his own toolbox, with responsibility for his own tools, but that didn't work out particularly well. When a hacker wants something on a machine adjusted, or wants to create a quick hardware hack, he'll use anything available, whether it belongs to a friend or whether it is one of Bill Bennett's pampered possessions. One time Nelson used the latter, a screwdriver, and in the course of his work marked it up somewhat. When Bennett came in the next day and found a damaged screwdriver, he went straight for Nelson.

Nelson was normally very quiet, but at times he would explode. Gosper later described it: "Nelson was an incredible arguer. If you cornered Nelson, he would turn from this mousy little guy to a complete savage." So, Gosper later recalled, Nelson and Bennett got into a shouting match, and during the course of it Nelson said that the screwdriver was just about "used up," anyway.

Used up? It was an incredibly offensive philosophy to Bennett. "This caused smoke to come out of Bennett's ears," Gosper later recounted. "He just blew up." To people like Bennett, things are not passed along from person to person until they are no longer useful. They are not like a computer program which you write and polish, then leave around so others—without asking your permission—can work on it, add new features, recast it in their own image, and then leave it for the next person to improve, the cycle repeating itself all over when someone builds from scratch a gorgeous new program to do the same thing. That might be what hackers believed, but Bill Bennett thought that tools were something you *owned,* something private. These hackers actually thought that a person was entitled to use a tool just because he thought he could do something useful with it. And when they were finished, they would just toss it away, saying it was . . . used up!

Considering these diametrically opposed philosophies, it was no surprise that Bennett blew up at Nelson. Bennett would later say that his outbursts were always quick, and followed by the usual good will that existed between himself and the hackers. But Nelson would later say that at the time he had been afraid the machinist might do him physical harm.

A few nights later Nelson wanted to perform some completely unauthorized adjustments to the power supply on a computer on the seventh floor of Tech Square, and needed a large screwdriver to do it. Naturally, he went into Bennett's locked cabinet for the tool. Somehow the breakers on the power supply were in a precarious state, and Nelson got a huge electrical jolt. Nelson survived nicely, but the shock melted the end off the screwdriver.

The next day Bill Bennett came back to his office and found his mangled screwdriver with a sign on it. The sign read USED UP.

6

WINNERS AND LOSERS

By 1966, when David Silver took his first elevator ride to the ninth floor of Tech Square, the AI lab was a showcase community, working under the hallowed precepts of the Hacker Ethic. After a big Chinese dinner, the hackers would go at it until dawn, congregating around the PDP-6 to do what was most important in the world to them. They would waddle back and forth with their printouts and their manuals, kibitzing around whoever was using the terminal at that time, appreciating the flair with which the programmer wrote his code. Obviously, the key to the lab was cooperation and a joint belief in the mission of hacking. These people were passionately involved in technology, and as soon as he saw them David Silver wanted to spend all his time there.

David Silver was fourteen years old. He was in the sixth grade, having been left back twice. He could hardly read. His classmates often taunted him. Later, people would reflect that his problem had been dyslexia; Silver would simply say that he "wasn't interested" in the teachers, the students, or anything that went on in school. He was interested in building systems.

From the time he was six or so, he had been going regularly to Eli Heffron's junkyard in Cambridge (where TMRC hackers also scavenged) and recovering all sorts of fascinating things. Once, when he was around ten, he came back with a radar dish, tore it apart, and rebuilt it so that it could pick up sounds—he rigged it as a parabolic reflector, stuck in a microphone, and was able to pick up conversations thousands of feet away. Mostly he used to listen to faraway cars, or birds, or insects. He also built a lot of audio equipment, and dabbled in time-lapse photography. Then he got interested in computers.

His father was a scientist, a friend of Minsky's and a teacher at MIT. He had a terminal in his office connected to the Compatible Time-sharing System on the IBM 7094. David began working with it—his first program was written in LISP, and translated English phrases into pig Latin. Then he began working on a program that would control a tiny robot—he called it a "bug"—which he built at home, out of old telephone relays that he got at Eli's. He hooked the bug to the terminal, and working in machine language he wrote a program that made the two-wheeled bug actually crawl. David decided that robotics was the best of all pursuits—what could be more interesting than making machines that could move on their own, see on their own . . . think on their own?

So his visit to the AI lab, arranged by Minsky, was a revelation. Not only were these people as excited about computers as David Silver was, but one of the major activities at the lab was robotics. Minsky was extremely interested in that field. Robotics was crucial to the progress of artificial intelligence; it let us see how far man could go in making smart machines do his work. Many of Minsky's graduate students concerned themselves with the theory of robotics, crafting theses about the relative difficulty of getting a robot to do this or that. The hackers were also heavily involved in the field—not so much in theorizing as in building and experimenting. Hackers loved robots for much the same reasons that David Silver did. Controlling a robot was a step beyond computer programming in controlling the system that was the real world. As Gosper used to say, "Why should we limit computers to the lies people tell them through keyboards?" Robots could go off and find out for themselves what the world was like.

When you program a robot to do something, Gosper would later explain, you get "a kind of gratification, an emotional impact, that is completely indescribable. And it far surpasses the kind of gratification you get from a working program. You're getting a physical confirmation of the correctness of your construction. Maybe it's sort of like having a kid."

One big project that the hackers completed was a robot that could catch a ball. Using a mechanical arm controlled by the PDP-6, as well as a television camera, Nelson, Greenblatt, and Gosper worked for months until the arm could finally catch a

Ping-Pong ball lobbed toward it. The arm was able to determine the location of the ball in time to move itself in position to catch it. It was something the hackers were tremendously proud of, and Gosper especially wanted to go further and begin work on a more mobile robot which could actually *play* Ping-Pong.

"Ping-Pong by Christmas?" Minsky asked Gosper as they watched the robot catch balls.

Ping-Pong, like Chinese restaurants, was a system Gosper respected. He'd played the game in his basement as a kid, and his Ping-Pong style had much in common with his hacking style: both were based on his love of the physically improbable. When Gosper hit a Ping-Pong ball, the result was something as looney as a PDP-6 display hack—he put so much English on the ball that complex and counterintuitive forces were summoned, and there was no telling where the ball might go. Gosper loved the spin, the denial of gravity that allowed you to violently slam a ball so that instead of sailing past the end of a table it suddenly curved down, and when the opponent tried to hit it the ball would be spinning so furiously that it would fly off toward the ceiling. Or he would chop at a ball to increase the spin so much that it almost flattened out, nearly exploding in mid-air from the centrifugal force. "There were times when in games I was having," Gosper would later say, "a ball would do something in mid-air, something unphysical, that would cause spectators to gasp. I have seen inexplicable things happen in mid-air. Those were interesting moments."

Gosper was obsessed for a while with the idea of a robot playing the game. The hackers actually did get the robot to hold a paddle and take a good swat at a ball lobbed in its direction. Bill Bennett would later recall a time when Minsky stepped into the robot arm's area, floodlit by the bright lights required by the vidicon camera; the robot, seeing the glare reflecting from Minsky's bald dome, mistook the professor for a large Ping-Pong ball and nearly decapitated him.

Gosper wanted to go all the way, have the robot geared to move around and make clever shots, perhaps with the otherworldly spin of a good Gosper volley. But Minsky, who had actually done some of the hardware design for the ball-catching machine, did not think it an interesting problem. He considered it no different from the problem of shooting missiles out of the sky with other missiles, a task that the Defense Department seemed to have under control. Minsky dissuaded Gosper from going ahead on the Ping-Pong project, and Gosper would later insist that that robot could have changed history.

Of course, the idea that a project like that was even *considered* was thrilling to David Silver. Minsky had allowed Silver to hang out on the ninth floor, and soon Silver had dropped out of school totally, so he could spend his time more constructively at Tech Square. Since hackers care less about people's age than about someone's potential contribution to hacking, fourteen-year-old David Silver was accepted, at first as sort of a mascot.

He immediately proved himself of some value by volunteering to do some tedious lock-hacking tasks. It was a time when the administration had installed a tough new system of high-security locks. Sometimes the slightly built teen-ager would spend a whole night crawling over false ceilings, to take apart a hallway's worth of locks, study them to see how the mastering system worked, and painstakingly reconstruct them before the administrators returned in the morning. Silver was very good at working with machinist's tools, and he machined a certain blank which could be fashioned into a key to open a particularly tough new lock. The lock was on a door protecting a room with a high-security safe which held . . . keys. Once the hackers got to that, the system "unraveled," in Silver's term.

Silver saw the hackers as his teachers—he could ask them anything about computers or machines, and they would toss him enormous chunks of knowledge. This would be transmitted in the colorful hacker jargon, loaded with odd, teddy-bearish variations on the English language. Words like *winnitude, Greenblattful, gronk,* and *foo* were staples of the hacker vocabulary, shorthand for relatively nonverbal people to communicate exactly what was on their minds.

Silver had all sorts of questions. Some of them were very basic: What are the various pieces computers are made of? What are control systems made of? But as he got more deeply into robotics he found that the questions you had to ask were double-edged. You had to consider things in almost cosmic terms before you could create reality for a robot. What is a point? What is velocity? What is acceleration? Questions about physics, questions about numbers, questions about information, questions about the representation of things . . . it got to the point, Silver realized later, where he was "asking basic philosophical questions like what am I, what is the universe, what are computers, what can you use them for, and how does that relate? At that time all those questions were interesting, because it was the first time I had started to contemplate. And started to know enough about computers, and was relating biological-, human-, and animal-type functions, and starting to relate them to science and technology and computers. I began to realize that there was this idea that you could do things with computers that are similar to the things intelligent beings do."

Silver's guru was Bill Gosper. They would often go off to one of the dorms for Ping-Pong, go out for Chinese food, or talk about computers and math. All the while, Silver was soaking up knowledge in this Xanadu above Cambridge. It was a school no one else knew about, and for the first time in his life he was happy.

The computer and the community around it had freed him, and soon David Silver felt ready to do serious work on the PDP-6. He wanted to write a big, complicated program: he wanted to modify his little robot "bug" so that it would use the television camera to actually "fetch" things that people would toss on the floor. The hackers were not fazed at the fact that no one, even experienced people with access to all sorts of sophisticated equipment, had really done anything similar. Silver went about it in his usual inquisitive style, going to ten or twenty hackers and asking each about a specific section of the vision part of the program. High-tech Tom Sawyer, painting a fence with assembly code. Hardware problems, he'd ask Nelson. Systems problems, Greenblatt. For math formulas, Gosper. And then he'd ask people to help him with a subroutine on that problem. When he got all the subroutines, he worked to put the program together, and he had his vision program.

The bug itself was a foot long and seven inches wide, made of two small motors strapped together with a plastic harness. It had erector-set wheels on either end, an erector-set bar going across the top, and copper welding bars sticking out in front, like a pair of antlers. It looked, frankly, like a piece of junk. Silver used a technique called "image subtraction" to let the computer know where the bug was at any time—the camera would always be scanning the scene to see what had moved, and would notice any change in its picture. Meanwhile the bug would be moving randomly until the camera picked it up, and the computer directed it to the target, which would be a wallet which someone tossed nearby.

Meanwhile, something was happening which was indicative of a continuing struggle in this hacker haven. David Silver was getting a lot of criticism. The criticism came from nemeses of the Hacker Ethic: the AI theorists and grad students on the eighth floor. These were people who did not necessarily see the process of computing as a joyful end in itself: they were more concerned with getting degrees, winning professional recognition, and the, ahem, advancement of computer science. They considered hackerism unscientific. They were always demanding that hackers get off the machine so they could work on their Officially Sanctioned Programs, and they were appalled at the seemingly frivolous uses to which the hackers put the computer. The grad students were all in the midst of scholarly and scientific theses and dissertations which pontificated on the difficulty of doing the kind of thing that David Silver was attempting. They would not consider any sort of computer-vision experiment without much more planning, complete review of previous experiments, careful architecture, and a setup which included pure white cubes on black velvet in a pristine, dustless room. They were furious that the valuable time of the PDP-6 was being taken up for this . . . toy! By a callow teen-ager, playing with the PDP-6 as if it were his personal go-cart.

While the grad students were complaining about how David Silver was never going to amount to anything, how David Silver wasn't doing proper AI, and how David Silver was never going to understand things like recursive function theory, David Silver was going ahead with his bug and PDP-6. Someone tossed a wallet on the grimy, crufty floor, and the bug scooted forward, six inches a second, moved right, stopped, moved forward. And the stupid little bug kept darting forward, right, or left until it reached the wallet, then rammed forward until the wallet was solidly between its "antlers" (which looked for all the world like bent shirt-hangers). And then the bug pushed the wallet to its designated "pen." Mission accomplished.

The graduate students went absolutely *nuts*. They tried to get Silver booted. They claimed there were insurance considerations springing from the presence of a fourteen-year-old in the lab late at night. Minsky had to stand up for the kid. "It sort of drove them crazy," Silver later reflected, "because this kid would just sort of screw around for a few weeks and the computer would start doing the thing they were working on that was really hard, and they were having difficulties and they knew they would never really fully solve [the problem] and couldn't implement it in the real world. And it was all of a sudden *happening* and I pissed them off. They're theorizing all these things and I'm rolling up my sleeves and doing it . . . you find a lot of that in hacking in general. I wasn't approaching it from either a theoretical point of view or an engineering point of view, but from sort of a fun-ness point of view. Let's make this robot wiggle around in a fun, interesting way. And so the things I built and the programs I wrote actually *did* something. And in many cases they actually did the very things that these graduate students were trying to do."

Eventually the grad students calmed down about Silver. But the schism was constant. The grad students viewed the hackers as necessary but juvenile technicians. The hackers thought that grad students were ignoramuses with their thumbs up their asses who sat around the eighth floor blindly theorizing about what the machine was like. They wouldn't know what The Right Thing was if it fell on them. It was an offensive sight, these incompetents working on Officially Sanctioned Programs which would be the subjects of theses and then tossed out (as opposed to hacker programs, which were used and improved upon). Some of them had won their sanctions by snow-jobbing professors who themselves knew next to nothing about the machines. The hackers would watch these people "spaz out" on the PDP-6, and rue the waste of perfectly good machine time.

One of these grad students, in particular, drove the hackers wild —he would make certain mistakes in his programs that would invariably cause the machine to try to execute faulty instructions, so-called "unused op-codes." He would do this for hours and days on end. The machine had a way of dealing with an unused op-code —it would store it in a certain place and, assuming you meant to define a new op-code, get ready to go back to it later. If you didn't *mean* to redefine this illegal instruction, and proceeded without knowing what you'd done, the program would go into a loop, at which point you'd stop it, look over your code, and realize what you'd done wrong. But this student, whom we will call Fubar in lieu of his long-forgotten name, could never understand this, and kept putting in the illegal instructions. Which caused the machine to loop wildly, constantly executing instructions that didn't exist, waiting for Fubar to stop it. Fubar would sit there and stare. When he got a printout of his program, he would stare at *that.* Later on, perhaps, after he got the printout home, he would realize his mistake, and come back to run the program again. Then he'd make the same error. And the hackers were infuriated because by taking his printout home and fixing it there all the time, he was wasting the PDP-6—doing thumb-sucker, IBM-style batch-processing instead of interactive programming. It was the equivalent of cardinal sin.

So one day Nelson got into the computer and made a hack that would respond to that particular mistake in a different way. People made sure to hang around the next time Fubar was signed up for the machine. He sat down at the console, taking his usual, interminably long time to get going, and sure enough, within a half hour, he made the same stupid mistake. Only this time, on the display screen, he saw that the program was not looping, but displaying the part of his code which had gone wrong. Right in the middle of it, pointing to the illegal instruction he'd put in, was a huge, gleaming, phosphorescent arrow. And flashing on the screen was the legend, "Fubar, you lose again!"

Fubar did not respond graciously. He wailed about his program being vandalized. He was so incensed that he completely ignored the information that Nelson's hack had given him about what he was doing wrong, and what he might do to fix it. He was not, as the hackers had somehow hoped, thankful that this wonderful feature had been installed to help him find the error of his ways. The brilliance of the hack had been wasted on him.

•

The hackers had a word to describe those graduate students. It was the same word they used to describe almost anyone who pretended to know something about computers and could not back it up with hacker-level expertise. The word was "loser." The hackers were "winners." It was a binary distinction: people around the AI lab were one or the other. The sole criterion was hacking ability. So intense was the quest to improve the world by understanding and building systems that almost all other human traits were disregarded. You could be fourteen years old and dyslexic, and be a winner. Or you could be bright, sensitive, and willing to learn, and still be considered a loser.

To a newcomer, the ninth floor was an intimidating, seemingly impenetrable passion palace of science. Just standing around the likes of Greenblatt or Gosper or Nelson could give you goose bumps. They would seem the smartest people in the world. And since only one person at a time could use the PDP-6, it took a lot of guts to sit down and learn things interactively. Still, anybody who had the hacker spirit in him would be so driven to compute that he would set self-doubt aside and begin writing programs.

Tom Knight, who drifted up to the the ninth floor as a startlingly tall and skinny seventeen-year-old freshman in 1965, went through that process, eventually earning winner status. To do that, he later recalled, "You have to pretty much bury yourself in that culture. Long nights looking over the shoulder of people who were doing interesting things that you didn't understand." What kept him going was his fascination with the machine, how it let you build complicated systems completely under your control. In that sense, Knight later reflected, you had the same kind of control that a dictator had over a political system. But Knight also felt that computers were an infinitely flexible artistic medium, one in which you could express yourself by creating your own little universe. Knight later explained: "Here is this object you can tell what to do, and with no questions asked, it's doing what *you* tell it to. There are very few institutions where an eighteen-year-old person can get that to happen for him."

People like Knight and Silver hacked so intensely and so well that they became winners. Others faced a long uphill climb, because once hackers felt that you were an obstacle to the general improvement of the overall system, you were a loser in the worst sense and should be either cold-shouldered or told to leave outright.

To some, that seemed cruel. A sensitive hacker named Brian Harvey was particularly upset at the drastically enforced standard. Harvey successfully passed muster himself. While working on the computer he discovered some bugs in the TECO editor, and when he pointed them out, people said, fine—now go fix them. He did, realized that the process of debugging was more fun than *using* a program you'd debugged, and set about looking for more bugs to fix. One day while he was hacking TECO, Greenblatt stood behind him, stroking his chin as Harvey hammered in some code, and said, "I guess we ought to start paying you." That was the way you were hired in the lab. Only winners were hired.

But Harvey did not like it when other people were fingered as losers, treated like pariahs simply because they were not brilliant. Harvey thought that Marvin Minsky had a lot to do with promulgating that attitude. (Minsky later insisted that all he did was allow the hackers to run things themselves—"the system was open and literally encouraged people to try it out, and if they were harmful or incompetent, they'd be encouraged to go away.") Harvey recognized that, while on the one hand the AI lab, fueled by the Hacker Ethic, was "a great intellectual garden," on the other hand it was flawed by the fact that *who* you were didn't matter as much as what kind of hacker you were.

Some people fell right into a trap of trying so hard to be a winner on the machine that they were judged instantly as losers: for instance, Gerry Sussman, who arrived at MIT as a cocky seventeen-year-old. Having been an adolescent electronics junkie and high school computer fan, the first thing he did when he arrived at MIT was to seek a computer. Someone pointed him to Tech Square. He asked a person who seemed to belong there if he could play with the computer. Richard Greenblatt said, go ahead, play with it.

So Sussman began working on a program. Not long after, this odd-looking bald guy came over. Sussman figured the guy was going to boot him out, but instead the man sat down, asking, "Hey, what are you doing?" Sussman talked over his program with the man, Marvin Minsky. At one point in the discussion, Sussman told Minsky that he was using a certain randomizing technique in his program because he didn't want the machine to have any preconceived notions. Minsky said, "Well, it has them, it's just that you don't know what they are." It was the most profound thing Gerry Sussman had ever heard. And Minsky continued, telling him that the world is built a certain way, and the most important thing we can do with the world is avoid randomness, and figure out ways by which things can be planned. Wisdom like this has its effect on seventeen-year-old freshmen, and from then on Sussman was hooked.

But he got off on the wrong foot with the hackers. He tried to compensate for his insecurity by excessive bravado, and everyone saw right through it. He was also, by many accounts, terrifically clumsy, almost getting himself flattened in a bout with the robot arm—which he had infinite trouble controlling—and once he accidentally crushed a special brand of imported Ping-Pong ball that Gosper had brought into the lab. Another time, while on a venture of the Midnight Computer Wiring Society, Sussman got a glob of solder in his eye. He was losing left and right.

Perhaps to cultivate a suave image, Sussman smoked a pipe, the utterly wrong thing to do on the smokeaphobic ninth floor, and one day the hackers managed to replace some of his tobacco with cut-up rubber bands of the same approximate color.

He unilaterally apprenticed himself to Gosper, the most verbally profound of the hackers. Gosper might not have thought that Sussman was much of a winner at that point, but he loved an audience, and tolerated Sussman's misguided cockiness. Sometimes the wry guru's remarks would set Sussman's head spinning, like the time Gosper offhandedly remarked that "Well, data is just a dumb kind of programming." To Sussman, that answered the eternal existence question, "What are you?" We are data, pieces of a cosmic computer program that is the universe. Looking at Gosper's programs,

Sussman divined that this philosophy was embedded in the code. Sussman later explained that "Gosper sort of imagined the world as being made out of all these little pieces, each of which is a little machine which is a little independent local state. And [each state] would talk to its neighbors."

Looking at Gosper's programs, Sussman realized an important assumption of hackerism: all serious computer programs are expressions of an individual. "It's only incidental that computers execute programs," Sussman would later explain. "The important thing about a program is that it's something you can show to people, and they can read it and they can learn something from it. It carries information. It's a piece of your mind that you can write down and give to someone else just like a book." Sussman learned to read programs with the same sensitivity that a literature buff would read a poem. There are fun programs with jokes in them, there are exciting programs which do The Right Thing, and there are sad programs which make valiant tries but don't quite fly.

These are important things to know, but they did not necessarily make you a winner. It was hacking that did it for Sussman. He stuck at it, hung around Gosper a lot, toned down his know-it-all attitude, and, above all, became an impressive programmer. He was the rare loser who eventually turned things around and became a winner. He later wrote a very complicated and much-heralded program in which the computer would move blocks with a robot arm; and by a process much like debugging, the program would figure out for itself which blocks it would have to move to get to the one requested. It was a significant step forward for artificial intelligence, and Sussman became known thereafter as more of a scientist, a planner. He named his famous program HACKER.

One thing that helped Sussman in his turnaround from loser to winner was a sense of what The Right Thing was. The biggest losers of all, in the eyes of the hackers, were those who so lacked that ability that they were incapable of realizing what the true best machine was, or the true best computer language, or the true best way to use a computer. And no system of using a computer earned the hackers' contempt as much as the time-sharing systems which, since they were a major part of Project MAC, were also based on the ninth floor of Tech Square. The first one, which was operating since the mid-sixties, was the Compatible Time-sharing System (CTSS). The other, long in preparation and high in expense, was called Multics, and was so offensive that its mere existence was an outrage.

Unlike the quiltwork of constantly improving systems programs operating on the PDP-6, CTSS had been written by one man, MIT Professor F. J. Corbató. It had been a virtuoso job in many respects, all carefully coded and ready to run on the IBM 7094, which would support a series of terminals to be used simultaneously. But to the hackers, CTSS represented bureaucracy and IBM-ism. "One of the really fun things about computers is that you have control over them," CTSS foe Tom Knight would later explain. "When you have a bureaucracy around a computer you no longer have control over it. The CTSS was a 'serious' system. People had to go get accounts and had to pay attention to security. It was a benign bureaucracy, but nevertheless a bureaucracy, full of people who were here from nine to five. If there was some reason you wanted to change the behavior of the system, the way it worked, or develop a program that might have only sometimes worked, or might have some danger of crashing the system, that was not encouraged [on CTSS]. You want an environment where making those mistakes is not something for which you're castigated, but an environment where people say, 'Oops, you made a mistake.' "

In other words, CTSS discouraged hacking. Add to this the fact that it was run on a two-million-dollar IBM machine that the hackers thought was much inferior to their PDP-6, and you had one loser system. No one was asking the hackers to use CTSS, but it *was* there, and sometimes you just have to do some hacking on what's available. When a hacker would try to use it, and a message would come on-screen saying that you couldn't log on without the proper password, he would be compelled to retaliate. Because to hackers, passwords were even more odious than locked doors. What could be worse than someone telling you that you weren't authorized to use his computer?

As it turned out, the hackers learned the CTSS system so well that they could circumvent the password requirements. Once they were on the system, they would rub it in a bit by leaving messages to the administrators—high-tech equivalents of "Kilroy Was Here." Sometimes they would even get the computer to print out a list of all current passwords, and leave the printout under an administrator's door. Greenblatt recalls that the Project MAC–CTSS people took a dim view of that, and inserted an official MAC memo which would flash when you logged in, basically saying, a password is your sanctity, and only the lowest form of human would violate a password. Tom Knight got inside the system and changed the heading of that memo from MAC to HAC.

But as bad as CTSS was, the hackers thought Multics was worse. Multics was the name of the hugely expensive time-sharing system for the masses being built and debugged on the ninth floor. Though it was designed for general users, the hackers evaluated the structure of any system in a very personal light, especially a system created on the very floor of the building in which they hacked. So MULTICS was a big topic of hacker conversation.

Originally, Multics was done in conjunction with General Electric; then Honeywell stepped in. There were all sorts of problems with it. As soon as the hackers heard that the system would run on teletype Model 33 terminals instead of fast, interactive CRT displays, they knew the system was a total loser. The fact that the system was written in an IBM-created computer language called PL/1 instead of sleek machine language was appalling. When the system first ran, it was incredibly sluggish. It was so slow that the hackers concluded the whole system must be brain-damaged, a term used so often to describe Multics that "brain-damaged" became a standard hackerese pejorative.

But the worst thing about Multics was the heavy security and the system of charging the user for the time. Multics took the attitude that the user paid down to the last nickel; it charged some for the memory you used, some more for the disk space, more for the time. Meanwhile the Multics planners, in the hacker view, were making proclamations about how this was the only way that utilities could work. The system totally turned the Hacker Ethic around—instead of encouraging more time on the computer (the only good thing about time-sharing as far as most hackers were concerned), it urged you to spend less time—and to use less of the computer's facilities once you were on! The Multics philosophy was a disaster.

The hackers plagued the Multics system with tricks and crashes. It was almost a duty to do it. As Minsky would later say, "There were people doing projects that some other people didn't like and they would play all sorts of jokes on them so that it was impossible to work with them . . . I think [the hackers] helped progress by undermining professors with stupid plans."

In light of the guerrilla tendencies of hackers, the planners in charge of the AI lab had to tread very lightly with suggestions that would impact the hacker environment. And around 1967, the planners wanted a whopper of a change. They wanted to convert the hackers' beloved PDP-6 into a time-sharing machine.

By that time, Minsky had turned many of his AI lab leadership duties over to his friend Ed Fredkin, Nelson's boss at Triple-I who himself was easing out of full-time business and into a professorship at MIT. (Fredkin would be one of the youngest full professors on the faculty, and the only full professor without a degree.) A master programmer himself, Fredkin was already close to the hackers. He appreciated the way the laissez-faire attitude allowed hackers to be dazzlingly productive. But he thought that sometimes the hackers could benefit from top-down direction. One of his early attempts to organize a "human wave" approach toward a robotics problem, assigning the hackers specific parts of the problem himself, had failed ignominiously. "Everyone thought I was crazy," Fredkin later recalled. He ultimately accepted the fact that the best way to get hackers to do things was to suggest them, and hope that the hackers would be interested enough. Then you would get production unheard of in industry or academia.

Time-sharing was something that Minsky and Fredkin considered essential. Between hackers and Officially Sanctioned Users, the PDP-6 was in constant demand; people were frustrated by long waits for access. But the hackers did not consider time-sharing acceptable. They pointed at CTSS, Multics, even at Jack Dennis' more amiable system on the PDP-1, as examples of the slower, less powerful access one would be stuck with when one shared the computer with others using it at the same time.

They noted that certain large programs could not be run at all with time-sharing. One of these was a monster program that Peter Samson had been working on. It was sort of an outgrowth of one of his first hacks on the TX-0, a program which, if you typed in the names of two subway stations on the MTA, would tell you the proper subway lines to take, and where to make the changes from one to another. Now, Samson was tackling the entire New York subway system . . . he intended to put the entire system in the computer's memory, and the full timetable of its trains on a data disk accessible by the computer. One day he ran the program to figure out a route by which a person could ride the entire subway system with one token. It got some media attention, and then someone suggested that they see if they could use the computer to actually *do* it, break a record previously set by a Harvard student for actually traveling to every stop on the New York subway system.

After months of hacking, Samson came up with a scheme, and one day two hackers made the run. A teletype was installed at the MIT Alumni Club in Manhattan, connected to the PDP-6. Two dozen or so messengers were stationed along the route, and they periodically ducked into pay phones, constantly updating schedule information, calling in late trains, reporting delays, and noting missed connections. The hackers at the teletype pounded in the information, and back in Cambridge the PDP-6 calculated changes in the route. As the travelers passed each station, Samson marked it off on a war-room map. The idea of these crew-cut madmen— stark contrast to the long-haired protesters making news in other sorts of activities—captured the imagination of the media for a day, and The Great Subway Hack was noted as one of the memorable uses of the PDP-6.

It underlined something that Greenblatt, Gosper, and the rest considered essential—the magic that could come only from programs using *all* of the computer. The hackers worked on the PDP-6, one by one, as if it were their own personal computer. They would often run display programs which ran in "real time" and required the computer to constantly refresh the screen; timesharing would make the display hacks run slower. And the hackers had gotten used to little frills that came from complete control of the PDP-6, like being able to track a program by the flashing lights (indicating which registers in the machine were firing). Those perks would be gone with time-sharing.

At heart, though, the time-sharing issue was an esthetic question. The very *idea* that you could not control the entire machine was disturbing. Even if the time-sharing system allowed the machine to respond to you in exactly the same way as it did in single-user mode, you would just *know* that it wasn't all yours. It would be like trying to make love to your wife, knowing she was simultaneously making love to six other people!

The hackers' stubbornness on this issue illustrated their commitment to the quality of computing; they were not prepared to compromise by using an inferior system that would serve more people and perhaps spread the gospel of hacking. In their view, hacking would be better served by using the best system possible. Not a time-shared system.

Fredkin was faced with an uphill political struggle. His strategy was to turn around the most vehement of the anti-time-sharing camp—Greenblatt. There was a certain affection between them. Fredkin was the only person on the ninth floor who called Greenblatt "Ricky." So he courted. He cajoled. He told Greenblatt how the power of the PDP-6 would be improved by a new piece of hardware which would expand its memory to a size bigger than any computer in the world. He promised that the time-sharing system would be better than any to date—and the hackers would control it. He worked on Greenblatt for weeks, and finally Ricky Greenblatt agreed that time-sharing should be implemented on the PDP-6.

Soon after that, Fredkin was in his office when Bill Gosper marched in, leading several hackers. They lined up before Fredkin's desk and gave him a collective icy stare.

"What's up?" Fredkin asked.

They kept staring him for a while longer. Finally they spoke.

"We'd like to know what you've done to Greenblatt," they said. "We have reason to believe you've hypnotized him."

Gosper in particular had difficulty accepting joint control of the PDP-6. His behavior reminded Fredkin of Rourke, the architect in Ayn Rand's *The Fountainhead* who designed a beautiful building; when Rourke's superiors took control of the design and compromised its beauty, Rourke blew up the building. Fredkin later recalled Gosper telling him that if time-sharing were implemented on the PDP-6, Gosper would be compelled to physically demolish the machine. "Just like Rourke," Fredkin later recalled. "He felt if this terrible thing was to be done, you would have to destroy it. And I understood this feeling. So I worked out a compromise." The compromise allowed the machine to be run late at night in single-user mode, so the hackers could run giant display programs and have the PDP-6 at their total command.

The entire experiment in time-sharing did not work out badly at all. The reason was that a special, new time-sharing system was created, a system that had the Hacker Ethic in its very soul.

•

The core of the system was written by Greenblatt and Nelson, in weeks of hard-core hacking. After some of the software was done, Tom Knight and others began the necessary adjustments to the PDP-6 and the brand-new memory addition—a large cabinet with the girth of two Laundromat-size washing machines, nicknamed Moby Memory. Although the administration approved of the hackers' working on the system, Greenblatt and the rest exercised full authority on how the system would turn out. An indication of how this system differed from the others (like the Compatible

Time-sharing System) was the name that Tom Knight gave the hacker program: the *In*compatible Time-sharing System (ITS).

The title was particularly ironic because, in terms of friendliness to other systems and programs, ITS was much more compatible than CTSS. True to the Hacker Ethic, ITS could easily be linked to other things—that way it could be infinitely extended so users could probe the world more effectively. As in any time-sharing system, several users would be able to run programs on ITS at the same time. But on ITS, one user could also run several programs at once. ITS also allowed considerable use of the displays, and had what was for the time a very advanced system of editing that used the full screen ("years before the rest of the world," Greenblatt later boasted). Because the hackers wanted the machine to run as swiftly as it would have done had it not been time-shared, Greenblatt and Nelson wrote machine language code which allowed for unprecedented control in a time-sharing system.

There was an even more striking embodiment of the Hacker Ethic within ITS. Unlike almost any other time-sharing system, ITS did not use passwords. It was designed, in fact, to allow hackers maximum access to *any* user's file. The old practice of having paper tapes in a drawer, a collective program library where you'd have people use and improve your programs, was embedded in ITS; each user could open a set of personal files, stored on a disk. The open architecture of ITS encouraged users to look through these files, see what neat hacks other people were working on, look for bugs in the programs, and fix them. If you wanted a routine to calculate sine functions, for instance, you might look in Gosper's files and find his ten-instruction sine hack. You could go through the programs of the master hackers, looking for ideas, admiring the code. The idea was that computer programs belonged not to individuals, but to the world of users.

ITS also preserved the feeling of community that the hackers had when there was only one user on the machine, and people could crowd around him to watch him code. Through clever crossbar switching, not only could any user on ITS type a command to find out who else was on the system, but he could actually switch himself to the terminal of any user he wanted to monitor. You could even hack in conjunction with another user—for instance, Knight could log in, find out that Gosper was on one of the other ports, and call up his program—then he could write lines of code in the program Gosper was hacking.

This feature could be used in all sorts of ways. Later on, after

Knight had built some sophisticated graphics terminals, a user might be wailing away on a program and suddenly on screen there would appear this six-legged . . . *bug*. It would crawl up your screen and maybe start munching on your code, spreading little phosphorous crumbs all over. On another terminal, hysterical with high-pitched laughter, would be the hacker who was telling you, in this inscrutable way, that your program was buggy. But though any user had the power not only to do that sort of thing, but to go in your files and delete ("reap," as they called it) your hard-hacked programs and valuable notes, that sort of thing wasn't done. There was honor among hackers on ITS.

The faith that the ITS had in users was best shown in its handling of the problem of intentional system crashes. Formerly, a hacker rite of passage would be breaking into a time-sharing system and causing such digital mayhem—maybe by overwhelming the registers with looping calculations—that the system would "crash." Go completely dead. After a while a hacker would grow out of that destructive mode, but it happened often enough to be a considerable problem for people who had to work on the system. The more safeguards the system had against this, the bigger the challenge would be for some random hacker to bring the thing to its knees. Multics, for instance, required a truly non-trivial hack before it bombed. So there'd always be macho programmers proving themselves by crashing Multics.

ITS, in contrast, had a command whose specific function was crashing the system. All you had to do was type KILL SYSTEM, and the PDP-6 would grind to a halt. The idea was to take all the fun away from crashing the system by making it trivial to do that. On rare occasions, some loser would look at the available commands and say, "Wonder what KILL does?" and bring the system down, but by and large ITS proved that the best security was no security at all.

Of course, as soon as ITS was put up on the PDP-6 there was a flurry of debugging, which, in a sense, was to go on for well over a decade. Greenblatt was the most prominent of those who spent full days "hacking ITS"—seeking bugs, adding new features, making sections of it run faster . . . working on it so much that the ITS environment became, in effect, a home for systems hackers.

In the world that was the AI lab, the role of the systems hacker was central. The Hacker Ethic allowed anyone to work on ITS, but the public consequences of systems hacking threw a harsh spotlight on the quality of your work—if you were trying to improve the

MIDAS assembler or the ITS-DDT debugger, and you made a hideous error, everyone's programs were going to crash, and people were going to find out what loser was responsible. On the other hand, there was no higher calling in hackerism than quality systems hacking.

The planners did not regard systems hacking with similar esteem. The planners were concerned with applications—using computers to go beyond computing, to create useful concepts and tools to benefit humanity. To the hackers, the system was an end in itself. Most hackers, after all, had been fascinated by systems since early childhood. They had set aside almost everything else in life once they recognized that the ultimate tool in creating systems was the computer: not only could you use it to set up a fantastically complicated system, at once byzantine and elegantly efficient, but then, with a "Moby" operating system like ITS, that same computer could actually *be* the system. And the beauty of ITS was that it opened itself up, made it easy for you to write programs to fit within it, begged for new features and bells and whistles. ITS was the hacker living room, and everyone was welcome to do what he could to make himself comfortable, to find and decorate his own little niche. ITS was the perfect system for building . . . systems!

It was an endlessly spiraling logical loop. As people used ITS, they might admire this feature or that, but most likely they would think of ways to improve it. This was only natural, because an important corollary of hackerism states that no system or program is ever completed. *You can always make it better.* Systems are organic, living creations: if people stop working on them and improving them, they die.

When you completed a systems program, be it a major effort like an assembler or debugger or something quick and (you hoped) elegant, like an interface output multiplexor, you were simultaneously creating a tool, unveiling a creation, and fashioning something to advance the level of your own future hacking. It was a particularly circular process, almost a spiritual one, in which the systems programmer was a habitual user of the system he was improving. Many virtuoso systems programs came out of remedies to annoying obstacles which hackers felt prevented them from optimum programming. (Real optimum programming, of course, could only be accomplished when every obstacle between you and the pure computer was eliminated—an ideal that probably won't be fulfilled until hackers are somehow biologically merged with computers.) The programs ITS hackers wrote helped them to program more easily, made programs run faster, and allowed programs to gain from the power that comes from using more of the machine. So not only would a hacker get huge satisfaction from writing a brilliant systems program—a tool which everyone would use and admire—but from then on he would be that much further along in making the next systems program.

To quote a progress report written by hacker Don Eastlake five years after ITS was first running:

> The ITS system is not the result of a human wave or crash effort. The system has been incrementally developed almost continuously since its inception. It is indeed true that large systems are never "finished." . . . In general, the ITS system can be said to have been designer implemented and user designed. The problem of unrealistic software design is greatly diminished when the designer is the implementor. The implementor's ease in programming and pride in the result is increased when he, in an essential sense, is the designer. Features are less likely to turn out to be of low utility if users are their designers and they are less likely to be difficult to use if their designers are their users.

The prose was dense, but the point was clear—ITS was the strongest expression yet of the Hacker Ethic. Many thought that it should be a national standard for time-sharing systems everywhere. Let every computer system in the land spread the gospel, eliminating the odious concept of passwords, urging the unrestricted hands-on practice of system debugging, and demonstrating the synergistic power that comes from shared software, where programs belong not to the author but to all users of the machine.

In 1968, major computer institutions held a meeting at the University of Utah to come up with a standard time-sharing system to be used on DEC's latest machine, the PDP-10. The Ten would be very similar to the PDP-6, and one of the two operating systems under consideration was the hackers' Incompatible Time-sharing System. The other was TENEX, a system written by Bolt Beranek and Newman that had not yet been implemented. Greenblatt and Knight represented MIT at the conference, and they presented an odd picture—two hackers trying to persuade the assembled bureaucracies of a dozen large institutions to commit millions of dollars of their equipment to a system that, for starters, had no built-in security.

They failed.

Knight would later say that it was political naïveté which lost it for the MIT hackers. He guessed that the fix was in even before the conference was called to order—a system based on the Hacker Ethic was too drastic a step for those institutions to take. But Greenblatt later insisted that "we could have carried the day if [we'd] really wanted to." But "charging forward," as he put it, was more important. It was simply not a priority for Greenblatt to spread the Hacker Ethic much beyond the boundaries of Cambridge. He considered it much more important to focus on the society at Tech Square, the hacker Utopia which would stun the world by applying the Hacker Ethic to create ever more perfect systems.

7

LIFE

THEY would later call it a Golden Age of hacking, this marvelous existence on the ninth floor of Tech Square. Spending their time in the drab machine room and the cluttered offices nearby, gathered closely around terminals where rows and rows of green characters of code would scroll past them, marking up printouts with pencils retrieved from shirt pockets, and chatting in their peculiar jargon over this infinite loop or that losing subroutine, the cluster of technological monks who populated the lab was as close to paradise as they would ever be. A benevolently anarchistic lifestyle dedicated to productivity and PDP-6 passion. Art, science, and play had merged into the magical activity of programming, with every hacker an omnipotent master of the flow of information within the machine. The debugged life in all its glory.

But as much as the hackers attempted to live the hacker dream without interference from the pathetically warped systems of the "Real World," it could not be done. Greenblatt and Knight's failure to convince outsiders of the natural superiority of the Incompatible Time-sharing System was only one indication that the total immersion of a small group of people into hackerism might not bring about change on the massive scale that all the hackers assumed was inevitable. It was true that, in the decade since the TX-0 was first delivered to MIT, the general public and certainly the other students on campus had become more aware of computers in general. But they did not regard computers with the same respect and fascination as did the hackers. And they did not necessarily regard the hackers' intentions as benign and idealistic.

On the contrary, many young people in the late 1960s saw computers as something evil, part of a technological conspiracy where the rich and powerful used the computer's might *against* the poor and powerless. This attitude was not limited to students protesting, among other things, the now exploding Vietnam war (a conflict fought in part by American computers). The machines which stood at the soul of hackerism were also loathed by millions of common, patriotic citizens who saw computers as a dehumanizing factor in society. Every time an inaccurate bill arrived at a home, and the recipient's attempts to set it right wound up in a frustrating round of calls—usually leading to an explanation that "the computer did it," and only herculean human effort could erase the digital blot—the popular contempt toward computers grew. Hackers, of course, attributed those slipups to the brain-damaged, bureaucratic, batch-processed mentality of IBM. Didn't people understand that the Hacker Ethic would eliminate those abuses by encouraging people to *fix* bugs like thousand-dollar electric bills? But in the public mind there was no distinction between the programmers of Hulking Giants and the AI lab denizens of the sleek, interactive PDP-6. And in that public mind all computer programmers, hackers or not, were seen either as wild-haired mad scientists plotting the destruction of the world or as pasty-skinned, glassy-eyed automatons, repeating wooden phrases in dull monotones while planning the next foray into technological big-brotherism.

Most hackers chose not to dwell on those impressions. But in 1968 and 1969 the hackers had to face their sad public images, like it or not.

A protest march that climaxed at Tech Square dramatically indicated how distant the hackers were from their peers. Many of the hackers were sympathetic to the anti-war cause. Greenblatt, for instance, had gone to a march in New Haven, and had done some phone line hookups for anti-war radicals at the National Strike Information Center at Brandeis. And hacker Brian Harvey was very active in organizing demonstrations; he would come back and tell in what low esteem the AI lab was held by the protesters. There was even some talk at anti-war meetings that some of the computers at Tech Square were used to help run the war. Harvey would try to tell them it wasn't so, but the radicals would not only disbelieve him but get angry that he'd try to feed them bullshit. The hackers shook their heads when they heard of that unfortunate misunderstanding. One more example of how people didn't understand! But one charge leveled at the AI lab by the anti-war movement was entirely accurate: all the lab's activities, even the most zany or anarchistic manifestations of the Hacker Ethic, had been funded by the Department of Defense. Everything, from the Incompatible Time-sharing System to Peter Samson's subway hack, was paid for by the same Department of Defense that was killing Vietnamese and drafting American boys to die overseas.

The general AI lab response to that charge was that the Defense Department's Advanced Research Projects Agency (ARPA), which funded the lab, never asked anyone to come up with specific military applications for the computer research engaged in by hackers and planners. ARPA had been run by computer scientists; its goal had been the advancement of pure research. During the late 1960s a planner named Robert Taylor was in charge of ARPA funding, and he later admitted to diverting funds from military, "mission-oriented" projects to projects that would advance pure computer science. It was only the rarest hacker who called the ARPA funding "dirty money."

Almost everyone else, even people who opposed the war, recognized that ARPA money was the lifeblood of the hacking way of life. When someone pointed out the obvious—that the Defense Department might not have asked for *specific* military applications for the Artificial Intelligence and systems work being done, but still expected a bonanza of military applications to come from the work (who was to say that all that "interesting" work in vision and robotics would not result in more efficient bombing raids?)—the hackers would either deny the obvious (Greenblatt: "Though our money was coming from the Department of Defense, it was not military") or talk like Marvin Minsky: "There's nothing illegal about a Defense Department funding research. It's certainly better than a Commerce Department or Education Department funding research . . . because that would lead to thought control. I would much rather have the military in charge of that . . . the military people make no bones about what they want, so we're not under any subtle pressures. It's clear what's going on. The case of ARPA was unique, because they felt that what this country needed was people good in defense technology. In case we ever needed it, we'd have it."

Planners thought they were advancing true science. Hackers were blithely formulating their tidy, new-age philosophy based on free flow of information, decentralization, and computer democracy. But the anti-military protesters thought it was a sham, since all that so-called idealism would ultimately benefit the War Machine that was the Defense Department. The anti-war people wanted to show their displeasure, and the word filtered up to the Artificial Intelligence lab one day that the protesters were planning a march ending with a rally right there on the ninth floor. There, protesters would gather to vividly demonstrate that all of them—hackers, planners, and users—were puppets of the Defense Department.

Russ Noftsker, the nuts-and-bolts administrator of the AI lab, took the threat of protesters very seriously. These were the days of the Weather Underground, and he feared that wild-eyed radicals were planning to actually blow up the computer. He felt compelled to take certain measures to protect the lab.

Some of the measures were so secretive—perhaps involving government agencies like the CIA, which had an office in Tech Square—that Noftsker would not reveal them, even a decade after the war had ended. But other measures were uncomfortably obvious. He removed the glass on the doors leading from the elevator foyer on the ninth floor to the area where the hackers played with computers. In place of the glass, Noftsker installed steel plates, covering the plates with wood so it would not look as if the area were as barricaded as it actually was. The glass panels beside the door were replaced with half-inch-thick bulletproof Plexiglas, so you could see who was petitioning for entry before you unlocked the locks and removed the bolts. Noftsker also made sure the doors had heavy-duty hinges bolted to the walls, so that the protesters would not try to remove the entire door, rush in, and storm the computers.

During the days preceding the demonstration, only people whose names were on an approved list were officially allowed entry to this locked fortress. On the day of the demonstration, he even went so far as to distribute around forty Instamatic cameras to various people, asking them, when they ventured outside the protected area, to take pictures of the demonstrators. If the demonstrators chose to become violent, at least there would be documentation of the wrongdoers.

The barricades worked insofar as the protesters—around twenty or thirty of them, in Noftsker's estimate—walked to Tech Square, stayed outside the lab a bit, and left without leveling the PDP-6 with sledgehammers. But the collective sigh of relief on the part of the hackers must have been mixed with much regret. While they had created a lock-less, democratic system within the lab, the hackers were so alienated from the outside world that they had to use those same hated locks, barricades, and bureaucrat-compiled lists to control access to this idealistic environment. While some might have groused at the presence of the locks, the usual free-access guerrilla fervor did not seem to be applied in this case. Some of the hackers, shaken at the possibility of a rout, even rigged the elevator system so that the elevators could not go directly to the ninth floor. Though previously some of the hackers had declared, "I will not work in a place that has locks," after the demonstrations were over, and after the restricted lists were long gone, the locks remained. Generally, the hackers chose not to view the locks as symbols of how far removed they were from the mainstream.

A very determined solipsism reigned on the ninth floor, a solipsism that stood its ground even when hackerism suffered some direct, though certainly less physically threatening, attacks in publications and journals. It was tough to ignore, however, the most vicious of these, since it came from within MIT, from a professor of Computer Science (yes, MIT had come around and started a department) named Joseph Weizenbaum. A former programmer himself, a thin, moustachioed man who spoke with a rolling eastern European accent, Weizenbaum had been at MIT since 1963, but had rarely interacted with the hackers. His biggest programming contribution to AI had been a program called ELIZA, which carried on a conversation with the user; the computer would take the role of a therapist. Weizenbaum recognized the computer's power, and was disturbed to note how seriously users would interact with ELIZA. Even though people knew it was "only" a computer program, they would tell it their most personal secrets. To Weizenbaum, it was a demonstration of how the computer's power could lead to irrational, almost addictive behavior, with dehumanizing consequences. And Weizenbaum thought that hackers—or "compulsive programmers"—were the ultimate in computer dehumanization. In what was to become a notorious passage, he wrote, in *Computer Power and Human Reason:*

. . . bright young men of disheveled appearance, often with sunken glowing eyes, can be seen sitting at computer consoles, their arms tensed and waiting to fire their fingers, already poised to strike, at the buttons and keys on which their attention seems to be riveted as a gambler's on the rolling dice. When not so transfixed, they often sit at tables strewn with computer printouts over which they pore like possessed students of a cabbalistic text. They work until they nearly drop, twenty, thirty hours at a time. Their food, if they arrange it, is brought to them: coffee, Cokes, sandwiches. If possible, they sleep on cots near the printouts. Their rumpled clothes, their unwashed and unshaven faces, and their uncombed hair all testify that they are oblivious to their bodies and to the world in which they move. These are computer bums, compulsive programmers . . .

Weizenbaum would later say that the vividness of this description came from his own experience as a hacker of sorts, and was not directly based on observations of the ninth-floor culture. But many hackers felt otherwise. Several thought that Weizenbaum had identified them personally, even invaded their privacy in his description. Some others guessed that Greenblatt had been unfairly singled out; indeed, Greenblatt did send Weizenbaum some messages objecting to the screed.

Still, there was no general introspection resulting from this or any other attack on the hacker life-style. That was not the way of the lab. Hackers would not generally delve into each other's psychological makeups. "There was a set of shared goals"—Tom Knight would later explain—"a set of shared intellectual excitement, even to a large degree a set of shared social life, but there was also a boundary which people were nervous to go beyond."

It was this unspoken boundary which came to bother hacker David Silver. He joined the lab as an adolescent and literally came to maturity there, and besides his productive hacking he spent time thinking about the relationship between hackers and computers. He came to be fascinated at how all of them got so attached to, so intimately connected with something as simple as the PDP-6. It was almost terrifying: thinking about this made David Silver wonder what it was that connected people together, how people found each other, why people got along . . . when something relatively simple like the PDP-6 drew the hackers so close. The whole subject made him wonder on the one hand whether people were just fancy kinds of computers, or on the other hand whether they were images of God as a spirit.

These introspections were not things he necessarily shared with his mentors, like Greenblatt or Gosper. "I don't think people had sort of warm conversations with each other," he would later say. "That wasn't the focus. The focus was on sheer brainpower." This was the case even with Gosper: Silver's apprenticeship with him was not so much a warm human relationship, he'd later reflect, as "a hacker relationship," very close in terms of what they shared in terms of the computer, but not imbued with the richness of a Real World friendship.

"There were many many many years that went by when all I did was hack computers, and I didn't feel lonely, like I was missing anything," Silver would say. "But I guess as I started to grow up more, round out more, change more, become less eccentric in certain ways, I started needing more input from people. [By not going to high school] I bypassed all that social stuff and went right into this blue-sky think tank . . . I spent my lifetime walking around talking like a robot, talking to a bunch of other robots."

Sometimes the hacker failure to be deeply personal had grim consequences. The lab might have been the ideal location for guru-level hackers, but for some the pressure was too much. Even the physical layout of the place promoted a certain high-tension feeling, with the open terminals, the constant intimidating presence of the greatest computer programmers in the world, the cold air and the endless hum of the air conditioners. At one point a research firm was called in to do a study of the excessive, inescapable noise, and they concluded that the hum of the air conditioner was so bothersome because there weren't *enough* competing noises—so they fixed the machines to make them give off a loud, continual hiss. In Greenblatt's words, this change "was not a win," and the constant hiss made the long hours on the ninth floor rather nerve-racking for some. Add that to other factors—lack of sleep, missed meals to the point of malnutrition, and a driving passion to *finish that hack*—and it was clear why some hackers went straight over the edge.

Greenblatt was best at spotting "the classical syndrome of various kinds of losses," as he called it. "In a certain way, I was concerned about the fact that we couldn't have people dropping dead all over the place." Greenblatt would sometimes tell people to go home for a while, take it easy. Other things were beyond him. For instance, drugs. One night, while driving back from a Chinese meal, a young hacker turned to him and asked, not kidding, if he wanted to "shoot up." Greenblatt was flabbergasted. The Real World was penetrating again, and there was little Greenblatt could do. One night not long afterward, that particular hacker leapt off the Harvard Bridge into the ice-covered Charles River and was severely injured. It was not the only suicide attempt by an AI lab hacker.

From that evidence alone, it would seem that Weizenbaum's point was well taken. But there was much more to it than that. Weizenbaum did not acknowledge the beauty of the hacker devotion itself . . . or the very idealism of the Hacker Ethic. He had not seen, as Ed Fredkin had, Stew Nelson composing code on the TECO editor while Greenblatt and Gosper watched: without any of the three saying a word, Nelson was entertaining the others, encoding assembly language tricks which to them, with their absolute mastery of that PDP-6 "language," had the same effect as hilariously incisive jokes. And after every few instructions there would be another punch line in this sublime form of communication . . . The scene was a demonstration of sharing which Fredkin never forgot.

While conceding that hacker relationships were unusual, especially in that most hackers lived asexual lives, Fredkin would later say that "they were living the future of computers . . . They just had fun. They knew they were an elite, something special. And I think they appreciated each other. They were all different, but each knew something great about the other. They all respected each other. I don't know if anything like [that hacker culture] has happened in the world. I would say they kind of loved each other."

The hackers focused on the magic of computers instead of human emotions, but they also could be touched by other people. A prime example would be the case of Louis Merton.* Merton was an MIT student, somewhat reserved, and an exceptional chess player. Save for the last trait, Greenblatt at first thought him well within the spectrum of random people who might wander into the lab.

The fact that Merton was such a good chess player pleased Greenblatt, who was then working to build an actual computer which would run a souped-up version of his chess program. Merton learned some programming, and joined Greenblatt on the project. He later did his own chess program on a little-used PDP-7 on the ninth floor. Merton was enthusiastic about chess and computers, and there was little to foreshadow what happened during the Thanksgiving break in late 1966, when, in the little theater-like AI "playroom" on Tech Square's eighth floor (where Professor Seymour Papert and a group were working on the educational

* A pseudonym.

LOGO computer language), Merton temporarily turned into a veg-
etable. He assumed a classic position of catatonia, rigidly sitting
upright, hands clenched into fists at his side. He would not respond
to questions, would not even acknowledge the existence of anything outside himself. People didn't know what to do. They called
up the MIT infirmary and were told to call the Cambridge police,
who carted poor Merton away. The incident severely shook the
hackers, including Greenblatt, who found out about the incident
when he returned from a holiday visit home.

Merton was not one of the premier hackers. Greenblatt was not
an intimate friend. Nonetheless, Greenblatt immediately drove out
to Westboro State Hospital to recover Merton. It was a long drive,
and the destination reminded Greenblatt of something out of the
Middle Ages. Less a hospital than a prison. Greenblatt became
determined not to leave until he got Merton out. The last step in
this tortuous process was getting the signature of an elderly, apparently senile doctor. "Exactly [like something] out of a horror film,"
Greenblatt later recalled. "He was unable to read. This random
attendant type would say, 'Sign here. Sign here.' "

It turned out that Merton had a history of these problems. Unlike most catatonics, Merton would improve after a few days, especially when he was given medicine. Often, when he went catatonic
somewhere, whoever found him would call someone to take him
away, and the doctors would give a diagnosis of permanent catatonia even as Merton was coming to life again. He would call up the
AI lab and say, "Help," and someone, often Greenblatt, would
come and get him.

Later, someone discovered in MIT records a letter from
Merton's late mother. The letter explained that Louis was a
strange boy, and he sometimes would go stiff. In that case, all you
needed to do was to ask, "Louis, would you like to play a game of
chess?" Fredkin, who had also taken an interest in Merton, tried
this. Merton one day stiffened on the edge of his chair, totally in
sculpture mode. Fredkin asked him if he'd like to play chess, and
Merton stiffly marched over to the chess board. The game got
under way, with Fredkin chatting away in a rather one-sided conversation, but suddenly Merton just stopped. Fredkin asked,
"Louis, why don't you move?" After a very long pause, Merton
responded in a guttural, slow voice, "Your . . . king's . . . in
. . . check." Fredkin had inadvertently uncovered the check from
his last move.

Merton's condition could be mitigated by a certain medicine, but for reasons of his own he almost never took it. Greenblatt would plead with him, but he'd refuse. Once Greenblatt went to Fredkin to ask him to help out; Fredkin went back with Greenblatt to find Merton stiff and unresponsive.

"Louis, how come you're not taking your medicine?" he asked. Merton just sat there, a weak smile frozen on his face. "Why won't you take it?" Fredkin repeated.

Suddenly, Merton reared back and walloped Fredkin on the chin. That kind of behavior was one of Merton's unfortunate features. But the hackers showed remarkable tolerance. They did not dismiss him as a loser. Fredkin considered Merton's case a good example of the essential humanity of the group which Weizenbaum had, in effect, dismissed as emotionless androids. "He's just crazy," Minsky would later say of Weizenbaum. "These [hackers] are the most sensitive, honorable people that have ever lived." Hyperbole, perhaps, but it was true that behind their single-mindedness there *was* warmth, in the collective realization of the Hacker Ethic. As much as any devout religious order, the hackers had sacrificed what outsiders would consider basic emotional behavior—for the love of hacking.

David Silver, who would eventually leave the order, was still in awe of that beautiful sacrifice years later: "It was sort of necessary for these people to be extremely brilliant and, in some sense, handicapped socially so that they would just kind of concentrate on this one thing." Hacking. The most important thing in the world to them.

•

The computer world outside Cambridge did not stand still while the Hacker Ethic flourished on the ninth floor of Tech Square. By the late 1960s, hackerism was spreading, partly because of the proliferation of interactive machines like the PDP-10 or the XDS-940, partly because of friendly programming environments (such as the one hackers had created at MIT), and partly because MIT veterans would leave the lab and carry their culture to new places. But the heart of the movement was this: people who wanted to hack were finding computers to hack on.

These computers were not necessarily at MIT. Centers of hacker culture were growing at various institutions around the country, from Stanford to Carnegie-Mellon. And as these other centers reached critical mass—enough dedicated people to hack a large system and go on nightly pilgrimages to local Chinese restaurants

—they became tempting enough to lure some of the AI lab hackers away from Tech Square. The intense MIT style of hackerism would be exported through these emissaries.

Sometimes it would not be an institution that hackers moved to, but a business. A programmer named Mike Levitt began a leading-edge technology firm called Systems Concepts in San Francisco. He was smart enough to recruit phone-and-PDP-1 hacker Stew Nelson as a partner; TX-0 music master Peter Samson also joined this high-tech hardware design-and-manufacture business. All in all, the small company managed to get a lot of the concentrated talent around Tech Square out to San Francisco. This was no small feat, since hackers were generally opposed to the requirements of California life, particularly driving and recreational exposure to the sun. But Nelson had learned his lesson earlier—despite Fredkin's repeated urgings in the mid-sixties, he'd refused to go to Triple-I's new Los Angeles headquarters until, one day, after emphatically reiterating his vow, he stormed out of Tech Square without a coat. It happened to be the coldest day of the Cambridge winter that year, and as soon as he walked outside his glasses cracked from the sudden change of temperature. He walked straight back to Fredkin's office, his eyebrows covered with icicles, and said, "I'm going to Los Angeles."

In some cases, a hacker's departure would be hastened by what Minsky and Ed Fredkin called "social engineering." Sometimes the planners would find a hacker getting into a rut, perhaps stuck on some systems problem, or maybe becoming so fixated on extracurricular activities, like lock hacking or phone hacking, that planners deemed his work no longer "interesting." Fredkin would later recall that hackers could get into a certain state where they were "like anchors dragging the thing down. Time had gone by them, in some sense. They needed to get out of the lab and the lab needed them out. So some surprising offer would come to those persons, or some visit arranged, usually someplace far, far away. These people started filtering out in the world to companies or other labs. It wasn't fate—I would arrange it."

Minsky would say, "Brave Fredkin," acknowledging the clandestine nature of Fredkin's activity, which would have to be done without the knowledge of the hacker community; they would not tolerate an organizational structure which actually dictated where people should go.

While the destination could be industry—besides Systems Concepts, Fredkin's Information International company hired many of the MIT hackers—it was often another computer center. The most desirable of these was the Stanford AI Lab (SAIL), which Uncle John McCarthy had founded when he left MIT in 1962.

In many respects SAIL was a mirror image of MIT's operation, distorted only by the California haze that would sometimes drift from the Pacific Ocean to the peninsula. But the California distortion was a significant one—demonstrating how even the closest thing to the MIT hacker community was only an approximation of the ideal; the hothouse MIT style of hackerism was destined to travel, but when exposed to things like California sunlight it faded a bit in intensity.

The difference began with the setting, a semicircular concrete-glass-and-redwood former conference center in the hills overlooking the Stanford campus. Inside the building, hackers would work at any of sixty-four terminals scattered around the various offices. None of the claustrophobia of Tech Square. No elevators, no deafening air-conditioning hiss. The laid-back style meant that much of MIT's sometimes constructive acrimony—the shouting sessions at the TMRC classroom, the religious wars between grad students and hackers—did not carry over. Instead of the battle-strewn imagery of shoot-'em-up space science fiction that pervaded Tech Square, the Stanford imagery was the gentle lore of elves, hobbits, and wizards described in J. R. R. Tolkien's Middle Earth trilogy. Rooms in the AI lab were named after Middle Earth locations, and the SAIL printer was rigged so it could handle three different Elven type fonts.

The California difference was reflected in the famous genre of computer games that the Stanford lab eventually developed after the heyday of MIT Spacewar. A Stanford hacker named Donald Woods discovered a kind of game on a Xerox research computer one day that involved a spelunker-explorer seeking treasure in a dungeon. Woods contacted the programmer, Will Crowther, talked to him about it, and decided to expand Crowther's game into a full-scale "Adventure," where a person could use the computer to assume the role of a traveler in a Tolkienesque setting, fight off enemies, overcome obstacles through clever tricks, and eventually recover treasure. The player would give two-word, verb-noun commands to the program, which would respond depending on how the command changed the universe that had been created inside the computer by Don Woods' imagination. For instance, the game began with the computer describing your opening location:

YOU ARE STANDING AT THE END OF A ROAD BEFORE A
SMALL BRICK BUILDING. AROUND YOU IS A FOREST. A
SMALL STREAM FLOWS OUT OF THE BUILDING AND
DOWN A GULLY.

If you wrote GO SOUTH, the computer would say:

YOU ARE IN A VALLEY IN THE FOREST BESIDE A
STREAM TUMBLING ALONG A ROCKY BED.

Later on, you would have to figure all sorts of tricks to survive.
The snake you encountered, for instance, could only be dealt with
by releasing a bird you'd picked up along the way. The bird would
attack the snake, and you'd be free to pass. Each "room" of the
adventure was like a computer subroutine, presenting a logical
problem you'd have to solve.

In a sense, Adventure was a metaphor for computer programming itself—the deep recesses you explored in the Adventure
world were akin to the basic, most obscure levels of the machine
that you'd be traveling in when you hacked in assembly code. You
could get dizzy trying to remember where you were in both activities. Indeed, Adventure proved as addicting as programming—
Woods put the program on the SAIL PDP-10 on a Friday, and
some hackers (and Real World "tourists") spent the entire weekend trying to solve it. Like any good system or program, of course,
Adventure was never finished—Woods and his friends were always
improving it, debugging it, adding more puzzles and features. And
like every significant program, Adventure was expressive of the
personality and environment of the authors. For instance, Woods'
vision of a mist-covered Toll Bridge protected by a stubborn troll
came during a break in hacking one night, when Woods and some
other hackers decided to watch the sun rise at a mist-shrouded
Mount Diablo, a substantial drive away. They didn't make it in
time, and Woods remembered what that misty dawn looked like,
and wrote it into the description of that scene in the game, which
he conceived of over breakfast that morning.

It was at Stanford that gurus were as likely to be faculty people
as systems hackers (among Stanford professors was the noted computer scientist Donald Knuth, author of the multivolume classic
The Art of Computer Programming). It was at Stanford that, before
the Adventure craze, the casual pleasures of Spacewar were honed
to a high art (Slug Russell had come out with McCarthy, but it was

younger hackers who developed five-player versions and options for reincarnation, and ran extensive all-night tournaments). It was at Stanford that hackers would actually *leave their terminals* for a daily game of volleyball. It was at Stanford that a fund-raising drive was successfully undertaken for an addition to the lab which would have been inconceivable at MIT: a sauna. It was at Stanford that the computer could support video images, allowing users to switch from a computer program to a television program. The most famous use of this, according to some SAIL regulars, came when SAIL hackers placed an ad in the campus newspaper for a couple of willing young coeds, and the women answering the ad became stars of a sex orgy at the AI lab, captured by a video camera and watched over the terminals by appreciative hackers. Something else that never would have occurred at MIT.

It was not as if the SAIL hackers were any less devoted to their hacking than the MIT people. In a paper summarizing the history of the Stanford lab, Professor Bruce Buchanan refers to the "strange social environment created by intense young people whose first love was hacking," and it was true that the lengths that hackers went to in California were no less extreme than those at Tech Square. For instance, it did not take long for SAIL hackers to notice that the crawl space between the low-hanging artificial ceiling and the roof could be a comfortable sleeping hutch, and several of them actually lived there for years. One systems hacker spent the early 1970s living in his dysfunctional car parked in the lot outside the building—once a week he'd bicycle down to Palo Alto for provisions. The other alternative for food was the Prancing Pony; named after a tavern in Middle Earth, this was the SAIL food-vending machine, loaded with health-food goodies and pot-stickers from a local Chinese restaurant. Each hacker kept an account on the Prancing Pony, maintained by the computer. After you made your food purchase, you were given the option to double-or-nothing the cost of your food, the outcome depending on whether it was an odd- or even-numbered millisecond when you made the gamble. With those kinds of provisions, SAIL was even more amenable than MIT for round-the-clock hacking. It had its applications people and its systems people. It was open to outsiders, who would sit down and begin hacking; and if they showed promise, Uncle John McCarthy might hire them.

SAIL hackers also lived by the Hacker Ethic. The time-sharing system on the SAIL machine, like ITS, did not require passwords, but, at John McCarthy's insistence, a user had the option to keep his files private. The SAIL hackers wrote a program to identify these people, and proceeded to unlock the files, which they would read with special interest. "Anybody that's asking for privacy must be doing something interesting," SAIL hacker Don Woods would later explain.

Likewise, SAIL was in no way inferior to MIT in doing important computer work. Just like their counterparts at MIT's AI lab, SAIL hackers were robotics fans, as implied by the sign outside SAIL: CAUTION, ROBOT VEHICLE. It was John McCarthy's dream to have a robot leave the funky AI lab and travel the three miles to campus under its own physical and mental power. At one point, presumably by mistake, a robot got loose and was careening down the hill when, fortunately, a worker driving to the lab spotted it, and rescued it. Various hackers and academics worked at SAIL in important planner fields like speech understanding and natural language studies. Some of the hackers got heavily involved in a computer music project that would break ground in that field.

Stanford and other labs, whether in universities like Carnegie-Mellon or research centers like Stanford Research Institute, became closer to each other when ARPA linked their computer systems through a communications network. This "ARPAnet" was very much influenced by the Hacker Ethic, in that among its values was the belief that systems should be decentralized, encourage exploration, and urge a free flow of information. From a computer at any "node" on the ARPAnet, you could work as if you were sitting at a terminal of a distant computer system. Hackers from all over the country could work on the ITS system at Tech Square, and the hacker values implicit in that were spreading. People sent a tremendous volume of electronic mail to each other, swapped technical esoterica, collaborated on projects, played Adventure, formed close hacker friendships with people they hadn't met in person, and kept in contact with friends at places they'd previously hacked. The contact helped to normalize hackerism, so you could find hackers in Utah speaking in the peculiar jargon developed in the Tool Room next to the Tech Model Railroad Club.

Yet even as the Hacker Ethic grew in the actual number of its adherents, the MIT hackers noted that outside of Cambridge things were not the same. The hackerism of Greenblatt, Gosper, and Nelson had been directed too much toward creating one Utopia, and even the very similar offshoots were, by comparison, losing in various ways.

"How could you go to California, away from the action?" people would ask those who went to Stanford. Some left because they tired of the winner-loser dichotomy on the ninth floor, though they would admit that the MIT intensity was not in California. Tom Knight, who hacked at Stanford for a while, used to say that you couldn't *really* do good work at Stanford.

David Silver went out there, too, and concluded that "the people at Stanford were kind of losers in their thinking. They weren't as rigorous in certain ways and they sort of were more fun-loving. One guy was building a race car and another was building an airplane in the basement . . ." Silver himself got into hardware at Stanford when he built an audio switch to allow people working at their terminals to listen to any of sixteen channels, from radio stations to a SAIL public-address system. All the choices, of course, were stored within the SAIL PDP-6. And Silver thinks that exposure to the California style of hacking helped loosen him up, preparing him to make the break from the closed society of the ninth floor.

The defection of Silver and the other MIT hackers did not cripple the lab. New hackers came to replace them. Greenblatt and Gosper remained, as did Knight and some other canonical hackers. But the terrifically optimistic energy that came with the opening explosion of AI research, of setting up new software systems, seemed to have dissipated. Some scientists were complaining that the boasts of early AI planners were not fulfilled. Within the hacker community itself, the fervid habits and weird patterns established in the past decade seemed to have solidified. Were *they* ossified as well? Could you grow old as a hacker, keep wrapping around to those thirty-hour days? "I was really proud," Gosper would say later, "of being able to hack around the clock and not really care what phase of the sun or moon it was. Wake up and find it twilight, have no idea whether it was dawn or sunset." He knew, though, that it could not go on forever. And when it could not, when there was no Gosper or Greenblatt wailing away for thirty hours, how far would the hacker dream go? Would the Golden Age, now drawing to its close, really have *meant* anything?

•

It was in 1970 that Bill Gosper began hacking LIFE. It was yet another system that was a world in itself, a world where behavior was "exceedingly rich, but not so rich as to be incomprehensible." It would obsess Bill Gosper for years.

LIFE was a game, a computer simulation developed by John

Conway, a distinguished British mathematician. It was first de-scribed by Martin Gardner, in his "Mathematical Games" column in the October 1970 issue of *Scientific American*. The game consists of markers on a checkerboard-like field, each marker representing a "cell." The pattern of cells changes with each move in the game (called a "generation"), depending on a few simple rules—cells die, are born, or survive to the next generation according to how many neighboring cells are in the vicinity. The principle is that isolated cells die of loneliness, and crowded cells die from overpopulation; favorable conditions will generate new cells and keep old ones alive. Gardner's column talked of the complexities made possible by this simple game and postulated some odd results that had not yet been achieved by Conway or his collaborators.

Gosper first saw the game when he came into the lab one day and found two hackers fooling around with it on the PDP-6. He watched for a while. His first reaction was to dismiss the exercise as not interesting. Then he watched the patterns take shape a while longer. Gosper had always appreciated how the specific bandwidth of the human eyeball could interpret patterns; he would often use weird algorithms to generate a display based on mathematical computations. What would appear to be random numbers on paper could be brought to life on a computer screen. A certain order could be discerned, an order that would change in an interesting way if you took the algorithm a few iterations further, or alter-nated the x and y patterns. It was soon clear to Gosper that LIFE presented these possibilities and more. He began working with a few AI workers to hack LIFE in an extremely serious way. He was to do almost nothing else for the next eighteen months.

The group's first effort was to try to find a configuration in the LIFE universe which was possible in theory but had not been dis-covered. Usually, no matter what pattern you began with, after a few generations it would peter out to nothing, or revert to one of a number of standard patterns named after the shape that the collec-tion of cells formed. The patterns included the beehive, honey farm (four beehives), spaceship, powder keg, beacon, Latin cross, toad, pinwheel, and swastika. Sometimes, after a number of generations, patterns would alternate, flashing between one and the other: these were called oscillators, traffic lights, or pulsars. What Gosper and the hackers were seeking was called a glider gun. A glider was a pattern which would move across the screen, periodically reverting to the same pointed shape. If you ever created a LIFE pattern which actually spewed out gliders as it changed shape, you'd have a glider gun, and LIFE's inventor, John Conway, offered fifty dollars to the first person who was able to create one.

The hackers would spend all night sitting at the PDP-6's high-quality "340" display (a special, high-speed monitor made by DEC), trying different patterns to see what they'd yield. They would log each "discovery" they made in this artificial universe in a large black sketchbook which Gosper dubbed the LIFE Scrapbook. They would stare at the screen as, generation by generation, the pattern would shift. Sometimes it looked like a worm snapping its tail between sudden reverses, as if it were alternating between itself and a mirror reflection. Other times, the screen would eventually darken as the cells died from aggregate overpopulation, then isolation. A pattern might end with the screen going blank. Other times things would stop with a stable "still life" pattern of one of the standards. Or things would look like they were winding down, and one little cell thrown off by a dying "colony" could reach another pattern and this newcomer could make it explode with activity. "Things could run off and do something incredibly random," Gosper would later recall of those fantastic first few weeks, "and we couldn't stop watching it. We'd just sit there, wondering if it was going to go on forever."

As they played, the world around them seemed connected in patterns of a LIFE simulation. They would often type in an arbitrary pattern such as the weaving in a piece of clothing, or a pattern one of them discerned in a picture or a book. Usually what it would do was not interesting. But sometimes they would detect unusual behavior in a small part of a large LIFE pattern. In that case they would try to isolate that part, as they did when they noticed a pattern that would be called "the shuttle," which would move a distance on the screen, then reverse itself. The shuttle left behind some cells in its path, which the hackers called "dribbles." The dribbles were "poison," because their presence would wreak havoc on otherwise stable LIFE populations.

Gosper wondered what might happen if two shuttles bounced off each other, and figured that there were between two and three hundred possibilities. He tried out each one, and eventually came across a pattern that actually threw off gliders. It would move across the screen like a jitterbugging whip, spewing off limp boomerangs of phosphor. It was a gorgeous sight. No wonder this was called LIFE—the program created life itself. To Gosper, Conway's simulation was a form of genetic creation, without the vile secretions and emotional complications associated with the Real

World's version of making new life. Congratulations—you've given birth to a glider gun!

Early the next morning Gosper made a point of printing out the coordinates of the pattern that resulted in the glider gun, and rushed down to the Western Union office to send a wire to Martin Gardner with the news. The hackers got the fifty dollars.

This by no means ended the LIFE craze on the ninth floor. Each night, Gosper and his friends would monopolize the 340 display running various LIFE patterns, a continual entertainment, exploration, and journey into alternate existence. Some did not share their fascination, notably Greenblatt. By the early seventies, Greenblatt had taken more of a leadership role in the lab. He seemed to care most about the things that *had to be done,* and after being the de facto caretaker of the ITS system he was actively trying to transform his vision of the hacker dream into a *machine* that would embody it. He had taken the first steps in his "chess machine," which responded with a quickness unheard of in most computers. He was also trying to make sure that the lab itself ran smoothly, so that hacking would progress and be continually interesting.

He was not charmed by LIFE. Specifically, he was unhappy that Gosper and the others were spending "unbelievable numbers of hours at the console staring at those soupy LIFE things" and monopolizing the single 340 terminal. Worst of all, he considered the program they were using as "clearly non-optimal." This was something the LIFE hackers readily admitted, but the LIFE case was the rare instance of hackers tolerating some inefficiency. They were so thrilled at the unfolding display of LIFE that they did not want to pause even for the few days it might take to hack up a better program. Greenblatt howled in protest—"the heat level got to be moderately high," he later admitted—and did not shut up until one of the LIFE hackers wrote a faster program, loaded with utilities that enabled you to go backward and forward for a specified number of generations, focus in on various parts of the screen, and do all sorts of other things to enhance exploration.

Greenblatt never got the idea. But to Gosper, LIFE was much more than your normal hack. He saw it as a way to "basically do science in a new universe where all the smart guys haven't already nixed you out two or three hundred years ago. It's your life story if you're a mathematician: every time you discover something neat, you discover that Gauss or Newton knew it in his crib. With LIFE you're the first guy there, and there's always fun stuff going on.

You can do everything from recursive function theory to animal husbandry. There's a community of people who are sharing these experiences with you. And there's the sense of connection between you and the environment. The idea of where's the boundary of a computer. Where does the computer leave off and the environment begin?"

Obviously, Gosper was hacking LIFE with near-religious intensity. The metaphors implicit in the simulation—of populations, generations, birth, death, survival—were becoming real to him. He began to wonder what the consequences would be if a giant supercomputer were dedicated to LIFE . . . and imagined that eventually some improbable objects might be created from the pattern. The most persistent among them would survive against odds which Gosper, as a mathematician, knew were almost impossible. It would not be randomness which determined survival, but some sort of computer Darwinism. In this game which is a struggle against decay and oblivion, the survivors would be the "maximally persistent states of matter." Gosper thought that these LIFE forms would have *contrived* to exist—they would actually have evolved into intelligent entities.

"Just as rocks wear down in a few billion years, but DNA hangs in there," he'd later explain. "This intelligent behavior would be just another one of those organizational phenomena like DNA which contrived to increase the probability of survival of some entity. So one tends to suspect, if one's not a creationist, that very very large LIFE configurations would eventually exhibit intelligent [characteristics]. Speculating what these things could know or could find out is very intriguing . . . and perhaps has implications for our own existence."

Gosper was further stimulated by Ed Fredkin's theory that it is impossible to tell if the universe isn't a computer simulation, perhaps being run by some hacker in another dimension. Gosper came to speculate that in his imaginary ultimate LIFE machine, the intelligent entities which would form over billions of generations might also engage in those very same speculations. According to the way we understand our own physics, it is impossible to make a perfectly reliable computer. So when an inevitable bug occurred in that super-duper LIFE machine, the intelligent entities in the simulation would have suddenly been presented with a window to the metaphysics which determined their own existence. They would have a clue to how they were really implemented. In that case, Fredkin conjectured, the entities might accurately conclude that they were part of a giant simulation and might want to pray to their implementors by arranging themselves in recognizable patterns, asking in readable code for the implementors to give clues as to what *they're* like. Gosper recalls "being offended by that notion, completely unable to wrap my head around it for days, before I accepted it."

He accepted it.

Maybe it is not so surprising. In one sense that far-flung conjecture was already reality. What were the hackers but gods of information, moving bits of knowledge around in cosmically complex patterns within the PDP-6? What satisfied them more than this power? If one concedes that power corrupts, then one might identify corruption in the hackers' failure to distribute this power—and the hacker dream itself—beyond the boundaries of the lab. That power was reserved for the winners, an inner circle that might live by the Hacker Ethic but made little attempt to widen the circle beyond those like themselves, driven by curiosity, genius, and the Hands-On Imperative.

Not long after his immersion in LIFE, Gosper himself got a glimpse of the limits of the tight circle the hackers had drawn. It happened in the man-made daylight of the 1972 Apollo 17 moon shot. He was a passenger on a special cruise to the Caribbean, a "science cruise" timed for the launch, and the boat was loaded with sci-fi writers, futurists, scientists of varying stripes, cultural commentators, and, according to Gosper, "an unbelievable quantity of just completely empty-headed cruise-niks."

Gosper was there as part of Marvin Minsky's party. He got to engage in discussion with the likes of Norman Mailer, Katherine Anne Porter, Isaac Asimov, and Carl Sagan, who impressed Gosper with his Ping-Pong playing. For real competition, Gosper snuck in some forbidden matches with the Indonesian crewmen, who were by far the best players on the boat.

Apollo 17 was to be the first manned space shot initiated at night, and the cruise boat was sitting three miles off Cape Kennedy for an advantageous view of the launch. Gosper had heard all the arguments against going to the trouble of seeing a liftoff—why not watch it on television, since you'll be miles away from the actual launching pad? But when he saw the damn thing actually lift off, he appreciated the distance. The night had been set ablaze, and the energy peak got to his very insides. The shirt slapped on his chest, the change in his pocket jingled, and the PA system speakers broke from their brackets on the viewing stand and dangled by their power cords. The rocket, which of course never could have held to so true a course without computers, leapt into the sky, hell-bent for the cosmos like some flaming avenger, a Spacewar nightmare; the cruise-niks were stunned into trances by the power and glory of the sight. The Indonesian crewmen went berserk. Gosper later recalled them running around in a panic and throwing their Ping-Pong equipment overboard, "like some kind of sacrifice."

The sight affected Gosper profoundly. Before that night, Gosper had disdained NASA's human-wave approach toward things. He had been adamant in defending the AI lab's more individualistic form of hacker elegance in programming, and in computing style in general. But now he saw how the Real World, when it got its mind made up, could have an astounding effect. NASA had not applied the Hacker Ethic, yet it had done something the lab, for all its pioneering, never could have done. Gosper realized that the ninth-floor hackers were in some sense deluding themselves, working on machines of relatively little power compared to the computers of the future—yet still trying to do it all, change the world right there in the lab. And since the state of computing had not yet developed machines with the power to change the world at large— certainly nothing to make your chest rumble as did the NASA operation—all that the hackers wound up doing was making Tools to Make Tools. It was embarrassing.

Gosper's revelation led him to believe that the hackers *could* change things—just make the computers bigger, more powerful, without skimping on expense. But the problem went even deeper than that. While the mastery of the hackers had indeed made computer programming a spiritual pursuit, a magical art, and while the culture of the lab was developed to the point of a technological Walden Pond, something was essentially lacking.

The world.

As much as the hackers tried to make their own world on the ninth floor, it could not be done. The movement of key people was inevitable. And the harsh realities of funding hit Tech Square in the seventies: ARPA, adhering to the strict new Mansfield Amendment passed by Congress, had to ask for specific justification for many computer projects. The unlimited funds for basic research were drying up; ARPA was pushing some pet projects like speech recognition (which would have directly increased the government's ability to mass-monitor phone conversations abroad and at home). Minsky thought the policy was a "losing" one, and distanced the AI lab from it. But there was no longer enough money to hire anyone who showed exceptional talent for hacking. And slowly, as MIT itself became more ensconced in training students for conventional computer studies, the Institute's attitude to computer studies shifted focus somewhat. The AI lab began to look for teachers as well as researchers, and the hackers were seldom interested in the bureaucratic hassles, social demands, and lack of hands-on machine time that came with teaching courses.

Greenblatt was still hacking away, as was Knight, and a few newer hackers were proving themselves masters at systems work . . . but others were leaving, or gone. Now, Bill Gosper headed West. He arranged to stay on the AI lab payroll, hacking on the ninth-floor PDP-6 via the ARPAnet . . . but he moved to California, to study the art of computer programming with Professor Donald Knuth at Stanford. He became a fixture at Louie's, the best Chinese restaurant in Palo Alto, but was missing in action at Tech Square. He was a mercurial presence on computer terminals there but no longer a physical center of attention, draped over a chair, whispering, "Look at *that,*" while the 340 terminal pulsed insanely with new forms of LIFE. He was in California, and he had bought a car.

With all these changes, some of the hackers sensed that an era was ending. "Before [in the sixties], the attitude was—'Here's these new machines, let's see what they can do,'" hacker Mike Beeler later recalled. "So we did robot arms, we parsed language, we did Spacewar . . . now we had to justify according to national goals. And [people pointed out that] some things we did were curious, but not relevant . . . we realized we'd had a Utopian situation, all this fascinating culture. There was a certain amount of isolation and lack of dissemination, spreading the word. I worried that it was all going to be lost."

It would not be lost. Because there was a second wave of hackers, a type of hacker who not only lived by the Hacker Ethic but saw a need to spread that gospel as widely as possible. The natural way to do this was through the power of the computer, and the time to do it was now. The computers to do it would have to be small and cheap—making the DEC minicomputers look like IBM Hulking Giants by comparison. But small and powerful computers in great numbers could truly change the world. There were people who had these visions, and they were not the likes of Gosper or Greenblatt: they were a different type of hacker, a second generation, more interested in the proliferation of computers than in hacking mystical AI applications. This second generation were hardware hackers, and the magic they would make in California would build on the cultural foundation set by the MIT hackers to spread the hacker dream throughout the land.

PART TWO

HARDWARE
HACKERS

NORTHERN CALIFORNIA:
The Seventies

8

REVOLT IN 2100

THE first public terminal of the Community Memory project was an ugly machine in a cluttered foyer on the second floor of a beat-up building in the spaciest town in the United States of America: Berkeley, California. It was inevitable that computers would come to "the people" in Berkeley. Everything else did, from gourmet food to local government. And if, in August 1973, computers were generally regarded as inhuman, unyielding, warmongering, and nonorganic, the imposition of a terminal connected to one of those Orwellian monsters in a normally good-vibes zone like the foyer outside Leopold's Records on Durant Avenue was not necessarily a threat to anyone's well-being. It was yet another kind of flow to go with.

Outrageous, in a sense. Sort of a squashed piano, the height of a Fender Rhodes, with a typewriter keyboard instead of a musical one. The keyboard was protected by a cardboard box casing, with a plate of glass set in its front. To touch the keys, you had to stick your hands through little holes, as if you were offering yourself for imprisonment in an electronic stockade. But the people standing by the terminal were familiar Berkeley types, with long stringy hair, jeans, T-shirts, and a demented gleam in their eyes that you would mistake for a drug reaction if you did not know them well. Those who did know them well realized that the group was high on technology. They were getting off like they had never gotten off before, dealing the hacker dream as if it were the most potent strain of sinsemilla in the Bay Area.

The name of the group was Community Memory, and according to a handout they distributed, the terminal was "a communication system which allows people to make contact with each other on the basis of mutually expressed interests, without having to cede judgement to third parties." The idea was to speed the flow of information in a decentralized, non-bureaucratic system. An idea born from computers, an idea executable only by computers, in this case a time-shared XDS-940 mainframe machine in the basement of a warehouse in San Francisco. By opening a hands-on computer facility to let people reach each other, a living metaphor would be created, a testament to the way computer technology could be used as guerrilla warfare for people *against* bureaucracies.

Ironically, the second-floor public area outside Leopold's, the hippest record store in the East Bay, was also the home of the musicians' bulletin board, a wall completely plastered with notices of vegetarian singers looking for gigs, jug bands seeking Dobro players, flutists into Jethro Tull seeking songwriters with similar fixations. The old style of matchmaking. Community Memory encouraged the new. You could place your notice in the computer and wait to be instantly and precisely accessed by the person who needed it most. But it did not take Berkeley-ites long to find other uses for the terminal:

FIND 1984, YOU SAY
HEH, HEH, HEH . . . JUST STICK AROUND ANOTHER
TEN YEARS
LISTEN TO ALVIN LEE
PART YOUR HAIR DIFFERENT
DROP ASPIRIN
MAKE A JOINT EFFORT
DRIFT AWAY
KEEP A CLEAN NOSE
HOME {ON THE RANGE}
QUIT KICKING YORE HEARTS SEE ME FEEL ME
U.S. GET OUT OF WASHINGTON
FREE THE INDIANAPOLIS 500
GET UP AND GET AWAY
FALL BY THE WAYSIDE
FLIP OUT
STRAIGHTEN UP

LET A SMILE BE YOUR UMBRELLA

. . . . . AND . . . . .

BEFORE YOU KNOW IT {}{}{}{}{}{}{}{}

1984

WILL

FIND

YOU!

AND ITS GO' BE RIGHTEOUS . . . . .

KEYWORDS: 1894   BENWAY TLALCLATLAN   INTERZONE
2-20-74

It was an explosion, a revolution, a body blow against the establishment, spearheaded by one demented User—userism, come to the people—who called himself Doctor Benway in tribute to a sadistically perverted character in Burroughs' *Naked Lunch.* This cat Benway was taking things further than even the computer radicals at Community Memory had suspected they would go, and the computer radicals were delighted.

None was happier than Lee Felsenstein. He was one of the founders of Community Memory and though he was not necessarily its most influential member, he was symbolic of the movement which was taking the Hacker Ethic to the streets. In the next decade, Lee Felsenstein was to promote a version of the hacker dream that would, had they known, appall Greenblatt and the Tech Square AI workers with its technological naïvete, political foundation, and willingness to spread the computer gospel through, of all things, the marketplace. But Lee Felsenstein felt he owed nothing to that first generation of hackers. He was a new breed, a scrappy, populist hardware hacker. His goal was to break computers out of the protected AI towers, up from the depths of the dungeons of corporate accounting departments, and let people discover themselves by the Hands-On Imperative. He would be joined in this struggle by others who simply hacked hardware, not for any political purpose but out of sheer delight in the activity for its own sake; these people would develop the machines and accessories through which the practice of computing would become so widespread that the very concept of it would change—it would be easier for everyone to feel the magic. Lee Felsenstein would come as close as anyone to being a field general to these rabidly anarchistic troops; but now, as a member of Community Memory, he was part of a collective effort to take the first few steps in a momentous battle that the MIT hackers had never considered worth fighting: to spread the Hacker Ethic by bringing computers to the people.

It was Lee Felsenstein's vision of the hacker dream, and he felt he had paid his dues in acquiring it.

•

Lee Felsenstein's boyhood might well have qualified him for a position among the hacker elite on the ninth floor of Tech Square. It was the same fixation with electronics, something that took hold so eerily that it defied rational explanation. Lee Felsenstein, though, would later try to give his love for electronics a rational explanation. In his reconstructions of his early years (reconstructions shaped by years of therapy), he would attribute his fascination with technology to a complex amalgam of psychological, emotional, and survival impulses—as well as the plain old Hands-On Imperative. And his peculiar circumstances guaranteed that he would become a different stripe of hacker than Kotok, Silver, Gosper, or Greenblatt.

Born in 1945, Lee grew up in the Strawberry Mansion section of Philadelphia, a neighborhood of row homes populated by first- and second-generation Jewish immigrants. His mother was the daughter of an engineer who had invented an important diesel fuel injector, and his father, a commercial artist, had worked in a locomotive plant. Later, in an unpublished autobiographical sketch, Lee would write that his father Jake "was a modernist who believed in the perfectability of man and the machine as the model for human society. In play with his children he would often imitate a steam locomotive as other men would imitate animals."

Lee's home life was not happy. Family tension ran high; there was sibling warfare between Lee, his brother Joe (three years older), and a cousin Lee's age who was adopted as the boys' sister. His father Jake's political adventures as a member of the Communist Party had ended in the mid-fifties when infighting led to Jake's losing his post as district organizer, but politics were central to the family. Lee participated in marches on Washington, D.C., at the age of twelve and thirteen, and once picketed Woolworth's in an early civil rights demonstration. But when things at home got too intense for him, he would retreat to a basement workshop loaded with electronic parts from abandoned televisions and radios. He would later call the workshop his Monastery, a refuge where he took a vow to technology.

It was a place where his brother's inescapable physical and academic superiority did not extend. Lee Felsenstein had a skill with electronics which allowed him to best his brother for the first time. It was a power he was almost afraid to extend—he would build things but never dare to turn them on, fearing a failure that would uphold his brother's contention that "those things are never going to work." So he'd build something else instead.

He loved the *idea* of electronics. He filled the cover of his sixth-grade notebook with electrical diagrams. He would go to his neighborhood branch of the Free Library of Philadelphia and thumb through the pages of the *Radio Amateur's Handbook*. He got the biggest thrill from a Heath Company instruction manual for building a shortwave receiver. The Heath Company specialized in do-it-yourself electronics projects, and this particular manual had very detailed diagrams of wires and connections. Comparing the actual parts for that five-tube project with the perfect diagram, with its octagons linked to other octagons, Lee saw the connection . . . *this* line of the schematic represented *that* pin on the tube socket. It gave him an almost sensual thrill, this linking of his fantasy electronics world to reality. He carried around the manual everywhere, a pilgrim toting a prayerbook. Soon he was completing projects, and was vindicated when at age thirteen he won a prize for his model space satellite—its name a bow to Mother Russia, the Felsnik.

But even though he was realizing himself in a way he never had before, each of Lee's new products was a venture in paranoia, as he feared that he might not be able to get the part to make it work. "I was always seeing these *[Popular Mechanics]* articles saying, 'Gee, if you have this transistor you could make a regular radio you always wanted, and talk to your friends and make new friends' . . . but I never could get that part and I didn't really know how to go about getting it, or I couldn't get the money to get it." He imagined the mocking voice of his brother, labeling him a failure.

When Lee was a freshman at Central High, Philadelphia's special academic high school for boys, brother Joe, a senior, drafted him to become chief engineer at the school's budding Computer Club, showing Lee a diagram of some obsolete flip-flops and challenging his younger brother to build them. Lee was too terrified to say no, and tried unsuccessfully to complete the project. The effort made him wary of computers for a decade afterward.

But high school uplifted Lee—he was involved in political groups, did some work on the school's cyclotron, and did some significant reading—particularly some novels by Robert Heinlein.

The slightly built, spectacled Jewish teen-ager somehow identified with the futuristic protagonists, particularly the virginal young soldier in *Revolt in 2100*. The novel's setting is a twenty-first-century dictatorship, where a devoted, idealistic underground is plotting to fight the forces of the Prophet, an omnipotent Orwellian thug supported by unthinking masses who worship him. The protagonist stumbles upon evidence of the Prophet's hypocrisy, and, forced to choose between good and evil, he takes the drastic step of joining the revolutionary Cabal, which provides him with the teachings to stir his imagination.

> For the first time in my life I was reading things which had not been approved by the Prophet's censors, and the impact on my mind was devastating. Sometimes I would glance over my shoulder to see who was watching me, frightened in spite of myself. I began to sense faintly that secrecy is the keystone of all tyranny.
>
> (from *Revolt in 2100)*

Reading that novel, and later reading *Stranger in a Strange Land,* in which Heinlein's extraterrestrial protagonist becomes a leader of a spiritual group which has a profound effect on society, Lee Felsenstein began to see his own life as something akin to a science-fiction novel. The books, he later said, gave him courage to dream big, to try out risky projects, and to rise above his own emotional conflicts. The great fight was not so much internal as broad—it was the choice between good and evil. Taking that romantic notion to heart, Lee saw himself as the ordinary person with potential who is seized by circumstances, chooses the difficult path of siding with the good, and embarks on a long odyssey to overthrow evil.

It was not long before Lee was able to apply this metaphor in reality. After graduation, he went to the University of California at Berkeley to matriculate in Electrical Engineering. He was unable to get a scholarship. His freshman year did not parallel that of a typical MIT hacker: he more or less toed the line, failing to qualify for a scholarship by a fraction of a grade point. But he got what seemed as good—a work-study job at NASA's Flight Research Center at Edwards Air Force Base, at the edge of the Mohave Desert. To Lee, it was admission to Paradise—the language people spoke there was electronics, rocket electronics, and the schematics he had studied would now be transmogrified into the stuff of science fiction come alive. He reveled in it, the brotherhood of engineers, loved wearing a tie, walking out of an office and seeing neat rows of other offices, and water coolers. Heinlein was forgotten—Lee was comforming, an engineer out of a cookie cutter. Deliriously happy in the service of the Prophet. Then, after two months of that "seventh heaven," as he later called it, he was summoned to a meeting with a security officer.

The officer seemed ill at ease. He was accompanied by a witness to the proceedings. The officer kept notes and had Lee sign each page as he finished it. He also had the form Lee had filled out upon entering Edwards, Security Form 398. The officer kept asking Lee if he knew anyone who was a member of the Communist Party. And Lee kept saying no. Finally he asked, in a gentle voice, "Don't you understand that your parents were Communists?"

Lee had never been told. He had assumed that "Communist" was just a term, red-baiting, that people flung at activist liberals like his parents. His brother had known—his brother had been named after Stalin!—but Lee had not been told. He had been perfectly honest when he had filled out Form 398 with a clear "no" on the line that asked if you knew any known Communists.

"So there I was, ejected from Paradise," Lee would later say, "and the security chief said, 'You keep your nose clean for a couple years more, you won't have any problem getting back in.' Now I'd always been setting myself up to be abandoned, always expected to be abandoned. Suddenly I *was*. Literally thrown out in the wilderness. There's the Mohave Desert out there, for God's sake!"

On the night of October 14, 1964, Lee Felsenstein, failed engineer, took a train back to Berkeley. Lee had heard radio reports of student demonstrations there beginning two weeks before; he had dismissed them as a modern version of the legendary panty raids that had occurred in 1952. But upon his return he found the whole community alive with the Free Speech Movement. "Secrecy is the keystone of all tyranny," said Heinlein's *Revolt in 2100* protagonist, voicing not only the cry of Berkeley revolution, but the Hacker Ethic. Lee Felsenstein made the leap—he joined the Cabal. But he would merge his fervor with his own particular talent. He would use technology to fuel the revolt.

Since he owned a tape recorder, he went to Press Central, the media center of the movement, and offered his talents as an audio technician. He did a little of everything: mimeographed, did shit work. He was inspired by the decentralized structure of the Free Speech Movement. On December 2, when over eight hundred students occupied Sproul Hall, Lee was there with his tape recorder. He was arrested, of course, but the administration backed down on the issues. The battle had been won. But the war was just beginning.

For the next few years, Lee balanced the seemingly incompatible existences of a political activist and a socially reclusive engineer. Not many in the movement were so technically inclined, technology and especially computers being perceived as evil forces. Lee worked furiously to organize the people in his co-op dorm, Oxford Hall—the most political on campus. He edited the activist dorm newspaper. But he was also learning more about electronics, playing with electronics, immersing himself in the logical environment of circuits and diodes. As much as he could, he merged the two pursuits—he designed, for instance, a tool which was a combination bullhorn and club to fend off cops. But unlike many in the movement who were also deeply into Berkeley's wild, freewheeling social activity, Lee shied away from close human contact, especially with women. An unwashed figure in work clothes, Lee self-consciously lived up to the nerdy engineer stereotype. He did not bathe regularly, and washed his unfashionably short hair perhaps once a month. He did not take drugs. He did not engage in *any* sex, let alone all the free sex that came with free speech. "I was afraid of women and had no way of dealing with them," he later explained. "I had some proscription in my personality against having fun. I was not allowed to have fun. The fun was in my work . . . It was as if my way of asserting my potency was to be able to build things that worked, and other people liked."

Lee dropped out of Berkeley in 1967, and began alternating between electronics jobs and work in the movement. In 1968, he joined the underground *Berkeley Barb* as the newspaper's "military editor." Joining the company of such other writers as Sergeant Pepper and Jefferson Fuck Poland, Lee wrote a series of articles evaluating demonstrations—not on the basis of issues, but on organization, structure, conformation to an elegant system. In one of his first articles, in March 1968, Lee talked of an upcoming demonstration for Stop-the-Draft Week, noting the probable result of insufficient planning and bickering among organizers: "The activity will be half-baked, chaotic, and just like all the other demonstrations. The movement politicians seem not to realize that in the real world action is carried on not by virtue of ideological hairsplitting, but with time and physical resources . . . it is my responsibility

as a technician not to simply criticize but to make suggestions
. . ."

And he did make suggestions. He insisted that demonstrations
should be executed as cleanly as logic circuits defined by the precise schematics he still revered. He praised demonstrators when
they smashed "the right windows" (banks, not small businesses).
He advocated attack only to draw the enemy out. He called the
bombing of a draft board "refreshing." His column called "Military Editor's Household Hints" advised: "Remember to turn your
stored dynamite every two weeks in hot weather. This will prevent
the nitroglycerin from sticking."

Heinlein's protagonist in *Revolt in 2100* said: "Revolution is not
accompanied by a handful of conspirators whispering around a
guttering candle in a deserted ruin. It requires countless supplies,
modern machinery, and modern weapons . . . and there must be
loyalty . . . and superlative staff organization." Lee Felsenstein in
1968 wrote: "Revolution is a lot more than a random street brawl.
It takes organization, money, dogged determination, and willingness to accept and build on past disasters."

Felsenstein had his effect. During the trial of the Oakland Seven,
the defense attorney Malcolm Burnstein said, "We shouldn't have
these defendants here . . . it should have been Lee Felsenstein."

•

In the summer of 1968, Lee Felsenstein placed an ad in the *Barb*.
The ad itself was less than explicit: Renaissance Man, Engineer
and Revolutionist, seeking conversation. Not long after, a woman
named Jude Milhon found the ad. Compared to the other sleazy
come-ons in the back pages of the *Barb* ("GIRLS ONLY! I crave
your feet!"), it looked as though it came from a decent man, she
thought. It was what Jude needed in that tumultuous year—a veteran of the civil rights movement and a long-time activist, she had
been dazed by 1968's political and social events. The very world
seemed to be coming apart.

Jude was not only an activist, but a computer programmer. She
had been close to a man named Efrem Lipkin who was also in the
movement, and he was a computer wizard who sent her puzzles for
entertainment—she would not sleep until she solved them. She
learned programming and found it delightful, though she never did
see why hackers found it obsessively consuming. Efrem was coming from the East to join her on the Coast in several months, but

she was lonely enough meanwhile to contact the man who wrote
the ad in the *Barb*.

Jude, a thin, plucky blond woman with steady blue eyes, immediately pegged Lee as a "quintessential technocreep," but solely of
his own making. Almost unwittingly, by her company, and particularly by her consistent straightforwardness, honed in countless
self-evaluation sessions in various collectives, Jude began the long
process of drawing out Lee Felsenstein's personality. Their friendship was deeper than a dating relationship, and continued well
after her friend Efrem arrived from the East Coast. Lee made
friends with Efrem, who was not only an activist but a computer
hacker as well. Efrem did not share Lee's belief that technology
could help the world; nevertheless, Lee's decade-long wariness
about computers was coming to an end. Because, in 1971, Lee had
a new roommate—an XDS-940 computer.

It belonged to a group called Resource One, part of the Project
One umbrella of Bay Area groups fostering community activism
and humanistic programs. "One" had been started by an architect-
engineer who wanted to give unemployed professionals something
useful to do with their skills, help the community, and begin to
dissipate the "aura of elitism, and even mysticism, that surrounds
the world of technology." Among the projects in One's five-story,
mustard-yellow warehouse in an industrial section of San Francisco, was the Resource One collective, formed of people "who
believe that technological tools can be tools of social change when
controlled by the people." Resource One people had cajoled the
Transamerica Corporation into lending an unused XDS-940 time-
sharing computer to the group, so One could start gathering alternative mailing lists and setting up its program of computer education, economic research projects, and "demystification for the general public."

The computer was a Hulking Giant, an $800,000 machine that
was already obsolete. It filled a room, and required twenty-three
tons of air-conditioning. It needed a full-time systems person to get
it going. Resource One needed a hacker, and Lee Felsenstein
seemed a logical choice.

The systems software was set up by a Xerox PARC (Palo Alto
Research Center) hacker who had written the original time-sharing
system for the 940 at Berkeley. He was a long-haired, bearded
Peter Deutsch, the same Peter Deutsch who at age twelve had
peered over the console of the TX-0 twelve years before. A Berke-

ley graduate, he had managed to blend the whole-earth California life-style with intense hacking at PARC.

But it was Lee who was the machine's caretaker. In his continual mythologizing of his life as a science-fiction novel, he saw this period as a re-immersion into the asocial role of a person whose best friend was a machine, a technological esthete sacrificing himself in the service of the Cabal. The monastery this time was in the basement of the Resource One warehouse; for thirty dollars a month he rented a room. It was below sewer level, had no running water, was filthy. For Lee it was perfect—"I was going to be an invisible servant. Part of this machine."

But Resource One failed Lee, who was far ahead of the group in realizing that the social uses of technology would depend on exercising something akin to the Hacker Ethic. The others in the group did not grow up yearning for hands-on technology . . . their connection to it was not visceral but intellectual. As a result, they would argue about how the machine should be used instead of throwing back the sheets and *using* it. It drove Lee crazy.

Lee later explained: "We were prigs, we were intolerable esthetes. Anybody who wanted to use the machine had to come argue their case before our meeting. They had to plead to use it." Lee wanted to change the group's outlook to a more hacker-like, hands-on openness, but did not have the pluck to make the social effort—his self-esteem had hit a low point. He rarely even had the courage to venture out of the building to face the world—when he did, he'd glumly note that the tenderloin district bums looked cleaner, more prosperous than he did. Other people in the collective tried to open him up; once during a meeting they borrowed a television camera from a video collective upstairs, and every time there was laughter in the group they would zoom in on Lee, invariably poker-faced. Looking at the tape afterward, he could see what he was becoming—heartless. "I felt like I couldn't afford to have a heart," he later said. "I could see this happening, but I was pushing them away."

After that experience, he tried to become more active in influencing the group. He confronted one goldbricker who spent most of the day slowly sipping coffee. "What have you been doing?" Felsenstein demanded. The guy began talking about vague ideas, and Lee said, "I'm not asking you what you *want* to do, I'm asking what have you *done?*" But he soon realized that calling people down for their bullshit was futile: like an inefficient machine, the group's architecture itself was flawed. It was a bureaucracy. And the hacker in Lee could not abide that. Fortunately around that time, the spring of 1973, Efrem Lipkin came to Resource One, to rescue Lee Felsenstein and get Community Memory off the ground.

Efrem Lipkin was the kind of person who could look at you with hooded eyes in a long, Semitic face, and without saying a word let you know that the world was sadly flawed and you were no exception. It was the air of a purist who could never meet his own exacting standards. Efrem had just gotten back from Boston, where he had been on the payroll of a computer consulting company. The company had been doing military-related contracting, and Efrem had stopped going to work. The idealistic programmer did not inform his employer—he just stopped, hoping that the project would grind to a halt because of his nonparticipation. After nine months during which the company assumed he was hacking away, it became clear that there was no program, and the president of the company came to his cockroach-infested Cambridge crash pad and asked him, "Why did you do this?" He told Efrem that he had started the company after Martin Luther King had died—to do *good*. He insisted the projects he took on would keep the country strong against the Japanese technological threat. Efrem saw only that the company they were under contract to had been involved in anti-personnel weapons during the war. How could he do work for that company? How could he be expected to do *any* computer work, considering its all too often harmful uses?

It was a question that had plagued Efrem Lipkin for years.

Efrem Lipkin had been a hacker since high school. His affinity for the machine was instant, and he found programming "the ultimate disembodied activity—I would forget to speak English. My mind works in computer forms." But unlike some of his companions in a special city-wide program for high school computerists in New York, Efrem also considered his uncanny talent for the computer a curse. Like Lee, he came from a virulently left-wing political family, and besides dazzling his math teachers, he'd been thrown out of class for not saluting the flag, and booted out of History for calling the teacher a liar. Unlike Lee, who sought to combine technology and politics, Efrem saw them in opposition—an attitude which kept him in constant turmoil.

"I love computers and hate what computers can do," he would say later. When he went to high school, he considered the commercial applications of big computers—sending bills and such—as merely uninteresting. But when the Vietnam war started, he began seeing his favorite toys as instruments of destruction. He lived in Cambridge for a while, and one day ventured up to the ninth floor at Tech Square. He saw the PDP-6, saw the perfect little beachhead of the Hacker Ethic that had been established there, saw the concentrated virtuosity and passion—but could think only of the source of the funding and the eventual applications of this unchecked wizardry. "I got so upset I started crying," he later said. "Because these people had stolen my profession. They made it impossible to be a computer person. They sold out. They sold out to the military uses, the evil uses, of the technology. They were a wholly owned subsidiary of the Department of Defense."

So Efrem drifted to California, then back East again, then back to California. It took a while for him to see how computers could be used for social good, and each time he glimpsed the possibilities he suspected betrayal. One interesting project he'd been involved with was the World Game. A group of California programmers, philosophers, and engineers constructed a simulation of the world. It was based on an idea by Buckminster Fuller, where you could try out all sorts of changes and see their effect on the world. For days, people ran around suggesting things and running the game on the computer. Not much came of it in terms of suggestions on how to run the world, but a lot of people met others with similar views.

Not long afterward, Efrem stumbled upon Resource One, with Lee mired in its bowels. He thought it was a crock. There was this great setup with a computer and some software for community data bases and switchboard, but the group wasn't doing all it could. Why not take that great setup to the streets? Efrem began to get excited about the idea, and for perhaps the first time in his life he saw how computers might really be used for some social good. He got Lee thinking about it, and brought in some other people he'd met in the World Game.

The idea was to form an offshoot of Resource One called Community Memory. Computers out on the streets, liberating the people to make their own connections. Felsenstein lobbied the Resource One people into paying for an office in Berkeley which would double as an apartment for him. So the Community Memory faction moved across the bay to Berkeley to get the system going. And Lee felt freed from his self-imposed institutionalization. He was part of a group imbued with the hacker spirit, ready to *do* something with computers, all charged up with the idea that access to terminals was going to link people together with unheard-of efficiency, and ultimately change the world.

•

Community Memory was not the only ongoing attempt to bring computers to the people. All over the Bay Area, the engineers and programmers who loved computers and had become politicized during the anti-war movement were thinking of combining their two activities. One place in particular seemed to combine an easygoing counterculture irreverence with an evangelical drive to expose people, especially kids, to computers. This was the People's Computer Company. True to the whimsical style of its founder, the People's Computer Company was not really a company. The organization, a misnomer if one ever existed, did publish a periodical by that name, but the only thing actually manufactured was an intense feeling for computing for its own sake. Lee Felsenstein often attended PCC's Wednesday night potluck dinners, which provided a common meeting ground for Bay Area computer counterculturists, as well as a chance to see Bob Albrecht try, for the umpteenth time, to teach everybody Greek folk dancing.

Bob Albrecht was the visionary behind the People's Computer Company. He was a man, Lee Felsenstein would later say, to whom "bringing a kid up to a computer was like child molesting." Like child molesting, that is, to an obsessive pederast.

In the spring of 1962, Bob Albrecht had walked into a classroom and had an experience which was to change his life. Albrecht, then working for the Control Data Company as a senior applications analyst, had been asked to speak to the high school math club at Denver's George Washington High School, a bunch of everyday, though well-mannered, Jewish achiever types. Albrecht, a large man with a clip-on tie, a beefy nose, and sea-blue eyes which could gleam with creative force or sag basset-like behind his square-rimmed lenses, gave his little talk on computers and casually asked if any of the thirty-two students might want to learn how to program a computer. Thirty-two hands waved in the air.

Albrecht had never seen any kind of response like that when he was teaching Remedial FORTRAN, his "one-day course for people who had been to IBM school and hadn't learned anything," as he later put it. Albrecht couldn't understand how IBM could have given those people classes and not let them *do* anything. He knew even then that the name of the game was Hands On, as it had always been since he had started with computers in 1955 at

Honeywell's aeronautical division. Through a succession of jobs, he had been constantly frustrated with bureaucracies. Bob Albrecht preferred a flexible environment; he was a student of serendipity in life-style and outlook. His hair was short, his shirt button-down, and his family profile—wife, three kids, dog—was unexceptional. Underneath it all, though, Bob Albrecht was a Greek dancer, eager to break out the ouzo and the bouzouki. Greek dancing, liquor, and computers—those were the elements for Bob Albrecht. And he was startled to find how eager the high school students were to indulge in the latter pleasure, the most seductive of the three.

He began teaching evening classes for the students at Control Data's office. Albrecht discovered that the youngsters' delight in learning to take control of the Control Data 160A computer was intense, addictive, visceral. He was showing a new way of life to kids. He was bestowing power.

Albrecht didn't realize it then, but he was spreading the gospel of the Hacker Ethic, as the students were swapping programs and sharing techniques. He began to envision a world where computers would lead the way to a new, liberating life-style. *If only they were available* . . . Slowly, he began to see his life's mission—he would spread this magic throughout the land.

Albrecht hired four of his top students to do programming for around a buck an hour. They would sit there at desks, happily typing in programs to solve quadratic functions. The machine would accept their cards and crunch away while they watched blissfully. Then Albrecht asked these ace students to teach their peers. "His idea was to make us multiply as fast as possible," one of the group, a redheaded kid named Bob Kahn, said later.

Albrecht used the four as "barkers" for a "medicine show" at their high school. The students were entirely in charge. Twenty math classes were involved in the program, for which Albrecht had convinced his employers to part with the 160A and a Flexowriter for a week. After showing the classes some math tricks, Kahn was asked if the computer could do the exercises in the back of a math text—and he proceeded to do that day's homework assignment, using the Flexowriter to cut a mimeograph form so that each student would have a copy. Sixty students were motivated by the medicine show to sign up for computer classes; and when Albrecht took the medicine show to other high schools, the response was just as enthusiastic. Soon Albrecht triumphantly presented his medicine show to the National Computer Conference, where his whiz kids astounded the industry's high priests. *We don't do that,* they told Albrecht. He rocked with glee. He *would* do it.

He convinced Control Data to allow him to take the medicine show across the country, and he moved his base to CD's Minnesota headquarters. It was there that someone showed him BASIC, the computer language developed by John Kemeny of Dartmouth to accommodate, Kemeny wrote, "the possibility of millions of people writing their own computer programs . . . Profiting from years of experience with FORTRAN, we designed a new language that was particularly easy for the layman to learn [and] that facilitated communication between man and machine." Albrecht immediately decided that BASIC was *it,* and FORTRAN was dead. BASIC was interactive, so that people hungry for computer use would get instant response from the machine (FORTRAN was geared for batch-processing). It used English-like words like INPUT and THEN and GOTO, so it was easier to learn. And it had a built-in random number generator, so kids could use it to write games quickly. Albrecht knew even then that games would provide the seductive scent that would lure kids to programming—and hackerism. Albrecht became a prophet of BASIC and eventually co-founded a group called SHAFT—Society to Help Abolish FORTRAN Teaching.

As he became more involved in the missionary aspects of his work, the Bob Albrecht simmering under the button-down exterior finally surfaced. As the sixties hit full swing, Albrecht swung into California—divorced, with long hair, blazing eyes, and a head full of radical ideas about exposing kids to computers. He lived at the top of Lombard Street (San Francisco's tallest, crookedest hill), and begged or borrowed computers for his evangelistic practice. On Tuesday nights he opened his apartment up for sessions that combined wine tasting, Greek dancing, and computer programming. He was involved with the influential Midpeninsula Free University, an embodiment of the area's do-your-own-thing attitude which drew people like Baba Ram Dass, Timothy Leary, and the former AI sage of MIT, Uncle John McCarthy. Albrecht was involved in starting the loosely run "computer education division" of the nonprofit foundation called the Portola Institute, which later spawned the *Whole Earth Catalog.* He met a teacher from Woodside High School on the peninsula, named LeRoy Finkel, who shared his enthusiasm about teaching kids computers; with Finkel he began a computer-book publishing company named Dymax, in honor of Buckminster Fuller's trademarked word "dymaxion," combining *dynamism* and *maximum*. The for-profit company was funded by Albrecht's substantial stock holdings (he had been lucky enough to get into DEC's first stock offering), and soon the company had a contract to write a series of instructional books on BASIC.

Albrecht and the Dymax crowd got hold of a DEC PDP-8 mini-computer. To house this marvelous machine, they moved the company to a new headquarters in Menlo Park. According to his deal with DEC, Bob would get a computer and a couple of terminals in exchange for writing a book for DEC called *My Computer Likes Me,* shrewdly keeping the copyright (it would sell over a quarter of a million copies). The equipment was packed into a VW bus, and Bob revived the medicine show days, taking his PDP-8 road show to schools. More equipment came, and in 1971 Dymax became a popular hangout for young computerists, budding hackers, would-be gurus of computer education, and techno-social malcontents. Bob, meanwhile, had moved to a forty-foot ketch docked off Beach Harbor, about thirty miles south of The City. "I had never done sailing in my life. I just had decided it was time to live on a boat," he later said.

Albrecht was often criticized by the hip, technology-is-evil Palo Alto crowd for pushing computers. So his method of indoctrinating people into the computer world became subtle, a sly dope-dealer approach: "Just take a hit of this game . . . feels good, doesn't it? . . . You can program this thing, you know . . ." He later explained: "We were covert. Unintentionally, we were taking the long-term view, encouraging anyone who wanted to to use computers, writing books that people could learn to program from, setting up places where people could play with computers and have fun."

But there was plenty of counterculture at Dymax. The place was full of long-haired, populist computer freaks, many of them of high school age. Bob Albrecht acted the role of bearded guru, spewing ideas and concepts faster than anyone could possibly carry them out. Some of his ideas were brilliant, others garbage, but all of them were infused with the charisma of his personality, which was often charming but could also be overbearing. Albrecht would take the crew on excursions to local piano bars where he would wind up with the microphone in hand, leading the group in songfests. He set up part of Dymax's offices as a Greek taverna, with blinking Christmas lights, for his Friday night dancing classes. His most demonic ideas, though, involved popularizing computers.

Albrecht thought that some sort of publication should chronicle this movement, be a lightning rod for new developments. So the group started a tabloid publication called *People's Computer Company*, in honor of Janis Joplin's rock group Big Brother and the Holding Company. On the cover of the first issue, dated October 1972, was a wavy drawing of a square-rigged boat sailing into the sunset—somehow symbolizing the golden age into which people were entering—and the following handwritten legend:

COMPUTERS ARE MOSTLY
USED AGAINST PEOPLE INSTEAD OF FOR PEO-
PLE
USED TO CONTROL PEOPLE INSTEAD OF TO
FREE THEM
TIME TO CHANGE ALL THAT—
WE NEED A . . .

PEOPLE'S COMPUTER COMPANY

The paper was laid out in similar style to the *Whole Earth Catalog*, only more impromptu, and sloppier. There could be four or five different type fonts on a page, and often messages were scribbled directly onto the boards, too urgent to wait for the typesetter. It was a perfect expression of Albrecht's all-embracing, hurried style. Readers got the impression that there was hardly any time to waste in the mission of spreading computing to the people—and certainly no time to waste doing random tasks like straightening margins or laying out stories neatly or planning too far ahead. Each issue was loaded with news of people infused with the computer religion, some of them starting similar operations in different parts of the country. This information would be rendered in whimsical missives, high-on-computer dispatches from the front lines of the people's computer revolution. There was little response from the ivory towers of academia or the blue-sky institutions of research. Hackers like those at MIT would not even blink at PCC—which, after all, printed program listings in *BASIC*, for God's sake, not their beloved assembly language. But the new breed of hardware hackers, the Lee Felsenstein types who were trying to figure out ways for more computer access for themselves and perhaps others, discovered the tabloid and would write in, offering program listings, suggestions on buying computer parts, or just plain encouragement. Felsenstein, in fact, wrote a hardware column for PCC.

The success of the newspaper led Dymax to spin off the operation into a nonprofit company called PCC, which would include not only the publication, but the operation of the burgeoning computer center itself, which ran classes and offered off-the-street computing for fifty cents an hour to anyone who cared to use it.

PCC and Dymax were located in a small shopping center on Menalto Avenue, in the space previously occupied by a corner drugstore. The space was furnished with diner-style booths. "Whenever someone wanted to talk to us, we'd go out and get a six-pack and talk in our booths," Albrecht later recalled. In the computer area next door was the PDP-8, which looked like a giant stereo receiver with flashing lights instead of an FM dial, and a row of switches in front. Most of the furniture, save for some chairs in front of the gray teletype-style terminals, consisted of large pillows which people variously used as seat cushions, beds, or playful weapons. A faded green rug covered the area, and against a wall was a battered bookshelf loaded with one of the best, and most active, paperback science-fiction collections in the area.

The air was usually filled with the clatter of the terminals, one hooked to the PDP-8, another connected to the telephone lines, through which it could access a computer at Hewlett-Packard, which had donated free time to PCC. More likely than not, someone would be playing one of the games that the growing group of PCC hackers had written. Sometimes housewives would bring their kids in, try the computers themselves, and get hooked, programming so much that husbands worried that the loyal matriarchs were abandoning children and kitchen for the joys of BASIC. Some businessmen tried to program the computer to predict stock prices, and spent infinite amounts of time on that chimera. When you had a computer center with the door wide open, anything could happen. Albrecht was quoted in the *Saturday Review* as saying, "We want to start friendly neighborhood computer centers, where people can walk in like they do in a bowling alley or penny arcade and find out how to have fun with computers."

It seemed to be working. As an indication of how captivating the machines could be, one reporter doing a story on PCC came in around five-thirty one day, and the workers sat him down at a teletype terminal running a game called Star Trek. "The next thing I remember," the reporter wrote in a letter to PCC, "is that somebody tapped me on the shoulder at 12:30 A.M. the next morning and told me it was time to go home." After a couple of days of hanging out at PCC, the reporter concluded, "I still have nothing to tell an editor beyond that I spent a total of twenty-eight hours so far just playing games on these seductive machines."

Every Wednesday night PCC had its potluck dinners. After a typically disorganized PCC staff meeting—Bob, with ideas zipping into his head like Spacewar torpedoes, could not easily follow an agenda—long tables would be covered with cloths, and gradually the room would fill up with a virtual who's who of alternative computing in Northern California.

Of the distinguished visitors dropping in, none was so welcome as Ted Nelson. Nelson was the self-published author of *Computer Lib*, the epic of the computer revolution, the bible of the hacker dream. He was stubborn enough to publish it when no one else seemed to think it was a good idea.

Ted Nelson had a self-diagnosed ailment of being years ahead of his time. Son of actress Celeste Holm and director Ralph Nelson ("Lilies of the Field"), product of private schools, student at fancy liberal arts colleges, Nelson was an admittedly irascible perfectionist, his main talent that of an "innovator." He wrote a rock musical —in 1957. He worked for John Lilly on the dolphin project, and did some film work. But his head was, he later explained, helplessly "swimming in ideas" until he came in contact with a computer and learned some programming.

That was in 1960. For the next fourteen years he would bounce from one job to another. He would walk out of his office in a job at a high-tech corporation and see "the incredible bleakness of the place in these corridors." He began to see how the IBM batch-process mentality had blinded people to the magnificent possibilities of computers. His observations about this went universally unheeded. Would no one listen?

Finally, out of anger and desperation, he decided to write a "counterculture computer book." No publisher was interested, certainly not with his demands on the format—a layout similar to the *Whole Earth Catalog* or the *PCC*, but even looser, with oversized pages loaded with print so small you could hardly read it, along with scribbled notations, and manically amateurish drawings. The book was in two parts: one was called "Computer Lib," the computer world according to Ted Nelson; and the other, "Dream Machines," the computer future according to Ted Nelson. Shelling out two thousand dollars out of pocket—"a lot to me," he would say later—he printed a few hundred copies of what was a virtual handbook to the Hacker Ethic. The opening pages shouted with urgency, as he bemoaned the generally bad image of computers (he blamed this on the lies that the powerful told about computers, lies he called "Cybercrud") and proclaimed in capital letters that THE PUBLIC DOES NOT HAVE TO TAKE WHAT IS DISHED OUT. He brazenly declared himself a computer *fan,* and said:

> I have an axe to grind. I want to see computers useful to individuals, and the sooner the better, without necessary complication or human servility being required. Anyone who agrees with these principles is on my side. And anyone who does not, is not.
>
> THIS BOOK IS FOR PERSONAL FREEDOM. AND AGAINST RESTRICTION AND COERCION . . .

A chant you can take to the streets:

> COMPUTER POWER TO THE PEOPLE!
> DOWN WITH CYBERCRUD!

"Computers are where it's at," Nelson's book said, and though it sold slowly, it sold, eventually going through several printings. More important, it had its cult following. At PCC, *Computer Lib* was one more reason to believe it would soon be no secret that computers were magic. And Ted Nelson was treated like royalty at potluck dinners.

But people were not coming to potluck dinners to see the wizards of the computer revolution: they were there because they were interested in computers. Some were middle-aged, hard-core hardware hackers, some were grammar-school kids who had been lured by the computers, some were long-haired teen-age boys who liked to hack the PCC PDP-8, some were educators, some were just plain hackers. As always, planners like Bob Albrecht would talk about the *issues* of computing, while the hackers concentrated on swapping technical data, or complained about Albrecht's predilection for BASIC, which hackers considered a "fascist" language because its limited structure did not encourage maximum access to the machine and decreased a programmer's power. It would not take many hours before the hackers slipped away to the clattering terminals, leaving the activists engaged in heated conversation about this development or that. And always, there would be Bob Albrecht. Glowing in the rapid progress of the great computer dream, he would be at the back of the room, moving with the climactic iterations of Greek folk dance, whether there was music or whether there was not.

•

In that charged atmosphere of messianic purpose, the Community Memory people unreservedly threw themselves into bringing their project on-line. Efrem Lipkin revised a large program that would be the basic interface with the users, and Lee set about fixing a Model 33 teletype donated by the Tymshare Company. It had seen thousands of hours of use and been given to CM as junk. Because of its fragility, someone would have to tend to it constantly; it would often jam up, or the damper would get gummy, or it wouldn't hit a carriage return before printing the next line. Later in the experiment, CM would get a Hazeltine 1500 terminal with a CRT which was a little more reliable, but someone from the collective still had to be there in case of a problem. The idea was for Lee to eventually develop a new kind of terminal to keep the project going, and he was already beginning to hatch ideas for that hardware project.

But that was for later. First they had to get CM on the streets. After weeks of activity, Efrem and Lee and the others set up the Model 33 and its cardboard box shell—protecting against coffee spills and marijuana ashes—at Leopold's Records. They'd drawn up posters instructing people how to use the system, bright-colored posters with psychedelic rabbits and wavy lines. They envisioned people making hard connections, for things like jobs, places to live, rides, and barter. It was simple enough so that anyone could use it —just use the commands ADD or FIND. The system was an affectionate variation of the hacker dream, and they found compatible sentiment in a poem which inspired them to bestow a special name on Community Memory's parent company: "Loving Grace Cybernetics." The poem was by Richard Brautigan:

ALL WATCHED OVER BY MACHINES OF LOVING GRACE

> I like to think (and
> the sooner the better!)
> of a cybernetic meadow
> where mammals and computers
> live together in mutually
> programming harmony

like pure water
touching clear sky

I like to think
       (right now, please!)
of a cybernetic forest
filled with pines and electronics
where deer stroll peacefully
past computers
as if they were flowers
with spinning blossoms.

I like to think
       (it has to be!)
of a cybernetic ecology
where we are free of our labors
and joined back to nature,
returned to our mammal
brothers and sisters,
and all watched over
by machines of loving grace.

That was no mere terminal in Leopold's—it was an instrument of Loving Grace! It was to shepherd the ignorant flock into a grazing meadow fertilized by the benevolent Hacker Ethic, shielded from the stifling influence of bureaucracy. But some within Community Memory had doubts. Even greater than Lee's nagging doubts of the terminal's durability was his fear that people would react with hostility to the idea of a computer invading the sacred space of a Berkeley record store; his worst fears saw the Community Memory "barkers" who tended the terminal forced to protect the hardware bodily against a vicious mob of hippie Luddites.

Unfounded fears. From the first day of the experiment, people reacted warmly to the terminal. They were curious to try it out, and racked their brains to think of something to put on the system. In the *Berkeley Barb* a week after the experiment began, Lee wrote that during the Model 33 teletype terminal's first five days at Leopold's, it was in use 1,434 minutes, accepting 151 new items, and printing out 188 sessions, 32 percent of which represented successful searches. And the violence level was nonexistent: Lee reported "100 percent smiles."

Word spread, and soon people came seeking important connections. If you typed in FIND HEALTH CLINICS, for instance, you would get information on any of eight, from the Haight-Ashbury Medical Research Clinic to the George Jackson People's Free Clinic. A request for BAGELS—someone asking where in the Bay Area one could find good New York–style bagels—got four responses: three of them naming retail outlets, another one from a person named Michael who gave his phone number and offered to show the inquirer how to make his or her *own* bagels. People found chess partners, study partners, and sex partners for boa constrictors. Passed tips on restaurants and record albums. Offered services like baby-sitting, hauling, typing, tarot reading, plumbing, pantomime, and photography ("MELLOW DUDE SEEKS FOLKS INTO NON-EXPLOITABLE PHOTOGRAPHY/MODELING/BOTH . . . OM SHANTI").

A strange phenomenon occurred. As the project progressed, users began venturing into uncharted applications. As the Community Memory people looked over the days' new additions they found some items which could fit into no category at all . . . even the keywords entered at the bottom of the item were puzzling. There were messages like "YOU ARE YOUR OWN BEST FRIEND," followed by keywords FRIEND, LOVER, DOG, YOU, WE, US, THANK YOU. There were messages like "ALIEN FROM ANOTHER PLANET NEEDS COMPETENT PHYSICIST TO COMPLETE REPAIRS AND SPACECRAFT. THOSE WITHOUT KNOWLEDGE OF GEOMAGNETIC INDUCTION NEED NOT APPLY." There were messages like "MY GOD WHY HAVE YOU FORSAKEN ME." There were messages that gave cryptic quotes from Ginsberg, The Grateful Dead, Arlo Guthrie, and Shakespeare. And there were messages from Doctor Benway and the mysterious Interzone.

Doctor Benway, the *Naked Lunch* character, was "a manipulator and coordinator of symbol systems, an expert on all phases of interrogation, brainwashing, and control." No matter. Whoever this demented user was, he began arranging the storage bits inside the XDS-940 into frazzled screeds, flip commentaries of the times spiked with unspeakable visions, calls to armed revolution, and dire predictions of big-brotherism—predictions rendered ironically by the use of 1984-style computer technology in a radical and creative fashion. "Benway here," he'd announce himself in a typical entry, "just a daytripper in the sands of this fecund data base." Benway was not the only one who took on weird personas—as hackers had already discovered, the computer was a limitless extension of one's own imagination, a non-judgmental mirror in which you could frame any kind of self-portraiture you desired. No matter what you wrote, the only fingerprints your message bore were those of your imagination. The fact that non-hackers were getting off on these ideas indicated that the very presence of computers in accessible places might be a spur for social change, a chance to see the possibilities offered by new technology.

Lee would later call it "an epiphany, an eye-opener. It was like my experience with the Free Speech Movement and People's Park. My God! I didn't know people could *do* this!"

Jude Milhon developed on-line personalities, wrote poems. "It was great fun," she'd later recall. "Your dreams incarnate." One CM regular swapped electronic missives with Benway, elaborating on the *Naked Lunch* theme to create a computer "Interzone," in honor of the decadent flesh market of the soul created by Burroughs. At first Benway's messages indicated surprise at this variation; then, almost as if realizing the democratic possibilities of the medium, he gave his blessing. "Certain nefarious pirates have spoken of cloning the Benway Logo . . . go right ahead . . . it's public domain," he wrote.

Jude Milhon met Benway. He was, as she described him, "very shy—but capable of functioning in the world of Community Memory."

The group flourished for a year and a half, moving the terminal at one point from Leopold's to the Whole Earth Access Store, and placing a second terminal at a public library in San Francisco's Mission District. But the terminals kept breaking down, and it became clear that more reliable equipment was essential. A whole new system was needed, since CM could only go so far with the Hulking Giant XDS-940, and in any case the relationship between CM and Resource One (its funding source) was breaking down. But there was no system waiting in the wings, and Community Memory, low in funds and technology, and quickly burning up the store of personal energy of its people, needed something soon.

Finally, in 1975, a burned-out group of Community Memory idealists sat down to decide whether to continue the project. It had been an exhilarating and exhausting year. The project "showed what could be done. It showed the way," Lee would later claim. But Lee and the others considered it "too risky" to continue the project in its present state. They had too much invested, technically and emotionally, to see the project peter out through a series of frustrated defections and random system crashes. The consensus was to submerge the experiment into a state of temporary remission. Still, it was a traumatic decision. "We were just developing when it got cut off," Jude Milhon later said, "[Our relationship to] Community Memory was like Romeo to Juliet—our other half-soul. Then all of a sudden—CHOP—it's gone. Nipped in early flower."

Efrem Lipkin went off and tried once more to think of a way he could get out of computers. Others got involved in various other projects, some technical, some social. But nobody, least of all Lee Felsenstein, gave up the dream.

9

EVERY MAN A GOD

In June 1974, Lee Felsenstein moved into a one-room apartment over a garage in Berkeley. It didn't have much in the way of amenities—not even a thermostat—but it only cost $185 a month, and Lee could fit a workbench in the corner, and call it home. He preferred low overhead, portability, utility in a place.

Felsenstein had a specific design project in mind. A computer terminal built on the Community Memory concept. Lee abhorred terminals built to be utterly secure in the face of careless users, black boxes which belch information and are otherwise opaque in their construction. He believed that the people should have a glimpse of what makes the machine go, and the user should be urged to interact in the process. Anything as flexible as computers should inspire people to engage in equally flexible activity. Lee considered the computer itself a model for activism, and hoped the proliferation of computers to people would, in effect, spread the Hacker Ethic throughout society, giving the people power not only over machines but over political oppressors.

Lee Felsenstein's father had sent him a book by Ivan Illich entitled *Tools for Conviviality,* and Illich's contentions bore out Lee's views ("To me, the best teachers tell me what I know is already right," Lee would later explain). Illich professed that hardware should be designed not only for the people's ease, but with the long-term view of the eventual symbiosis between the user and the tool. This inspired Felsenstein to conceive of a tool which would embody the thoughts of Illich, Bucky Fuller, Karl Marx, and Robert Heinlein. It would be a terminal for the people. Lee dubbed it the Tom Swift Terminal, "in honor of the American folk hero most likely to be found tampering with the equipment." It would be Lee Felsenstein bringing the hacker dream to life.

Meanwhile, he would live off income from free-lance engineering contracts. One place he sought work was Systems Concepts, the small company which employed MIT veterans Stew Nelson (the phone wizard and coding genius), and TMRC and TX-0 alumnus Peter Samson. Felsenstein was leery of anything to do with MIT; typical of hardware hackers, he was offended at what he considered the excessive purity of those hackers, particularly their insouciance when it came to spreading the technology among the "losers." "Anyone who's been around artificial intelligence is likely to be a hopeless case," he'd later explain. "They're so far removed from reality that they cannot deal with the real world. When they start saying, 'Well, essentially all you need to do is dot dot dot,' I just glaze over and say, 'OK, buddy, but that's the easy part. Where *we* do our work is the rest of that.' "

His suspicions were confirmed when he met diminutive but strong-willed Stew Nelson. Almost instantly, they were involved in a disagreement, an arcane technical dispute which Lee later termed an "I'm-smarter-than-you-are, typical hacker dispute." Stew was insisting that you could pull off a certain hardware trick, while Lee, whose engineering style was shaped by his early childhood paranoia that things might not work, said he wouldn't risk it. Sitting in the big, wooden, warehouse-like structure that housed Systems Concepts, Lee felt that these guys were not as interested in getting computer technology out to the people as they were in elegant, mind-blowing computer pyrotechnics. To Lee, they were technological Jesuits. He was unconcerned about the high magic they could produce and the exalted pantheon of canonical wizards they revered. What about the *people?*

So when Stew Nelson, the archetypal MIT hacker type, gave Felsenstein the equivalent of an audition, a quick design test for a hardware product, Lee did not play the game. He could care less about producing the technological *bon mot* which Stew was looking for. Lee walked out.

He'd look for work elsewhere. He figured he could make it if he brought in eight thousand dollars a year. Because of the recession, work had been hard to find, but things were picking up. Fifty miles south of Berkeley, Silicon Valley was beginning to come alive.

The twenty miles or so between Palo Alto on the peninsula and San Jose at the lower end of San Francisco Bay had earned the title "Silicon Valley" from the material, made of refined sand, used to make semiconductors. Two decades before, Palo Alto had been the spawning ground of the transistor; this advance had been parlayed into the magic of integrated circuits (ICs)—tiny networks of transistors which were compressed onto chips, little plastic-covered squares with thin metallic connectors on the bottom. They looked like headless robot insects. And now, in the early 1970s, three daring engineers working for a Santa Clara company called Intel had invented a chip called a microprocessor: a dazzlingly intricate layout of connections which duplicated the complex grid of circuitry one would find in the central processing unit (CPU) of a computer.

The bosses of these engineers were still pondering the potential uses of the microprocessor.

Lee Felsenstein, in any case, was reluctant to take a chance on brand-new technology. His "junk-box" style of engineering precluded using anything but products which he knew would be around for a while. The success of the microchip, and the rapid price-cutting process that occurred after the chips were manufactured in volume (it cost a fortune to design a chip and make a prototype; it cost very little to produce one chip after an assembly line existed to churn them out), resulted in a chip shortage in 1974, and Felsenstein had little confidence that the industry would keep these new microprocessors in sufficient supply for his design. He pictured the users of his terminal treating it the way hackers treat a computer operating system, changing parts and making improvements . . . "a living system rather than a mechanical system," he'd later explain. "The tools are part of the regenerative process." These users would need steady access to parts. So while waiting for clear winners in the microchip race to develop, he took his time, pondering the lessons of Ivan Illich, who favored the design of a tool "that enhances the ability of people to pursue their own goals in their unique way." On sunny days in laid-back Berkeley, Lee would take his drawing board down to People's Park, the strip of greenery which he had helped liberate in the not-too-distant sixties, and make sketches of schematics, getting a sunburn from the reflection off the white drafting paper.

Felsenstein was only one of hundreds of engineers in the Bay Area who somewhere along the line had shed all pretenses that their interest was solely professional. They loved the hands-on aspects of circuitry and electronics, and even if many of them worked by day in firms with exotic names like Zilog and Itel and National Semiconductor, they would come home at night and build, build fantastic projects on epoxy-based silk-screened boards loaded with etched lines and lumpy rows of ICs. Soldered into metal boxes, the boards would do strange functions: radio functions, video functions, logic functions. Less important than making these boards perform tasks was the *act* of making the boards, of creating a system that got something done. It was hacking. If there was a goal at all, it was constructing a computer in one's very own home. Not to serve a specific function, but to play with, to explore. The ultimate system. But these hackers of hardware would not often confide their objective to outsiders, because, in 1974, the idea of a regular person having a computer in his home was patently absurd.

Still, that's where things were going. You could sense an excitement everywhere these hardware hackers congregated. Lee would get involved in technical discussions at the PCC potlucks. He also attended the Saturday morning bullshit sessions at Mike Quinn's junk shop.

Quinn's was the Bay Area counterpart of Eli Heffron's at Cambridge, where the Tech Model Railroad hackers scrounged for crossbar switches and step relays. Holding court at the shop, a giant, battleship gray, World War II vintage, hangar-like structure on the grounds of the Oakland Airport, was Vinnie "the Bear" Golden. At a counter cluttered with boxes of resistors and switches marked down to pennies, Vinnie the Bear would bargain with the hardware hackers he lovingly referred to as "reclusive cheapskates." They'd haggle over prices on used circuit boards, government surplus oscilloscopes, and lots of digital clock LEDs (light emitting diodes). Moving around the mammoth structure's wellworn wooden floor, the hacker-scavengers would pick through the rows of boxes holding thousands of ICs, capacitors, diodes, transistors, blank circuit boards, potentiometers, switches, sockets, clips, and cables. A sign in Gothic letters read IF YOU CAN NOT FIND IT DIG FOR IT and it was advice well taken. A hundred failed companies used Quinn's to dump excess, and you might stumble on a giant gas control unit, a stack of used computer tapes, or even a used computer tape drive the size of a file cabinet. Vinnie the Bear, a bearded, big-bellied giant, would pick up the parts you offered for his observations, guess at the possible limits of their uses, wonder if you could pull off a connection with this part or that, and adhere to the legend on the sign above him: "Price Varies as to Attitude of Purchaser." All sorts of technical discussions would rage on, ultimately ending with Vinnie the Bear mumbling vague insults about the intelligence of the participants, all of whom would come back the next week for more junk and more talk.

Next door to Mike Quinn's was the operation of Bill Godbout, who bought junk on a more massive scale—usually government surplus chips and parts which were rejected as not meeting the exacting standards required for a specific function, but perfectly acceptable for other uses. Godbout, a gruff, beefy, still-active pilot who hinted at a past loaded with international espionage and intrigues for government agencies whose names he could not legally utter, would take these parts, throw his own brand name on them, and sell them, often in logic circuitry kits which you could buy by mail order. From his encyclopedic knowledge about what companies were ordering and what they were throwing out, Godbout seemed to know everything going on in the Valley, and as his operation got bigger he supplied more and more parts and kits to eager hardware hackers.

Lee got to know Vinnie and Godbout and dozens of others. But he developed a particularly close relationship with a hardware hacker who had contacted him via the Community Memory terminal before the experiment went into indefinite remission. It was someone Lee had known vaguely from his Oxford Hall days at Berkeley. His name was Bob Marsh.

Marsh, a small, Pancho Villa–moustached man with long dark hair, pale skin, and a tense, ironic way of talking, had left a message for Lee on the terminal asking him if he wanted to get involved in building a project Marsh had read about in a recent issue of *Radio Electronics.* An article by a hardware hacker named Don Lancaster described how readers could build what he called a "TV Typewriter"—something that would allow you to put characters from a typewriter-style keyboard onto a television screen, just like on a fancy computer terminal.

Marsh had been a hardware freak since childhood; his father had been a radio operator, and he worked on ham sets through school. He majored in engineering at Berkeley, but got diverted, spending most of his time playing pool. He dropped out, went to Europe, fell in love, and came back to school, but not in engineering—it was the sixties, and engineering was extremely uncool, almost right-wing. But he did work in a hi-fi store, selling, fixing, and installing stereos, and he kept working at the store after graduating with a biology degree. Infused with idealism, he wanted to be a teacher of poor kids, but this did not last when he realized that no matter how you cut it, school was regimented—students sitting in precise rows, not able to talk. Years of working in the free-flow world of electronics had infused Marsh with the Hacker Ethic, and he saw school as an inefficient, repressive system. Even when he worked at a radical school with an open classroom, he thought it was a sham, still a jail.

So, after an unsuccessful try at running a stereo shop—he wasn't a very good businessman—he went back to engineering. A friend named Gary Ingram who worked at a company called Dictran got him a job, working on the first digital voltmeter. After a couple of years at that, he got into the idea of computers, and was amazed to see Lancaster's article. He figured he might use the TV Typewriter as a terminal to hook up to a computer.

Buying parts from Mike Quinn's to enhance the equipment in the kit offered in the magazine, he worked for weeks on the project, trying to improve on the design here and there. He never did get it working 100 percent, but the point was *doing* it, learning about it. He later explained: "It was the same as ham radio. I didn't want to spend my money to get on the air bragging about my equipment. I wanted to build things."

Lee responded to Marsh's message on CM and they met at the storefront headquarters of the group. Lee told him of the Tom Swift Terminal, a terminal which would use a home TV set as a character display, a "cybernetic building block" which could expand into almost anything. Marsh was impressed. He was also unemployed at the time, spending most of his time hacking the TV Typewriter in a rented garage on Fourth Street, near the bay. Marsh was married and had a kid—money was running low. He asked Lee to split the $175 garage rent with him, and Lee moved his workbench down there.

So Marsh worked on his project, while also cooking up a scheme to buy digital clock parts from Bill Godbout and mount them in fancy wooden cases. He had a friend who was a great woodworker. Meanwhile, Lee, president of the one-man LGC Engineering Company (named after Loving Grace Cybernetics), was working on his terminal, which was as much a philosophic venture as a design project.

Unlike your usual design in which all the parts would be controlled by one central chip, Lee's project had a complex multi-backup way of operating. It would have a "memory"—a place where characters could be stored—and that memory would be on a circuit "card," or board. Other cards would get the characters from the keyboard and put characters on the screen. Instead of a processor directing the flow, the cards would constantly be sending or receiving—"Gimme, gimme, gimme," they'd say, in effect, to the inputs such as the keyboard. The memory would be the terminal's crossroads. Even if you put a microprocessor on the terminal later on, to do computer-like functions, that powerful chip would be connected to the memory, not running the whole show—the task to which microprocessors are accustomed. It was a design that enshrined the concept of decentralization. It was also Felsenstein's paranoia coming to the fore. He wasn't ready to cede all the power to one lousy chip. *What if this part fails? What if that one does?* He was designing as if his brother were still looking over his shoulder, ready to deliver withering sarcasm when the system crashed.

But Lee had figured out how the Tom Swift Terminal could extend itself unto eternity. He envisioned it as a system for people to form clubs around, the center of little Tom Swift Terminal karasses of knowledge. It would revive Community Memory, it would galvanize the world, it would be the prime topic of conversation at Mike Quinn's and PCC potlucks, and it would even lay a foundation for the people's entry into computers—which would ultimately topple the evil IBM regime, thriving on Cybercrud and monopolistic manipulation of the marketplace.

But even as Lee's nose was reddening from the reflection of the sun on the schematics of his remarkable terminal, the January 1975 issue of *Popular Electronics* was on its way to almost half a million hobbyist-subscribers. It carried on its cover a picture of a machine that would have as big an impact on these people as Lee imagined the Tom Swift Terminal would. The machine was a computer. And its price was $397.

•

It was the brainchild of a strange Floridian running a company in Albuquerque, New Mexico. The man was Ed Roberts and his company was named MITS, short for Model Instrumentation Telemetry Systems, though some would come to believe it an acronym for "Man In The Street." Ed Roberts, an enigma even to his closest friends, inspired that kind of speculation. He was a giant, six feet four and over two hundred and fifty pounds, and his energy and curiosity were awesome. He would become interested in a subject and devour it wholesale. "I tend to consume shelves in libraries," he'd later explain. If one day his curiosity was aroused about photography, within a week he would not only own a complete color developing darkroom but be able to talk shop with experts. Then he would be off studying beekeeping, or American history. The subject that enthralled him most was technology and its uses. His curiosity made him, as an early employee of MITS named David Bunnell would say, "The world's ultimate hobbyist." And those days, being a hobbyist in digital electronics meant you were probably a hardware hacker.

It was model rocketry that led him to start MITS, which initially produced light flashers for hobbyist rocket ships, so backyard von Brauns could photograph the trajectories of their attempts to poke holes in the sky. From there, Roberts took MITS into test equipment—temperature sensors, audio sweep generators, and the like. Then Roberts became interested in things using LEDs, so MITS made digital clocks, both assembled and in kits, and his company was perfectly placed to take advantage of advances in microchip technology that made small digital calculators possible. He sold those in kits, too, and the company took off, expanding to nearly one hundred employees. But then the "Big Boys" came in, giant companies like Texas Instruments making their own microchips, and smaller companies reacted by cutting calculator prices so low that MITS could not compete. "We went through a period where our cost to ship a calculator was thirty-nine dollars and you could buy one in a drugstore for twenty-nine dollars," Roberts later recalled. It was devastating. By mid-1974, Ed Roberts' company was three hundred sixty-five thousand dollars in debt.

But Ed Roberts had something up his sleeve. He knew about Intel's new microprocessor chips and knew it was possible to take one and build a computer around it. A computer. Ever since he'd first had contact with them, during his time in the Air Force, he had been in awe of their power and disgusted with the convoluted steps one had to take to get access to them. Around 1974, Ed Roberts would talk often to his boyhood friend from Florida, Eddie Currie, so much so that to keep phone bills down they had taken to exchanging cassette tapes. The tapes became productions in and of themselves, with sound effects, music in the background, and dramatic readings. One day Eddie Currie got this tape from Ed Roberts which was unlike any previous one. Currie later remembered Ed, in the most excited cadences he could muster, speaking of building a computer for the masses. Something that would eliminate the Computer Priesthood for once and for all. He would use this new microprocessor technology to offer a computer to the world, and it would be so cheap that no one could afford not to buy it.

He followed up the tape with calls to Currie. Would you buy it if it were five hundred dollars? *Four* hundred? He talked it over with what staff was left in his failing company (the staff had shrunk to a relative handful) and, MITS employee David Bunnell would later recall, "We thought he was off the deep end."

But when Ed Roberts had his mind made up, no force could compel him to reconsider. He would build a computer, and that was it. He knew that Intel's current chip, the 8008, was not powerful enough, but when Intel came out with a new one, the 8080, which could support a good deal of memory as well as other hardware, Roberts called up the company for some horse-trading. Bought in small lots, the chips would cost $350 each. But Roberts was not thinking in small lots, so he "beat Intel over the head" to get the chips for $75 apiece.

With that obstacle cleared, he had his staff engineer Bill Yates design a hardware "bus," a setup of connections where points on the chip would be wired to outputs ("pins") which ultimately would support things like a computer memory, and all sorts of peripheral devices. The bus design was not particularly elegant—in fact, later on hackers would universally bitch about how randomly the designer had chosen which point on the chip would connect to which point on the bus—but it reflected Ed Roberts' dogged determination to get this job done *now*. It was an open secret that you *could* build a computer from one of those chips, but no one had previously dared to do it. The Big Boys of computerdom, particularly IBM, considered the whole concept absurd. What kind of nut would want a little computer? Even Intel, which made the chips, thought they were better suited for duty as pieces of traffic-light controllers than as minicomputers. Still, Roberts and Yates worked on the design for the machine, which Bunnell urged Roberts to call "Little Brother" in an Orwellian swipe at the Big Boys. Roberts was confident that people would buy the computer once he offered it in kit form. Maybe even a few hundred buyers in the first year.

While Ed Roberts was working on his prototype, a short, balding magazine editor in New York City was thinking along the same lines as Roberts was. Les Solomon was a vagrant from a Bernard Malamud story, a droll, Brooklyn-born former engineer with a gallows sense of humor. This unremarkable-looking fellow boasted a past as a Zionist mercenary fighting alongside Menachem Begin in Palestine. He would also talk of strange journeys which led him to the feet of South American Indian *brujos,* or witch doctors, with whom he would partake of ritual drugs and ingest previously sheltered data on the meaning of existence. In 1974, he was looking for someone who'd designed a computer kit so that the electronics-crazy readers of the magazine he worked for, *Popular Electronics,* would be in the vanguard of technology and have plenty of weird projects to build. Later on, Solomon would attempt to shrug off any cosmic motives. "There are only two kinds of gratification that a human being can possess," he would say, "ego and wallet. That's it, baby. If you got those you're in business. It was my job to get articles. There was another magazine *[Radio Electronics],* which was also doing digital things. They came out with a computer kit based on the Intel 8008. I knew the 8080 could run rings around it. I talked to Ed Roberts, who had published things about his calculators in our magazine, about his computer, and I realized it would be a great project in the magazine. Hopefully, I would get a raise."

But Solomon knew that this was not just another project, and in fact there were many factors here beyond ego and wallet. This was a computer. Later on, when coaxed, Les Solomon would speak in hushed terms of the project he was about to introduce to his readers: "The computer is a magic box. It's a tool. It's an art form. It's the ultimate martial art . . . There's no bullshit in there. Without truth, the computer won't work. You can't bullshit a computer, God damn it, the bit is there or the bit ain't there." He knew of the act of creation that is a natural outgrowth of working with the computer with a hacker's obsessive passion. "It's where every man can be a god," Les Solomon would say.

So he was eager to see Ed Roberts' machine. Ed Roberts sent him the only prototype via air freight, and it got lost in transit. The only prototype. So Solomon had to look at the schematics, taking Roberts' word that the thing worked. He believed. One night, he flippantly asked his daughter what might be a good name for this machine, and she mentioned that on the TV show "Star Trek" that evening, the good ship Enterprise was rocketing off to the star called Altair. So it was that Ed Roberts' computer was named Altair.

Roberts and his design helper Bill Yates wrote an article describing it. In January 1975, Solomon published the article, with the address of MITS, and the offer to sell a basic kit for $397. On the cover of that issue was a phonied-up picture of the Altair 8800, which was a blue box half the size of an air conditioner, with an enticing front panel loaded with tiny switches and two rows of red

LEDs. (This front panel would be changed to an even spiffier variation, anchored by a chrome strip with the MITS logo and the legend "Altair 8800" in the variegated type font identified with computer readouts.)

Those who read the article would discover that there were only 256 bytes (a "byte" is a unit of eight bits) of memory inside the machine, which came with no input or output devices; in other words, it was a computer with no built-in way of getting information to or from the world besides those switches in front, by which you could painstakingly feed information directly to the memory locations. The only way it could talk to you was by the flashing lights on the front. For all practical purposes, it was deaf, dumb, and blind. But, like a totally paralyzed person whose brain was alive, its noncommunicative shell obscured the fact that a computer brain was alive and ticking inside. It was a computer, and what hackers could do with it would be limited only by their own imaginations.

Roberts hoped that perhaps four hundred orders would trickle in while MITS perfected its assembly line to the point where it was ready to process reliable kits to the dedicated hobbyists. He knew he was gambling his company on the Altair. In his original brainstorm he had talked about spreading computing to the masses, letting people interact directly with computers, an act that would spread the Hacker Ethic across the land. That kind of talk, he later admitted, had an element of promotion in it. He wanted to save his company. Before the article came out he would rarely sleep, worrying about possible bankruptcy, forced retirement.

The day the magazine reached the subscribers it was clear that there would be no disaster. The phones started ringing, and did not stop ringing. And the mail bore orders, each one including checks or money orders for hundreds of dollars' worth of MITS equipment—not just computers, but the add-on boards that would make the computers more useful. Boards which hadn't even been designed yet. In one afternoon, MITS took orders for four hundred machines, the total response that Ed Roberts had dared hope for. And there would be hundreds more, hundreds of people across America who had burning desires to *build their own computers*. In three weeks, MITS' status with its bank went from a negative value to plus $250,000.

How did Les Solomon describe the phenomenon? "The only word which could come into mind was 'magic.' You buy the Altair, you have to build it, then you have to build other things to plug into it to make it work. You are a weird-type person. Because only weird-type people sit in kitchens and basements and places all hours of the night, soldering things to boards to make machines go flickety-flock. The worst horror, the horrifying thing is, here's a company in Albuquerque, New Mexico, that nobody ever heard of. And they put together a machine which is a computer. And a magazine who publishes this article and puts it on the cover says, 'Now you can build your own computer for four hundred bucks. All you gotta do is send a check to MITS in Albuquerque and they will send you a box of parts.' Most people wouldn't send fifteen cents to a company for a flashlight dial, right? About two thousand people, sight unseen, sent checks, money orders, three, four, five hundred dollars apiece, to an unknown company in a relatively unknown city, in a technically unknown state. These people were different. They were adventurers in a new land. They were the same people who went West in the early days of America. The weirdos who decided they were going to California, or Oregon, or Christ knows where."

They were hackers. They were as curious about systems as the MIT hackers were, but, lacking daily access to PDP-6s, they had to build their own systems. What would come out of these systems was not as important as the act of understanding, exploring, and changing the systems themselves—the act of creation, the benevolent exercise of power in the logical, unambiguous world of computers, where truth, openness, and democracy existed in a form purer than one could find anywhere else.

Ed Roberts later spoke of the power: "When you talk about wealth, what you're really saying is, 'How many people do you control?' If I were to give you an army of ten thousand people, could you build a pyramid? A computer gives the average person, a high school freshman, the power to do things in a week that all the mathematicians who ever lived until thirty years ago couldn't do."

Typical of the people who were galvanized by the Altair article was a thirty-year-old Berkeley building contractor with long blond hair and gleaming green eyes named Steve Dompier. A year before the *Popular Electronics* article had come out he had driven up the steep, winding road above Berkeley which leads to the Lawrence Hall of Science, a huge, ominous, bunker-like concrete structure which was the setting for the movie *The Forbin Project,* about two intelligent computers who collaborate to take over the world. This museum and educational center was funded by a grant to support literacy in the sciences, and in the early 1970s its computer education program was run by one of Bob Albrecht's original medicine-show barkers, Bob Kahn. It had a large HP time-sharing computer connected to dozens of gunmetal-gray teletype terminals, and when Steve Dompier first visited the hall he stood in line to buy a fifty-cent ticket for an hour of computer time, as if he were buying a ride on a roller coaster. He looked around the exhibits while waiting for his turn on a terminal, and when it was time he stepped into a room with thirty clattering teletypes. It felt like being inside a cement mixer. He flicked on the terminal, and with violent confidence the line printer hammered out the words, HELLO. WHAT'S YOUR NAME. He typed in STEVE. The line printer hammered out HI STEVE WHAT DO YOU WANT TO DO, and Steve Dompier was blown away.

He later described it: "It was the magic machine that had intelligence. Of course I didn't understand how it worked. But on everybody's face you could see the same thing for the first four or five months until they understood it really wasn't intelligent. That's the addictive part, that first magic where this machine talks back to you and does mathematics incredibly fast." For Steve Dompier, the addiction continued. He played games on the system, like Star Trek, or carried on a dialogue with a version of Joseph Weizenbaum's ELIZA program. He got a book of BASIC programming and worked on making little routines. He read *Computer Lib* and got technologically politicized. He bought a teletype for his home so he could access Lawrence Hall's computer by phone, where he'd play the new space game Trek '73 for hours on end. And then he heard about the Altair.

He was instantly on the phone to Albuquerque, asking for their catalog, and when he got it, everything looked great—the computer kit, the optional disk drives, memory modules, clock modules. So he sent for everything. Four thousand dollars' worth. His excuse to himself was that he would use his new computer system to catalog all his *Popular Science* magazines; if he wondered where that article about, say, heat pipes was, he'd type HEAT PIPES on the computer and it would say, ISSUE 4, PAGE 76, STEVE! Ten years and many computers later, he still wouldn't have gotten around to that task. Because he really wanted a computer to hack on, not to make any stupid index.

MITS wrote back to him saying he sent too much money; half the equipment he ordered was only in vague planning stages. The other half of the equipment he ordered didn't exist either, but MITS was working on those products. So Steve Dompier waited.

He waited that January, he waited that February, and in early
March the wait had become so excruciating that he drove down to
the airport, got into a plane, flew to Albuquerque, rented a car,
and, armed only with the street name, began driving around Albuquerque looking for this computer company. He had been to various firms in Silicon Valley, so he figured he knew what to look for
. . . a long, modernistic one-story building on a big green lawn,
sprinklers whirring, with a sign out front with "MITS" chiseled in
rustic wood. But the neighborhood where the address seemed to be
was nothing like that. It was a shabby industrial area. After he
drove back and forth a few times he saw a little sign, "MITS," in
the corner of a window in a tiny shopping center, between a mas-
sage parlor and a Laundromat. If he'd looked in the parking lot
nearby, he would have seen a trailer that some hacker had been
living in for the past three weeks while waiting for his machine to
be ready for delivery.

Dompier went in and saw that MITS headquarters was two tiny
offices, with one secretary trying to cope with a phone that would
ring as soon as the receiver was hung up. She was assuring one
phone caller after another that yes, one day the computer would
come. Dompier met Ed Roberts, who was taking all this with good
cheer. Roberts spun a golden tale of the computer future, how
MITS was going to be bigger than IBM, and then they went into
the back room, piled to the ceiling with parts, where an engineer
held up a front panel in one hand and a handful of LEDs in the
other. And that was all there was of the Altair so far.

The MITS system of kit delivery did not quite conform to
United States postal regulations, which frowned upon accepting
money through the mail for items that did not exist except in
pictures on magazine covers. But the post office did not receive
many complaints. When Ed Roberts' friend Eddie Currie joined
the company to help out in the crunch, he found that his experience with some MITS customers in Chicago was typical: one guy
in particular complained about sending over a thousand dollars
more than a year before, with no response. "You guys are ripping
me off, not even offering me my money back!" he shouted. Currie
said, "Fine, give me your name, I'll have the accounting department issue you a check immediately, with interest." The man
quickly turned humble. "Oh, no. I don't want that." He wanted his
equipment. "That was the mentality," Currie later recalled. "It was
incredible how badly people wanted this."

Ed Roberts was on a high, too busy trying to get things done to worry about how far behind in orders his company was. He had over a million dollars in orders, and plans which were much bigger than that. Every day, it seemed, new things appeared to make it even clearer that the computer revolution had occurred right there. Even Ted Nelson, author of *Computer Lib,* called with his blessing. Bob Albrecht also called, and said he'd write a book about games on the Altair, if Roberts would send him a working model to review for *PCC.*

Eventually, MITS managed to get some kits out the door. Steve Dompier had left the office only after Roberts had given him a plastic bag of parts he could begin working with, and over the next couple of months more parts would arrive by UPS, and finally Dompier had enough parts to put together an Altair with a serial number of four. Number three went to the guy in the parking lot who would work with a battery-powered soldering system. Every time he had a problem he would leap out of the trailer and bug a MITS engineer until he understood the problem. An even earlier assembled prototype went to PCC, which had the fantastic advantage of getting an already constructed model.

It was not easy to put an Altair together. Eddie Currie later acknowledged this when he said, "One of the nice things about the kit [from MITS' point of view] was you didn't have to test the parts you sent, you didn't have to test the subunits, you didn't have to test the finished units. You just put all the stuff in envelopes and shipped them. It was left to the poor customer to figure out how to put all those bags of junk together." (Actually, Ed Roberts would explain, it would have been cheaper to assemble the things at the factory, since frustrated hobbyists would often send back their semi-completed machines to MITS, which would finish the task at a loss.)

It was an education in itself, a course of digital logic and soldering skills and innovation. But it could be done. The problem was that, when you were finished, what you had was a box of blinking lights with only 256 bytes of memory. You could put in a program only by flicking octal numbers into the computer by those tiny, finger-shredding switches, and you could see the answer to your problem only by interpreting the flickety-flock of the LED lights, which were also laid out in octal. Hell, what did it matter. It was a start. It was a computer.

Around the People's Computer Company, the announcement of the Altair 8800 was cause for celebration. Everybody had known about the attempts to get a system going around the less powerful Intel 8008 chip; the unofficial sister publication of *PCC* was the "Micro-8 Newsletter," a byzantinely arranged document with microscopic type published by a teacher and 8008 freak in Lompoc, California. But the Altair, with its incredibly low price and its 8080 chip, was spoken about as if it were the Second Coming.

The first issue of *PCC* in 1975 devoted a page to the new machine, urging readers to get hold of the *Popular Electronics* article, and including a handwritten addendum by Bob Albrecht: "We will put our chips on the chip. If you are assembling a home computer, school computer, community memory computer . . . game-playing-fun-loving computer . . . using an Intel 8008 or Intel 8080, please write a letter to the PCC Dragon!"

Lee Felsenstein, who was doing hardware reviews for *PCC*, was eager to see the machine. The biggest thing before that had been the TV Typewriter that his garage-mate Bob Marsh had been working on, and Lee had been corresponding with its designer, Don Lancaster. The design seemed to have the fatal flaw of blanking out at the end of each page of text—a "whirling dervish" scheme of erasing what went before when the screen was refreshed with a new output—and Lee had been thinking of designing a board to fix that. But when the Altair came out all bets were off. Felsenstein and Marsh read the *Popular Electronics* article, and they instantly realized that the model pictured in the magazine was a dummy, and that even when the real Altair was ready, it would be a box with flashing lights. There was nothing in it! It was just a logical extension of what everyone knew and no one had dared to take advantage of.

This did not upset Lee in the least; he knew that the significance of the Altair was not as a technological advance, or even as a useful product. The value would be in the price and the promise—both of which would entice people to order kits and build their own computers. Lee, who had no respect for the elitist ivory-tower universities like MIT, was exultant at the opening of the first college with a major in hardware hacking: University of Altair. Your degree would come after completing courses in Soldering, Digital Logic, Technical Improvisation, Debugging, and Knowing Whom to Ask for Help. Then you would be ready for a lifelong matriculation toward a Ph.D. in Getting the Thing to *Do* Something.

When Altair sent one of the first assembled computers to PCC,

Bob Albrecht lent it to Lee for a week. He took it to Efrem Lipkin's place and they set it down, treating it as a curiosity, a piece of sculpture. Lee got the thing apart and began dreaming of things to put in it to make a system out of the machine. In his review of the machine in *PCC*, which ran with a picture of lightning striking a small town, he wrote: "The Altair 8800 has two things (at least) going for it: it's here and it works. These facts alone will guarantee that it is THE amateur computer for at least the next year . . ."

PCC devoted pages to the machine, which was the center of the now imminent revolution. But as enthusiastic as Bob Albrecht was about the Altair, he still felt that the key thing his operation had to offer was the initial magic of computing itself, not the hard-wired craziness experienced by the hardware hackers rushing to order Altairs. There were plenty of hardware people hanging out at PCC, but when one of them, Fred Moore, an idealist with some very political ideas about computers, asked Albrecht if he could teach a PCC class in computer hardware, Albrecht demurred.

It was a classic hacker-planner conflict. Albrecht the planner wanted magic spread far and wide, and considered the intense fanaticism of high-level hacking as secondary. Hardware hackers wanted to go all the way into the machines, so deep that they reached the point where the world was in its purest form, where "the bit is there or it ain't there," as Lee Solomon put it. A world where politics and social causes were irrelevant.

It was ironic that it was Fred Moore who wanted to lead that descent into hardware mysteries, because in his own way Moore was much more a planner than a hacker.

Fred Moore's interest in computers was not only for the pleasure they gave to devoted programmers, but also for their ability to bring people together. Fred was a vagabond activist, a student of nonviolence who believed that most problems could be solved if only people could get together, communicate, and share solutions. Sometimes, in the service of these beliefs, Fred Moore would do very strange things.

One of his more notable moments had come four years earlier, in 1971, during the demise party of the *Whole Earth Catalog*. Editor Stewart Brand had thrown this farewell-to-the-*Catalog* bash into turmoil by announcing that he was going to give away twenty thousand dollars: it was up to the fifteen hundred party-goers to decide whom he should give it to. The announcement was made at 10:30 P.M., and for the next ten hours the party turned, variously, from town meeting to parliamentary conference, to debate, to brawl, to circus, and to bitching session. The crowd was dwindling: around 3 A.M. the I Ching was thrown, with inconclusive results. It was then that Fred Moore spoke. Described later by a reporter as "a young man with wavy hair and a beard and an intense, earnest expression," Moore was upset that money was being labeled a savior and people were being bought. He thought the whole thing was getting to be a downer. He announced to the crowd that more important than the money was the event occurring right then. He noted that a poet had asked for money to publish a book of poems and someone had said, "We know where you can get paper," and someone else had suggested a cheap printer . . . and Fred thought that maybe people didn't need money to get what they wanted, just themselves. To illustrate the point, Fred began setting fire to dollar bills. Then people decided to take a vote whether to bother to spend the money; Moore opposed the vote, since voting in his view was a way of dividing people against each other. His opposition to the concept of voting so confused the issue that polling the audience didn't work. Then, after much more talk, Moore began circulating a petition which said, in part, "We feel the union of people here tonight is more important than money, a greater resource," and he urged people to sign their names to a piece of paper to keep in contact through a pragmatic networking. Finally, well after dawn, when there were around twenty people left, they said to hell with it, and gave the money to Fred Moore. To quote a *Rolling Stone* reporter's account, "Moore seemed to get the money by default, by persistence . . . Moore wandered around for a while, bewildered and awed, trying to get riders to accompany him back to Palo Alto and wondering aloud whether he should deposit the money in a bank account . . . then realized he had no bank account."

Fred Moore never did put the money in a bank ("They make war," he said), but eventually distributed thousands of dollars to worthy groups. But the experience showed him two things. One, he knew: money was evil. The other was the power of people getting together, how they could do things *without* money, just by banding together and using their natural resources. That was why Fred Moore got so excited about computers.

Moore had been involved with computers for a few years, ever since wandering into the computer center at the Stanford Medical Center in 1970. He was traveling around then in a Volkswagen bus with his young daughter, and he would sometimes leave her in the bus while he played with the computer. Once he got so wrapped up in the machine that a policeman came to the computer center asking if anyone knew anything about the little girl left out in the parking lot . . .

He saw the computer as an incredible facilitator, a way for people to get control of their environment. He could see it in the kids he taught games to, in classes at PCC. The kids would just play and have a good time. Fred was teaching about thirteen of these classes a week, and thinking a lot about how computers might keep alternative people together in big data bases. And then the Altair was announced, and he thought that people should get together and teach each other how to use it. He didn't know much about hardware, had little idea how to build the thing, but he figured that people in the class would help each other, and they'd get things done.

Bob Albrecht did not like the idea, so there was no hardware class.

Fred Moore got to talking about this with another frustrated hanger-on in the PCC orbit, Gordon French, the consulting engineer who'd built—"homebrewed," as the hardware hackers called it—a computer which more or less worked, centered on the Intel 8008 chip. He named his system Chicken Hawk. Gordon French liked to build computers the way people like to take engines out of automobiles and rebuild them. He was a gangly fellow with a wide, crooked smile and long, prematurely gray hair. He loved to talk computers, and it sometimes seemed, when Gordon French got going on the subject, a faucet opened up that would not stop until a squad of plumbers with big wrenches and rubber coats came to turn off the flow. A yearning to meet people with similar likes led him to PCC, but French was unsuccessful in his application to be on the PCC board of directors. He was also unhappy that the Wednesday potlucks seemed to be phasing out. The Altair was for sale, people were going crazy, it was time to get together, and there was no way to do it. So French and Moore decided to start up a group of people interested in building computers. Their *own* hardware group, and it would be full of good computer talk, shared electronic technique, and maybe a demonstration or two of the latest stuff you could buy. Just a bunch of hardware hackers seeing what might come of a somewhat more than random meeting.

So on crucial billboards in the area—at PCC, at Lawrence Hall, at a few schools and high-tech corporations—Fred Moore tacked up a sign that read:

AMATEUR COMPUTER USERS GROUP
HOMEBREW COMPUTER CLUB . . . you name it

Are you building your own computer? Terminal? TV Typewriter? I/O device? or some other digital black magic box?

Or are you buying time on a time-sharing service?

If so, you might like to come to a gathering of people with likeminded interests. Exchange information, swap ideas, help work on a project, whatever . . .

The meeting was called for March 5, 1975, at Gordon's Menlo Park address. Fred Moore and Gordon French had just set the stage for the latest flowering of the hacker dream.

10

THE HOMEBREW COMPUTER CLUB

THE fifth of March was a rainy night in Silicon Valley. All thirty-two participants in the first meeting of the yet unnamed group could hear the rain while sitting on the hard cement floor of Gordon French's two-car garage.

Some of the people at the meeting knew each other; others had come into random contact through the flier that Fred Moore had posted. Lee Felsenstein and Bob Marsh had driven down from Berkeley in Lee's battered pickup truck. Bob Albrecht had come over to give the group his blessing, and to show off the Altair 8800 that MITS had loaned PCC. Tom Pittman, a free-lance engineer who'd built an improbable homebrew computer around the early Intel 4004 chip, had met Fred Moore at a computer conference the previous month and had been looking forward to meeting others with similar interests. Steve Dompier, still waiting for the rest of his Altair parts, had seen the notice posted at Lawrence Hall. Marty Spergel had a small business selling electronic parts and figured it would be a good idea to rap to some engineers about chips. An engineer at Hewlett-Packard named Alan Baum had heard about the meeting and wondered if the talk would be of the new, low-cost computers; he dragged along a friend he'd known since high school, a fellow HP employee named Stephen Wozniak.

Almost every person in the garage was passionate about hardware, with the possible exception of Fred Moore, who envisioned

sort of a social group in which people would "bootstrap" themselves into learning about hardware. He didn't quite realize this
was, as Gordon French would later put it, "the damned finest
collection of engineers and technicians that you could possibly get
under one roof." These were people intensely interested in getting
computers into their homes to study, to play with, to create with
. . . and the fact that they would have to build the computers was
no deterrent. The introduction of the Altair had told them that
their dream was possible, and looking at others with the same goal
was a thrill in itself. And in the front of Gordon French's cluttered
garage workshop—you could never have fit a car in there, let alone
two—there it was, an Altair. Bob Albrecht turned it on and the
lights flashed and everyone knew that inside that implacable front
panel there were seething little binary bits, LDA-ing and JMP-ing
and ADD-ing.

Fred Moore had set up a table in the front and took notes, while
Gordon French, who was unspeakably proud of his own homebrew
8008 setup, moderated. Everybody introduced himself, and it
turned out that six of the thirty-two had built their own computer
system of some sort, while several others had ordered Altairs.
Right away, there was some debate about the relative merits of
chips, particularly the 8008. In fact, there were endless topics for
debate: hex (base sixteen numbers) versus octal (base eight); operating codes for the 8080; paper tape storage versus cassette versus
paper and pencil listings . . . They discussed what they wanted in
a club, and the words people used most were "cooperation" and
"sharing." There was some talk about what people might do with
computers in the home, and some suggested games, control of
home utilities, text editing, education. Lee mentioned Community
Memory. Albrecht distributed the latest issue of *PCC.* And Steve
Dompier told about his pilgrimage to Albuquerque, how MITS
was trying to fill four thousand orders, and how they were so busy
trying to get basic kits out the door that they were unable to even
think of shipping the extra stuff that would enable the machine to
do more than flash its lights.

Fred Moore was very excited about the energy the gathering
generated. It seemed to him that he had put something in motion.
He did not realize at the time that the source of the intellectual
heat was not a planner-like contemplation of the social changes
possible by mass computing, but the white-hot hacker fascination
with technology. Buoyed by the willingness everyone seemed to
have to work together, Moore suggested the group meet every fort-

night. As if to symbolize the concept of free exchange that the group would embody, Marty Spergel, the electric parts supplier who would be known as "the Junk Man" within the group, held up an Intel 8008 chip, just as everyone was leaving. "Who wants this?" he asked, and when the first hand went up, he tossed the chip, the fingernail-sized chunk of technology that could provide a good percentage of the multimillion-dollar power of the TX-0.

Over forty people came to the second meeting, which was held at the Stanford AI lab in the foothills, home of Uncle John Mc-Carthy's Tolkien-esque hackers. Much of the meeting was taken up by a discussion of what the group should be called. Suggestions included Infinitesimal Computer Club, Midget Brains, Steam Beer Computer Club, People's Computer Club, Eight-Bit Byte Bangers, Bay Area Computer Experimenters' Group, and Amateur Computer Club of America. Eventually people decided on Bay Area Amateur Computer Users Group—Homebrew Computer Club. The last three words became the de facto designation. In true hacker spirit the club had no membership requirement, asked no minimum dues (though French's suggestion that anyone who wanted to should give a dollar to cover meeting notice and newsletter expenses had netted $52.63 by the third meeting), and had no elections of officers.

By the fourth meeting, it was clear that the Homebrew Computer Club was going to be a hacker haven. Well over a hundred people received the mailing which announced the meeting would be held that week at the Peninsula School, an isolated, private school nestled in a wooded area of Menlo Park.

Steve Dompier had built his Altair by then: he had received the final shipment of parts at ten one morning, and spent the next thirty hours putting it together, only to find that the 256-byte memory wasn't working. Six hours later he figured out the bug was caused by a scratch on a printed circuit. He patched that up, and then tried to figure out what to do with it.

It seems that the only option supplied by MITS for those who actually finished building the machine was a machine language program that you could key into the machine only by the row of tiny switches on the front panel. It was a program which used the 8080 chip instructions LDA, MOV, ADD, STA, and JMP. If everything was right, the program would add two numbers together. You would be able to tell by mentally translating the code of the flashing LEDs out of their octal form and into a regular decimal number. You would feel like the first man stepping on the moon, a figure in history—you would have the answer to the question stumping mankind for centuries: What happens when you add six and two? Eight! "For an engineer who appreciates computers, that was an exciting event," early Altair owner and Homebrew Club member Harry Garland would later say, admitting that "you might have a hard time explaining to an outsider why it was exciting." To Steve Dompier it was thrilling.

He did not stop there. He made little machine language programs to test all the functions of the chips. (They had to be little programs, since the Altair's memory was so minuscule.) He did this until his own ten "input devices"—his fingers—had thick calluses. The 8080 chip had a 72-function instruction set, so there was plenty to do. An amateur pilot, Dompier listened to a low-frequency radio broadcasting the weather while he worked, and after he tested a program to sort some numbers, a very strange thing happened when he hit the switch to "run" the program: the radio started making ZIPPPP! ZIIIP! ZIIIIIIIPPPP! noises. It was apparently reacting to the radio frequency interference caused by the switching of bits from location to location inside the Altair. He brought the radio closer, and ran the program again. This time the ZIPs were louder. Dompier was exultant: he had discovered the first input/output device for the Altair 8800 computer.

Now the idea was to control the device. Dompier brought his guitar over and figured out that one of the noises the computer made (at memory address 075) was equivalent to an F-sharp on the guitar. So he hacked away at programming until he figured the memory locations of other notes. After eight hours or so, he had charted the musical scale and written a program for writing music. Although it was a simple program, nothing like Peter Samson's elegant music program on the PDP-1, it took Dompier a hell of a long (and painful) time to enter it by those maddening switches. But he was ready with his rendition of the Beatles' "Fool on the Hill" (the first piece of sheet music he came across) for the meeting of Homebrew at the Peninsula School.

The meeting was held in a room on the second floor of the school, a huge, ancient wooden building straight out of "The Addams Family." Dompier's Altair was, of course, the object of much adoration, and he was dying to show them the first documented application. But when Dompier tried to turn on the Altair, it wouldn't work. The electrical outlet was dead. The nearest working outlet was on the first floor of the building, and after locating an extension cord long enough to stretch from there to the second floor, Dompier finally had his Altair plugged in, though the cord was not quite long enough, and the machine had to stand a bit outside the doorway. Dompier began the long process of hitting the right switches to enter the song in octal code, and was just about finished when two kids who had been playing in the hallway accidentally tripped over the cord, pulling it out of the wall. This erased the contents of the computer memory which Dompier had been entering bit by bit. He started over, and finally shushed everyone up in preparation for the first public demonstration of a working Altair application.

He hit the RUN switch.

The little radio on top of the big, menacing computer box began to make raspy, buzzy noises. It was music of a sort, and by the time the first few plaintive bars of Paul McCartney's ballad were through, the room of hackers—normally abuzz with gossip about the latest chip—fell into an awed silence. Steve Dompier's computer, with the pure, knee-shaking innocence of a first-grader's first recital, was playing a song. As soon as the last note played, there was total, stunned silence. They had just heard evidence that the dream they'd been sharing was real. A dream that only a few weeks before had seemed vague and distant.

Well before they had a chance to recover . . . *the Altair started to play again.* No one (except Dompier) was prepared for this reprise, a rendition of "Daisy," which some of them knew was the first song ever played on a computer, in Bell Labs in 1957; that momentous event in computer history was being matched right before their ears. It was an encore so unexpected that it seemed to come from the machine's genetic connection to its Hulking Giant ancestors (a notion apparently implicit in Kubrick's *2001* when the HAL computer, being dismantled, regressed to a childlike rendition of that very song).

When the Altair finished, the silence did not last for long. The room burst into wild applause and cheers, the hackers leaping to their feet as they slammed hands together. The people in Homebrew were a mélange of professionals too passionate to leave computing at their jobs, amateurs transfixed by the possibilities of technology, and techno-cultural guerrillas devoted to overthrowing an oppressive society in which government, business, and especially IBM had relegated computers to a despised Priesthood. Lee Felsenstein would call them "a bunch of escapees, at least temporary escapees from industry, and somehow the bosses weren't watching. And we got together and started doing things that didn't matter because that wasn't what the big guys were doing. But we knew this was our chance to do something the way we thought it should be done." This involved no less than a major rewriting of computer history, and somehow this simple little music recital by Steve Dompier's Altair seemed the first step. "It was a major achievement in computer history, in my estimation," Bob Marsh later said. Dompier wrote up the experience, along with the machine language code for the program, in the next issue of *PCC* under the title "Music, of a Sort," and for months afterward Altair owners would call him in the middle of the night, sometimes three at once on conference calls, playing him Bach fugues.

Dompier got over four hundred calls like that. There were a lot more hackers out there than anyone imagined.

•

Bob Marsh, Lee Felsenstein's unemployed garage-mate, left the first meeting of Homebrew almost dazed with excitement from what he'd been a part of in that little garage. He knew that until now only a tiny number of people had dared to conceive of the act of personal computing. Now here was long-haired Steve Dompier saying that this random company, MITS, had *thousands* of orders. Bob Marsh realized right then and there that the hacker brotherhood was going to grow exponentially in the next few years. But like a raging fire, it needed fuel. The flashing LEDs on the Altair were exciting, but he knew that—hackers being hackers—there would be a demand for all sorts of peripheral devices, devices this MITS company obviously could not provide.

But *someone* would have to, because the Altair was the basis for a fantastic system to build new systems, new worlds. Just as the PDP-1, or the PDP-6, had arrived at MIT as a magic box without a satisfactory operating system, and just as the MIT hackers had supplied it with assemblers, debuggers, and all sorts of hardware and software tools to make it useful in creating new systems and even some applications, it was up to these as yet unorganized hardware hackers to make their own mark on the Altair 8800.

Bob Marsh understood that this was the beginning of a new era, and a terrific opportunity. Sitting on the cold floor in Gordon French's garage, he decided that he would design and build some circuit boards that would plug into one of the blank slots on the Altair bus.

Bob Marsh wasn't the only one with that idea. In fact, right there in Palo Alto (the town next to Menlo Park, where the meet-

ing was being held), two Stanford professors named Harry Garland
and Roger Melen were already working on add-on boards to the
Altair. They hadn't heard about the meeting, but would come to
the second meeting of hardware enthusiasts, and be regulars thereafter.

The two Ph.D.s had first heard about the Altair when Melen, a
tall, heavy man whose wittiness was only slightly impeded by a
recurrent stutter, was visiting Les Solomon in late 1974 at the New
York office of *Popular Electronics*. Melen and Garland had done
articles outlining hobbyist projects for the magazine in their spare
time, and were just putting to bed an article telling how to build a
TV-camera control device.

Melen noticed a strange box on Solomon's desk and asked what
it was. Solomon informed him that the box, the prototype Altair
that Ed Roberts had sent to replace the one lost in air freight, was
an 8080 microcomputer that sold for under four hundred dollars.
Roger Melen did not think that such a thing was possible, and Les
Solomon told him that if he doubted it, he should call Ed Roberts
in Albuquerque. Melen did this without hesitation, and arranged
to make a stopover on his way back West. He wanted to buy two of
those computers. Also, Ed Roberts had previously licensed a project that Melen and Garland had written about in *Popular Electronics*, and had never gotten around to paying them royalties. So there
were two things that Melen wanted to talk to Roberts about.

The Altair computer was the more important by far—the right
toy at the right time, Melen thought—and he was so excited about
the prospect of owning one that he couldn't sleep that night. When
he finally got to MITS' modest headquarters, he was disappointed
to find that there *was* no Altair ready to take home. But Ed Roberts was a fascinating fellow, a dyed-in-the-wool engineer with a
blazing vision. They talked until five in the morning about the
technical aspects of this vision. This was before the *Popular Electronics* article was out, though, and Roberts was concerned at what
the response might be. He figured it would not hurt to have some
people manufacturing boards to put into the Altair to make it
useful, and he agreed to send Melen and Garland an early prototype, so they could make something to connect a TV camera to the
machine, and then a board to output a video image as well.

So Garland and Melen were in business, naming their company
Cromemco, in honor of the Stanford dorm they'd once lived in,
Crowthers Memorial. They were delighted to find similar spirits at
the Homebrew Club, among them Marsh, who had talked his

friend Gary Ingram into helping start a company called Processor Technology.

Marsh knew that the biggest immediate need of an Altair owner was a memory bigger than the lousy 256 bytes that came with the machine, so he figured he'd make a board which would give 2K of memory. (Each "K" equals 1,024 bytes.) MITS had announced its own memory boards, and had delivered some to customers. They were nice memory boards, but they didn't work. Marsh borrowed the PCC's Altair and looked it over carefully, read the manual backward and forward. This was a necessity because he couldn't initially afford to spend the money to make a Xerox copy. He figured that he would run the company the way Roberts was apparently running MITS—announce his product first, then collect the money required to design and manufacture the product.

So on April Fools' Day, Marsh and Ingram, a reclusive engineer who didn't go to Homebrew meetings ("It's not the kind of thing he did," Marsh later explained), officially inaugurated the company. Marsh was able to scrape up enough money to Xerox fifty fliers explaining the line of proposed products. On April 2, Marsh stood up at the third Homebrew meeting, handed out the fliers, and announced a 20 percent discount to anyone who ordered in advance. After a week, he hadn't heard anything. As Marsh later said, "Despair had set in. We felt, we've blown it, it's not going to work. Then our first order came in, for a ROM [memory] board costing only forty-five dollars. A purchase order asking 'Net 30 terms,' from this company called Cromemco. We thought, 'Who is this Cromemco? And why don't they pay cash?' Despair set in once more. IT'S NOT GOING TO FLY! The next day three orders came in, and within a week after that we had twenty-five hundred dollars cash. We took a thousand, ponied up for a sixth-page ad in *Popular Electronics,* and all hell broke loose after that. It took us only two months to get a hundred thousand dollars in orders."

The irony was that Marsh and the other hacker-run operations were not setting up to be huge businesses. They were looking for a way to finance their avocation of playing with electronics, of exploring this new realm of little bitty computers. For Marsh and the others who left the first few Homebrew meetings with board-building fervor, the fun was beginning: designing and building stuff, expressing themselves by the twists and tangles of a digital logic integrated circuit board to be attached to Ed Roberts' byzantine bus.

As Marsh found out, building a board for the Altair was the Homebrew hacker's equivalent of attempting a great novel. It would be something that harsh Homebrew reviewers would examine carefully, and they would not only note whether it worked or not but judge the relative beauty and stability of its architecture. The layout of circuits on the board was a window into the designer's personality, and even superficial details like the quality of the holes by which one mounted the board would betray the designer's motives, philosophy, and commitment to elegance. Digital designs, like computer programs, "are the best pictures of minds you can get," Lee Felsenstein once said. "There are things I can tell about people from hardware designs I see. You can look at something and say, 'Jesus Christ, this guy designs like an earthworm—goes from one place through to the end and doesn't even know what it was he did in the middle.' "

Bob Marsh wanted Processor Technology to be known for quality products, and he spent the next few months in a frazzled state, trying not only to finish his projects, but to do them right. It was important for the company and for his pride as well.

The process was not a terribly simple one. After figuring out what your board would do, you would spend long nights designing the layout. Looking in the manual that described the workings of the 8080 chip, you would jot down the numbers for the various sections you wanted—designating this section for an input, that one for memory—and the labyrinthine grid inside that piece of black plastic would begin to reshape inside your head. The effectiveness of your choice of which sections to access would depend on how well and how accurately you kept that vision up there. You would make a pencil drawing of those connections, with the stuff destined to go on one side of the board written in blue, stuff for the other side in red. Then you would get sheets of Mylar, lay them on a grid on a light table, and begin laying out the outline of the connections, using crepe paper tape. You might find out that your scheme had some problems—too much traffic in one part, the interconnections too tight—and have to realign some things. One mistake could blow everything. So you'd be sure to do an overlay of the schematic: placing that on top of your taped-up design, you could see if you made some grievous error, like hooking three things together. If the schematic itself was in error, forget it.

You would design it so that the board would have several layers; a different set of connections on the top and the bottom. You would flip the layout back and forth as you worked, and sometimes the tape would peel off, or you would have little pieces of tape left over, or a hair would get stuck somewhere: any of these uncalled-for phenomena would be faithfully duplicated in the sepia reproductions made for you at a blueline house (if you didn't have money for that, you'd do a careful Xerox), and result in a disastrous short circuit. Then you'd mark up the layout for the board company, telling where to drill and what needed gold-plating, and so on.

Finally, you'd go to a local board house with drawings in hand. You'd give it to them. Since it was still a recession, they would be happy for the business, even business coming from a scruffy, small-time, glassy-eyed hardware hacker. They would put the thing on a digitizer, drill the holes, and produce on greenish epoxy material a mess of silvery interconnections. That was the deluxe method—Bob Marsh at first could not afford that, so he hand-etched the board over the kitchen stove, using printed circuit laminate material, making barely discernible lines that the material would melt into. That method was a tortuous courting of the bitch goddess Disaster, but Marsh was a compulsively careful worker. He later explained: "I really get into it. I become one with my schematic design."

For this first memory board, Marsh was under particular pressure. Every other week at the Homebrew meeting, every day on the phone, frantic people were gasping for static memory boards like divers gasping for air. Marsh later recalled their cries: "Where's my board? I need it. I GOTTA HAVE IT."

Finally Marsh was done. There wasn't time for a prototype. He had his board, which was the green epoxy rectangle with a little protrusion of etched gold connectors underneath, sized to fit into a slot in the Altair bus. He had the chips and wires which the kit-builders would solder onto it. (Processor Tech would only sell unassembled boards at first.) Marsh had it all ready—and no Altair to test it out on. So despite the fact that it was three in the morning he called that guy Dompier he knew from Homebrew and told him to bring the machine over. Dompier's Altair was at least as valuable to him as a human infant offspring would be if he weren't in Bachelor Mode, so he carefully wrapped it up in a little red blanket to bring it over. Dompier had gone by the book in assembling the machine, even wearing a copper bracelet around his wrist when he soldered (to keep static down), and taking care not to touch the fragile 8080 heart of the machine. So he was stunned, after lovingly setting the machine down in Marsh's workshop, when the hardware veterans Marsh and Ingram began handling

chips like a couple of garage mechanics installing a muffler. They'd
grab chips with their grubby fingers and throw chips around and
pull chips out and stuff them back in. Dompier watched in horror.
Finally they had the board all ready, and Ingram flicked the switch
on, and Steve Dompier's precious computer fizzled into uncon-
sciousness. They'd put the board in backward.

It took a day to fix Dompier's Altair, but Steve Dompier harbored no anger: in fact, he loaned his machine to Processor Technology for future testing. It was indicative of Homebrew behavior.
These were a different breed of hacker than the unapproachable
wizards of MIT, but they still held to the Hacker Ethic that subli-
mated possession and selfishness in favor of the common good,
which meant anything that could help people hack more efficiently.
Steve Dompier was nervous about his Altair, but he wanted little
in the world more than a memory board, so he could run some real
programs on the machine. And then he wanted i/o devices, display
devices . . . so that he could write utilities to make the machine
more powerful. Tools to Make Tools, to go deep into the world
that centered on the mysterious 8080 microprocessor inside his
machine. Bob Marsh and the others in Homebrew, whether they
were offering products for sale or were simply curious hackers like
himself, were all in this together, and together they formed a community that may not have been as geographically centered as
MIT's PDP-6 community was—it stretched from Sacramento to
San Jose—but was strongly bonded nonetheless.

When Bob Marsh showed up at a Homebrew meeting in early
June with the first shipment of boards, the people who ordered
them were so thankful you might think that he'd been giving them
away. He handed over the little plastic blister-wrapped packets of
board and ICs, along with the instruction manual Lee Felsenstein
had written. "Unless you are an experienced kit-builder," Lee
warned, "don't build this kit."

There was very little experience in the world at building those
kinds of things, but much of the experience that did exist in the
world was centered in that meeting room, which was now the
auditorium at the Stanford Linear Accelerator (SLAC). It was four
months after the first casual meeting of the club, and its membership had grown almost tenfold.

•

The little club formed by Fred Moore and Gordon French had
grown to something neither could have imagined. It was the van-

guard of a breed of hardware hackers who were "bootstrapping" themselves into a new industry—which, they were sure, would be different from any previous industry. The microcomputer industry would be ruled by the Hacker Ethic. (The term "bootstrap" was indicative of the new jargon spoken by these hackers: the term literally describes the process by which a computer program feeds itself into a machine when the machine is first turned on, or "booted." Part of the program will feed the code into the computer; this code will program the machine to tell itself to feed the rest of the code in. Just like pulling yourself up by your bootstraps. It is symbolic of what the Homebrew people were doing—creating a niche in the world of small computer systems, then digging deeper to make the niche a cavern, a permanent settlement.)

But the club's founders were both soon outdistanced by the technical brilliance around them. In French's case, he suffered from what seemed to be a latent bureaucratic attitude. In some respects, his mania to keep the club progressing in an orderly, controlled manner was helpful. He acted as secretary and librarian, keeping a list of everyone's phone number and what equipment everyone owned. As he later recalled, "My phone rang off the hook. It was incredible. Everybody needed information, and they needed each other in order to get going because there was an absolute paucity of equipment. For example: 'If you have a terminal could I borrow it for a couple days while I get my program in it so it'll read my punch paper tape reader?' That sort of thing."

But in other respects, particularly in the way he moderated the meetings, French's style was not consistent with the hacker spirit brewing in Homebrew. "Gordon was a didactic sort," Lee Felsenstein would later recall. "He would try to push the discussion to where he wanted it to go. He wanted it to be an educational event, holding lectures, teaching people about certain things, especially stuff he was expert on. He was very upset if the discussion strayed from people literally teaching other people in a schoolish sense. He would jump into whatever people were saying and get involved in the content, injecting his opinions and telling them 'There's an important point that shouldn't be missed, and I know more about this kind of stuff.'" After the first part of the meeting, in which people would introduce themselves and say what they were working on, Gordon would stand up in front of the room and give what amounted to a tutorial, explaining the way the machine uses the code you feed into it, and informing the restless members how learning good coding habits will save you headaches in the future

. . . and sooner or later people would get so impatient they'd slip out of the meetings and start exchanging information in the hall. It was a touchy situation, the kind of complex human dilemma that hackers don't generally like to confront. But the feeling emerged that a new moderator should take over.

The logical choice might have been Fred Moore, who sat in the front of the room for the first few months of Homebrew with his tape recorder and notebook, capturing the meeting so he could summarize highlights in the newsletter he put out every month. He was putting a lot of his time into the group, because he saw that the hackers and their Altairs were on the verge of what might be a significant social force. "By sharing our experience and exchanging tips we advance the state of the art and make low-cost computing possible for more folks," he wrote in the newsletter, adding his social commentary: "The evidence is overwhelming that people want computers, probably for self-entertainment and education usage. Why did the Big Companies miss this market? They were busy selling overpriced machines to each other (and the government and the military). They don't want to sell directly to the public. I'm all in favor of the splash MITS is having with the Altair because it will do three things: (1) force the awakening of other companies to the demand for low-cost computers in the home . . . (2) cause local computer clubs and hobby groups to form to fill the technical knowledge vacuum, (3) help demystify computers . . ."

Moore explicitly identified the purpose of the club as an information exchange. Like the unfettered flow of bits in an elegantly designed computer, information should pass freely among the participants in Homebrew. "More than any other individual, Fred Moore knew what sharing was all about," Gordon French later recalled. "That was one of the expressions he was always using— sharing, sharing, sharing."

But the majority of the club preferred a path that diverged from Fred Moore's. Fred was always harping on applications. Every so often in the early meetings he would urge the members of this basically anarchistic group to get together and do something, though he was usually vague on what that something might be. Maybe using computers to aid handicapped people, maybe compiling mailing lists for draft resistance. Moore might have been correct in perceiving that the thrust of the club was in some way political, but his view seemed at odds with the reality that hackers do not generally set about to create social change—hackers act like hackers. Moore was less fascinated with the workings of computer systems than with the idea of bringing about a sharing, benevolent social system; he seemed to regard Homebrew not as a technical stronghold of people hungry for the pyramid-building power of in-home computers, but as a cadre devoted to social change, like the draft resistance or anti-nuke groups he'd been involved in. He would suggest cake sales to raise funds for the group, or publish cute little poems in the newsletter like "Don't complain or fuss / It is up to each of us / To make the Club do / What we want it to." Meanwhile, most of the club members would be turning to the back of the newsletter to study the schematics in the contribution called "Arbitrary Logic Function Generation Via Digital Multiplexers." *That* was the way to change the world, and a lot more fun than a cake sale.

Lee Felsenstein later reflected that he didn't think Moore "got his politics straight. At the surface level he remained at the point of the protest or the gesture of protest. But we were much more interested in what you might call the Propaganda of the Deed."

So when an opening fortuitously appeared to make the meetings more compatible with the free-flowing hacker spirit—Gordon French, doing consulting work for the Social Security Administration, was temporarily called to Baltimore—it was not Moore that some club members asked to moderate, but Lee Felsenstein. He turned out to be an ideal choice, since he was as much a hardware hacker as any, but also a political computerist. He looked upon the call to moderate these meetings as a significant elevation. He could now be the point man of the revolution on the hardware front, allowing the meetings to progress with just the right blend of anarchism and direction, continuing his own guerrilla hardware design schemes which would lead to the triumph of the Tom Swift Terminal, and participating in the resurrection of the dormant Community Memory concept—a process which was beginning that summer with the publication of a mimeographed periodical called *Journal of Community Communication,* which would spread the concept of microcomputer devices "created and used by people in their daily lives as members of communities."

When he first stood in front of the room at a June 1975 meeting of Homebrew, though, he was terrified. As he recalls it, someone asked who the new moderator would be, and Marty Spergel, the "Junk Man" who owned the M&R Electronics supply house, suggested Lee, and "the cry went up." It was as if he'd been crowned. Nervous as he was, it was a chance he could not pass up. As usual for Lee, the risks of failing were less intimidating than the risks that came from not trying at all.

He knew a bit about running a forum. During his student radical days in1968, he'd been listening to a Berkeley radio call-in show which was so badly engineered, with inaudible callers and fuzz and things, that he ran over to the studio waving his portable radio and saying, "Listen to this, you idiots!" He wound up helping run the show, and part of his role was to prime the guests before they went on the air. He thought that his role in Homebrew could draw from that; he urged people not familiar with addressing any audience larger than a tableful of electronic parts to talk to other humans about their interests. As Fred Moore sensed, this was to be the heart of the meeting, the exchange of information. So Lee, creating an architecture for the meeting as if he were tackling an electronic design problem, flowcharted the session. There would be a time to go around the room and let people say what they were doing or what they wanted to know—that would be the "mapping" section, akin to drawing a schematic. Then there would be a "random access" section, where you would drift over to the people who suggested things that interested you, or could answer your questions, or seemed to have information you wanted, or just seemed interesting to talk to. After that, there would be perhaps a brief talk, or someone would demonstrate a system or show a new product, and then there would be more mapping, and more random access. When Lee saw that people were reluctant to return from the first random access section—sometimes you could get lost in some technical point, or some religious issue like a technique for wire-wrapping a board or something—he changed the structure to include only one random access section, at the end of the meeting. Thus debugged, the structure worked fine.

Lee found that standing in front of a group of people who accepted him and were appreciative of his role as a "stack pointer"— the computer function which determines the order by which computational tasks get done—helped his conscious effort to bring himself out of his mole-like shell. Soon into his tenure as moderator, he felt confident enough to give the group a talk on his Tom Swift Terminal; scrawling on the blackboard at the front of the small auditorium at SLAC, he talked of video displays, hardware reliability, Ivan Illich, and the idea of incorporating the user in the design. It was a good blend of social commentary and technical esoterica, and the Homebrewers appreciated it. Lee found himself talented in the ready quip, and eventually hacked a little routine that he'd deliver at the beginning of each meeting. He came to take a fierce pride in his job as club master of ceremonies: in his thinking he was now the ringmaster of a hacker movement, a group that was central in shaping a microprocessor way of life.

Not long after Lee took over, a troubled Fred Moore resigned his roles as treasurer, secretary, and editor of the newsletter. He was having some personal problems; the woman he'd been seeing had left him. It was a rough time for him to leave: he felt that the club had been his legacy, in a sense, but it was probably clear by then that his hopes of it being devoted to public service work were futile. Instead there was the Propaganda of the Deed, and, more disturbing, some people who came to meetings, Fred later recalled, "with dollar bill signs in their eyes, saying, 'Wow, here's a new industry, I'll build this company and make these boards, and make a million . . .'" There were other computer-related social issues Moore wanted to pursue, but he had come to realize, he later explained, that "the people in the club were way ahead [of him] as far as their knowledge of electronics or computing, [and because of this] the people were enamored with those very devices, devices which were very seductive." So Fred was unhappy at how blindly people accepted technology. Someone had told Fred about the cheap female labor in Malaysia and other Asian countries who physically assembled those magical chips. He heard how the Asian women were paid pitiful wages, worked in unsafe factories, and were unable to return to their villages, since they never had a chance to learn the traditional modes of cooking or raising a family. He felt he should tell the club about it, force the issue, but by then he realized that it was not the kind of issue that the Homebrew Club was meant to address.

Still, he loved the club, and when his personal problems forced him to bow out and go back East, he would later say it was "one of the saddest days of my life." A small, wistful figure, he stood at the blackboard at a mid-August meeting and wrote down his duties, asking who would do the newsletter, who would do the treasury, the notes . . . And someone came up and began writing "Fred Moore" beside each item. It broke his heart, yet he felt for him it was over, and while he couldn't share all his reasons he had to let his brothers know he couldn't be there any more.

"I saw myself as a person who had helped those people get together and share their skills and energy," Moore said later. And those goals had been reached. Indeed, each meeting seemed to crackle with spirit and excitement as people swapped gossip and

chips, bootstrapping themselves into this new world. At the mapping period, people would stand up and say that they had a problem in setting up this or that part of the Altair, and Lee would ask,
"Who can help this guy?" and three or four hands would go up.
Fine. Next? And someone would say that he needed a 1702 chip.
Someone else might have an extra 6500 chip, and there'd be a
trade.

Then there would be people standing up to announce the latest
rumors in Silicon Valley. Jim Warren, a chunky former Stanford
computer science grad student, was a particularly well-connected
gossipmonger who would pop up in the random access period and
go on for ten minutes about this company and the next, often
slipping in some of his personal views on the future of computer
communications by digital broadcasts.

Another notorious purveyor of this weird form of gossip was a
novice engineer named Dan Sokol, who worked as a systems tester
at one of the big Valley firms. His tidbits were often startlingly
prescient (to keep them guessing, Sokol later admitted, he'd fabri-
cate about half his rumors). Sokol, a long-haired, bearded digital
disciple who threw himself into Homebrew with the energy of the
newly converted, quickly adhered to the Hacker Ethic. He considered no rumor too classified to share, and the more important the
secret the greater his delight in its disclosure. "Is anybody here
from Intel?" he might ask—and, if there wasn't, he would divulge
the news of the chip that Intel had previously been successful in
shielding from every company in the Valley (and perhaps from a
cadre of Russian spies).

Sometimes Sokol, an inveterate barterer, would actually reach
into his pocket and produce the prototype of a chip. For instance,
one day at work, he recalled, some men from a new company
called Atari came in to test some chips. They were extremely secretive, and didn't say what the chips were. Sokol examined them:
some were marked Syntech, some AMI. Sokol knew guys at both
companies, and they told him the chips were custom parts, laid out
and designed by the Atari people. So he took one home, put it on a
board, and tested it out. The chip turned out to contain a program
to play the new video game "Pong"—the new Atari firm was just
beginning to put together a home setup to play that game, in which
two people control "paddles" of light on a TV screen and try to
keep a blip-like "ball" in play. Sokol laid out the design on a circuit
board, took it to Homebrew and displayed it. He took a few extra
chips along with him, and traded the chips with others, eventually

winding up with a keyboard and a few RAM chips. "We're talking outright thievery," he later explained; but in Homebrew terms, Sokol was liberating a neat hack from the proprietary oppressors. Pong was neat, and should belong to the world. And in Homebrew, exchanges like that were free and easy.

Years earlier, Buckminster Fuller had developed the concept of synergy—the collective power, more than the sum of the parts, that comes of people and/or phenomena working together in a system—and Homebrew was a textbook example of the concept at work. One person's idea would spark another person into embarking on a large project, and perhaps beginning a company to make a product based on that idea. Or, if someone came up with a clever hack to produce a random number generator on the Altair, he would give out the code so everyone could do it, and by the next meeting someone else would have devised a game that utilized the routine.

The synergy would continue even after the meeting, as some of the Homebrew people would carry on their conversations till midnight at The Oasis, a raucous watering hole near the campus. (The location had been suggested by Roger Melen; Jim Warren, a virulent anti-smoker, once tried to lure people over to the no-smoking section at The Village Host, but that never caught on.) Piling into wooden booths with tables deeply etched with the initials of generations of Stanford students, Garland and Melen and Marsh and Felsenstein and Dompier and French and whoever else felt like showing up would get emboldened by the meeting's energy and the pitchers of beer. They would envision developments so fantastic that no one ever believed they could be more than fantasies, far-flung fancies like the day when home computers with TV displays would engender pornographic programs—SMUT-ROMs, they called them—which would not be illegal because they'd only be pornographic if you scanned them the way the computer did. How could the raw computer code be pornographic? It was just one of dozens of perversely improbable musings that would be not only realized but surpassed within a few years.

Synergy: Marty Spergel, the Junk Man, knew exactly how that worked. A tanned, middle-aged haggler with a disarmingly wide smile, he thought that Homebrew was like "having your own little Boy Scout troop, everybody helping everybody else. I remember I had trouble with a teletype machine at my office and one guy [at Homebrew] said he'd check it out. Not only did he check it out but he came out with a little kit and he put in four or five different parts, oiled it, lubed it, adjusted all the gears. I said, 'How much do I owe you?' He said, 'Nothing.' " To the Junk Man, that was the essence of Homebrew.

Spergel always kept track of what parts people needed; he'd sometimes bring a box of them to a meeting. After the Tom Swift Terminal talk, he asked Lee if he cared to build one for Spergel's company, M&R Electronics. Well, the Swift terminal wasn't ready, Lee told him, but how about this design for a modem—a device which enables computers to communicate by the phone lines—that Lee had done a couple of years back? "He probably even knew what a modem was, though that was not clear from the way he reacted," Lee said later. Modems sold then for four to six hundred dollars, but Marty was able to construct Lee's cleanly designed "Pennywhistle" modem to sell for $109. They sent a copy of the schematics to Lee Solomon at *Popular Electronics* and he put a picture of Lee's modem on the cover.

Synergy. The increasing number of Homebrew members who were designing or giving away new products, from game joysticks to i/o boards for the Altair, used the club as a source of ideas and early orders, and for beta-testing of the prototypes. Whenever a product was done you would bring it to the club, and get the most expert criticism available. Then you'd distribute the technical specifications and the schematics—if it involved software, you would distribute the source code. Everybody could learn from it, and improve on it if they cared to and were good enough.

It was a sizzling atmosphere that worked so well because, in keeping with the Hacker Ethic, no artificial boundaries were maintained. In fact, every principle of that Ethic, as formed by the MIT hackers, was exercised to some degree within Homebrew. Exploration and hands-on activities were recognized as cardinal values; the information gathered in these explorations and ventures in design were freely distributed even to nominal competitors (the idea of competition came slowly to these new companies, since the struggle was to create a hacker version of an industry—a task which took all hands working together); authoritarian rules were disdained, and people believed that personal computers were the ultimate ambassadors of decentralization; the membership ranks were open to anyone wandering in, with respect earned by expertise or good ideas, and it was not unusual to see a seventeen-year-old conversing as an equal with a prosperous, middle-aged veteran engineer; there was a keen level of appreciation of technical elegance and digital artistry; and, above all, these hardware hackers were seeing in a vibrantly different and populist way how computers could change lives. These were cheap machines that they knew were only a few years away from becoming actually useful.

This, of course, did not prevent them from becoming totally immersed in hacking these machines for the sake of hacking itself, for the control, the quest, and the dream. Their lives were directed to that moment when the board they designed, or the bus they wired, or the program they keyed in would take its first run . . . One person later referred to that moment as akin to backing up a locomotive over a section of track you'd just fixed, and running it over that track at ninety miles an hour. If your track wasn't strong, the train would derail calamitously . . . smoke . . . fire . . . twisted metal . . . But if you hacked well, it would rush through in an exhilarating rush. You would be jolted with the realization that thousands of computations a second would be flashed through that piece of equipment with your personal stamp on it. You, the master of information and lawgiver to a new world.

Some planners would visit Homebrew and be turned off by the technical ferocity of the discussions, the intense flame that burned brightest when people directed themselves to the hacker pursuit of building. Ted Nelson, author of *Computer Lib*, came to a meeting and was confused by all of it, later calling the scruffily dressed and largely uncombed Homebrew people "chip-monks, people obsessed with chips. It was like going to a meeting of people who love hammers." Bob Albrecht rarely attended, later explaining that "I could understand only about every fourth word those guys were saying . . . they were hackers." Jude Milhon, the woman with whom Lee remained friends after their meeting through the *Barb* and their involvement in Community Memory, dropped in once and was repelled by the concentration on sheer technology, exploration, and control for the sake of control. She noted the lack of female hardware hackers, and was enraged at the male hacker obsession with technological play and power. She summed up her feelings with the epithet "the boys and their toys," and like Fred Moore worried that the love affair with technology might blindly lead to abuse of that technology.

None of these concerns slowed down the momentum of Homebrew, which was growing to several hundred members, filling the auditorium of SLAC, becoming the fortnightly highlight in the lives of well over a hundred hard-core Brewers. What they had started was almost a crusade now, something that Ted Nelson, whose book was filled with anti-IBM screeds, should have appreciated. While IBM and the Big Guys never gave a thought to these random hackers in computer clubs with their ideas of owning computers, the Homebrew people and others like them were hacking away not only at 8080 chips, but at the now crumbling foundations of the Batch-processed Tower of Bit-Babble. "We reinforced each other," Lee Felsenstein later explained. We provided a support structure for each other. We bought each other's products. We covered each other's asses, in effect. There we were—the industrial structure was paying no attention to us. Yet we had people who knew as much as anyone else knew about this aspect of technology, because it was so new. We could run wild, and we did."

•

By the time Les Solomon, the New York guru of this movement, arrived for a visit to the West Coast, the golden age of the Homebrew Computer Club was gleaming its brightest. Solomon first checked on Roger Melen and Harry Garland, who had just finished the prototype of the Cromemco product that would be on the cover of *Popular Electronics* in November 1975—an add-on board for the Altair which would allow the machine to be connected to a color television set, yielding dazzling graphic results. In fact, Melen and Garland were calling the board "the Dazzler." Les went over to Roger's apartment to see it, but before they put the board into Roger's Altair the three of them got to drinking, and they were pretty well lubricated by the time the board was in and the color TV was on.

There were two Altair programs that could take advantage of the Dazzler then. One was called Kaleidoscope, and it shimmered and changed shape. It was a great moment for Solomon, seeing the computer he had helped bring to the world making a color television set run beautiful patterns.

Then they tried another program: LIFE. The game-that-is-more-than-a-game, created by mathematician John Conway. The game which MIT wizard Bill Gosper had hacked so intently, to the point where he saw it as potentially generating life itself. The Altair version ran much more slowly than the PDP-6 program, of course, and with none of those elegantly hacked utilities, but it followed the same rules. *And it did it while sitting on the kitchen table.* Garland put in a few patterns, and Les Solomon, not fully knowing the rules of the game and certainly not aware of the deep philosophical and mathematical implications, watched the little blue, red, or green stars (that was the way the Dazzler made the cells look) eat the other little stars, or make more stars. *What a waste of time,* he thought. *Who cares?*

Then he began idly playing with the machine, sketching out a pattern to run. He happened, in his inebriation, to put up somethng resembling the Star of David. He later recalled: "I ran the program and watched the way it ate itself up. It took about ten minutes and finally it died. I thought, 'Gee that's interesting—does that mean the Jewish religion is about to go after 247 generations?' So I drew a crucifix. That went for 121 generations. Does this somehow mean that Judaism will outlast Christianity?" Soon he was putting up crescents and stars and symbols of different meanings, and the three of them—four of them, including the Altair—were exploring the mysteries of the world's religions and nationalities. "Who the hell needs philosophy at three o'clock in the morning, drinking?" Solomon later said. *"It was a computer.* It was there."

But Les Solomon had more magic to transmit. One of the stories he would tell, stories so outrageous that only a penny-pincher of the imagination would complain of their improbability, was of the time he was exploring in pursuit of one of his "hobbies," pre-Colombian archeology. This required much time in jungles, "running around with Indians, digging, pitching around in the dirt . . . you know, finding things." It was from those Indians, Les Solomon insisted, that he learned the vital principle of *vril,* a power which allows you to move huge objects with very little force. Solomon believed that it was the power of *vril* which enabled the Egyptians to build the pyramids. (Perhaps *vril* was the power that Ed Roberts was talking about when he realized that his Altair would give people the power of ten thousand pyramid-building Egyptians.) According to his story, Solomon met a venerable Indian *brujo* and asked if he might learn this power. Could the *brujo* teach him? And the *brujo* complied. Now, after the drunken evening with the LIFE program, Solomon attended a Homebrew meeting at SLAC where he was accorded the respect of an honored guest— the midwife of Ed Roberts' Altair. And after the meeting, Solomon was telling the hardware hackers about *vril.* There was some skepticism.

Outside of SLAC were huge orange picnic tables with concrete bases. Solomon had the Homebrew people touch their hands on one of the tables, and he touched it, too. They simply had to think it would rise.

Lee Felsenstein later described the scene: "He'd said, 'Hey, let me show you . . .' We were hanging on his every word, we'd do anything. So about six people surrounded the table, put their hands on. He put his hand on top, squinted his eyes and said, 'Let's go.' *And the table raised about a foot.* It rose like a harmonic motion, [as elegantly as] a sine wave. It didn't feel heavy. It just *happened.*''

Afterward, even the participants, save Solomon, were not sure that it had really happened. But Lee Felsenstein, seeing another chapter close in that earth-shattering science-fiction novel that was his life, understood the mythic impact of this event. They, the soldiers of the Homebrew Computer Club, had taken their talents and applied the Hacker Ethic to work for the common good. It was the act of working together in unison, hands-on, without the doubts caused by holding back, which made extraordinary things occur. Even impossible things occur. The MIT hackers had discovered that when their desire to hack led them to persist so single-mindedly that the barriers of security, exhaustion, and mental limits seemed to shrink away. Now, in the movement to wipe away generations of centralized, anti-hacker control of the computer industry, to change the world's disapproving view of computers and computer people, the combined energy of hardware hackers working together could do anything. If they did not hold back, not retreat within themselves, not yield to the force of greed, they could make the ideals of hackerism ripple through society as if a pearl were dropped in a silver basin.

Homebrew Club was sitting atop the power of *vril.*

11

TINY BASIC

WHILE the hunger to build and expand the Altair was as insatiable in the hardware hackers of the seventies as the desire to hack PDP-1s and 6s was to the MIT hackers of the sixties, a conflict was developing around the Homebrew Computer Club which had the potential to slow the idealistic, bootstrapping process and stem the rising tide lifting them all. At the heart of the problem was one of the central tenets of the Hacker Ethic: the free flow of information, particularly information that helped fellow hackers understand, explore, and build systems. Previously, there had not been much of a problem in getting that information from others. The "mapping section" time at Homebrew was a good example of that—secrets that big institutional companies considered proprietary were often revealed. And by 1976 there were more publications plugging into what was becoming a national pipeline of hardware hackers—besides *PCC* and the Homebrew newsletter there was now *Byte* magazine in New Hampshire—you could always find interesting assembly language programs, hardware hints, and technical gossip. New hacker-formed companies would give out schematics of their products at Homebrew, not worrying about whether competitors might see them; and after the meetings at The Oasis the young, blue-jeaned officers of the different companies would freely discuss how many boards they shipped, and what new products they were considering.

Then came the outcry over Altair BASIC. It would give the

hardware hackers a hint of the new fragility of the Hacker Ethic. And indicate that—as computer power did come to the people— other, less altruistic philosophies might prevail.

It all started out as a typical hacker caper. Among the products that MITS had announced, but not yet sent out to those who had ordered it, was a version of the BASIC computer language. Among the tools an Altair owner could have, this was to be one of the most highly coveted: because, once you had a BASIC on your Altair, the machine's power to implement systems, to move mental pyramids, would improve "by orders of magnitude," as the expression went. Instead of having to laboriously type in machine language programs onto paper tape and then have to retranslate the signals back (by then many Altair owners had installed i/o cards which would enable them to link the machines to teletypes and paper-tape readers), you would have a way to write quick, useful programs. While software hackers (and certainly such ancient assembly-language zealots as Gosper and Greenblatt) disdained BASIC as a fascist language, to hardware hackers trying to extend their systems it was an incredibly valuable tool.

The problem was that at first you couldn't get a BASIC. It was particularly maddening because MITS supposedly had one, though no one at Homebrew had seen it run.

Indeed, MITS did have a BASIC. It had had the language running since early spring 1975. Not long before MITS began shipping Altairs to computer-starved *Popular Electronics* readers, Ed Roberts had gotten a phone call from two college students named Paul Allen and Bill Gates.

The two teen-agers hailed from Seattle. Since high school the two of them had been hacking computers; large firms paid them to do lucrative contract programming. By the time Gates, a slim, blond genius who looked even younger than his tender years, had gone off to Harvard, the two had discovered there was some money to be made in making interpreters for computer languages like BASIC for new computers.

The Altair article, while not impressing them technically, was exciting to them: it was clear microcomputers were the next big thing, and they could get involved in all the action by writing BASIC for this thing. They had a manual explaining the instruction set for the 8080 chip, and they had the *Popular Electronics* article with the Altair schematics, so they got to work writing something that would fit in 4K of memory. Actually, they had to write the interpreter in less than that amount of code, since the memory would not only be holding their program to interpret BASIC into machine language, but would need space for the program that the user would be writing. It was not easy, but Gates in particular was a master at bumming code, and with a lot of squeezing and some innovative use of the elaborate 8080 instruction set, they thought they'd done it. When they called Roberts, they did not mention they were placing the call from Bill Gates' college dorm room. Roberts was cordial, but warned them that others were thinking of an Altair BASIC; they were welcome to try, though. "We'll buy from the first guy who shows up with one," Roberts told them.

Not long afterward, Paul Allen was on a plane to Albuquerque with a paper tape containing what he and his friend hoped would run BASIC on the machine. He found MITS a madhouse. "People would work all day long, rush home, eat their dinner and come back," MITS executive Eddie Currie later recalled. "You could go in there any hour of the day or night and there would be twenty or thirty people, a third to half the staff [excluding manufacturing]. And this went on seven days a week. People were really caught up in this because they were giving computers to people who were so appreciative, and who wanted them so badly. It was a grand and glorious crusade."

Only one machine at MITS then had 4K of memory, and that barely worked. When Paul Allen stuck the tape in the teletype reader and read the tape in, no one was sure what would happen. What happened was that the teletype it was connected to said, READY. Ready to program! "They got very excited," Bill Gates later said. "Nobody had ever seen the machine *do* anything."

The BASIC was far from a working version, but it was close enough to completion and its routines were sufficiently clever to impress Ed Roberts. He hired Allen and arranged to have Gates work from Harvard to help get the thing working. When, not long afterward, Gates finally took off from school (he would never return) to go to Albuquerque, he felt like Picasso stumbling upon a sea of blank canvases—here was a neat computer without utilities. "They had nothing!" he said later, awed years after the fact. "I mean, the place was not sophisticated, as far as software went. We rewrote the assembler, we rewrote the loader . . . we put together a software library. It was pretty trashy stuff, but people could have fun using the thing."

The difference between the Gates-Allen software library and the software library in the drawer by the PDP-6 or the Homebrew

Club library was that the former was for sale only. Neither Bill Gates nor Ed Roberts believed that software was any kind of sanctified material, meant to be passed around as if it were too holy to pay for. It represented work, just as hardware did, and Altair BASIC was listed in the MITS catalog like anything else it sold.

Meanwhile, the hunger at Homebrew for an Altair BASIC was getting unbearable. As it turned out, Homebrew members were perfectly capable of writing BASIC interpreters, and some of them would do just that. Others, though, had ordered Altair BASIC and were impatiently awaiting delivery, just as they had impatiently awaited delivery of other MITS products. Patience with MITS was getting thin, especially since the debacle with the dynamic memory boards which Ed Roberts insisted should work and never did. People who had been burned by buying memory boards began to snort and pout when they spoke of Ed Roberts' company, especially since Roberts himself, who had attained legendary status as a reclusive genius who never left Albuquerque, was spoken of as a greedy, power-mad foe of the Hacker Ethic. It was even rumored that he wished ill on his competitors. The proper hacker response to competitors was to give them your business plan and technical information, so they might make better products and the world in general might improve. Not to act as Ed Roberts did at the First World Altair Convention, held at Albuquerque a year after the machines were introduced, when the strong-willed MITS president refused to rent display booths to competitors, and, according to some, raged with fury when he heard that companies like Bob Marsh's Processor Technology had rented suites at the convention hotel and were entertaining prospective customers.

So when the MITS Caravan came to the Rickeys Hyatt House in Palo Alto in June of 1975, the stage was set for what some would call a crime and others would call liberation. The "Caravan" was a MITS marketing innovation. Some of the MITS engineers would travel in a motor home, dubbed the MITS-mobile, from city to city, setting up Altairs in motel seminar rooms and inviting people to see the amazing low-cost computers at work. The turnout would largely be people who ordered Altairs and had questions on when they could expect delivery. People who owned them would want to know where they went wrong in assembling the monster. People who owned MITS memory boards would want to know why they didn't work. And people who'd ordered Altair BASIC would complain that they hadn't gotten it.

The Homebrew Computer Club crowd was out in force when

the Caravan met at the Rickeys Hyatt on El Camino Real in Palo Alto in early June, and were amazed when they found that the Altair on display was running BASIC. It was connected to a teletype which had a paper-tape reader, and once it was loaded anyone could type in commands and get responses instantly. It looked like a godsend to those hackers who had already sent in several hundred dollars to MITS and were impatiently waiting for BASIC. There is nothing more frustrating to a hacker than to see an extension to a system and not be able to keep hands-on. The thought of going home to an Altair without the capability of that machine running in the pseudo-plush confines of the Rickeys Hyatt must have been like a prison sentence to those hackers. But hands-on prevailed. Years later, Steve Dompier tactfully described what happened next: "Somebody, I don't think anyone figured out who, borrowed one of their paper tapes lying on the floor." The paper tape in question held the current version of Altair BASIC written by Bill Gates and Paul Allen.

Dan Sokol later recalled that vague "someone" coming up to him and, noting that Sokol worked for one of the semiconductor firms, asking if he had any way of duplicating paper tapes. Sokol said yes, there was a tape-copying machine available to him. He was handed the tape.

Sokol had all sorts of reasons for accepting the assignment to copy the tapes. He felt that MITS' price for the BASIC was excessive. He thought that MITS was greedy. He had heard a rumor that Gates and Allen had written the interpreter on a big computer system belonging to an institution funded in part by the government, and therefore felt the program belonged to all taxpayers. He knew that many people had paid MITS for the product already, and their getting an early copy wouldn't hurt MITS financially. But most of all, it seemed *right* to copy it. Why should there be a barrier of ownership standing between a hacker and a tool to explore, improve, and build systems?

Armed with this philosophical rationale, Sokol took the tape to his employer's, sat down at a PDP-11, and threaded in the tape. He ran it all night, churning out tapes, and at the next Homebrew Computer Club meeting he came with a box of tapes. Sokol charged what in hacker terms was the proper price for software: nothing. The only stipulation was that if you took a tape, you should make copies and come to the next meeting with *two* tapes. And give them away. People snapped up the tapes, and not only brought copies to the next meeting but sent them to other computer clubs as well. So that first version of Altair BASIC was in free-flowing circulation even before its official release.

There were two hackers, however, who were far from delighted at this demonstration of sharing and cooperation—Paul Allen and Bill Gates. They had sold their BASIC to MITS on a basis that earned them royalties for every copy sold, and the idea of the hacker community blithely churning out copies of their program and giving them away did not seem particularly Utopian. It seemed like stealing. Bill Gates was also upset because the version that people were exchanging was loaded with bugs that he was in the process of fixing. At first he figured that people would just buy the debugged version. But even after MITS did release the debugged BASIC, it became clear that Altair users were not buying as many copies as they would if they hadn't had a "pirated" BASIC already running. Apparently, they were either putting up with the bugs or, more likely, having a grand old hacker time debugging it themselves. Gates was becoming very upset, and when David Bunnell (who was then editing the newly begun *Altair Users' Newsletter* for MITS) asked him what he wanted to do about it, Gates, then nineteen and imbued with a cockiness that comes from technical virtuosity and not necessarily social tact, said maybe he should write a letter. Bunnell promised him he could get the letter out to the troublemakers.

So Gates wrote his letter, and Bunnell not only printed it in the Altair newsletter but sent it to other publications, including the Homebrew Computer Club newsletter. Entitled an "Open Letter to Hobbyists," it explained that while he and Allen had received lots of good feedback about the interpreter, most of the people praising it *hadn't bought it.* The letter got to the heart of the matter quickly:

> Why is this? As the majority of hobbyists must be aware, most of you steal your software. Hardware must be paid for, but software is something to share. Who cares if the people who worked on it get paid?

Gates went on to explain that this "theft" of software was holding back talented programmers from writing for machines like the Altair. "Who can afford to do professional work for nothing? What hobbyist can put 3 man-years into programming, finding all the bugs, documenting his product and distributing for free?"

Though fairly impassioned, the letter, carefully edited by Bunnell, was far from a screed. But all hell broke loose in the hacker community. Ed Roberts, though agreeing philosophically with Gates, couldn't help but notice the bad feelings, and was upset that Gates hadn't consulted him before publishing the letter. The Southern California Computer Society threatened to sue Gates for calling hobbyists "thieves." Gates received between three and four hundred letters, only five or six containing the voluntary payment he suggested that owners of pirated BASIC send him. Many of the letters were intensely negative. Hal Singer, editor of the *Micro-8 Newsletter*, which received Gates' letter via special delivery, wrote that "the most logical action was to tear the letter up and forget about it."

But the "software flap," as it came to be known, could not easily be forgotten. When MIT hackers were writing software and leaving it in the drawer for others to work on, they did not have the temptation of royalties. Slug Russell's Spacewar, for instance, had no market (there were only fifty PDP-1s made, and the institutions that owned them would hardly spend money to buy a space game). With the growing number of computers in use (not only Altairs but others as well), a good piece of software became something which could make a lot of money—if hackers did not consider it well within their province to pirate the software. No one seemed to object to a software author getting something for his work—but neither did the hackers want to let go of the idea that computer programs belonged to everybody. It was too much a part of the hacker dream to abandon.

Steve Dompier thought that Bill Gates was merely whining. "Ironically, Bill complaining about piracy didn't stop anything. People still believed, 'If you got it, you could run it.' It was like taping music off the air. BASIC had spread all over the country, all over the world. And it helped Gates—the fact that everybody had Altair BASIC and knew how it worked and how to fix it meant that when other computer companies came on line and needed a BASIC, they went to Gates' company. It became a de facto standard."

People around the Homebrew Computer Club tried to ease into this new era, in which software had commercial value, without losing the hacker ideals. One way to do that was by writing programs with the specific idea of distributing them in the informal, though quasi-legal, manner by which Altair BASIC was distributed—through a branching, give-it-to-your-friends scheme. So software could continue being an organic process, with the original author launching the program code on a journey that would see an endless round of improvements.

•

The best example of that organic process came in the proliferation of "Tiny BASIC" interpreters. When PCC's Bob Albrecht first looked over his Altair, he immediately realized that the only way to program it then was with the ponderous machine language of the 8080 chip. He also saw how limited the memory was. So he went to Dennis Allison, a PCC board member who taught computer science at Stanford, and asked him to make some design notes for a stripped-down BASIC that would be easy to use and wouldn't take up much memory. Allison wrote up a framework for a possible interpreter, labeling his article a "participatory project," soliciting help from anyone else interested in writing "a minimal BASIC-like language for writing simple programs." Allison later recalled the reaction to the *PCC* article: "Three weeks later we got responses, including one sent from two guys from Texas who had written an entirely corrected and debugged Tiny BASIC, with a complete code listing in octal." The Texas duo had put a BASIC in 2K of memory and had sent it off, just like that, to be printed in *PCC.* Albrecht complied, running the entire source code, and in a few weeks Altair owners began sending in "bug reports" and suggestions for improvement. This was before any i/o boards for the Altair existed; *PCC* readers had been switching in the two thousand numbers by hand, repeating the process each time they turned the machine on.

Various hackers deluged *PCC* with new dialects of Tiny BASIC and interesting programs written in the language. Albrecht, always more planner than hacker, was worried that running all that code would make *PCC* too much a technical journal, so he devised a plan to publish a temporary offshoot of *PCC* called *Tiny BASIC Journal.* But the response was so heavy that he realized an entire new magazine was called for, devoted to software. He called on Jim Warren to edit it.

Warren was the portly, mercurial computer science student who refused to go to The Oasis after Homebrew because he couldn't stand the smoke. He was a veteran of the Midpeninsula Free University. In addition to several academic degrees, he had about eight years of consulting experience in computers, and was chairman of several special interest groups of the Association for Computer Machinery. *PCC* offered him $350 a month for the job, and he took it right away. "It looked like fun," he later explained. Knowing some people were militantly opposed to BASIC, he insisted that the journal not be limited to BASIC but publish software in general, to help all those hardware hackers who had set up their machines and wanted the incantations to move the bits around inside them.

The journal's very name was indicative of the atmosphere around PCC and Homebrew around then: because Tiny BASIC saves bytes of memory, it was dubbed "The Dr. Dobbs Journal of Computer Calisthenics and Orthodontia . . . Running Light Without Overbyte." Why not?

Dr. Dobbs Journal (DDJ) would be, Warren editorialized in the premier issue, about "free and very inexpensive software." In a letter sent out to explain the magazine, he elaborated: "There is a viable alternative to the problems raised by Bill Gates in his irate letter to computer hobbyists concerning 'ripping off' software. When software is free, or so inexpensive that it's easier to pay for it than duplicate it, then it won't be 'stolen.' "

Warren saw *DDJ* as a flagship of the hacker dream. He wanted it to be a clearinghouse for assemblers, debuggers, graphics, and music software. Also, he saw it as a "communication medium and intellectual rabble-rouser." But things were happening so fast by 1976 that more often than not the hardware news he heard or the software solution to a problem couldn't wait for publication, and he would rush to the next meeting of Homebrew—where he became a familiar figure, standing up and spouting all the news that had come over his desk that week.

Warren's vocal lobbying for a public-domain approach to software was not the only course of action. Perhaps the most characteristic hacker response to the threat that commercialization might change the spirit of hacking came from an adamantly independent software wizard named Tom Pittman. Pittman was not involved in any of the major projects then in progress around Homebrew. He was representative of the middle-aged hardware hackers who gravitated toward Homebrew and took pride in associating with the microcomputer revolution, but derived so much satisfaction from the personal joys of hacking that they kept their profiles low. Pittman was Lee Felsenstein's age, and had even been at Berkeley at the same time, but did not live the swashbuckling internal life of Felsenstein.

Pittman had been going faithfully to Homebrew since the first meeting, and without making much effort to communicate he became known as one of the purest and most accomplished engineers in the club. He was a slightly built fellow with thick glasses and a wide, flickering smile which signaled, despite an obvious shyness, that he'd always be willing to indulge in conversation about hardware. He had built an improbably useful computer system based on the relatively low-power Intel 4004 chip, and for a time maintained the Homebrew mailing list on it. He took a perverse pleasure in evoking astonishment from people when he told them what he had done with the system, making it perform tasks far beyond its theoretical limits.

Pittman had dreamed of having his own computer since his high school days in the early sixties. All his life he had been a self-described "doer, not a watcher," but he worked alone, in a private world dominated by the reassuring logic of electronics. "I'm not very sensitive to other people's thought patterns," he said later. He would go to the library to take out books on the subject, go through them, then take out more. "I couldn't read long before I'd set the book down and *do* things—in my head if nowhere else."

By the time he had arrived at Berkeley, he had already taken college-level courses on all sorts of math and engineering subjects. His favorite course during his freshman year was Numerical Analysis. While the Free Speech Movement was raging around him, Pittman was blithely tangling with the problems in the lab section of the course, systematically wrestling each mathematical conundrum to the ground till it howled for mercy. But he was bored by the lecture part of the course; it didn't seem "interesting," and his mark in Numerical Analysis was split between an A in lab and an F in lecture. He had identical results upon repeating the course. Perhaps he was not destined to fit into the organized structure of a university.

Then he found his escape. A sympathetic professor helped him get a job at a Department of Defense laboratory in San Francisco. He worked on computers there, helping on game simulations that gauged the radiation effect from hypothetical nuclear explosions. He had no ethical problem with the job. "Being basically insensitive to political issues, I never even noticed," he later said. His beliefs as a devout Christian led him to declare himself a "semiobjector." He later explained: "It means I was willing [to serve] but not willing to shoot people. I worked there at the laboratory to serve my country. I had a lot of fun."

He welcomed the chance to finally become addicted to computers; though his work hours officially ended at six, he would often work much later, enjoying the peace of being the only one there. He would work until he was too tired to go on; one night driving home to the East Bay he fell asleep and woke up in a rosebush on the side of the road. He learned the computer system at the lab so well that he became the unofficial systems hacker; whenever people had a problem with the machine they came to Tom. He was crushed when, after the war ended and defense funds withered, the lab closed.

But by then the possibility of making his own computer had materialized. He went down to Intel, maker of the first microprocessor, the 4004 chip, and offered to write an assembler for it. He would take the parts to build a computer in exchange for the job. Scrunching code like a master, he did a compact assembler, then wrote a debugger in exchange for more parts. The people at Intel began to send any 4004 buyers who needed programming down to Tom. By the time he began going to Homebrew meetings, he had moved to San Jose, having built a considerable consulting business to support himself and his wife, who accepted his computer fanaticism only grudgingly.

While he was fascinated by the technological brotherhood of Homebrew, Tom Pittman was among those who never considered going into business as Bob Marsh did with Processor Technology. Nor did he think of working at any of those energetic start-up firms. "I never hit it off with anyone there. The people didn't know me—I'm a loner," he later said. "Besides, I don't have managerial skills. I'm more a software person than an electronic engineer."

But after the "software flap" caused by Bill Gates' letter, Pittman decided to take public action. "Gates was moaning about the ripoffs, and people were saying, 'If you didn't charge $150, we'd buy it.' I decided to prove it." He had been following the Tiny BASIC news in *Dr. Dobbs Journal,* and understood the guidelines of writing a BASIC. And he noted that there were some new computers, competitors to MITS, coming out that used the Motorola 6800 chip instead of the Intel 8080, and there was no BASIC interpreter written to work on them. So he decided to write a 6800 Tiny BASIC interpreter and sell it for the sum of five dollars, a fraction of the MITS price, to see if people would buy instead of stealing.

Being a true hacker, Pittman was not satisfied with running just any kind of Tiny BASIC: he was a captive of the beast he called "the creepy feature creature," which stands behind the shoulder of every hacker, poking him in the back and urging, "More features! Make it better!" He put in things that some people thought impossible in a "tiny" language—like room to insert helpful remarks, and utilization of a full command set. Inside of two months he had his interpreter running, and he got lucky when he sold it to the AMI company for $3,500, on the condition that the sale be non-exclusive. He still wanted to sell it to hobbyists for five dollars a shot.

He sent an ad to *Byte* magazine, and within days of its appearance he had fifty dollars in his mailbox. Some people sent in ten dollars or more, saying the five was too little. Some sent in five dollars with a note saying not to ship anything to them—they'd already copied it from a friend. Pittman kept sending them out. His costs included twelve cents for the paper tape, and fifty cents for printing the manual he'd written. He would sit on the couch of his modest home at night, listening to the Christian radio station in San Jose or tape cassettes of speakers at Christian conferences, and fold paper tapes, having mastered the skill of folding every eight inches. Then he'd go to the post office, and send the packages off. It was all done by hand, with the help of his wife, who had been skeptical about the whole enterprise.

It was a triumph for hackerism, but Tom Pittman did not stop there. He wanted to tell people about it, show them the example by which they could grow. He later gave a presentation at a Homebrew meeting, and when he loped to the front of the auditorium, Lee saw that his body was knotted with tension. Lee tried to loosen him up—"They call you Tiny Tom Pittman, but you're really not so small," he said. "Why is that?" Tom, not used to public repartee, did not respond with more than a laugh. But when he began speaking he gained strength, coiling and uncoiling his body, chopping his arm in the air to make points about free software. It had a certain drama to it, this normally taciturn technician speaking with heartfelt openness about an issue that obviously mattered to him: the free flow of information.

Not long after Tiny BASIC he went a step further, announcing his intention to write a FORTRAN for microcomputers and sell it for twenty-five dollars. This was to be another gung-ho full-time enterprise, and he was still hacking away when, as he later put it, "my computer widow left me. She decided she didn't want to be married to an addict."

It was a jolt that many Homebrew members—those who had convinced a woman to marry a computer addict in the first place—would experience. "I would say the divorce rate among computerists is almost 100 percent—certainly in my case," Gordon French later said. That did not make things easier for Tom Pittman. He had no heart to finish the FORTRAN. He did a lot of thinking about the devotion he'd given to the machine, and where it came from, and sat down to write something, not in machine language, but in English.

He called the essay "Deus Ex Machina, or The True Computerist" (one might use the last word interchangeably with "hacker"), and it was a telling explanation of what bound together the hardware hackers of Silicon Valley and the artificial intelligence hackers of Cambridge. He wrote about the certain feeling one gets after hacking something. "In that instant," he wrote, "I as a Christian thought I could feel something of the satisfaction that God must have felt when He created the world." He went on to compile the creed of the computerist—the hardware hacker—which included such familiar "articles of faith" (to Homebrew people) as:

The computer is more interesting than most people. I love to spend time with my computer. It is fun to write programs for it, play games on it, and to build new parts for it. It is fascinating to try to figure out what part of the program it is in by the way the lights flicker or the radio buzzes. It beats dull conversation any day.

The computer needs just a little more (memory) (speed) (peripherals) (better BASIC) (newer CPU) (noise suppression on the bus) (debugging on this program) (powerful editor) (bigger power supply) before it can do this or that.

There is no need to buy this software package or that circuit board; I can design one better.

Never miss a club meeting. This is where it's at. The juicy little news bits, the how-to-fixits for the problem that has been bugging me the last two weeks . . . that is the real thing! Besides, they might have some free software.

Pittman's tone shifted at that point. He forced himself to take exception to those articles of faith, testifying that he had "been there" and seen the problems with them. Point by point he demonstrated the folly of hacking, and concluded by writing: "By now the computer has moved out of the den and into the rest of your life. It will consume all of your spare time, and even your vacation, if you let it. It will empty your wallet and tie up your thoughts. It will drive away your family. Your friends will start to think of you as a bore. And what for?"

Shaken by the breakup of his marriage, Tom Pittman decided to change his habits. And he did. He later described the transformation: "I take a day of rest now. I won't turn on the computer on Sunday.

"The other six days, I'll work like a dog."

•

Lee Felsenstein was gaining confidence and purpose through his role as toastmaster of the Homebrew Computer Club. His express desire was to allow the club to develop as an anarchist community, a society of non-joiners wed, whether they knew it or not, by the Propaganda of the Deed. He saw what Moore and French didn't: for maximum political effect in the war of the hardware hackers against the evil forces of IBM and such, the strategy should reflect the style of hackerism itself. This meant that the club would never be run like a formal bureaucracy.

If he desired a blueprint for failure, he need only look to the south, at the Southern California Computer Society. Starting up a few months after Homebrew's first meeting, SCCS took advantage of the hobbyists in the electronics-intensive area (almost all the high-tech defense contractors are in Southern California) to quickly boost its membership to *eight thousand.* Its leaders were not happy with the mere exchange of information: they envisioned group buying plans, a national magazine, and an influence which would allow hobbyists to dictate terms to the growing microcomputer industry. Homebrew had no steering committee to confer on goals and directions; it only incorporated as an afterthought, almost a year after inception; it had no real dues requirements—only a suggested contribution of ten dollars a year to get its modest newsletter. But SCCS had a formal board of directors, whose regular meetings were often sparked by acrimonious debates on What the Club Should Be. It wasn't long before SCCS was publishing a slick magazine, had a growing group buying program (as much as forty thousand dollars a month), and was considering changing its name to the *National* Computer Society.

Bob Marsh, hawking Processor Technology boards, often flew down to the packed SCCS meetings, and even sat on the SCCS board for a few months. He later described the difference between the two groups: "Homebrew was a place where people came together mysteriously, twice a month. It never was an organization.

But SCCS was more organized. Those guys had megalomania. The politics were terrible, and ruined it." Somehow, the particulars never became clear, a lot of money was misplaced in the buying scheme. The editor they hired to run the slick magazine felt justified in dropping the publication's relationship with the club and going off on his own with the magazine (still publishing as *Interface Age*); a lawsuit resulted. The board meetings became incredibly tempestuous, and the bad feelings spread to the general membership meetings. Eventually the club faded away.

Though Lee's plans were no less ambitious than those of the leaders of SCCS, he realized that this war must not be waged in a bureaucratic, follow-the-leader fashion. He was perfectly happy dealing with an army of Bob Marshes and Tom Pittmans, some changing the world by dint of useful products manufactured in the spirit of hackerism and others just going their way, being hackers. The eventual goal would be a mass distribution of the wonderment that Lee Felsenstein had experienced in his basement monastery. An environment conducive to the Hands-On Imperative. As Lee told a conference of the Institute of Electrical and Electronic Engineers in 1975, "The industrial approach is grim and doesn't work: the design motto is 'Design by Geniuses for Use by Idiots,' and the watchword for dealing with the untrained and unwashed public is KEEP THEIR HANDS OFF! . . . The convivial approach I suggest would rely on the user's ability to learn about and gain some control over the tool. The user will have to spend some amount of time probing around inside the equipment, and we will have to make this possible and not fatal to either the equipment or the person."

The piece of equipment to which Felsenstein referred was his Tom Swift Terminal, which still had not been built in 1975. But it was getting close. Bob Marsh, eager to expand the scope of his booming Processor Technology company, offered Lee a deal he couldn't refuse. "I'll pay you to design the video portion of the Tom Swift Terminal," he told him. That sounded all right to Lee, who had been doing work in documentation and schematics for Processor Technology all along. Bob Marsh, in the company's first year of business, was adhering to the Hacker Ethic. The company distributed schematics and source code for software, free or at nominal cost. (In partial reaction to MIT's high-priced BASIC, Processor Technology would develop its own and sell it, along with source code, for five dollars.) For a time, the company had a socialistic salary structure of $800 a month for all employees. "We didn't pay attention to profits or management of almost any kind."

Lee was not an employee, choosing to work on a contract basis. "I'd quote them a price," Lee later recalled, and "they had to get the price up by a factor of ten, since I was such a small-time thinker. In terms of money."

In less than three months, Lee had done a working prototype. Lee's "video display module" (VDM) embodied a different philosophy than the other video board for Altair, Cromemco's Dazzler. The Dazzler used color, and produced its flashy effects by constantly going back to the memory in the main chip of the Altair (or any of the other new computers that used a similar hardware bus). Steve Dompier liked to use his Dazzler while running BASIC: it threw up patterns on the screen that gave a Rorschach-like visual impression of the computer memory at a given time—a cryptic output which gave clues to program operation, much like the aural impression given of the TX-0's memory by the speaker under the console.

Lee's video display module, though, was a more stridently focused piece of equipment, designed with the eventual re-formation of Community Memory in mind. Its output was black and white, and instead of using dots it actually formed alphanumeric characters. (Lee considered adding another alternative—hexagrams, as found in the I Ching—but that idea got shelved somehow.) The cleverest thing about Lee's VDM, though, was the way it used the speed of new microprocessor chips to allow the machine's memory to be shared between computational duties and display duties. It worked like a mini-time-sharing system, where the two users were the video display and the computer itself. The VDM, along with an Altair and other expansion cards, made the promise of the TV Typewriter a reality, and was an instant success, even though it was, like almost every Processor Technology product, not ready till somewhat after the promised delivery date, in late 1975.

One person particularly impressed by the VDM was Les Solomon in New York. He was not content to bask in the reflected glory of launching Ed Roberts' seminal machine. His magazine had followed up on the coup, he had delivered more computer-related cover stories, and now he was hoping to present a complete computer video display terminal—a self-contained item which would have the power of the computer as well as a display capability. It would be the next step beyond the Altair, a combination computer-teletype with video. No more goddamn bloody fingers from the flicking switches on the Altair front panel. In pursuit of the product, Solomon went to Phoenix to visit Don Lancaster, inventor of the TV Typewriter (the one Bob Marsh had tried to build in Berkeley), and convinced him to drive down to Albuquerque to meet Ed Roberts; maybe the two giants might combine on a terminal project. As Solomon later described it, the meeting was "bang, clash. A clash of egos. Don refused to change his design to match Ed's computer because he said Ed's was inefficient. Ed said, 'No way, I can't redesign it.' They immediately decided to kill each other on the spot, and I separated them."

So Solomon went to Bob Marsh, whose Processor Technology company already offered the VDM and memory boards and even a "motherboard" which could replace the basic circuitry of the Altair, and asked, "Why don't you put them all together? Let's make something we can look at." If Marsh could deliver an "intelligent terminal" in thirty days, Solomon would put it on the cover.

Bob talked to Lee, who agreed to do most of the design, and as they discussed it they realized that what Les Solomon wanted was not merely a terminal, but a complete computer. In the year since the Altair had been announced, "hobbyist" computers, sold either in kits or assembled, had appeared, most notably one called the IMSAI, put out by a company whose employees had taken Werner Erhard's *est* training. Almost all of these computers used the 100-pin Altair bus as their base. Almost all looked like the Altair, an oversized stereo receiver with lights and switches instead of an FM dial. All required some sort of terminal, usually a klunky teletype, for the user to do anything with it.

For that month, December of 1975, Lee and Bob worked on the design. Marsh wanted to use an 8080 chip, an idea which Lee at first still opposed for political reasons (why one centralized silicon dictator?) but came to accept as he realized that a truly "intelligent" terminal—one which gave you all the power of a computer—would need a brain. Lee figured he would use his junkyard-paranoid style to balance out the rest of the design, so that the brain would not be tempted to run amok. Marsh would often interrupt Lee's design-in-progress to reveal his latest inspiration from the "feature creature."

Lee later recounted this process in a magazine article: "When [Marsh] had little else with which to concern himself, he was continually turning up with new features and economies that he suddenly wanted incorporated in the design. He would explain the problem or opportunity and then preface his technical solution with an inevitable, 'All's ya gotta do is . . .' Were the designer a prima donna, the relationship would terminate after the second such incident, with the designer fuming about 'professionalism' and 'interference.' Of course since my workshop was in the same room as his, I could not have gotten very far if I had wanted to stamp out in a rage."

Marsh, like Lee, was thinking of the machine as a political tool as well as a good, fun product to design. "We wanted to make the microcomputer accessible to human beings," he later said. "The public didn't know it yet, but the computer was the coming thing and every home would have one and people could use computers for useful things. We really weren't sure what they were [but] we felt we were participating in a movement, in a way."

Lee suggested that since they were putting the wisdom of Solomon into the machine, it should be called the Sol. (Les Solomon later commented: "If it works, they'll say Sol means "sun" in Spanish. If it don't work, they're gonna blame it on the Jewish guys.")

Completing the Sol was a process that took six weeks of fourteen- to seventeen-hour days, seven days a week. Lee, just about living on orange juice, spent endless hours staring at the Mylar spaghetti of the layout on the fluorescent light table. Meanwhile, one of Bob Marsh's woodworker friends had managed to get a bargain on center-cut pieces of walnut, and it was determined that the sides of the Sol would be made of that classy material. The prototype boards were finally finished, only fifteen days after Les Solomon's original deadline. Two weeks later, a day before the newly scheduled delivery date in late February 1976 in New York, they were racing to get all the workings to fit on an Altair-style bus, along with a kluged-up power supply, a keyboard, and even some preliminary software. The operating system was written by Processor Tech's head of software development, Homebrewer Steve Dompier.

Ever frugal, Marsh had booked himself and Lee on a night flight. Finishing just in time, they had to race to a heliport in order to make the plane. They arrived at Kennedy around 6 A.M., frazzled, with the Computer of the Common Man distributed between two paper bags. Nothing was open at the airport, even for coffee, so Solomon invited them over to his home in Flushing for breakfast. By then Les Solomon's home, particularly his basement workshop, was achieving legendary status as a proving ground for thrilling new breakthroughs. He would often entertain the young hardware hackers who designed these products, and his wife would always recognize them at a glance. "Because they all had the same thing," Solomon would later explain. "That little burning inside the eyeball. She used to say there was an inside personality, and though they looked like disreputable bums, you looked them in the face, you looked in those eyes and you knew who they were. She'd look at them and what would come out was the brightness, the intenseness."

The brightness dimmed on that cold February morning: Marsh and Felsenstein's terminal didn't work. After a quick day-trip to New Hampshire to meet the folks at the new hobbyist magazine *Byte,* Lee was able to get to a workbench and find the problem—a small wire had come loose. They went back to the offices of *Popular Electronics* and turned it on. "It looked like a house on fire," Solomon later said. He had immediately grasped that he was looking at a complete computer.

The resulting *Popular Electronics* article spoke of an intelligent computer terminal. But it was clearly a computer, a computer that, when Processor Technology packaged it in its pretty blue case with walnut sides, looked more like a fancy typewriter without a platen. There were new schematics for the revised kit (under one thousand dollars), which of course were provided to anyone who wanted to see how the thing worked. Marsh later estimated that they got thirty to forty *thousand* requests for schematics. Orders for the kit kept pouring in. It looked like the Sol would be the machine that broke the computer out of the hobbyist market and brought hacking into the home.

The first public display of the Sol was at a show in Atlantic City called PC '76. It was an odd affair, the first time the tradesmen of this hobbyist-computer business all got together to show their collective wares. The site was the Shelbourne Hotel, and in those pre-gambling days the hotel's glory was visibly faded. There were holes in the walls, some of the doors to the rooms had no knobs, the air-conditioning didn't work. Some indignant elderly retirees living at the hotel almost attacked Steve Dompier in the elevator when they saw his long hair. Still, it was an exhilarating experience. Almost five thousand people attended, many of them traveling from other parts of the country (SCCS ran a large group excursion which many Bay Area people took advantage of). Homebrew-inspired companies like Processor Tech and Cromemco finally met similar souls from other parts of the country, and everybody stayed up far into the night, swapping technical hints and plotting the future.

The Sol got lots of notice. The hackers all seemed to agree that with its low profile, its typewriter-style built-in keyboard, and its video display, the Sol was the next step. Not long afterward, Processor Tech managed to get a Sol on television—on Tom Snyder's "Tomorrow" show. The normally abrasive television personality came face to face with the newest manifestation of the hacker dream—a Sol computer running a game program written by Steve Dompier. The game was called "Target," and it consisted of a little cannon on the bottom of the screen by which the user could shoot down a series of alien spaceships, made of alphanumeric characters, sailing across the top of the screen. It was a clever little hack, and Steve Dompier, as he later said, "basically gave it away." After all, the point of writing those games was to see people have fun with the machine.

"Target" was perfect for showing Tom Snyder and a television audience a new way to look at those monsters shrouded in evil, computers. Imagine these grungy post-hippies being able to bring a computer over to a television studio, set it up, and have a total technical illiterate like Tom Snyder do something with it. Tom went along, and before you could say "commercial break" he was deeply involved—not in the least kidding—in shooting down aliens, which would zip across the screen in greater numbers as the game progressed, and even dispatch little parachutists loaded with grenades. It gave you a challenge you felt compelled to rise to. As you shot down the aliens, Tom Snyder was noticing, there was this feeling of . . . *power.* A feeling that gave you a small taste of what it must be like to use this machine to actually create. What mysteries lay within this typewriter-shaped machine? Even something as simple as "Target" could get someone thinking about that. "No one's given it a definition yet," Steve Dompier later said, "but I think there's a piece of magic there." In any case, as Dompier later recalled, "they had to drag Tom Snyder off the computer to have him finish the show."

12

WOZ

STEVE Wozniak did not sit near the front of the SLAC auditorium along with Lee Felsenstein during Homebrew meetings. His participation in the mapping sessions were infrequent. He had no great social scheme, did not incubate plans for a Community Memory–style assault on the foundations of the batch-processed society. Meeting after meeting, Steve Wozniak would be at the back of the room, along with a loose contingent of followers of his digital exploits—mostly high school–age computer nuts drawn by the sheer charisma of his hacking. He looked like a bum. His hair fell haphazardly on his shoulders, he had the kind of beard grown more to obviate the time-consuming act of shaving than to enhance appearance, and his clothes—jeans and sports shirts, with little variation —never seemed to fit quite right.

Still, it was Steve Wozniak, known to his friends as "Woz," who would best exemplify the spirit and the synergy of the Homebrew Computer Club. It was Wozniak and the computer he'd design that would take the Hacker Ethic, at least in terms of hardware hacking, to its apogee. It would be the legacy of the Homebrew.

Stephen Wozniak did not reach his views of hackerism through personal struggle and political rumination as Lee Felsenstein did. He was more like Richard Greenblatt and Stew Nelson: a born hacker. He grew up in Cupertino, California, amidst the curving streets lined with small single-family homes and the one-story, sparsely windowed buildings that sowed the crop of silicon which would be so central to his existence. Even in grammar school, Wozniak could get so engrossed in mathematical ponderings that his mother had to rap on his head to bring him back to the real world. He won a science contest at thirteen for building a computer-like machine which could add and subtract. His friend Alan Baum later remembered him at Homestead High School: "I saw a guy scribbling these neat diagrams on a piece of paper. I said, 'What's that?' He said, 'I'm designing a computer.' He had taught himself how to do it."

Baum was impressed enough to join this unusual classmate in a quest for computer access, and through contacts in the engineering-rich Silicon Valley they managed to get on various time-sharing computers. Every Wednesday they would leave school and have a friend sneak them into a computer room at the Sylvania company. They'd program the machine to do things like printing out all the powers of two and finding the primes. The two followed the computer industry with the serious passion with which fanatic sports fans might follow favorite teams. Every time they heard of a new minicomputer being released, they would write to the manufacturer, be it Digital or Control Data or whoever, and request the manual, a request often routinely fulfilled. When the manual came, they would devour it. They would instantly turn to the part which described the computer's instruction set. They would note how many registers the machine had, how it added, how it did multiplication, division. They could discern from the instruction set the character of the machine, how easy it would be to use. Was this a machine to fantasize about? If it was, Woz later recalled, he would "spend hours in class writing code without ever being able to test it." Once, after receiving a manual for a Data General Nova computer, he and Baum took it upon themselves to redesign it, even sending their new design to the company, in case Data General wanted to implement the suggestions of two high school kids.

"It just seemed *neat* [to design computers]," Baum later recalled. "It seemed like an important thing to do. The glamour appealed to us. It was fun." As high school progressed, and Wozniak scrounged more time on computers to perfect his skills, Baum would often be astounded at the programming tricks Woz would come up with. "He seems to have invented all the tricks on his own," Baum later said. "Steve looks at things a different way. He says, 'Why don't I try this?' He's driven to use all the problem-solving techniques he can because ordinary design isn't good enough. He has to be the best. He'll do things no one's thought of, use every trick. Sometimes, using every trick, you find better ways to do things."

Woz graduated from high school before Baum did, and went off to college. But a few years later, both wound up working at the same company, the Hewlett-Packard computer firm. An extremely high-tech operation, devoted to high-performance computers which were like Mercedes cars compared to IBM's clunky Caddies, this was truly the big leagues, and Woz was very happy there. He was married, but computers still were his number one priority. Besides his work at HP designing arithmetic logic for calculator chips, he also did some extra design work for the Atari game company, where another high school friend, Steve Jobs, worked. This provided side benefits, like the time he went into a bowling alley and encountered a coin-operated videogame with a sign promising a pizza to anyone who scored over a certain level. After a number of pizzas, his amazed companion asked him how he had beaten the game so easily. "I designed it," said Wozniak between spasms of laughter.

A prankster with an unsettling, sometimes sophomoric sense of humor, Woz ran a free "dial-a-joke" service from his home, dispensing a seemingly endless supply of Polish jokes. That was not the only amusement he derived from the phone. He and Jobs became inspired after reading a 1971 article in *Esquire* about a legendary fellow known as Captain Crunch who was a devoted builder of blue boxes—these were devices which allowed one to make long distance calls for free. Jobs and Woz built their own, and not only used them to make free calls but at one point sold them door-to-door at the Berkeley dorms. Woz once used his box to see if he could phone the Pope; he pretended he was Henry Kissinger, and almost reached His Eminence before someone at the Vatican caught on.

It was a freewheeling life Woz lived, centered on hacking for HP, hacking on his own, and playing games. He loved to play games, especially electronic ones like Pong. He also played tennis; like Bill Gosper playing Ping-Pong, Wozniak got a kick out of putting spin on the ball. As he later told an interviewer, "The winning isn't as important as the running after the ball." A sentiment which applied to hacking computers as well as tennis.

He dreamed, always, of that computer he might design for himself. He had already homebrewed his own TV Typewriter, a good first step. His goal was, of course, a computer built to encourage more hacking—a Tool to Make Tools, a system to create systems. It would be cleverer than any preceding it.

It was 1975, and most people, had they heard his dream, would have thought he was nuts.

Then Alan Baum saw the notice for the Homebrew meeting on a bulletin board and told Woz about it. They both went. Baum, admittedly too lazy to build a computer when he was surrounded with state-of-the-art machines at HP, wasn't terribly excited. But Woz was thrilled. Here were thirty people *like him*—people quixotically fixated on building their own computers. When Marty Spergel passed out data sheets on the 8008 chip, Woz took one home and examined it until he realized that those minicomputers he was thinking of designing—big machines like the ones Digital Equipment made—were unnecessary. You could do it with microchips, like that Altair he had seen that night. He got hold of all the literature he could on microprocessors and wrote for more information, started files on all sorts of i/o devices and chips, and began designing circuits for this eventual computer. The second Homebrew Computer Club newsletter printed his report on current activities:

Have TVT my own design . . . have my own version of Pong, a videogame called breakthrough, a NRZI reader for cassettes very simple! Working on a 17-chip TV chess display (includes 3 stored boards); a 30-chip TV display. Skills: digital design, interfacing, I/O devices, short on time, have schematics.

The Homebrew atmosphere was perfect for Steve Wozniak; there was activity and energy focusing on the experimentation and electronic creativity which were as essential to him as the air he breathed or the junk food he ate. And even a person not normally taken to socializing could find himself making friends. Woz often used his home terminal to access the account that had been set up for Homebrew members on the Call Computer service. (Call Computer was a service that allowed people with home terminals to access a mainframe computer by phone.) There was a program on the computer much like the function on the MIT ITS system, where two people could "chat" to each other while on the computer, sharing information. Woz not only used this to communicate electronically with people, but he hacked into the depths of the system and discovered a way to break in on other people's electronic conversations. So when Gordon French, for instance, was flaming about his new trick with the 8008 Chicken Hawk, his home terminal would inexplicably begin printing out these semi-obscene *Polish jokes,* and he never did figure out that somewhere miles away Steve Wozniak was doubled up in laughter.

Woz also met Randy Wigginton, an athletic, blond-haired fourteen-year-old computer kid who had managed to get a job at Call Computer. Wigginton lived just down the street from the cluttered garden apartment Wozniak shared with his wife, and Woz would drive the youngster to Homebrew meetings. Since before high school, Wigginton had been in love with computers. He came to almost idolize Woz for his profound understanding of computers, and deeply appreciated the fact that the twenty-five-year-old Woz "would talk to anybody about any technical thing," even to a fourteen-year-old like Wigginton. Though Randy's parents worried at the fact that computers were taking over their son's life, his obsession deepened, fueled by Woz's informal tutorials at Denny's restaurant on Foothill Drive on the way back from meetings. They would be driving in Woz's beat-up Malibu with its mounds of trash on the back seat—dozens of McDonald's bags and technical journals, all soggy from Woz's strange reluctance to roll up the windows when it rained—and stop for Cokes, fries, and onion rings. "I would ask Woz any dumb question just to get him talking—'How does a BASIC interpreter work?'—and just listen to him as long as he talked," Wigginton later recalled.

Wozniak soon got to know another Homebrew member who worked at Call Computer—John Draper. A semi-employed engineer, John Draper was better known as "Captain Crunch," the "phone phreak" hero of that *Esquire* article that excited Woz in 1971. Draper, whose unmodulated voice could drone like the last whines of a fire alarm, a scraggly dresser who never seemed to put a comb to his long dark hair, got that moniker after he discovered that when one blew the whistle that came in the breakfast cereal by that name, the result would be the precise 2,600-cycle tone that the phone company used to shuttle long-distance traffic over the phone lines. John Draper, then an airman stationed overseas, used this knowledge to call friends at home.

But Draper's interest went beyond free calls—as an engineer with a latent hacker tendency toward exploration which would soon prove overwhelming, he became fascinated with the phone company system. "I do [phreaking] for one reason and one reason only," he told the *Esquire* reporter who made him famous in 1971.

"I'm learning about a system. The phone company is a System. A computer is a System. Do you understand? If I do what I do, it is only to explore a System. That's my bag. The phone company is nothing but a computer." It was the same fascination shared by the Tech Model Railroad Club hackers, particularly Stew Nelson (the MIT hacker who had hacked phones since childhood); but, not having Nelson's access to sophisticated tools to explore it, Draper had to devise his own jerry-rigged means of access. (The one time Nelson did meet Draper, the MIT hacker was unimpressed by Draper's technical ability.) Draper was helped by discovering a network of phone phreaks with similar interests, many of them blind men who could easily identify the tones which could whizz one through the system. Draper was astonished that there were alternate phone systems from which you could get into test boards, verification trunks for breaking into people's conversations (he once startled a woman he fancied by angrily interrupting her phone chat with another man), and overseas switching units. He soon figured out how to jump from one circuit to another, and mastered the secrets of "blue boxes," which like Stew Nelson's adjustment to the PDP-1 a decade earlier, could send tones over phone lines to get unlimited, free long-distance calls.

But John Draper, who sometimes acted so impulsively that he would seem an overgrown infant, wailing for his mother's milk of systems knowledge, did not have the focused resolve of the MIT hackers—he could easily be cajoled into yielding the information about blue boxes to people who wanted to sell the boxes to people who wanted free calls—as Wozniak and Jobs had done door-to-door in the Berkeley dorms.

Draper's own phone excursions were more benign. A typical caper would be to seek out and "map" various access codes for foreign countries, and he would use those codes to leapfrog from one trunk line to another, listening to a series of edifying clicks as his signal bounced from one communications satellite to the next. After the *Esquire* article, though, authorities targeted him, and in 1972 he was caught in the act of illegally calling a Sydney, Australia, number which gave callers the names of the top tunes Down Under. For this first offense, he was given a suspended sentence.

He turned to computer programming, and soon was a regular hacker. People would later recall him at People's Computer Company potlucks, filling his plate sky-high and stuffing himself. A virulent anti-smoker, he would also scream almost painfully when someone lit a cigarette. He was still interested in phone hacking, and among the subjects he'd talk about at the potlucks were things like getting ARPAnet access, something he considered eminently justifiable—"I had some integrations I had to do analytically. The MIT computer [had a program to help me do it]. So I used it," he would later explain.

When the potlucks ended, he gravitated to Homebrew. He was a consultant to Call Computer, and had arranged for the Homebrew Club to get its account. He became a huge fan of Wozniak's hacking, and Wozniak was thrilled to meet the famous phone phreak who had inspired his own blue box escapades. It was not unusual to see them together at the back of the room, as they were one night in late 1975 when Dan Sokol approached them. Sokol was the long-haired, blond guy who would stand up at Homebrew, check that no one from Intel was around, and barter off 8080 chips to anyone with good equipment to trade.

Sokol at that time was going broke from using his home terminal to access the Call Computer account. Since Sokol lived in Santa Cruz, and Call Computer was in Palo Alto, his phone bill was outrageous; he was accessing the computer for forty to fifty hours a week. The solution came one day at the back of the SLAC auditorium when Sokol was introduced to Wozniak and John Draper.

Not Captain Crunch?

"Yeah, that's me!" Draper volunteered, and Sokol immediately peppered him with questions on building a blue box, which would enable him to make the Santa Cruz–Palo Alto phone calls for free. Though Draper's probation specified that he refuse to divulge his phone-hacking secrets, he was unable to resist when people asked; the hacker in his blood just let the information flow. "In the next fifteen minutes, he proceeded to tell me everything I needed to know [to build a blue box]," Sokol later said. But when Sokol put the blue box together it didn't work; he let Draper know and that next Saturday, Draper, accompanied by Steve Wozniak, came over. They looked over Sokol's box. "Looks OK," said Draper, and began adjusting the tones by ear. This time, when Sokol tried the blue box, it worked. Sokol would use the box only for connecting to the computer—a practice which in the hacker mind justifies lawbreaking—and not for personal gain in trivial matters like calling distant relatives.

Wozniak took a look at Sokol's "kluge," the computer he'd gotten from bartering liberated parts, and they both lamented the high cost of hardware hacking. Woz complained that even though he worked for Hewlett-Packard the sales people wouldn't part with any chips for him. At the next Homebrew meeting, Dan Sokol presented Wozniak with a box full of parts that would work with a Motorola 6800 microprocessor. Woz got a 6800 manual and began designs for a computer that would interface with the TV Typewriter he'd built. When someone brought a computer to a Homebrew meeting that had video included, he knew that his computer. would have to have video built in, too. He liked the idea of a computer you could play a videogame on. Around that time the Wescon computer show was being held, and Wozniak went by the MOS Technology booth and found that they were selling early models of their new microprocessor chip, the 6502, for only twenty dollars. Since the chip wasn't much different from the Motorola 6800, he bought a handful, and decided that the 6502 would be the heart of his new machine.

Wozniak was not thinking of building a computer to sell. He was building a computer to have fun with, to show to his friends. He would mention what he was doing to his friend Steve Jobs at Atari, who was interested in terminals and thinking about setting up a company that made them. Every two weeks Woz would go to Homebrew and see or hear what was new, never having any problem in following up on technical details because everyone was free with information. Some things he would incorporate into the computer; for instance, when he saw the Dazzler board, he knew he wanted color graphics. He knew, of course, that he wanted a BASIC, and since the only BASIC that ran on the 6502 then was Tom Pittman's Tiny BASIC, and Woz wanted a "big" BASIC, he wrote his own. He gave out the code to anyone who wanted it, and would even print some of his subroutines in *Dr. Dobbs Journal.*

By the time he was finished, he had a computer which was not really a kit or an assembled computer, but one board loaded with chips and circuitry. With just that board, you could do nothing, but when you attached a power supply and a keyboard and a video monitor and a cassette tape player to the board, you would have a working computer with video display, mass storage, and input/output. You could then load in Steve Wozniak's "Integer BASIC" and write programs. There were several amazing things about his computer, not the least of which was that he had delivered the power and capabilities of an Altair and several boards on one much smaller board. What it took other people two chips to do, Woz did in one. This was not only fiscally prudent, but a sort of technical machismo reminiscent of the code-bumming of TMRC days, when

Samson, Saunders, and Kotok would attempt to whittle a subroutine down to the fewest instructions.

Wozniak later explained why the board used so few chips: "I'm into it for esthetic purposes and I like to consider myself clever. That's my puzzle, and I do designs that use one less chip than the last guy. I would think how could I do this faster or smaller or more cleverly. If [I work on something] considered a good job using six instructions, I try it in five or three, or two if I want to win [big]. I do tricky things that aren't normal. Every problem has a better solution when you start thinking it differently than the normal way. And I see them—every single day I see several problems, I ask if it's a hardware problem, I start looking at a lot of techniques I've done before, counters and feedback or chip registers . . . a bottom-line approach, looking for little specific end points from a hierarchy . . . it creates basically a sort of different mathematics. The discoveries did increase my motivation because I would have something to show off and I hoped that other people would see them and say, 'Thank God, that's how I want to do it,' and that's what I got from the Homebrew Club."

Wozniak brought the board, along with the hardware to make it work, to Homebrew. He didn't have a cassette recorder, and while the meeting went on he sat outside, frantically typing in the hexadecimal code—3,000 bytes' worth—of the 3K BASIC interpreter into the machine. He would run a test on part of the program, and the test might clobber it and he'd start over again. Finally it was running, though it was only a preliminary version which didn't have the full command set, and when people drifted over Wozniak would explain, in his breathless, high-speed drone, what the thing could do.

It was not long before Wozniak addressed the entire Homebrew Computer Club, holding his board in the air and fielding questions from the members, most of them asking how he did this or if he was going to put this feature or that into it. They were good ideas, and Wozniak brought his setup every two weeks, sitting in the back of the auditorium where the electrical outlet was, getting suggestions for improvements and incorporating those improvements.

Woz's friend Steve Jobs was very excited about the board; he thought that, like Processor Technology and Cromemco, they should make the boards in quantity and sell them. Jobs, at twenty-two, was a couple of years younger than Wozniak, and not much cleaner. He had what was described as a "Fidel Castro beard," often went shoeless, and had a Californian interest in Oriental philosophies and vegetarianism. He was a tireless promoter, silver-tongued, a deft persuader. Soon the pair was known as "the two Steves," and Wozniak's computer was known as the Apple, a name conceived by Jobs, who once worked in an orchard. Though the official address of the as yet unincorporated Apple company was a mail drop, Jobs and Wozniak really worked out of a garage. For capital, Jobs sold his Volkswagen bus and Woz sold his HP programmable calculator. Jobs placed ads in hobbyist publications and they began selling Apples for the price of $666.66. Anyone in Homebrew could take a look at the schematics for the design, Woz's BASIC was given away free with purchase of a piece of equipment that connected the computer to a cassette recorder, and Woz published the routines for his 6502 "monitor," which enabled you to look into memory and see what instructions were stored, in magazines like *Dr. Dobbs*. The Apple ad even said, "our philosophy is to provide software for our machines free or at minimal cost."

While the selling was going on, Steve Wozniak began working on an expanded design of the board, something that would impress his Homebrew peers even more. Steve Jobs·had plans to sell many computers based on this new design, and he started getting financing, support, and professional help for the day the product would be ready. The new version of Steve Wozniak's computer would be called the Apple II, and at the time no one suspected that it would become the most important computer in history.

•

It was the fertile atmosphere of Homebrew that guided Steve Wozniak through the incubation of the Apple II. The exchange of information, the access to esoteric technical hints, the swirling creative energy, and the chance to blow everybody's mind with a well-hacked design or program . . . these were the incentives which only increased the intense desire Steve Wozniak already had: to build the kind of computer he wanted to play with. Computing was the boundary of his desires; he was not haunted by visions of riches and fame, nor was he obsessed by dreams of a world of end users exposed to computers. He liked his work at HP, and loved the heady atmosphere of being around the gentleman engineers atop the computer industry. At one point Wozniak asked his bosses at HP if they wanted him to design the Apple computer for them—they thought it was unmarketable, and gave him a release to sell it on his own. When it looked like HP would be setting up a small computer division, Wozniak applied for a transfer; but, according to Alan Baum, "the head of the lab wasn't impressed. He had no degree." (Woz had left Berkeley before graduation.)

So he worked on the Apple II, often until 4 A.M.—he would soon be one more Homebrew member divorced by a computer widow. Designing the Apple II was no picnic. There were hundreds of problems in making a ready-to-program, self-contained computer-and-terminal combination; Wozniak did not have even the moderate resources and cash flow that Bob Marsh and Lee Felsenstein had when they designed the Sol, the first computer-terminal combination and one of many inspirations for the Apple II. But he had a vision of what he wanted his computer to be, and could draw on help from Homebrew and other experts in the Valley. Finally he had a prototype working. He and Randy Wigginton carried it—a loose but fully connected jumble of parts and boards —over to a December 1976 Homebrew meeting in a couple of boxes, along with a klunky Sears color TV.

Years later, the people attending that Homebrew meeting would recall different versions of the reaction to Stephen Wozniak's presentation of the Apple II. Wozniak, and the other fans of the 6502 chip, came out with the impression that the computer had thrilled everyone. Others thought it was simply one more advance in the frantic climb toward an ultimate homebrewed computer. As Lee Felsenstein put it, "The people in Homebrew were not sitting around waiting for the Apple to happen: people were making stuff, talking about stuff, showing stuff off."

One thing that did not excite the members was the fact that the production models of the Apple would come only in fully assembled form—why buy a computer, hardware hackers thought, if you could not build it yourself? The hard-core old-liners, who respected the solidity and predictability of the Processor Technology and Cromemco products, thought the Apple interesting, especially in its economical circuitry and its color capabilities, but not as good a machine as the Sol, which was based on the familiar Altair bus (newly named the S-100 bus by a consensus of manufacturers, notably Marsh and Garland, who were sick of referring to a part of their computers with the name of a competitor who in most unhackerish spirit seemed to resent their existence). The Apple had an entirely new bus and a brand-new operating system, both designed by Woz; plus, there was the unfamiliar 6502 chip as its brain. Also, a proven company like Processor Technology seemed more likely to be able to support a machine in the field than did Apple, which apparently consisted only of two kids in a garage.

Basically, though, the disagreement came down to religious issues of design. The Sol reflected Lee Felsenstein's apocalyptic fears, shaped by post-holocaust science fiction, that the industrial infrastructure might be snatched away at any time, and people should be able to scrounge parts to keep his machine going in the rubble of this devastated society; ideally, the machine's design would be clear enough to allow users to figure out where to put those parts. "I've got to design so you can put it together out of garbage cans," Felsenstein once said. "In part because that's what I started from, but mostly because I don't trust the industrial structure—they might decide to suppress us weirdos and try to deny us the parts we need." This philosophy was expressed in the VDM and the Sol itself, both of which were products which did their job cleanly, in a not overly flashy manner, and with a proletarian lack of sentimentality.

Steve Wozniak's Apple was another story. Growing up in a conventional family in the sheltered, suburban California world of single homes, science fairs, and McDonald's burgers, Wozniak had inbred security. He felt comfortable taking chances, letting the design go as far as his imagination could take him. He created an esthetic wonder by optimizing a limited number of off-the-shelf electronic parts so that, very ingeniously laid out and wired, they delivered not only the power of a PDP-1, but color, motion, and sound.

If Woz had his way, he would add features forever. Just two days before the meeting, he had jimmied up the machine so that it could display special, high-resolution color graphics. He did this not by the usual way of adding special chips to do it, but by figuring out a way to wire the machine so that the central processing unit, the 6502, could do double duty.

Woz's genius for optimization sometimes had odd effects. For example, the way the Apple filled the screen with an image was much different than the Sol's method, which filled things in by a proper order; the Apple drew its screen in a seemingly haphazard, crazy-quilt manner. It did this not by chance, but because Woz figured out that doing it that way would save an instruction for each line put on the screen. A clever trick, disdained by some who thought it indicative of the Apple's unpredictability and "flakiness," but much admired by those who could appreciate the beauty of a maximized design. All in all, the design reflected a tour de force of hacking, and a very savvy engineer could see the clever twists of plot, the optimistic flights of fancy, and the eccentrically cosmic jokes embodied in the machine.

One person who thought that the Apple II was just super was Chris Espinosa, a young acquaintance of Randy Wigginton. Espinosa was a skinny, pale fourteen-year-old high school kid who loved computers and flunked math classes because he felt that doing homework was a non-optimal use of time. He was enthralled by this computer of Steve Wozniak's. From the explanation of the syntax of Woz's special BASIC commands which came out in the talk, and the explanation of sketches of the machine's innards distributed all around, Espinosa jotted down some BASIC programs, and during the random access period of the meeting, when people crowded around this new machine, he took over the keyboard and frantically hammered in some programs which created flashy color displays on the big old Sears television set Wozniak had dragged along. Wozniak was thrilled: "I didn't think somebody else could come up and show me—'Look!'—and get excited and show other people and say, 'Look, this is easy, you just put this command in and you do this.' " Here was this high school kid, running programs on this little computer Wozniak had built. Steve Jobs' reaction was more pragmatic—he hired Chris Espinosa as one of the company's first employees. Like the other teen-age software specialist, Randy Wigginton, he would earn three dollars an hour.

Steve Jobs was concentrating full-time on building up the Apple company to get ready to deliver the Apple II the following year and make a big splash in the marketplace. Jobs was a brilliant talker who, according to Alan Baum, "worked his tail off . . . he told me about the prices he was getting for parts, and they were favorable to the prices HP was paying." As an engineer, Jobs was mediocre; his strength was as a planner, someone with vision to see how computers could extend to a point of usefulness beyond that dreamed of by pure hackers like Steve Wozniak. He was also wise enough to realize that as a long-haired twenty-two-year-old whose customary garb was jeans and bare feet, he was not the person to head a major computer corporation; most of all, he lacked management and marketing experience. He decided that he would hire top-notch, high-priced management talent to run Apple Computer.

This was no easy conclusion in those days, when engineers like Ed Roberts and Bob Marsh thought that building a quality machine was the main ingredient for success, and management might take care of itself. Ed Roberts learned the folly of this, the hard way. By mid-1976, Roberts had tired of the "soap opera" (in his words) that MITS had become, with frustrated customers, a confusing line of several new and improved versions of the Altair, hundreds of employees, vicious internal politics, perpetually panicked dealers, hopelessly muddled finances, and not a decent night's sleep in over a year. He had been designing an exciting new Altair 2 computer—a high-powered, compact machine which could fit in a briefcase—but most of his energies were spent in management squabbles. So he decided to call it, he later said, "a page in my life—it was time to move on to the next page," and he stunned the world of hardware hackers by selling the company to a big firm called Pertec. By the end of the year, Roberts, with his million-dollar-plus buy-out, left the business and became a farmer in southern Georgia.

The moral of the story was that engineers can't necessarily run companies. But finding people who can isn't easy, especially when your company, on the surface at least, looks like a small coven of hippies and high school kids. Chris Espinosa later noted that, in early 1977, Jobs looked so slovenly that "they wouldn't let him on to minibuses and airplanes, much less into the corridors of power of the semiconductor industry," yet he pulled off a major coup by getting Mike Markkula on the Apple team. Markkula was a former marketing whiz, now in his mid-thirties, who'd retired from Intel a few years back; he had been spending his time since then in various pursuits, some business-oriented, some as odd as inventing a wheelchart to show different fingering positions for guitar chords. Jobs asked him to help draw a business plan for the Apple, and Markkula wound up helping to get venture capital for the company and signing up as its first chairman of the board. It was through Markkula that Jobs also got a nuts-and-bolts manager from Fairchild Semiconductor named Mike Scott to become president of the firm. So, while the most prominent company with a terminal-computer on the market, Processor Technology, was struggling with the inexperienced management of hardware hackers Bob Marsh and Gary Ingram, Apple was set for growth.

This real-world activity hadn't really sunk in as far as Steve Wozniak was concerned. Chris Espinosa and Randy Wigginton would come over to his house from playing with Wigginton's half-built version of the Apple II, and there, on the living room floor of Woz's small place, they would debug programs and hardware, write tone generation programs, solder boards. It was fun. Meanwhile, in his own garage, Jobs was running the day-to-day operations. "He would come by every once in a while and see what we were doing, make recommendations, but he didn't do any designing," Espinosa later said. "He would pass judgment, which is his major talent: over the keyboards, the case design, the logo, what parts to buy, how to lay out the PC board to look nice, the arrangement of parts, the dealers we chose . . . the method of assembly, the distribution method, everything."

He was guided in this by the experienced hand of Mike Markkula, who was taking the Apple venture very seriously. One thing he apparently recognized was that Steve Wozniak's commitment was to the computer rather than to the company. To Woz, the Apple was a brilliant hack, not an investment. It was his art, not his business. He got his payment by solving puzzles, saving chips, impressing people at Homebrew. This was fine for hacking, but Markkula wanted, at the least, Wozniak's full-time participation in the company. He told Jobs to tell his partner that if Woz wanted there to be an Apple Computer company, he must quit HP for all-out work on pre-production of the Apple II.

It was a tough decision for Wozniak. "This was different than the year we spent throwing the Apple I together in the garage," Wozniak later recalled. "This was a real *company*. I designed a computer because I like to design, to show off at the club. My motivation was not to have a company and make money. Mike was giving me three days to say yes or no, was I going to leave HP. I liked HP. They were a good company and I was secure and there was a lot of good work. I didn't want to leave, and I said no."

Steve Jobs heard the decision, and called Wozniak's friends and relatives, begging them to persuade Woz to quit HP and work for Apple full-time. Some of them did, and as Woz heard the arguments he reconsidered. Why not work to let the Apple II go out into the world? But even as he agreed to quit HP and work with Jobs full-time, he told himself that what he was doing was no longer pure hacking. The truth was that starting a company had nothing to do with hacking or creative design. It was about making money. It was "stepping over the boundary," as Wozniak later put it. Not in any kind of rip-off—Wozniak believed in his computer and had confidence in the team that would produce and sell it—but "there's no way I would associate Apple with doing good computer design in my head. It wasn't the reason for starting Apple. The reason for starting Apple after the computer design is there's something else—that's to make money."

It was a crucial decision that would symbolize the shift taking place in small computers. Now that hackers like Wozniak were building machines with terminals and keyboards, machines which might presumably be useful to people other than hobbyists, the direction of the budding industry was no longer in the hands of those hackers. It was almost twenty years after the TMRC hackers had been introduced to the TX-0. Now, going into business was The Right Thing.

In January of 1977, the half-dozen or so employees of this new firm, which would not incorporate until that March, moved into a cramped space on Stevens Creek Boulevard in Cupertino, within stone-throwing distance of a 7-Eleven and a Good Earth health food restaurant. Wozniak preferred to walk down the street to go to Bob's Big Boy. First thing in the morning, he and Wigginton would go there, order a cup of coffee, take a sip out of it, and talk about how bad the coffee was, leaving the almost full cup on the table. It was sort of a ritual. Woz had a fondness for taking packets of Fizine, a bubbling antacid, and emptying them into the sugar containers at Bob's, where he would wait until some unsuspecting customer put what he thought was sugar in his coffee. It would erupt like a small volcano, and Woz would get a big kick out of it. But often Woz would just talk, mostly technical stuff, and sometimes about Apple. Wigginton and Espinosa, both still in high school, had taken some of Jobs' planner-like hyperbole to heart—they all had to some degree—and believed that the Homebrew crusade was focused right there on Stevens Creek Boulevard. "Everybody was so much into it," Wigginton later said. "We were motivated more by a dream of what was going to happen than by what was actually happening. That we would be a successful company and were going to come out with the neatest product that had ever been produced."

They would often work around the clock, soldering, designing, and programming. One of Woz's friends hired as a hardware specialist would make bird calls as he worked. Woz would pull pranks, play games, and then do an incredible amount of work in a brief burst. Woz and his friends were preparing a different kind of computer than the previous bestsellers, the Altair, Sol, and IMSAI. Steve Jobs and Mike Markkula felt that the Apple's market went well beyond hobbyists, and to make the machine *look* friendlier, Jobs hired an industrial designer to construct a sleek, low-profile plastic case in a warm beige earth color. He made sure that Woz's layout would be appealing once the lid of the case was lifted. The Apple bus, like the S-100 bus, was capable of accepting extra cir-

cuit boards to make it do interesting things, but Woz had taken
some advice from his friend Alan Baum and made it so that the
eight "expansion slots" inside the Apple were especially easy for
manufacturers to make compatible circuit boards for. They would
be helped, of course, by the "open" architecture of the machine;
true to the Hacker Ethic, Woz made sure the Apple had no secrets
to prevent people from creating on it. Every twist and turn of his
design, every coding trick in his BASIC interpreter (which would
be included inside this machine, hard-wired into a custom circuit
chip) would be documented and distributed to anyone who wanted
to see.

At certain points, Woz and Jobs relied on their Homebrew connections for help. A good example was what happened with a
potential problem in getting FCC approval of the computer. Rod
Holt, an engineer from Atari who had been helping design the
power supply, sadly declared that the machine's connector to a
television set—called the Radio Frequency (RF) Modulator—gave
off too much interference, and would never pass muster with the
FCC. So Steve Jobs went to Marty Spergel, the Junk Man.

Spergel would often show up at Homebrew meetings, holding
some esoteric part and giving it away. "I'd look through my junk
box and say, 'Here's a box full of A through Z,' and people would
run over at six hundred miles an hour and before I could even let
go of the box it was gone." He had a nose for niches in the electronics market, and had recently made a killing by importing joy-
stick controllers from Hong Kong so that people could play games
like Steve Dompier's "Target" on Altairs and Sols. At one point,
his company, M&R Electronics, even introduced a computer kit,
but that product never really caught on. One day Marty visited the
one-room Apple headquarters in Cupertino and talked to Woz,
Jobs, and Rod Holt about the modulator situation. It was clear
that Apple could not ship the computers with the current modulators, so it was decided that Holt would give Marty Spergel the
specifications for the modulator, and *he* would build them. "My
part was keeping the FCC away from Apple Computer," Spergel
later said. "So what I did was ship modulators out of my door,
Apple shipping Apples out of their door. But when they got to the
dealers, the dealers would sell a modulator to the end user, and
when the end user [went] home he could plug in the modulator.
Consequently, it's now the end user's responsibility [to prevent RF
interference]."

It was a classic case of Homebrew sharing, with everybody benefiting, to get around a bureaucratic obstacle. Spergel asked Jobs about how many modulators, which M&R would sell under the name "Sup'r Mod" for about thirty dollars each, would be required. Jobs promised it would be high volume. Perhaps even fifty units a month.

Several years later, Spergel estimated he had sold four hundred thousand Sup'r Mods.

•

In early 1977, Homebrew Computer Club member and editor of *Dr. Dobbs Journal* Jim Warren was hatching a rather large scheme himself. Warren was the short-haired, wide-faced, bearded fellow who collected "technogossip" as a hobby, and saw Homebrew as an outlet to spew all sorts of rumors about firms in the "Silicon Gulch," as he called it. Often, his rumors were accurate. In addition to his editorial duties and his activities as a silicon *yenta,* Warren was in a self-described "dissertation mode" at Stanford. But the quantum growth rate of the personal computer interested him more than a doctorate. He was a fan, regarding the homebrew computer movement as a sort of post–Free University, take-your-clothes-off-and-get-dirty, humanistic lovefest.

His attendance at the PC '76 computer show in Atlantic City had reinforced that belief. He hadn't wanted to go at first, considering that faded resort as "the crotch of the nation," but the show's promoter had called him up and told him about all the exciting people who'd be there, adding how great it would be for the editor of *Dr. Dobbs* to be in attendance, and Jim Warren felt somewhat frustrated because, with Bob Albrecht paying him only $350 a month to edit the magazine, he had to beg for the money for the trip. He figured that the big show should be right there, in California. One night he was talking to Bob Reiling, an engineer at Philco who had quietly taken over Fred Moore's duties as editor of the Homebrew newsletter. Warren asked why the hell all that stuff was happening on the wrong coast when the undisputed center of the microcomputer world was right here. Reiling agreed, and Warren decided that they should do it, put on a show which would also, in hacker spirit, be an exchange of information, equipment, technical knowledge, and good vibrations. It could have the idyllic atmosphere of the annual "Renaissance Faire" in Marin County—a genuine "Computer *Faire.*"

He was thinking about this show when he got to Atlantic City, which despite the horrid humidity and the dilapidated facilities was, he later said, "a complete turn-on. [You met] all the people you'd talked to on the phone or gotten a letter from who were doing things . . . [you had] tremendous excitement over meeting the people who were doing the deeds." They were a powerful new interfacing feature, these face-to-face meetings, which provided much fresher information than you got in publications. *"Dr. Dobbs* had a six-week lead time and it was driving me crazy. Hell, six months was half a generation of machines. The opportunity to talk to people about what they were doing *that week* was a radical improvement. So it was in that kind of environment that I announced that we were going to do a Computer Faire on the West Coast."

With Reiling as his partner, Warren set out to organize the event. He was soon daunted by the fact that the ideal location, the Civic Auditorium in San Francisco, charged a considerable rental fee. Thousands of dollars a day! After hearing this, Warren and Reiling drove down to the peninsula, stopping at Pete's Harbor, an open-air café by the bayside marina, a favorite haunt of Albrecht and the PCC crowd. Warren recalls: "I remember saying, 'Boy, we're really getting in deep. Can we afford this?' And I pulled a napkin out of a big napkin holder and began scribbling. How many exhibits to expect. How many attendees. If they drew thirty-five hundred in Atlantic City, we should double that . . . maybe draw as many as seven thousand. How much to charge for exhibitors and attendees? Multiply it out. Add it up . . ." And Jim Warren was astonished to find out that not only could they afford it, but they could make a *profit* out of it. And certainly there was nothing wrong with that.

Jim Warren got on the phone and began calling the presidents of the biggest companies in the industry, most of whom he knew personally from Homebrew or his magazine work. "I phoned up Bob Marsh and said, 'Hey, we're going to do a Computer Faire, are you interested?' and he said, 'Hell yeah.' 'Okay, send some money and we'll get you exhibit space. Far out.' We phoned up Harry Garland from Cromemco. 'This is Jim Warren, we're doing a Computer Faire. Want in on it?' 'Sure, fine.' 'Yeah, well, we'll get a booth plan to you as soon as we get a chance. Send us the money because we need some.' I think it took us four days before we were in the black."

Warren turned out to have considerable talents as a promoter. He began a tabloid newspaper specifically to pump up excitement about the Faire, and, incidentally, to spread his brand of technogossip. It was called *Silicon Gulch Gazette,* and there were stories about what the Faire would be like and little profiles of some of the speakers, and also a profile of "chaircreature" Jim Warren. The paper boasted of the Faire's "co-sponsorship" arrangements with nonprofit groups like the Homebrew Computer Club, SCCS, PCC and its offshoot, Community Computer Center (CCC), and others. (Joanne Koltnow, who helped out the Faire from her job at CCC, later said that "everyone was shocked" when they later discovered that the Faire was a for-profit organization.) With a staff of two secretaries, Warren and his partners worked almost around the clock as the Faire progressed.

Also working frantically before the Faire were the eight employees of Apple Computer. Apple had taken space for two of the $350 ten-foot-square booths and somehow managed to wangle the prime space near the entrance to the exhibit hall. The idea was to take advantage of that break to officially introduce the Apple II at the Faire. Though many around the Homebrew Club did not take Apple as a serious entry in the market (Gordon French came by one day and went away scoffing that the company was still basically two guys in a garage), there was now serious money behind Apple. One day the new president, Mike Scott, had told Chris Espinosa to copy the demo software that ran a "Breakout" game. It was a game Jobs had done for Atari and Woz had rewritten for Apple BASIC, and at the end of the game, the program rated your score with a comment. Scott said, by the way, could Chris also change the comments, making the screen say "Not Good" instead of "Pure Shit"? The reason was, some Bank of America people were coming to talk about a line of credit.

So the Apple people were prepared to spend for the show. They hired a decorator to design the booth, and they prepared professional-looking signs with their spiffy new logo, a rainbow-colored apple with a bite out of it. They worked frantically down to the last minute before they had to drive the machines up to San Francisco; they had planned to have four Apple IIs running, and those would be the only existing prototypes. On the night of April 15, the cases arrived, fresh from being made out of injection molds. As everyone worked to put the innards of the computers into those cases, it was clear how different the Apple II was from the competition (with the possible exception of the Sol). Everyone else's computer looked like the kind of thing that a combat radio operator might have strapped to his back. The Apple had no visible screws or bolts (the ten screws mainly hooked from underneath): just a sleek, warm, friendly variation of a typewriter, futuristic in its low slope, but not so harshly angled that it looked menacing. Inside the machine was the evidence of Woz's hackerish tinkering. He had gotten the number of chips down to an astonishing sixty-two, including the powerful 6502 central processing unit. In fact, when you opened the snap-on lid of the machine, what you saw was Woz's "motherboard"—the chip-loaded green circuit card that was the Apple I, souped up—a silvery power supply the size of a stack of Ritz crackers, and the eight expansion slots which indicated the infinite uses to which you might apply the machine. By the time the screws and rivet holes were inserted in the case, and the motherboards attached, and the base plates bolted, and everything was tested and the lids were snapped on, it was one in the morning of the Apple's official world debut.

On time that morning, the Apples were in the booth, near the entrance. Most every other company relied on the tried and true yellow-curtained backdrop with pasted-on cardboard signs spelling out the company name in block letters. But Apple's booth gleamed with its six-color Plexiglass logo.

Jim Warren was at the site very early that morning, of course, riding on adrenaline after his nonstop sixteen-hour days of preparation. Just two days before, he and Reiling had incorporated the Faire as a for-profit organization. Though he considered it a "load of bureaucratic bullshit legalistic crap," Reiling had pointed out that as a partnership they were individually liable for any damages, and Warren had gone along. There was really no doubt as to where Jim Warren was headed by then—as a person who knew the Hacker Ethic well, he also could see what was happening in his own Silicon Gulch backyard. The Real World had arrived, and it was time for a merger between the two cultures, hacker and industrial, because if there was a clash there would be no question who would lose. The hardware hackers had let the microcomputer cat out of the bag, and the multimillion-dollar yearly grosses at MITS, Processor Technology, and IMSAI in 1976 were irrefutable proof that this was a growth industry, worthy of heavy money and the changes that implied. Jim Warren loved the hacker spirit, but he was a survivor, too. If he lost money, or suffered some sort of disaster by sticking to his post-hippie, idealistic, antibureaucratic phobias, it would not help hackerism one bit. Whereas his making money would perhaps not be harmful at all to the Hacker Ethic. So even though, as he later put it, he "didn't care diddly shit about booths and power and contracts and all that stuff," he went with it.

The micro world was changing. He needed no further evidence of this than the scene at the ticket booths outside of the grand, Greek-columned edifice that was the San Francisco Civic Center.

On that sunny, bright April day in 1977, there were thousands of people standing in five long lines, snaking around both sides of the block-long auditorium and meeting in the back. A block-long beaded necklace of hackers, would-be hackers, people curious about hackers, or people wanting to know what was *going on* in this freaky new world where computers meant something different than a guy in a white shirt and black tie and fat billfold and dulled-out expression which all added up to IBM. True, the lines were there in large part because Jim Warren's inexperience had resulted in a total screw-up in preregistration and ticket sales. For instance, instead of one fixed price for day-of-sale entry, there were different rates—eight dollars for general public, four dollars for students, five dollars for Homebrew Computer Club members, and so on. And because it cost ten dollars an hour for cashiers, Warren had decided not to hire too many extras. Now, with almost twice as many people arriving as anticipated, and everyone seeming to have arrived early, it was the kind of situation which could get out of hand.

But it did not get out of hand. Everyone was looking around in disbelief that *all these people were into computers,* that the secret hacker lust they'd had for machines, often as solipsistic little kids, tiny Greenblatts or Wozniaks, was not so aberrant after all. Loving computers was no longer a forbidden public practice. So it was no ordeal at all, standing with these people waiting to get into the First Annual West Coast Computer Faire. As Jim Warren later recalled: "We had these lines running all around the fucking building and nobody was irritated. Nobody was pushy. We didn't know what we were doing and the exhibitors didn't know what they were doing and the attendees didn't know what was going on, but everybody was excited and congenial and nondemanding and it was a tremendous turn-on. People just stood and talked—'Oh, you've got an Altair? Far out!' 'You solved this problem?' And nobody was irritated."

When people got inside the hall, it was wall-to-wall techno-freak, the sounds of voices mingling with the clatter of printers and the tinny tones of three or four different strains of computer-generated music. If you wanted to move from one place to another, you would have to gauge which part of the constant flow of people was moving in which direction, and you would shoulder your way into the proper stream and go with it until you reached your destination. Almost every one of the nearly two hundred exhibitors had packed booths. Particularly Processor Technology, which was running Steve Dompier's "Target" game on Sol computers. People were also pushing into IMSAI's booth to get biorhythms charted. And right there at the entrance, the wave of the future, was Apple, running a kaleidoscopic video graphics program on a huge Advent display monitor. "It was crazy," Randy Wigginton, who was working in the booth with Woz and Chris Espinosa and the others, later recalled. "Everybody was coming by and asking for demonstrations, and it was fun because people were excited about it."

It wasn't only the Apple that people were excited about. It was the triumph of the hardware hackers in making their passion into an industry. You could see the excitement as people looked around disbelievingly at their sheer numbers—all these people?—and there was a huge roar when Jim Warren got on the public-address system and announced the attendance—the weekend's total was almost thirteen thousand. He was immediately followed by *Computer Lib* author Ted Nelson, feeling no doubt like a once lonesome guru who in one fell swoop was united with a sea of disciples. "This is Captain Kirk," Nelson said. "Prepare for blastoff!"

Warren himself was long past lift-off. He shot around the Faire on a pair of roller skates, marveling at how far the movement had come. For him, as for the people at Apple, Processor Technology, and dozens of other places, this success had very welcome financial implications; soon after the Faire was over, after recovering from a period of what he would later call "ecstatic collapse," Warren would be considering whether to sink his profits into a Mercedes SL. He would finally decide to buy forty acres of land he was coveting in the hills overlooking Woodside, and within a few years he would have built a huge wooden structure with a redwood deck and hot tub overlooking the Pacific; it would be his home and computerized work quarters, from which a staff of over a dozen would prepare a small empire of publications and computer shows. Jim Warren understood the future.

The first Computer Faire was to the hardware hackers an event comparable to Woodstock in the movement of the sixties. Like the concert at Max Yasgur's farm, this was both a cultural vindication and a signal that the movement had gotten so big that it no longer belonged to its progenitors. The latter revelation was slow to sink in. Everyone was flying, moving from booth to booth, seeing all sorts of ground-breaking hardware and mind-blowing software, meeting people you could swap subroutines and wire-wrapping schemes with, and attending some of the nearly one hundred workshops, which included Lee Felsenstein on the Community Memory movement, Tom Pittman on computer languages, Bob Kahn on the Lawrence Hall of Science computing program, Marc LeBrun on computer music, and Ted Nelson on the triumphant future.

Nelson was one of the keynote speakers at a banquet held at the nearby St. Francis Hotel. The name of his talk was "Those Unforgettable Next Two Years," and looking over that mass of people drawn by micros, he opened by saying, "Here we are at the brink of a new world. Small computers are about to remake our society, and you know it." As far as Nelson was concerned, the battle was won—the hackers had overthrown the evil Prophet. "IBM will be in disarray," Nelson crowed. It was truly a wonderful world about to unfold:

> For now, though, the dinky computers are working magic enough. They will bring about changes in society as radical as those brought about by the telephone or the automobile. The little computers are here, you can buy them on your plastic charge card, and the available accessories include disc storage, graphic displays, interactive games, programmable turtles that draw pictures on butcher paper, and goodness knows what else. Here we have all the makings of a fad, it is fast blossoming into a cult, and soon it will mature into a full-blown consumer market.
>
> FAD! CULT! CONSUMER MARKET! The rush will be on. The American manufacturing publicity machine will go ape. American society will go out of its gourd. And the next two years will be unforgettable.

13

SECRETS

TED Nelson's speech was not the crazed outburst of a planner overdosing on large-scale integration. The unforgettable next two years were indeed marked by unprecedented growth in the industry that was almost unwittingly started by the hardware hackers. The hackers in Homebrew either went into business, trotted off to one of the new companies forming in the opening stages of this microcomputer boom, or kept doing what they had always been doing: hacking. The planners, those who had seen the advent of the small computer as a means of spreading hacker spirit, generally did not pause to evaluate the situation: things were moving too fast for contemplation. Left by the wayside were purists like Fred Moore, who once wrote in a treatise entitled "Put Your Trust in People, Not Money" that money was "obsolete, valueless, anti-life." Money was the means by which computer power was beginning to spread, and the hackers who ignored that fact were destined to work in (perhaps blissful) solipsism, either in tight, ARPA-funded communities or in meager collectives where the term "hand-to-mouth" was a neat analogy for a "chip-to-machine" existence.

The West Coast Computer Faire had been the resounding first step of hardware hackers making their move from Silicon Valley garages into the bedrooms and dens of America. Before the end of 1977, the other shoe dropped. Megamillion-dollar companies introduced computer-terminal combinations requiring no assembly, computers to be sold like appliances. One of those machines was the Commodore PET, designed by the man who devised the same 6502 chip that was the core of the Apple. Another was the Radio Shack TRS-80 computer, a computer stamped in plastic, assembly-lined, and sold *en masse* in hundreds of Radio Shack stores across the country.

No longer was it a struggle, a learning process, to make computers. So the pioneers of Homebrew, many of whom had switched from building computers to *manufacturing* computers, had not a common bond, but competition to maintain market share. It retarded Homebrew's time-honored practice of sharing all techniques, of refusing to recognize secrets, and of keeping information going in an unencumbered flow. When it was Bill Gates' Altair BASIC that was under consideration, it was easy to maintain the Hacker Ethic. Now, as major shareholders of companies supporting hundreds of employees, the hackers found things not so simple. All of a sudden, they had secrets to keep.

"It was amazing to watch the anarchists put on a different shirt," Dan Sokol later recalled. "People stopped coming. Homebrew [still moderated by Lee Felsenstein, who kept the hacker fire burning] was still anarchistic: people would ask you about the company, and you'd have to say, 'I can't tell you that.' I solved that the way other people did—I didn't go. I didn't want to go and not tell people things. There would be no easy way out where you would feel good about that."

Homebrew still drew hundreds to its meetings, and its mailing list was over fifteen hundred—but there were many novices there, with problems that weren't challenging to old hands who'd built machines when machines were nearly impossible to build. It no longer was *essential* to go to meetings. Many of the people involved in companies like Apple, Processor Tech, and Cromemco were too damned busy. And the companies themselves provided the communities around which to share information.

Apple was a good example. Steve Wozniak and his two young friends, Espinosa and Wigginton, were too busy with the young firm to keep going to Homebrew. Chris Espinosa later explained: "[After the Computer Faire] our attendance at Homebrew started dropping off and ended completely by the end of the summer of 1977. We, in effect, created our own computer club [at Apple] that was more focused, more dedicated to producing things. When we started getting involved with Apple, we found what we wanted to work on and we wanted to spend all our time perfecting it, expanding it, doing more for it, and we wanted to go into one subject deeper rather than covering the field and finding out what everybody was doing. And that's how you make a company."

In some senses, the "computer club" at Apple's Cupertino headquarters reflected the same community feeling and sharing of Homebrew. The company's formal goals were traditional—making money, growing, gaining market share—and some secretiveness was required even of Steve Wozniak, who considered openness the central principle of the Hacker Ethic he fervently subscribed to. But this meant that the people within the company could be even closer. They had to depend on each other to swap suggestions for floating-point BASIC or parallel printer cards. And sometimes, the community was loose enough to accept some old Homebrew friends. For instance, in mid-1977, John Draper appeared.

The former "Captain Crunch" was in a bad way. Apparently certain authorities had objected to his willingness to share phone company secrets with anyone who bothered to ask; FBI agents trailed him and, according to his accounts of the incident, planted an informer who talked him into a blue-box escapade while agents waited to bust him. For this second conviction, he was sentenced to a brief jail term, and incarceration did not agree with the normally contentious Captain, a person taken to screaming like a six-foot-tall hyena if someone lit a cigarette twenty feet away from him. After his release, he needed legitimate work badly, and Woz got him hired as a consultant, designing a telephone interface board, something that would plug into one of the Apple's expansion slots to allow you to connect the phone to your computer.

Draper happily worked on the board. The people at Apple were amused by his programming style, which alternated bursts of brilliance with bizarre pedantic detours. Draper was a "defensive" programmer. Chris Espinosa, who had the unenviable task of trying to keep an eye on the unpredictable Captain, would later explain: "Say you're writing a program and you discover you've done something wrong, like every time you try to use the program, a button pops up. Most programmers go in, analyze their program, find out what causes the button to pop up and cure it so it doesn't do that. Draper would go in and code around the button so when the bug occurs, the program knows it's made an error and fixes it, rather than avoiding the error in the first place. The joke is, if Draper were writing math routines for addition and he came up with the answer $2 + 2 = 5$, he would put a clause in the program, if $2 + 2 = 5$, then that answer is 4. That's generally the way he writes programs."

But while the hackers at Apple were amused that the strange style of John Draper was turning out a featureful product, the people in charge of the business end of Apple got wind of the capabilities of Draper's design. They did not like it. Apple was not a showcase for tricks; this was not Homebrew. And John Draper's board could do some considerably neat tricks; not only did it interface with the phone, but it generated official phone company tones —it was a computer-driven blue box. What Stew Nelson had done with the PDP-1 over a decade ago could now be done in the home. The hacker instinct would have been to explore the capabilities of this hardware, which would enable you to explore systems all over the world. But though Apple felt it could benefit by the Hacker Ethic in distributing information about the innards of the machine, and distributing its computers as complete systems to explore, it was not in the business of promoting pure hackerism. It was, after all, a business, with a line of credit and a truckload of venture capital provided by men in three-piece suits who did not relate to concepts like phone hacking. "When Mike Scott discovered what [Draper's board] could do," Espinosa later said, "he axed the project instantly. It was much too dangerous to put out in the world for anybody to have."

Killing that project was well in keeping with the propriety of the booming Apple Computer Company, which was selling computers like mad, and becoming respectable at a pace which had the Homebrew alumni dazzled. Randy Wigginton, for instance, realized by late summer in 1977 that this company had far eclipsed your normal growth story. That was when everyone went to Mike Markkula's for a party to celebrate shipping a quarter-million dollars' worth of equipment that month. It was only the beginning of a climb that turned Apple into a billion-dollar company within five years.

During this period when everybody at Apple was celebrating the increasing revenues—piles of money that would make many of them so rich that they would be *beyond* millionaires, in the ozone of Croesus Mode, where wealth is counted in units of tens of millions—John Draper was at home, playing with his Apple. He set the completed board into his Apple II. He connected it to the telephone line. And he set it up so that it would "scan" entire telephone exchanges, looking for telltale tones which would inform him that a computer was on the other side of the line. A virgin computer that a hacker could enter and explore. He had hacked a program by which the computer could dial on its own. "It seemed like an innocent thing to do," he later said. On its own, the computer began making a hundred and fifty calls an hour. Every time it discovered a computer at the other end of the line, the teletype printer attached to the machine would grind out the telephone number. After nine hours, John Draper would have a printout of every computer number in an entire three-digit exchange. "I just collected them," he would later explain. The setup could also detect WATS Extenders service numbers, with which one could make free long-distance calls. (It was John Draper's system which later would be the model for a young hacker's computer break-in in the movie *WarGames.*)

Unfortunately, the ever vigilant system that was the phone company had developed some new phone-hacking detection equipment. John Draper's unprecedented output of over twenty thousand phone calls in under a week not only signaled that something was awry, but also exhausted the paper supply in the phone company printer which logged such irregularities. John Draper was confronted with another visit from the authorities. It was his third conviction, his first using a home computer. An inauspicious beginning for a new era of phone hacking with personal computers.

•

Some thought that the establishment of an industry of low-cost personal computers meant the war was won. They believed the widespread proliferation of computers and their innate lessons of openness and creative innovation would, in and of itself, spur the Hacker Ethic. But for Lee Felsenstein, the war was just beginning. His consuming passion was the resurrection of Community Memory. He still stuck to the dream whose glory he had glimpsed in the experiment at Leopold's Records. It was perhaps exquisite irony that the development of the small computer industry had been aided in part by the introduction of the Pennywhistle modem, the VDM video board, and the Sol computer, all pieces of the mythic Tom Swift Terminal, a machine which could reach fruition only in the publicly accessed terminals of Community Memory branches. Irony, because a growing consensus among Lee's peers held that the once bold Community Memory concept—and the Tom Swift Terminal itself—had been supplanted by the rapid acceptance of home computers. It was fine to desire a public terminal to be the heart of an information center that would be an "amalgam of branch libraries, game arcades, coffee houses, city parks, and post offices." But why would people leave the house to go to a CM terminal when they could use an Apple Computer, along with a telephone interface right there at home, to communicate with any data base in the world?

The Tom Swift Terminal itself might have been shelved, but Lee still held to his goals. The science-fiction novel in which he was protagonist was taking bolder plot twists, confirming that it was a major work indeed. In the two "unforgettable years" since the triumphant Computer Faire, he had seen a company crumble. Processor Technology had suffered too much growth and too little sound management to survive. Through the whole year of 1977, orders for the Sol came in at a rate beyond the capacity of the company to fulfill them. In that fiscal year, Bob Marsh later estimated, the company did five and a half million dollars' worth of sales, selling perhaps eight thousand machines. It moved into a clean, thirty-six-thousand-square-foot headquarters east of the Bay Area.

But even as the future looked bright, with Bob Marsh and Gary Ingram figuring that if sales got up to fifteen or twenty million they'd sell out and get rich, the company was doomed by lack of planning and failure to address the competition of the new, cheaper, sleeker machines like the Apple, the PET, the TRS-80. Marsh later said that the company was thinking of going into that lower end of the market, but was intimidated by the power of the competing firms that had announced complete computers in the $1,000-and-under range. He figured that PT could sell the Sol as a more expensive, quality item, like MacIntosh amplifiers in the audio business. But the company missed the chance to extend its equipment effectively when its disk drive storage system proved to be unreliable. And it was unable to deliver software for its machines on time. There would be announcements of upcoming products in the PT newsletter, a spirited publication which mixed bug reports with cryptic quotations (" 'There are no Jewish midgets'— Lenny Bruce"). Months later, the products, either software programs or hardware peripherals, would still be unavailable. When PT had an offer to sell Sol computers through a new chain of computer stores called Computerland, Marsh and Ingram refused, suspicious because the owners of the chain were the same people who ran the company (also struggling, soon to be bankrupt) which made the IMSAI computer. Instead of Sols being sold as computer-terminals at Computerland, Apples were.

"It's embarrassing to think how Mickey Mouse we were sometimes," Marsh admitted later. There was no business plan. Things would not get delivered on time, credit would not be extended to priority customers, and the constant PT errors in delivery and unprofessionalism with suppliers gave the company a reputation for arrogance and greediness.

"We were just violating some of the basic laws of nature," Marsh later said. When sales flattened, the money to run the company wasn't there. For the first time they looked for investors. Adam Osborne, an already established gadfly of the young industry, introduced them to people who were willing to invest, but Marsh and Gary Ingram did not want to give up a substantial percentage of the company. "Greedy," Osborne later said. Some months later, when the company was almost bankrupt, Marsh came back to accept the offer. It was no longer open.

"We could have been Apple," Bob Marsh said, years later. "A lot of people say that 1975 was the year of the Altair, '76 was the IMSAI, and 1977 was the Sol. The dominant machines." But by the end of those "unforgettable two years," the engineer-managed companies that made those machines, machines available in kit form as well as assembled, machines which hardware hackers loved to play with . . . were gone. The dominant small computers in the market were Apples, PETs, TRS-80s, in which the act of hardware creation was essentially done for you. People bought these machines to hack software.

Lee Felsenstein was perhaps the biggest financial beneficiary in Processor Technology's short history. He had never been an official employee, and his royalties on the Sol eventually totaled over one hundred thousand dollars. He was never paid the last twelve thousand in royalties. Most of the money went toward the new incarnation of Community Memory, which had set up a headquarters in a large, two-level, barn-like loft structure in a West Berkeley industrial area. Efrem Lipkin and Jude Milhon of the original group were among the dedicated members of the new CM Collective, all of whom vowed to work for long hours and subsistence wages to establish permanently the thrilling experiment they'd worked on earlier in the decade. It required extensive work in developing a new system; the collective decided that funding could come, in part, by writing software products for these small computers.

Meanwhile, Lee was broke. "The rational thing for me to do would have been to shut down [my engineering] business and get a job. But I didn't," he later said. Instead, he worked for almost nothing, designing a Swedish version of the Sol. His energies were divided between that, the hopelessly earnest Community Memory meetings, and monthly Homebrew meetings, which he still proudly moderated. The club was famous now that microcomputers were being acclaimed as the chief growth industry of the country. And the prime example of this was Apple Computer, which would gross $139 million in 1980, the year it went public, making Jobs and Wozniak worth a combined sum of well over $300 million. Croesus Mode.

That was the year that Lee Felsenstein ran into Adam Osborne at the Computer Faire. Jim Warren's show was now an annual event pulling in fifty thousand people in a weekend. Osborne was a trim, Bangkok-born Englishman in his forties with a thin brown moustache and an imperious vanity which propelled his column in trade magazines (entitled "From the Fountainhead") to notoriety. A former engineer, he made a fortune publishing books on microcomputers when no one else was. He would sometimes bring boxes of them to Homebrew meetings and go home with empty boxes and wads of cash. His books eventually sold hundreds of thousands, McGraw-Hill bought his publishing house, and now, "with the money burning a hole in my pocket," as he said, he was looking to go into the manufacture of computers.

Osborne's theory was that all the current products were too much oriented toward hackers. He did not believe that people cared to know about the magic that hackers found within computers. He had no sympathy for people who wanted to know how things worked, people who wanted to explore things, people who wanted to improve the systems they studied and dreamed about. In Adam Osborne's view, there was nothing to be gained by spreading the Hacker Ethic; computers were for simple applications, like word processing or financial calculation. His idea was to provide a no-frills computer which would come with all you needed to get going—Osborne thought people were happiest when relieved of anxiety-producing choices, like which word-processing program to buy. It would be cheap, and small enough to carry on a plane. A portable Volkscomputer. He asked Lee Felsenstein to design it. Because the machine he wanted need only be "adequate," designing it should not be too hard a task. "Five thousand people on the peninsula could have done it," Osborne later said. "I happened to know Lee."

So for twenty-five percent of this as yet unformed company, Lee Felsenstein designed the machine. He chose to interpret Osborne's requirement that the machine be "adequate" to mean he could do his usual job of junkyard engineering, making sure that the design was solid enough to support well-tested components in an architecture that eschewed tricks and detours. "To be able to make a design that is good and adequate, works well, and is buildable and cheap and contains nothing fancy is an artistic problem," he later said. "I had to be crazy enough and broke enough [to try it]." But Lee knew that he could fulfill the requirements. As usual, there was fear in the equation: Lee had an admittedly irrational fear of Adam Osborne; he guessed he identified Adam with the authority figures of his childhood. There was no way that these two could communicate deeply. Once Lee tried to explain Community Memory to him—his *real* career—and Osborne "didn't get it," lamented Lee. "He may be one of the last people to get what Community Memory is about when he sees it, uses it." Yet Lee worked hard for Adam Osborne, working in a space in the Community Memory headquarters, and in six months he was done. He had fulfilled, he thought, the technical requirements as well as the artistic ones in building the machine which was known as the Osborne 1. Critics would later say that the plastic-cased machine had an uncomfortably small five-inch screen, and note other small problems, but when the computer first came out praise was plentiful and the Osborne Computer was soon a multimillion-dollar company. And, out of nowhere, Lee Felsenstein was worth over twenty million dollars. On paper.

He did not radically change his life-style. He still lived in the spartan second-floor apartment renting for under two hundred a month. He still washed his clothes in dimly lit Laundromats near Osborne's offices in Hayward. The only concession was his driving a company car, a new BMW. But perhaps due to age, some therapy sessions, and maturity, as well as his tangible success, he had grown in other ways. In his late thirties, he described himself as "still catching up, undergoing experiences you typically undergo in your early twenties." He had a steady girlfriend, a woman who worked at Osborne.

Of the Osborne stock that Lee sold, almost all went to Community Memory. Which, in the middle of the microcomputer boom, was going through some rough times.

Much of the collective's energies were going toward developing software to sell to make money for the establishment of the non-profit Community Memory system. But a debate was raging within the group as to the propriety of selling the software to anyone who cared to use it, or restricting it so that it would not benefit any military efforts. It was not clear that the military were clamoring to buy this software, which included a data base and communications applications more useful for small businesses than weapon-bearers. But these were hardened Berkeley radicals, and discussions like these were to be expected. The person worrying most about the military was Efrem Lipkin, the hacker blessed with computing wizardry and cursed with a loathing for the uses to which computers were put.

Lee and Efrem were not getting along. Efrem was not charmed with the personal computer industry, which he considered "luxury toys for the middle class." He considered the Osborne computer "disgusting." He resented Lee's working for Osborne while he and the others were working for slave stipends at CM. The fact that much of the money for CM came from Lee's work on that machine bothered Lipkin like a bug in a program, a fatal error which could not be coded away. Lipkin was a hacker purist; while he and Lee agreed on the spirit of Community Memory—using computers to bring people together—he could not accept certain things. Efrem Lipkin told the group that one thing he could not accept was any sales of the software he'd written to the military.

The problem ran deeper than that. Personal computers like the Apple and the Osborne, along with modems in the style of Lee's Pennywhistle, had engendered other examples of the kind of thing Community Memory was attempting. People *were* using computers for communication. And the original mythos of Community Memory, the ideal of machines of loving grace in a field watching over us, had been largely fulfilled—in less than ten years, computers had been demystified. They were no longer evil black boxes to be feared. They were even hip—in due time, computer technology would not only be commonplace around Leopold's Records, but would probably be sold there, in software that replaced records in some of the racks. Jude Milhon, close friend to both Lee and Efrem, a person who'd given a substantial portion of her life to Community Memory, could hardly get the words out when she discussed it, but she knew: they'd blown it. The Revolt in 2100 was over, and it wasn't even 1984 yet. Computers were accepted as convivial tools, and the power of computers was accessible at thousands of retail stores, for those who could pay.

Racked with frustration, Efrem Lipkin blew up during a meeting. He laid down what he considered the failure of the group. "Basically I thought the thing was falling apart," he later said. He was particularly hard on the topic of Lee's money financing the group.

Lee told him that this tainted money was paying Efrem's salary. "Not anymore," said Efrem. And the hacker was gone.

Less than a year later, there was no more Osborne Computer. Management bungling worse than at Processor Technology had made the firm the first of many major financial disasters in what would be called "The Great Computer Shakeout." Lee's paper millions would be gone.

But he would still have his dreams. One great battle had been won. Now, perhaps two thirds into the epic science-fiction novel, it was time to gather forces for a final spin into greatness. Sometime before Osborne Computer went bankrupt, Lee had been lamenting the opaque nature of the most recent computers, the lack of necessity that would lead people to actually go inside the chips and circuit boards and wire them. Hardware construction, he was saying, is an objectified way of thinking. It would be a shame if that went by the wayside, were limited only to the few. He did not think it would be gone. "[The magic] will always be in there to a certain extent. You talk about deus ex machina, well, we're talking about deus *in* machina. You start by thinking there's a god in the box. And then you find there isn't anything in the box. *You* put the god in the box."

Lee Felsenstein and the hardware hackers had helped make the transition from the world of the MIT hacker, where the Hacker Ethic could flourish only within the limited, monastic communities around the machine, to a world where the machines were everywhere. Now, millions of computers were being made, each one an invitation to program, to explore, to mythologize in machine language, to change the world. Computers were rolling off assembly lines as blank slates; a new generation of hackers would be seduced by the power to fill the slates; and the software they created would be presented to a world which saw computers in quite a different way than it had a decade before.

PART THREE

GAME HACKERS

THE SIERRAS:
The Eighties

14

THE WIZARD
AND THE PRINCESS

DRIVING northeast out of Fresno on Route 41 toward the South Gate of Yosemite, you climbed slowly at first, through low fields dotted with huge, pitted boulders. About forty miles out was the town of Coarsegold; soon after, the road rose steeply, topping a mountain called Deadwood. Only after beginning the descent from Deadwood did one see how Route 41 formed the center strip of Oakhurst. Population under six thousand. A modern poly-mart named Raley's (everything from health foods to electric blankets). A few fast-food joints, several clusters of specialty stores, two motels, and a real estate office with a faded brown fiberglass statue of a bear outside it. After a mile or so of Oakhurst, the road continued its climb to Yosemite, thirty miles away.

The bear could talk. Push a button on its base, and you got a low, growling welcome to Oakhurst, a pitch on the price of land. The bear did not mention the transformation of the town by the personal computer. Oakhurst had seen hard times, but in 1982 it boasted one major success story. A company built, in a sense, by the hacker dream, and made possible only by the wizardry of Steve Wozniak and his Apple Computer. A company that symbolized how the products of hacking—computer programs which are works of art—had been recognized as such in significant sectors of the Real World. The hackers who played Spacewar at MIT did not envision it, but the offspring of that PDP-1 program, now that the hardware hackers had liberated the computer and made it personal, had spawned a new industry.

Not far from Talking Bear was an inconspicuous two-story building constructed for offices and shops. Except for a small beauty parlor, a lawyer's office, and the tiny local office of Pacific Gas and Electric, the entire building was occupied by the Sierra On-Line company. Its main product was code, lines of assembly-language computer code written on floppy disks which, when inserted into personal computers like the Apple, magically turned into fantastic games. A specialty of the company was "Adventure" games, like that perfected by Don Woods at the Stanford AI lab; this company had figured out how to add pictures to the game. It sold tens of thousands of these disks.

As of this August day in 1982, On-Line had around seventy employees. Things changed so quickly that on any given day it was difficult to give an exact figure, but this was over triple the employees it had a year ago. A year before that, there were only the two founders, Ken and Roberta Williams, who were, respectively, twenty-five and twenty-six when they started the company in 1980.

Ken Williams was sitting in his office. Outside was his red Porsche 928. It was another day to make some history and have some fun. Ken's office today was relatively neat; the piles of papers on the desk were only several inches high, the sofa and chairs facing the desk were clear of floppy disks and magazines. On the wall was a lithograph, an homage to Rodin's Thinker: instead of that noble human frozen in cerebration was a depiction of a robot contemplating a rainbow-colored Apple.

Ken Williams, meanwhile, was characteristically sloppy. He was a burly, big-gutted man, with swollen features that overwhelmed his friendly blue eyes. There was a hole in his red T-shirt and a hole in his jeans. His shoulder-length, dark-blond hair covered his head in an uncombed matting. He sat draped over his tall, brown executive armchair like some post-counterculture King Cole. In a pleasant California cadence punctuated by self-effacing comments that wistfully tripped off his tongue, he was explaining his life to a reporter. He had covered the tremendous growth of his company, his pleasure in spreading the gospel of computers to the world through the software his company sold, and now was discussing the changes that had come when the company became big, something much more than an operation of hackers in the hills. He was in touch with Real World power now.

"The things I do on a daily basis blow my mind," he said.

He talked about eventually going public. In 1982, a lot of people who owned companies spawned by the revolution that the hardware hackers had started were talking about this. Computers had become the jewel of the economy, the only area of real growth in a recessionary period. More and more people were seeing the magic first glimpsed in batch-processed monasteries by the Hands-On visionaries; in the power harnessed by the PDP-1 artists; in the accessible mastery of information provided by Ed Roberts and proselytized by Lee Felsenstein. As a result, companies like Sierra On-Line, started on shoestrings, were now big enough to contemplate public share offerings. Ken Williams' talk was reminiscent of that heard several years before, when, using the same self-consciously nonchalant cadences, people would speak of one day getting rolfed: in both circumstances, an act once approached with evangelistic gravity was now regarded as somewhat of a delicious inevitability. Going public was something you naturally considered, at least when you had gone from being an ambitious computer programmer to an owner of a $10-million-a-year computer game company in a little over two years.

It was a crucial time for Ken Williams' company. It was also a crucial time for the computer games industry, a crucial time for the computer industry as a whole, and a crucial time for America. The elements had conspired to put Ken Williams, a self-described former hacker, into the driver's seat of more than a Porsche 928.

Ken Williams left his office and went to a large room two doors down in the same building. There were two rows of cubicles in this plaster-walled, industrially carpeted room. In each cubicle was a small computer and a monitor. This was the programming office, and this was where a young hacker had come to show his game off to Ken Williams. The hacker was a cocky-looking kid; he was short, had a smile of bravado on a pug-nosed face, and his chest jutted out, bantam-like, under a faded blue T-shirt. He had driven up from L.A. this morning, so high that he could have filled up the tank with his excess adrenaline.

On the monitor was a prototype of a game called "Wall Wars," written in the past few months in intense bursts between midnight and eight in the morning. While the hacker had worked in a small apartment, his stereo had blared out music by Haircut 100. Wall Wars involved a stream of colorful, brick-like pieces forming a kinetic wall in the middle of the screen. On the top and the bottom of the screen were equally dazzling robot-like creatures. A player would control one of the robots, shoot through the wall by knocking out enough bricks to form a moving gap, and destroy the other robot, who of course would be trying to accomplish the same task, with the player as the victim.

The hacker had promised himself that if Ken Williams bought his game concept, he'd quit his job as a programmer for Mattel and go independent, joining the ranks of an elite group who were already being referred to as Software Superstars. They were the apogee of a Third Generation of hackers who had learned their programming artistry on small computers, who had never bootstrapped themselves up by way of a community. Who dreamed not only of the ultimate hack, but of fame, and big royalty checks.

Ken Williams ambled into the room and leaned an elbow on the edge of the cubicle. The young hacker, masking his nervousness, began to explain something about the game, but Ken didn't seem to be listening.

"This is all so far?" Ken said.

The hacker nodded and started to explain how the game would eventually play. Ken interrupted him.

"How long will it take you to finish?"

"I'm going to quit my job," said the hacker. "I can do it in a month."

"We'll figure two months," said Ken. "Programmers always lie." He spun around and started walking away. "Drop into my office and we'll have you sign a contract."

It was reminiscent of an old-time entertainment mogul giving the nod to an auditioning starlet. It was indicative of the massive change in the way people thought of computers, used computers, and interacted with computers. The story of the MIT hackers and the Homebrew Club had led to this: Sierra On-Line and aspiring software stars.

The Hacker Ethic had met the marketplace.

•

Ken Williams was never a pure hacker. He certainly did not take the appellation as a badge of pride; the idea of an aristocracy of computer excellence never occurred to him. He'd stumbled into computing. Only incidentally did he develop a relationship with the machine, and it was not until he thought himself its master that he even began to appreciate what kinds of changes the computer could make in the world.

At first, the computer had him totally stymied. It was at California Polytechnic, Pomona Campus, which Ken Williams was attending because (a) it cost only twenty-four dollars a quarter plus books and (b) he was only sixteen, and it was close to home. His major was physics; he had trouble with classes. Though Ken had always slid by academically on high aptitude, things like trigonometry and calculus weren't as easily mastered as the subjects in high school were. Now there was this computer course, geared to programming in FORTRAN.

Ken Williams was intimidated by computers, and that intimidation triggered an odd reaction in him. He had always resisted preset curricula—while refusing to do his homework in junior high, he would almost compulsively read, everything from the Hardy Boys to what became his favorite genre, the rags-to-riches stories of Harold Robbins. He identified with the underdog. Williams' father was a television repairman for Sears, a rugged man who had moved to California from Cumberland County, Kentucky; his co-workers nicknamed him "Country." Ken grew up in a fairly tough neighborhood in Pomona, at times sharing a bedroom with his two brothers. He avoided fights assiduously, later cheerfully admitting he was "a coward." "I wouldn't hit back" he once explained, as if the rites of dominance and macho posturing were alien to him.

But when he read about those struggles in big, melodramatic novels, he was enraptured. He loved the idea of some poor kid making a bundle and getting all the girls. He was susceptible to the hyperbolic charms of a life like that of Jonas Cord, the young, ruthless, Howard Hughes–like figure in *The Carpetbaggers* who built his inheritance into an aviation and filmmaking empire. "That's where I got my role model," Williams later explained. Maybe it was some of Jonas Cord's kind of ambition that led Ken Williams to become more active in high school, where he joined the band, had a girlfriend, learned how to play the game of good grades, and worked up schemes to make money. (He would later boast that he won so many sales contests on his paper route that he was on a first-name basis with the ticket-takers at Disneyland.) Ken's inclination toward self-deprecation and his seemingly casual independence masked a fierce determination that showed up even as he was backed into a corner by an ornery Control Data computer in FORTRAN class.

For weeks he struggled, lagging behind his classmates. He had set a problem for himself: to simulate a little mouse running through a maze, following a wall, and getting out of the maze. (It called for a program similar to the old "Mouse in the Maze" program on the TX-0, where the little mouse tries to find the martini glasses.) With six weeks gone in the nine-week course, Ken was headed toward an F. And there was nothing that Ken Williams, even then, liked about failure. So he kept at it until one day he came to a sudden realization. The computer really wasn't so smart at all. It was just some dumb beast, following orders, doing what you told it to in exactly the order you determined. You could control it. You could be God.

Power, power, power! Up here where the world was like a toy beneath me. Where I held the stick like my cock in my hands and there was no one . . . to say me no!
        —Jonas Cord, in Harold Robbins' *Carpetbaggers*

The mouse got through the maze. Ken Williams got through the course. It was as if a light had gone on in his head, and everyone in the class could see it from the ease with which he turned out code. Ken Williams had something going with the Dumb Beast.

A more important relationship to Ken at the time was his romance with a girl named Roberta Heuer. He had met her in high school, when she was dating a friend of his. Out of the blue, two months after a double date, Ken called her, nervously reminded her who he was and asked her out. Roberta, a demure, passive girl, later said that she hadn't been that impressed with Ken at first. "He was cute, but I thought he acted kind of dumb. He was shy but [to compensate for it] he would go overboard, acting too aggressive. He carried cigarettes in his pocket, but didn't smoke. He asked me to go steady the first week [we went out]."

Roberta had been seeing a boy who lived upstate; Ken tried to force her into choosing between them. Roberta might well have decided against this insecure, pushy boy, but one day Ken opened up to her. "He was talking about physics," Roberta later recalled. "I figured he really was a bright guy. All the boyfriends I'd had before were rather dumb. Ken was talking about real things, responsibility." She stopped seeing the other boy, and almost instantly Ken pushed for a permanent commitment. "I didn't want to be alone," he later reflected.

Roberta talked to her mother about it: "He's going to go someplace," she said. "To really make it. *Be* something."

Finally Ken told her, "We're getting married, and that's it." She didn't fight it. She was nineteen; he was a year younger.

Within a year, Roberta was pregnant, and Ken was pulling D's and worrying about supporting a family. He knew from reading the want ads that there were a lot more jobs in computer programming than there were in physics, so he figured, just like it said on the matchbook covers, that he would find a career for himself in electronic data processing. Roberta's dad co-signed a student loan for $1,500, tuition for a trade school called Control Data Institute.

The world Ken Williams was entering was nothing like the holy preserve of the MIT AI lab. His would-be colleagues in the business computing field had little of the hands-on hunger that drove the class of Altair graduates who hacked hardware. In the early 1970s the business computer field that Ken was entering was considered the creepiest in America. It was a joke, an occupation where meek little moles did things—who knows what those things were?—to the punch cards and whirring wheels of Hulking Giant computers. As far as the public was concerned, there wasn't even much difference between the drones who mechanically punched the cards and hammered at the keyboards, and the skilled technicians who programmed the machines to put the cards in their places. They were all seen as the white-shirted, Coke-bottle-glasses moles in the computer room. Creatures of the disembodied age.

If Ken and Roberta had been part of a wide circle of friends, they might have had to confront that stereotype, which Ken did not resemble in the least. But Ken and Roberta did not bother to put down roots or establish close friendships. As a computer programmer, Ken was less a Richard Greenblatt or a Lee Felsenstein than he was Jonas Cord. Later, he would jauntily say, "I guess greed would summarize me better than anything. I always want more."

Ken Williams was far from a dazzling programmer when he finished Control Data Institute, but he was certainly prepared to do anything required of him. And more. As much work as possible, to help him go as high as he could. Then take on another, more demanding job, whether or not he was qualified. Instead of cleanly breaking with the previous employer, Ken tried to keep on the payroll, in consultant mode.

He would claim to know computer languages and operating systems he knew nothing about, reading a book about the subject hours before a job interview and bullshitting his way into the position. "Well, we're looking for a programmer in BAL," they would tell him, referring to an esoteric computer language, and he would laugh almost derisively.

"BAL? I've been programming in BAL for three years!"

Then he would immediately rush out to get hold of some books, since he had never even *heard* of BAL. But by the time the job started he would have procured documentation, uniformly buried in dense, cheaply printed looseleaf manuals, to fake expertise in the "BAL environment," or at least buy time until he could get into the machine and divine the secrets of BAL.

No matter where he worked, in any number of nameless service companies in the yawning valley above Los Angeles, Ken Williams did not meet one person who deserved an iota of his respect. He would observe people who'd been programming computers for years and he would say to himself, "Give me a book and in two hours I'll be doing what they're doing." And sure enough, stackloads of manuals and a few fourteen-hour days later, he would at least appear to be one hotshot programmer.

He'd come into the heavily air-conditioned computer sanctums at weird hours of the night to fix a bug, or get the computer back up when one of his programs accidentally fed on itself and tripped the millions of calculations up in such a fury of misunderstanding that nothing the regular crew could think of could revive the machine. But Ken, confident that the stupidity of his colleagues was dwarfed only by the astounding compliance of the Dumb Beast whom he could feed and befriend with his programming skills, would work three days straight, forgetting to even stop for a meal, until the Dumb Beast was back on the job. Ken Williams, hero of the day, tamer of the Dumb Beast, would go home, sleep for a day and a half, then return to work, ready for another marathon. Employers noticed, and rewarded him.

Ken was rising at quantum speed—Roberta figured they moved to various locations in the L.A. area about twelve times in that go-go decade, always making sure that they turned a profit on the house. They had no time for making friends. They felt like loners and misfits, usually the only white-collar family in a blue-collar neighborhood. The consolation was money. "Wouldn't it be nice to make another two hundred dollars a week?" Roberta would ask, and Ken would get a new job or take on more consulting work . . . but even before Ken had settled into this new job, he and Roberta would be sitting in the tiny living room of whatever house they happened to be living in, and saying, "Wouldn't it be nice to earn two hundred dollars *more?*" The pressure never stopped, especially since Ken Williams had idle dreams of fantastic sums of money, money enough to goof off with for the rest of his life—not only all the cash that he and Roberta could spend but all that his kids could spend, too (Roberta was pregnant by then with the second Williams son, Chris). *Wouldn't it be nice,* he thought, *to retire at thirty?*

By then something else was changing: his relationship with the Dumb Beast. When Ken had time, he would often pull out some of those dense, cheaply printed looseleaf manuals, trying to figure out what made the big Burroughs or IBM or Control Data machine *really* tick. As he gained proficiency in his profession, he began to respect it more, see how it could approach art. There were layers of expertise that were way beyond what Williams had previously come to assume. A programming pantheon did exist, almost like some sort of old-time philosophical brotherhood.

Ken had gotten a taste of this more exotic realm when he fast-talked his way into a job as systems programmer for Bekins Moving and Storage. Bekins was switching then from a Burroughs computer to a bigger and slightly more interactive IBM machine. Ken baldly fabricated a career history of IBM wizardry for himself, and landed the job.

At Bekins, Ken Williams became hooked on pure programming. His task was installing a heavy-duty telecommunications system on the IBM that would allow one computer to support eight or nine hundred users in the field across the country, and the problems and complications were beyond anything he'd confronted so far. He would experiment with three or four languages that had nothing to do with his job, fascinated with the techniques and mind-frames required with each language. There was a whole world inside this computer . . . a way of thinking. And maybe for the first time Ken Williams was being drawn to the process of computing more than to the goal of completing a task. In other words, hacking.

As a consequence of his sustained interest, Ken remained at Bekins longer than at most of his other employers: a year and a half. It was time well spent, since his next job presented him with an even greater challenge, as well as contacts and ideas which would soon enable him to act out his wildest fantasies.

•

The company was called Informatics. It was one of a number of firms that sprang up in the mid-sixties to take advantage of a gap in the mainframe computer software field. More and more big companies and government agencies were getting computers, and almost none of the software that the behemoth computer companies supplied could artfully execute the tasks the computers were supposed to perform. So each company had to hire its own programming staff, or rely on highly paid consultants who invariably would disappear just when the system crashed and valuable data came out looking like Russian. A new team of programmers or consultants would then come out to untangle the mess, and the process would repeat itself: starting from scratch, the new team would have to reinvent the wheel.

Informatics and companies like it were set up to sell software that made the Hulking Giants a little more comprehensible. The idea was to invent the wheel once and for all, slam a patent on it, and sell it like crazy. Their programmers would toil away at the assembly level and finally come up with a system which would allow low-level programmers, or even in some cases nonprogrammers, to perform simple computer tasks. After all, these commercial systems all did pretty much the same thing—you had something coming in from a clerk or a branch office on paper which got keypunched and entered into a system which modified some preexisting file. Informatics came up with a pre-programmed system called Mark 4. Sometime in the seventies it became the largest-selling mainframe computer software product of all time, approaching at one point $100 million in yearly revenue.

In the late seventies, one of the managers in charge of Informatics' new products was Dick Sunderland, a former FORTRAN programmer who was climbing the corporate ladder after reluctantly foregoing a late-in-life stab at law school. In place of the law, Sunderland had determined to pursue a romance with a bright and holy concept of management. To be a leader of men, a deft builder of competent, well-meshed employee teams, a persuasive promoter, and a constructive manipulator . . . this was what Dick Sunderland aspired toward.

A small, chalk-complexioned man with hooded eyes and a contemplative drawl, Sunderland considered himself a natural manager. He had always been interested in the advertising, selling, promoting of things. Psychology fascinated him. And he was especially enamored of the idea of choosing the right people to work together so that their joint output dwarfed the measly sum of their individual inputs.

Dick was trying to do that at Informatics with his new product team. He already had one genuine wizard on the staff, a lean, quiet man in his forties named Jay Sullivan. Jay was a former jazz pianist who had come to Informatics from a more mundane job in his native Chicago. He later explained why: "Systems software [at Informatics] was much more interesting. You didn't have to worry about mundane things like applications or payrolls. It was much more *real programming* to me; you dealt more in the essence of what programming was about. The actual techniques of programming are more important than the specifics of the job at a specific time." In other words, he could hack there.

In his programming, Sullivan worked like a vacationer who, having planned his trip carefully, educating himself on the subtle characteristics of the local scenery, followed the itinerary with enhanced consciousness. Yet he still retained the curiosity to stray from the plan if circumstances seemed to call for it, and derived pleasure from the careful exploration that such a fork in his path would involve, not to mention the sense of accomplishment when the detour proved successful.

As with many hackers, Sullivan's immersion in programming had taken its social toll. Sullivan later explained that with computers "you can create your own universe, and you can do whatever you want within that. You don't have to deal with people." So while he was a master in his work, Sullivan had the infuriating kind of programmer personality that led him to get on splendidly with computers but not pay much attention to the niceties of human interaction. He would casually insult Dick, and nonchalantly go about his business, doing brilliant things with the operating system, but often would see his innovations die because he was not adept at politicking, a process necessary at the large company. Dick Sunderland had forced himself to be patient with Sullivan, and eventually they had arrived at a seller-inventor relationship which produced two lucrative improvements to the Mark 4 line.

Dick was looking for more master programmers, calling recruiters and making it quite clear that he was looking for cream-of-the-crop people, nothing less. One recruiter mentioned Ken Williams to him. "This kid's a genius type," the recruiter said.

Sunderland called in Ken for an interview and made sure that his true genius, Jay Sullivan, would be there to test the mettle of this Williams person. Dick never before had seen anyone stand toe-to-toe with Jay Sullivan, and was curious to see what might come of the interview.

Dick and Jay were talking about a problem in implementing a new, user-friendly language that Informatics was working on when Ken showed up, wearing slacks and a sport shirt which fit so badly that it was obvious T-shirts were his norm. The discussion had been fairly technical, focusing on the problem that to make a language a nonprogrammer would understand—a language like English—one would have to avoid any kind of ambiguous words or acronyms.

Suddenly Jay Sullivan turned to Ken and said, "What do you think of the word 'any'?"

Without hesitation, Ken correctly asserted that it was a very valuable word, but an ambiguous word nonetheless . . . and then extemporaneously tossed off ideas about how that word might be handled.

It seemed to Dick that he was witnessing a classic battle—the cheeky Pomona Kid versus venerable Chicago Slim. While Ken had a charismatic quality to him, and obviously knew computers, Dick still had his money on Jay. Jay did not let him down. After Ken stopped, Jay, speaking quietly and methodically, "sliced Ken up with a razor blade," Dick later recalled, enumerating the errors and incompleteness of Ken's thoughts. Yet it was impressive to Dick—and even to Jay—that this college dropout could even think such thoughts. What's more, rather than being dissuaded by Jay's broadside, Ken came right back. Dick watched the two pick up threads of each other's ideas and weave them into more refined concepts. This was synergy, the manager's holy grail. Dick decided to hire Ken Williams.

Dick put Ken under Jay's supervision, and the two of them would chatter about programming arcana for hours. For Ken it was an education: he was learning the psychology of computerdom in a way he never had. Of course, one part of the job that Ken Williams did not like was having a boss; Ken in this regard was a typical anti-bureaucratic hacker. So he came to dislike Dick, with all his schedules and fixation on managerial details—obstacles to the free flow of information.

Ken and Jay would be talking about the intricacies of some aspect of programming language—like trying to figure out, when somebody says "List by customer," what that really means. Does it mean "SORT by customer," or perhaps "List ALL customers"? Or maybe "List ANY customers"? (That word again.) The computer had to be programmed so it wouldn't screw up on any of those interpretations. At the very least it should know when to ask users to clarify their meaning. This took a language of considerable flexibility and elegance, and though Ken and his new guru Jay might not have said it out loud, a task of that sort goes a bit beyond technology and into primal linguistics. After all, once you get waist-deep into a discussion about the meaning of the word "any," it's only a short step to thinking philosophically about existence itself.

Somewhere in the midst of one of these conversations Dick would come in, eager to witness some synergy among his troops. "We'd try to supersubset it so that a two-year-old would understand, ask Dick's opinion, he'd give it, and we'd chase him out of the room," Ken later recalled. "Dick never understood what we were putting up. He was obviously out of his league."

At those times Ken might have felt superior to Dick, but in retrospect he had to admit that Dick was smart enough to recognize talent. Ken realized that he was one of the weaker members of a superteam of programmers who were doing great stuff for Informatics. Sometimes Ken figured that Dick must have gotten lucky, accidentally corralling five of the most creative people around for his new products team. Either that or he was the best manager in the world, or at least the best talent evaluator.

Ken, always needing more money, began moonlighting. Sunderland was refusing his constant requests for raises, and when Ken suggested that he might like to head a programming group, Dick, a little astounded perhaps at the chutzpah of this brilliant but scattershot kid, flatly denied the request. "You have no talent for management," said Dick, and Ken Williams never forgot that. Ken was regularly going home to Roberta and complaining about Dick—how mean he was, how strict, how he had no understanding of people and their problems—but it was less a dissatisfaction with his boss than his desire for more money, money for a bigger house, a faster car, a CB radio, a motorcycle, a hot tub, more electronic gadgets, that led him to double and even triple up on work, often phasing into a no-sleep mode. Eventually the outside work got to be more than the inside work, and he left Informatics in 1979, becoming an independent consultant.

First there was a guy with a scheme to do tax returns for big companies like General Motors and Shell, and then there was some work with Warner Brothers, programming a system for the record company to keep artists' royalties straight. There was a bookkeeping system he constructed for Security Pacific Banks, something about foreign tax plans. Ken was becoming a finance guru; the thirty thousand a year he was pulling down looked to be only the beginning, if Ken kept hustling.

He and Roberta began weaving a little fantasy. At night—the nights Ken wasn't out consulting for someone—they would sit in the hot tub and talk about splitting the Simi Valley suburban trap and moving to the woods. Where they would go water skiing, snow skiing . . . just goof off. Of course there weren't nearly as many hours in a day to make money to turn *that* kind of trick, no matter how many companies Ken set up tax programs for. So the fantasy was just that, a fantasy.

Until Ken's little brother Larry got an Apple Computer.

Larry brought it over to Ken's office one day. To Ken, who had been dealing with telecommunications networks that handled two thousand people all at once, who had invented entire computer *languages* with mainframe wizards the likes of Jay Sullivan, the idea of this sleek, beige machine being a computer seemed in one sense ludicrous. "It was a toy compared to the computers I'd been using," he later explained. "A piece of junk, a primeval machine."

On the other hand, there were plenty of things that the Apple offered that Ken's Hulking Giants did not provide. Up till the time he worked at Informatics, his computers had been batch-processed, loading dread punch cards. The Apple at least was interactive. And when you got down to it, it was fairly powerful, especially compared to the big machines of less than a decade ago. (MIT's Marvin Minsky once estimated that an Apple II had the virtual power of the PDP-1.) And it ran pretty fast, almost comparable to a big machine, because on a time-sharing mainframe you're fighting for CPU time with eight hundred people all trying to grind their code through at once, with the Dumb Beast sweating silicon trying to parcel out nanoseconds to each user. You shared your Apple with no one. In the middle of the night, it was just sitting there in the house, waiting for you and you alone. Ken Williams decided he had to have one.

So in January 1980 he scraped together "every cent I had," as he later told it, and bought an Apple II. But it took a while to understand how significant a machine it was. Ken figured that everybody with an Apple was like him, a technician or engineer. It seemed logical that what these people really wanted was a powerful language to run on their computer. No one had yet done FORTRAN for the Apple. Hardly anyone had done *anything* on the Apple at that point, but Ken was thinking like a hacker, unable to envision anything neater than something to use the computer *with*. The Tools-to-Make-Tools syndrome. (Richard Greenblatt's first big project on the PDP-1 was a FORTRAN implementation, for much the same reason.) At that point Ken was unable to conceive that the Apple and small machines like it had opened the field of recreational computing to others besides hackers.

The irony of it was that, even as Ken planned to write a FOR-
TRAN for the Apple, this more significant revolution in computing was happening right there in his own house.

•

For most of her life Roberta Williams had been timid. There was
a dreamy quality about her, and her doll-like brown eyes, long
brown hair, and frilly, feminine wardrobe—bell sleeves, suede
boots, Peter Pan collars—indicated that this was a woman who'd
had a childhood rich in fantasy. In fact, Roberta Williams' early
daydreaming had taken on almost supernatural proportions. She
had always pictured herself in strange situations. At night she
would lie in bed and construct what she referred to as "my movies." One night pirates would kidnap her and she would devise
elaborate escape plans, often involving some dashing savior. Another night she would be in ancient Greece. Always dreaming of
things happening to her.

Daughter of a frugal agricultural inspector in Southern California, she was painfully shy, and the relative isolation of her rural
home reinforced that. "I never really liked myself," she would later
reflect. "I always wanted to be someone else." She felt her parents
doted on her younger brother, who suffered from epilepsy. Her
form of entertainment was telling stories that would enthrall her
elders, and enrapture her brother, who took the stories literally.
But as she got older, and coped with dating and the grown-up
world, "all that got thrown out the window," as she says now.
When she and Ken married, she passively expected him to make a
living; as for herself, she was so shy she "could hardly make a
phone call." The storytelling remained buried.

Then one night Ken, who had brought a computer terminal
home, called Roberta over to show her this program that someone
had put on the IBM mainframe computer he was connected to.
"Come on over here, Roberta," he urged, sitting on the green-
carpeted floor of the spare bedroom where he'd put the terminal.
"See this—it's a really fun game."

Roberta didn't want anything to do with it. First of all, she
didn't like games too much. Second, it was on a computer. Though
much of Ken's life was spent communicating with computers, they
were still unfriendly ciphers to Roberta. But Ken was persistent,
and finally cajoled her to sit at the terminal to see what this thing
was about. This is what she saw:

YOU ARE STANDING AT THE END OF A ROAD BEFORE A
SMALL BRICK BUILDING. AROUND YOU IS A FOREST. A
SMALL STREAM FLOWS OUT OF THE BUILDING AND
DOWN A GULLY.

It was "Adventure," the game written at the Stanford AI lab by
hacker Don Woods, the Tolkienesque game which lured hackers
and users into immersing themselves in a magical dungeon world.
And from the moment Roberta Williams tentatively poked GO
EAST she was totally and irrevocably hooked. "I just couldn't
stop. It was compulsive. I started playing it and kept playing it. I
had a baby at the time, Chris was eight months old; I totally ignored him. I didn't want to be bothered. I didn't want to stop and
make dinner." She didn't want to do anything except figure out
how to get to Witt's End or get around the snake. She would be up
until four in the morning, trying to figure out how to get around
the damn snake to get to the giant clams. And then she would sit
up in bed thinking, *What didn't I do? What else could I have done?
Why couldn't I open that stupid clam? What's in it?*
    At first Ken participated, but he soon lost interest. Roberta
thought this was because Ken never liked it when Adventure got
sarcastic. You would say KILL DRAGON and it would come
back and say WHAT, WITH YOUR BARE HANDS? You
couldn't get mad, you had to ignore it. And you certainly couldn't
be sarcastic back, just say, "Yes." And it said WITH YOUR
BARE HANDS YOU KILL THE DRAGON AND HE'S
LYING DEAD AT YOUR FEET. You killed the dragon! You
could go on. Roberta approached the game with methodical intensity, drawing elaborate maps and anticipating what was around
every turn. Ken thought it was amazing that one day Roberta
couldn't stand computers and the next day he couldn't get her
away from the terminal. Finally, after a month of ratiocination
about trolls, axes, misty caverns, and vast halls, Roberta solved
Adventure. She was desperate to find more games like it.
    By then, Ken had bought the Apple. Despite her newfound in-
terest in computers, Roberta was less than thrilled at the two-
thousand-dollar purchase. If Ken wanted it so badly, she told him,
he should try to make money from it. This coincided perfectly with
Ken's desires at the time, which were to write a FORTRAN compiler for the Apple and sell it for bundles of money to the engineers
and technicians who wanted Tools to Make Tools. He hired five
part-time programmers to help him implement the compiler. Ken's

house, a typical Simi Valley four-bedroom, two-thousand-square-foot tract home, became headquarters for the FORTRAN project.

Meanwhile Roberta had heard that there were some Adventure-style games available for the Apple. Roberta bought some at a computer store in nearby Northridge in the San Fernando Valley, but she found them too easy. She wanted her newly awakened imagination to be as taxed and teased as it was before. She began sketching out an adventure game of her own.

She started by writing out a story about a "mystery house," and things that happened in it. The story had much to do with Agatha Christie's *Ten Little Indians;* another inspiration was the board game "Clue." Instead of just finding treasures as in Adventure, this game would have you do some detective work. Roberta mapped out the story just as she mapped out an adventure game when she played it. Along the way, she devised puzzles, character traits, events, and landmarks. After a couple of weeks she had a stack of papers with maps and dilemmas and plot turns and twists and she flopped it down in front of Ken and said, "Look what I did!"

Ken told Roberta that her little stack of papers was very nice and she should run along and finish it. No one really wanted to use a personal computer as a game machine—they were for engineers who wanted to figure out how to design circuits or solve triple-x exponential equations.

Not long after, Ken and Roberta were at the Plank House in the Valley, a redwood-walled steak house where they often dined, and there he finally listened to his delicate wife describing how her game put you in an old Victorian house in which your friends were being killed off one by one. She described a few of the dilemmas, and told of a secret passageway. It began to sound good to Ken. Ken Williams could usually smell some money to be made, and he thought that there might be enough bread in this for a trip to Tahiti or some new furniture.

"This sounds great," he told her, "but to really sell you need more. An angle. Something different."

As it happened, Roberta had been thinking lately how great it would be if an adventure game were accompanied by pictures on the computer screen. You could see where you were instead of just reading it. She had no idea if this was possible on an Apple or any kind of computer. How would you even get a picture *into* a computer?

Ken guessed they could try.

As it happened, a device called a VersaWriter had just been released. It was a tablet that you drew on and it registered the shapes into an Apple computer. But it didn't draw very accurately, and it was hard to control the writing mechanism, which was like the clunky base of a desk lamp. Worst of all, it cost two hundred dollars. Ken and Roberta decided to shoot the dice and spring for it. Ken then reprogrammed the whole thing so Roberta could do something with it. Eventually she made a few dozen black-and-white pictures of rooms inside the Mystery House, with people drawn only slightly better than stick figures. Then Ken coded the game logic, after figuring out how to pack seventy pictures onto one floppy disk, a task which any programmer in the least familiar with the Apple would have guessed was impossible. The secret was not storing data for entire pictures, but using assembly-language commands which stored coordinates of the individual lines in each picture; as each new picture was due to appear, the computer would follow the commands to draw the picture. It was a dazzling program bum that characterized Ken's facility for top-level hacking.

The whole thing took a month.

•

Ken scrapped the FORTRAN project and took the game to a software distributing company called Programma. It was the biggest distributor of Apple software in the world. In early 1980, that was not saying too much. It sold a range of programs with names like "Biorhythm," "Nude Lady," "Vegas Style Keno," "State Capitals," and "Apple Flyswatter." Most of the games were written in BASIC (as opposed to the much faster-running assembly language) and could entertain only a toddler or a person in love with the idea of playing with a computer. There were enough of the latter to jack Programma's gross up to $150,000 a month.

The Programma people loved Mystery House. Here was an assembly-language Adventure game that was well planned, challenging—and had pictures. The fact that the pictures were in black and white and looked like something young D. J. Williams (age six) might have drawn was irrelevant. No one else had done anything like it. They offered Ken a 25 percent royalty on the $12 wholesale price, and assured him they could sell five hundred copies a month for six months, which at $3 a copy would be $9,000. This was almost twice the amount that Ken had been promised for the FORTRAN compiler—before splitting it with his five programmers. All for Roberta's silly game.

Ken Williams also considered selling the game directly to Apple Computer. He sent a sample, but waited over a month and got no reply. (A year later, Apple—now a large company with a slow-moving bureaucracy, wrote back and said, yes, maybe we might like to consider buying this. This said a lot more about what Apple Computer had become than it did about Mystery House.) Ken and Roberta did not take Programma's offer. Ken and Roberta wanted *all* the money. Why not try to sell it independently? If it doesn't work, *then* take it to Programma.

So the Williamses started taking Mystery House around to the few computer stores in the area. The people at the stores would be skeptical at first—after all, excited new computer fanatics, intoxicated with the power lent them by their new Apples and Radio Shack TRS-80s and PET computers, were always trying to sell strange programs. But then Roberta's game would boot with a picture of an old house drawn on the computer's high-resolution (hi-res) screen rather than the computer's clunky, block-oriented lo-res one. The people at the stores would ask how Ken *did* that. After a few experiences like that, Ken and Roberta figured they might be able to make as much as one or two thousand dollars a month from this software-selling thing.

The next step was advertising the product in a magazine. But as long as they were doing that, they figured, why not offer a couple more games, and look like a *real* company? They already had a name: On-Line Systems—a holdover from Ken's vision of selling the respectable kind of business software for the Apple that he did in his consulting for on-line computer firms. Ken went to a friend and asked him to be On-Line's first outside programmer. In return for eventual royalties, the friend did a simple black-and-white shoot-one-dot-with-another-dot game called "Skeet Shoot." They printed up some advertising fliers and documentation sheets—unwilling to pay the one-hundred-dollar typesetting fee, Roberta cut the individual letters out of magazines and got that "master" printed by a local copy shop. It came back with little lines that betrayed its cut-and-paste origin, but they had already spent five hundred dollars. Anyway, that form of packaging was state of the art at that time. This was the computer world, where the packaging didn't matter. What mattered was the magic that happened when all those binary connections were made. Marketing was second to substance.

Mystery House, or "Hi-Res Adventure #1," was priced at $24.95. Ken and Roberta, in a fit of optimism, had bought a box of one hundred blank disks at the nearby Rainbow Computing store, and once the fliers were sent to computer stores and the ad placed for a reluctantly paid two-hundred-dollar fee in the May 1980 issue of a small magazine called *MICRO,* they waited. The phone rang, on that first day in May, and then there was a break and then it rang again. And from then on, it would be a long time before Ken and Roberta could count on their phone not ringing.

Ken and Roberta made eleven thousand dollars that May. In June, they made twenty thousand dollars. July was thirty thousand. Their Simi Valley house was becoming a money machine. Ken would go off to work at Financial Decisions, where he was now programming for around forty-two thousand a year, and Roberta would copy disks and put the disks, along with the fliers and inserts, into a Ziploc bag. She would also take care of the kids and put the programs in boxes and keep the house clean and send programs out by U.P.S. At night Roberta was designing a longer and better adventure game based on the world of fairy tales.

Every few minutes the phone would ring and it would most likely be someone ready to absolutely die unless they got a hint to unstick them from a seemingly hopeless situation in Mystery House. People who called the number shown on the flier included in the Ziploc bag with the floppy disk were under the impression that On-Line was some big conglomerate, and they couldn't believe their luck in somehow connecting with the actual author of the program. "I'm talking to the person who *wrote* the game?" Yeah, in her kitchen. Roberta would give them a hint—never a straight answer: part of the fun was working it out for yourself—and chat with them a while. The energy level was contagious. People were going looney over playing with computers.

Ken Williams was carrying a full work load at Financial Decisions, developing a complicated finance system and heading the data processing department. At night, he would work on the Apple, hacking a new machine-language system for Roberta's new adventure game. On weekends, Ken would make the rounds of the computer stores. It was clear that the software business required his full time.

Roberta thought that as long as Ken was thinking of quitting, they might as well live out their longtime dream of moving to the woods. Her parents lived near Yosemite, above the town of Oakhurst, and it was even more rural and quiet than the place Roberta grew up in and still remembered fondly. It would be perfect for the kids. So they did it. "I'm going to move to the mountains," he told an astounded Dick Sunderland at a party in mid-1980. Dick and Ken were in a room a bit away from the party noise, and Ken said, "Here I am, twenty-five years old, and the Apple Computer has enabled me to fulfill my dream: living in the woods and living in a log cabin and writing software."

Ken and Roberta bought the first country house they looked at, a three-bedroom, rustic, wooden A-frame cabin on Mudge Ranch Road just outside Coarsegold, California.

By then, they had finished Roberta's fairy-tale game, "Wizard and the Princess." It was twice as long as Mystery House, and ran faster thanks to Ken's improvements on the program logic. Ken had developed a whole new assembly-language interpreter for writing adventure games; he called it ADL, or Adventure Development Language. Also, this "Hi-Res Adventure #2" had over one hundred and fifty pictures. Ken had devised subroutines that allowed Roberta to enter the pictures into the computer as easily as if she were drawing on a regular tablet. This time the pictures were in color; Ken used a technique called "dithering" to blend the six colors of the Apple, mixing dot by dot, to get twenty-one colors. He was performing stunts on the Apple that Steve Wozniak never dreamed of. Magic stuff.

The game's only problem was the first puzzle, where the adventurer, on his way to rescue Princess Priscilla of Serenia from Wizard Harlin, had to get past a snake. The answer was rather obscure: you had to pick up a rock and use it to kill the snake, but unless you chose a rock in one specific location (they all looked alike) you got bit by a scorpion and died. Most people started banging their heads against the wall at the third or fourth scorpion bite. Eventually, after countless frustrated adventurers made calls to Roberta's kitchen in Coarsegold (East Coast people sometimes would call at 6 A.M. California time), On-Line began supplying a hint to that dilemma in every package.

Snake or not, Wizard and the Princess eventually sold over sixty thousand copies at $32.95. Ken and Roberta would sit in the hot tub they'd installed and shake their heads, saying, "Do you believe this?"

On December 1 of that first year, after the business had already changed their lives, got them a new house, and made them the rising stars of the Apple world, they finally moved the business out of the house to a space on the second floor of a two-story building in Oakhurst, seven miles up Route 41. Their neighbor was a religious promoter who was unsuccessfully trying to book Little Richard on a national preaching tour. You could hear him shouting through the thin walls.

Early in 1981, less than a year after the company began with a few floppy disks and a $150 ad in a little magazine, Roberta described the situation in a letter to another small magazine: "We opened an office December 1, 1980, and hired our first employee to help us with the shipping and the phones. Two weeks later, we hired somebody to help her, one week after that we hired somebody to help them. We just hired a full-time programmer this week, and we need at least another programmer. Our business is growing by leaps and bounds, and there's no end in sight."

15

THE BROTHERHOOD

THE Hacker Ethic was changing, even as it spread throughout the country. Its emissaries were the small, low-cost computers sold by Apple, Radio Shack, Commodore (the PET), and Atari. Each was a real computer; the sheer proliferation created a demand for more innovative programs that previous distribution methods could not address. A hacker could no longer distribute clever programs by leaving them in a drawer, as he had at MIT, nor could he rely on a Homebrew Computer Club system of swapping programs at club meetings. Many people who bought these new computers never bothered to join clubs. Instead they relied on computer stores, where they happily paid for programs. When you were desperate for something to fulfill the promise of this thrilling new machine, spending twenty-five dollars for Mystery House seemed almost a privilege. These pioneering computer owners in the early eighties might learn enough about their machines to appreciate the beauty of an unencumbered flow of information, but the Hacker Ethic, microcomputer-style, no longer necessarily implied that information was free.

As companies like On-Line wrote and sold more programs, people who had no desire to become programmers, let alone hackers, began to buy computers, intending only to run packaged software on them. In a way, this represented a fulfillment of the hacker dream—computers for the masses, computers like record players: you'd go to the software store, choose the latest releases, and spin away. But did you really benefit from your computer if you did not program it?

Still, in the early eighties, everyone with a computer had to delve into the hacker mentality to some degree. Doing the simplest things on your machine required a learning process, a search for gurus who could tell you how to copy a disk or find the proper connecting cables to hook up the printer. Even the process of buying ready-to-run software had a funky, hacker feel to it. The programs were packaged in Ziploc bags, the graphics on the so-called documentation were mostly on the level of Roberta Williams' stick-figure primitives, and more often than not the labels on the disk would be typewritten and stuck on by hand . . . there was an aura of the illegitimate about the product, only slightly more respectable than hard-core porno books.

An excursion to the local computer store was a journey to the unknown. The salesman, more often than not some kid working at minimum wage, would take your measure, as if you were a potential obstacle in an Adventure game, testing you by tossing off the jargon of Ks, bytes, nibbles, and RAM cards. You would try to get him to explain, say, why this accounting package ran better than that one, and he would come back with some gibberish about protocols and macros. Finally you'd ask him the question that almost every Apple owner asked in 1980 or 1981: *"What's the hot new game?"* Games were the programs which took greatest advantage of the machine's power—put the user in control of the machine, made him the god of the bits and bytes inside the box (even if he wasn't sure of the difference between a bit and a byte). The kid would sigh, nod, reach under the counter for the current Ziploc-bag phenomenon, and, if you were lucky, boot it on the screen and race through a few rounds, so you could see what you were buying. Then you would plunk down your twenty or twenty-five or even thirty-five dollars and go home for what was the essential interface with the Apple. Playing games.

In early 1980, the Hot New Game would most likely be written in deadly-slow BASIC. Most of the Apples at that time used cassette recorders; the difficulty of using an assembler with a cassette recorder made it nearly impossible to go down into the deepest recess of the machine, the 6502 chip, to speak in the Apple's assembly language.

This was changing: Steve Wozniak had recently hacked a brilliant design for a disk-drive interface for the Apple, and the company was able to offer low-cost floppy-disk drives which accessed thousands of bytes a second, making assembling easy for those few who knew how to program on that difficult level. Those infected with the Hands-On Imperative, of course, would soon join that elite in learning the system at its most primal level. Programmers, would-be programmers, and even users buying Apples would invariably purchase disk drives along with them. Since Steve Wozniak's Apple adhered to the Hacker Ethic in that it was a totally "open" machine, with an easily available reference guide that told you where everything was on the chip and the motherboard, the Apple was an open invitation to roll your sleeves up and get down to the hexadecimal code of machine level. To hack away.

So Ken Williams was not the only one catching the glory train by hacking Apple machine language in the spring of 1980. Technological pioneers all over the country were sensing what hackers had known all along: *computers could change your life.* In Sacramento, a Vietnam vet named Jerry Jewell, who had sandy hair, a matching moustache, and a perpetually addled, slightly pissed-off look about him, had bought an Apple to see if he could switch from the insurance business to something more lucrative. Two weeks after he got the machine, he enrolled in an assembly-language class at Lawrence Hall of Science taught by Andy Herzfeld, one of Apple's top programmers. Jewell had no disk drive and could not run the sample programs that were distributed each week. For eight weeks, he didn't have the slightest idea what Herzfeld was talking about, and not even brief tutorials from the assistant instructor—John Draper, alias Captain Crunch—could crack the code. Eventually, after Jewell got a disk drive and listened to the tapes he'd made of the class, he caught on.

Jewell got a job managing a local computer store. All kinds of people came into computer stores those days. It was almost like a statement in BASIC: IF you own a computer THEN you're probably a little crazy. Because even then, four years after the Altair, you still couldn't do many useful tasks with a personal computer. There was a simple word-processing program called "Easy Writer" written by John Draper (Jewell bought one of the first copies at the 1980 Computer Faire), and some accounting stuff. But mostly people hacked Tools to Make Tools. Or games. And they would come into computer stores to show off their hacks.

So it was not surprising when an Arabic-looking college student named Nasir Gebelli strode up to Jewell in the store and booted a slide-show program he'd written. Jewell liked it, and worked with

Gebelli to make a spin-off, a graphics-drawing program they called "E-Z-Draw." Jewell began making the rounds of computer stores in L.A. and the Bay Area to sell it.

Then Nasir, a computer science major who was doing poorly in his classes, began to write games. Nasir's use of color and a technique called "Page Flipping" made the current crop of games look sick. Page Flipping used a duplicate screen ("page") for everything that was displayed on the Apple; using machine-language instructions, you were flipping between the two pages thousands of times each second, in order to eliminate the flickering that made microcomputer graphics look so unappealing. Nasir was also unafraid to enlist everything and anything as "invader" in his games, which almost always used one basic scenario: you've got to shoot lots of stuff before some of it shoots back at you. It re-created the addictive, pyrotechnic state of siege that was hugely popular in coin-operated games, which had special microchips to create spectacular graphic effects, and only when Nasir showed them did people realize that some of these effects could be achieved on the Apple.

Nasir wrote twelve games that year. Jewell and the owner of the computer store formed a company called Sirius Software to sell the games. Jewell would look at Nasir's preliminary version of a game and suggest outlandish changes. One game that Nasir wrote was quite similar to "Space Invaders," a popular coin-operated arcade game where aliens irrevocably inch down the screen in waves to attack the player's little tank. Jewell suggested that weapons fired by the invaders should not be shells, but eggs—and the invaders should be, in turn, monsters, space wolves, giant-bomb-throwing lips, and the most dangerous of all, killer fuzz balls. Killer fuzz balls that bounce and shake and move toward you with frantic inevitability. "Space Eggs" was a runaway bestseller for Sirius Software.

•

Another company breaking into the market then was the brainchild of a former corporate lawyer from Wisconsin. Doug Carlston had been unhappy working for a big law firm on the eighty-second floor of the Sears Building in Chicago; he missed his college hacking days, when he and his friends would stuff chewing gum in the lock of the computer room door so the staff couldn't keep them out; at night fifteen of them would sneak in and hack. Even after he'd set up a small law practice in rural Maine, his heart remained in computing. Then the soft-spoken, contemplative Carlston heard that Radio Shack was selling a computer for under two thousand dollars. He bought one on a Friday and didn't come up for air, he remembers, until that Sunday night. Eventually he began writing a gigantic strategy game on the TRS-80, one which involved an entire imaginary universe. Your mission was to protect the interstellar good guys: the Brøderbund. (This was Scandinavian for "Brotherhood.")

It was early 1980, and Carlston, like Williams and Jewell, saw his life in software. He enlisted his brother Gary, who had been working in a job so desirable that grown men gasped when he mentioned it—coach of a Scandinavian women's basketball team. Together they set up Brøderbund Software to sell Galactic Saga. The idea was to translate the Saga from TRS-80 to the Apple.

The Saga did not fare too well at first. The seven thousand dollars that Doug and Gary began with was down to around thirty-two dollars at one point. They were living on Gary's VISA card. It wasn't until Doug drove across the country, stopping at every computer store he found and showing them the game, letting them soak in some of the program's fine points, and calling in seventeen thousand dollars' worth of business in his nightly calls back to Gary that things picked up.

But the really big break came at the 1980 Computer Faire, where the Carlstons had scraped the money together to show the Saga in a low-cost "microbooth," an innovation of Jim Warren's to allow small, often nonprofit companies to display without shelling out the spiraling exhibitor's fees on the main floor. A conservative Japanese businessman took a liking to these clean-living, religious Carlstons, and allowed them to distribute the work of some Japanese programmers he handled. The games were faithful copies of current coin-operated arcade games. And the very first Apple program he gave them, a brilliant rip-off of the arcade game "Galaxian"—they named it, unapologetically, "Apple Galaxian"—became a top hit, selling tens of thousands of disks. And though Brøderbund began to recruit programmers in the United States to write games, for months the Japanese product accounted for most of its business.

On-Line, Brøderbund, and Sirius were the fastest risers of dozens of companies springing up to cater to new computer users, particularly those in what came to be known as the Apple World. The formerly dominant Programma had overextended itself and eventually was folded into a bigger company, which was not as much of a market force. But newer firms with names like Continental and Stoneware and Southwestern Data were out of the gate like wild quarter horses, too. The distinguishing characteristic of these companies was that, like the hardware firms forming out of the Homebrew Computer Club, the impetus seemed to be as much to get software *out there* as it was to cash in on a budding trend. Hitting the marketplace seemed to be the best way to show off one's hacks.

Significantly, a new magazine which became closely identified with the brash new wave of Apple World software companies, was started by people who were not terribly experienced in publishing, but were fanatic proselytizers of the Apple computer.

Margot Tommervik, a Los Angeles free-lance textbook editor with brown hair worn long and straight in true sixties-refugee style, had loved games long before she touched her first computer. In early 1980, she appeared on the television game show "Password," and despite being paired with a couple of soap opera personalities who, she later recalled, "had no idea that Virginia was south and New Hampshire was north," she came out of a deftly played "lightning round" with fifteen thousand dollars. She and her husband Al, a copy editor at *Variety,* made a list of things to do with the money, and it turned out they needed twice as much as that to make a dent in the list. So they said to hell with it and went out to buy a computer.

The best-known home computer those days was the TRS-80. But while Margot and Al were waiting for a salesman in the local Radio Shack, a store employee—a kid who was standing near Al—said, "What's that smell?" Al was a stumpy, redheaded, long-bearded man who resembled a toll-taker at a bridge in Middle Earth, and it was unimaginable to picture him without his briar pipe. The kid, perhaps with an MIT-style smoke aversion in his hacker blood, said to Al Tommervik, "Mister, you shouldn't smoke that pipe, it's making me sick." The Tommerviks walked out of Radio Shack, and a week later bought an Apple.

Margot and Al, in her words, "became addicted" to the Apple. She enjoyed the games it played, but her satisfaction went deeper. Without any technical background, Margot Tommervik was able to extract the Hacker Ethic from this sleek piece of machinery in her home. She believed that her Apple had its own personality, life-loving and kind of daffy, in a positive way. She later explained: "The very idea of naming it Apple—it's wonderful. It's much better than [giving it a name like] 72497 or 9R. It says, 'Hey, this is

more than just a piece of machinery. You can get more out of it.'
Even the little beep it emits when you turn it on shows a special
enthusiasm.''

Margot Tommervik learned the story of how Apple Computer
began, and she marveled at how the machine conveyed Steve
Wozniak's "life-loving spirit into the computer. He had that ability
to bite all the big pieces of life and chew it up and savor every bit.
He put the spirit into it as he built. He made the machine do as
many things as he could think of it to do . . .'' Margot believed
that if you spent enough time with your Apple, you would realize
that *you* could also do anything you could think of. To her, the
Apple embodied the essence of pioneering, of doing something
brand new, having the courage and the willingness to take risks,
doing what's not been done before, trying the impossible and pulling it off with joy. The joy of making things work. In short, the joy
of hackerism, for the first time transparent to those not born with
the Hands-On Imperative.

Margot saw it in everyone who used the Apple. They just fell in
love with it. Her plumber, for example, got an Apple, and as
Margot watched the plumber's wife playing a game on it, Margot
swore she was actually seeing a mind expanding. You could get
some of this excitement even just setting up an Apple, when you
got your first disk to boot, and the disk drive came on, whirring
happily, with the little red "in use" light glowing. By God, you did
it! *You caused something to happen.* You caused the disk drive to
run, you caused this to happen, and then as you started to set real
tasks for your Apple and construct your tiny universes, you started
to solve things. You saw your power tremendously increased. All
the people she talked to in the Apple world, and certainly Margot
herself, showed that joy. She believed it was no less than the joy in
one's own humanity.

Margot Tommervik loved the new kinds of software coming out,
and though she and Al did some BASIC programming, the machine was mostly used to play these new games she would buy.
One day she dropped by Rainbow Computing and saw a notice
that a new Adventure-style program was coming out, and would
be put on sale at ten o'clock on a certain Friday; the first one who
solved it would win a prize. Margot was there with $32.95 that
Friday, and by noon Saturday she was back at the store with the
solution. The game was Mystery House.

Sometime later Margot stumbled across a publishing house
which had started a magazine about software, and was looking for

a partner. Margot and Al said they'd put up some money and do the magazine if they were promised full control. So the remains of the "Password" money went into this new incarnation of the magazine, a magazine devoted to the world of the Apple computer. It would be called *Softalk*.

When Margot started drumming up advertisers she called up On-Line and told Roberta, who was still handling corporate business from her Simi Valley kitchen, about wanting a completely professional magazine that would reflect the spirit of the Apple computer. Margot's enthusiasm was obvious. And when Margot mentioned that it was she who had won that contest to solve Mystery House, Roberta howled, "*You're* the one! We thought it would take months to do it." Roberta talked to Ken, and On-Line decided to take out four quarter-page ads in the first issue. They called up other companies and urged them to take out ads, too.

Softalk came out in September 1980 at thirty-two pages, including the covers. Eventually the people in the cottage industry of supplying products for the Apple began to realize the value of a magazine whose readers were their direct target audience. By the end of 1981, there were well over a hundred advertising pages in an issue.

•

These pioneering Apple World companies were bound by an unspoken spiritual bond. They all loved the Apple computer, and the idea of mass computing in general. Somehow, they all believed that the world would be better when people got their hands on computers, learned the lessons that computers had to teach, and especially got software that would help expedite this process.

In pursuit of this common goal, On-Line, Sirius, and Brøderbund became almost a Brotherhood of their own. Jewell and the Williamses and the Carlstons got to know each other very well, not only at computer shows and trade events, but at each other's parties, where the three staffs gathered, along with people from other Apple-oriented firms in California.

This was in high contrast to some not-so-old but already moribund companies. Particularly Atari, the company which started as the first purveyor of the computer game and sold millions of dollars of software for the Atari "VCS" game machine (which could not be programmed like a computer) and its own competitor to the Apple, the Atari Home Computer. Since its acquisition by the huge Warner Communications conglomerate, Atari had shorn itself of the hacker-like openness of its founders. You almost had to be a KGB agent to find out the *name* of one of its programmers, so terrified was Atari that someone would raid its ranks. And the thought of programmers getting together and comparing notes was even more frightening. What if one of its programmers realized that he could do better somewhere else? No such secrets for the Brotherhood, who in 1981 most often paid their programmers on a 30 percent royalty basis, a rate well known to all three companies and all the programmers working in the field.

The cooperation went deeper than partying. Almost as if they had unconsciously pledged to adhere to at least part of the Hacker Ethic, there were no secrets between them. Almost every day, Ken, Doug, and Jerry would talk on the phone, sharing information about this distributor or that floppy disk manufacturer. If some retailer didn't pay off one of the companies, the others would know immediately, and not deliver to that retailer. "We had this unwritten code," Jerry Jewell later recalled. "We would let each other know what we were working on so we wouldn't do the same projects. If I was working on a racing car game, we would tell them, so they wouldn't start one."

Some might look at this interaction and call it restraint of trade, but that would be an Old Age interpretation. This Brotherhood was no cartel banding together to the detriment of the user and the technology. The user benefited by getting a wider range of games. And if a programmer from one of the companies couldn't figure out some assembly-language trick with zero page graphics, the fact that he could get in touch with a programmer at another company was only the application of the Hacker Ethic to commerce. Why hide helpful information? If neat tricks were widely disseminated, the quality of all the software would rise, and people would get more out of computers, and it would be good for all the companies in the long run.

Maybe it was time to scrap the divisive practices of corporate business and adopt a more hacker-like approach, one which might, by its successes in the software field, spread through all of America and revitalize the entire country, long spinning in a Darwinian, litigious, MBA-dominated maelstrom. Substance might then prevail over cloudy "corporate image," in a world free of the insane, anti-productive practice of *owning* concepts and trade secrets which could be distributed far and wide. A world without all that destructive, cutthroat *seriousness.* The attitude in the Apple World seemed to be "If it's not fun, if it's not creative or new, it's not worth it." That's what you would hear from Ken and Roberta Williams, from Doug and Gary Carlston, from Jerry Jewell.

This spirit reached its peak during the summer of 1981 in a scene imbued with all the gusto of a cola commercial: a white-water raft trip down the Stanislaus River. It was Ken Williams' idea, a joint vacation trip for the whole industry. Ken joked that he did it only to put leaks into his competitors' boats; but the very absurdity of that statement underlined the difference between this industry and others. Instead of sabotaging competitors, Ken Williams would forge his way through fierce waters alongside them.

The river was idyllic, but one participant later explained to a reporter that even more idyllic than the isolated pine-treed and high-canyon-walled setting was the feeling among the adventurers, who of course swapped all sorts of product, technological, and financial information: "We all sort of feel like we beat the system: we got to microcomputers before IBM did. We're all competitors but we like to cooperate."

Even the boatmen had to tell the participants, which included the heads of over six software firms, like Ken and Roberta, or the Carlstons, or Steve Dompier (the Homebrew member who was independently writing software now that Processor Tech was out of business) to *stop talking shop*. Sometimes they did stop. They stopped at the end of the ride as they approached the last rapid. Not for the first time, Ken Williams rammed his raft into someone else's. Some people on that raft tumbled onto another one, and people from all ten rafts used their paddles and buckets to splash one another, and the Brotherhood exploded in a mist of white water, laughter, and thrilling camaraderie.

16

THE THIRD GENERATION

THERE were still the born hackers, those blessed with the unrelenting curiosity, the Hands-On Imperative. The last chosen in basketball, and the first in arithmetic class to divine the mysteries of fractions. The fifth-graders who would mumble, when adults pressed them for explanation, that they "like numbers." The cowlicked kids in the back of the junior high classroom who got so far ahead of the class that the math teachers gave up on them, let them skip to future chapters in the text, and finally allowed them to leave the room and wander downstairs to discover, with much the same wonder as Peter Samson stumbling upon the EAM room at MIT, a terminal connected to a time-sharing computer at some university. A gray teletype terminal in the basement of a suburban school, a terminal which held, wonder of wonders, games. You could play the games, but if you were hacker-born, that would not be enough. You would ask, "Why can't the game do *this?*" "Why can't it have *that* feature?" And since this was a computer, for the first time in your life you would have the power to change *this* into *that.* Someone would show you some BASIC, and the system would be at your command.

It happened exactly like that with John Harris. Though he was tall and not unattractive, a towheaded blond with a goofily appealing smile and the breathless verbal delivery of someone whose enthusiasm runs too high to acknowledge cycle-wasting grammatical interrupts, he was a social outcast. He would later admit cheerfully that he had been "the worst English student in school and the worst in P.E." His roots were in the upper middle class of San Diego. His father was a bank officer. His siblings, a younger brother and two older twin sisters, were uninterested in technical matters. "I was completely, a hundred percent technical," John later said with endearing redundancy. It seemed he had no more intimate confidant than the remote computer—he did not even know its location—connected to his school's time-sharing terminal.

John Harris was not one of those methodical, plodding geniuses who dazzled folks in science fairs. Impressing adults was not his forte. John Harris' art hinged on impressing people who shared his passions, which were few and well defined: Science fiction (films and comics—not books, because John was not much of a reader). Games. And hacking.

At one time, the apex of existence for a person like John Harris might have been to find his way into a computer center like the MIT AI lab, where he would have loitered and learned until he got his chances at a terminal. It might have felt like delivery into heaven, as it had felt to fourteen-year-old David Silver when he was initiated by the ninth-floor hackers and allowed to take the sacrament of the PDP-6. But Harris came of high school age after the revolution that began with the Altair. John Harris' generation was the first that did not have to beg, borrow, or steal computer time from a distant mainframe attached to teletype terminals. In the lush suburbs around San Diego, it was not uncommon for a high school kid in 1980 to cajole his parents, or even earn enough money from a part-time job, for a large purchase. Most kids wanted cars. But as the early computer store owners knew well, other kids were asking for computers.

When John Harris was in eleventh grade, a senior he knew let him use his Commodore PET computer. John later recalled: "I started playing games on his system and started programming on his system, a Star Trek game. And a couple of other things in BASIC that I had learned and that were a lot more fun than any of the time-sharing stuff was. It was quicker, was much more interactive, had graphics and sound effects . . . Teletypes were OK, but I hadn't known anything else existed, and I went, 'Wow, this is great . . .' "

For John Harris' Third Generation, which followed the pioneering generation of mainframe hackers and the second generation of hardware hackers who liberated computers from the institutions, access to computers was easy. You could own one, or use a friend's. The computers were not as powerful as those in institutions and there were no communities of wizards, no Greenblatts or Gospers to urge you to abandon loserdom and engage in The Right Thing until you could be called a winner. But those facts of life did not bother this Third Generation. They could get hands on computers *now.* In their bedrooms. And whatever they learned about hacking, and whatever elements of the Hacker Ethic they picked up, would be determined by a learning process that grew from the hacking itself.

John Harris was fascinated with the PET. You could *do* things so much more easily with a personal computer. John was particularly impressed with the full-screen editing capability, a great improvement on the teletype-style edit-one-line-at-a-time process he'd been stuck at before. But the best part of the PET and other personal computers were the games.

"I'm obsessed with all forms of games," John Harris later said. "It's just *me,* I guess!" It was only natural that a junior high school electronics junkie would be dazzled by the batch of space warfare arcade games appearing in the late seventies: Harris did not know that their inspiration was Slug Russell's Spacewar hack. For a time after that, John fell in love with a game called "Crazy Climber," where you try to get a guy to the top of a building, avoiding dropped flowerpots, people who close windows on your hand, and a giant gorilla who tries to swat you off. What impressed him about Crazy Climber was its groundbreaking creation of a unique and artful scenario. It did something that no one had ever done before.

John Harris strove for that level of originality. His attitude toward games was similar to his attitude toward computer languages, or his preference for a certain computer over another: an intense personal identification, and a tendency to take offense at an inefficient, sub-optimal way of doing things. John came to feel that games should have a certain degree of innovation, a certain degree of graphic razzle-dazzle, and a certain degree of challenge. His standards of "playability" were rigid. He took personal offense at cases where a programmer *could have* made the game better in some obvious (to John Harris) way, but did not, whether because of technical ignorance, a lapse in perception, or—worst of all—laziness. Details made a game really great, and John adopted the firm belief that a game author should include every possible frill to make the game more enjoyable. Not neglecting, of course, to perfect the basic structure of the game so that it was essentially bug-free.

To fulfill his own exacting standards, John needed his own computer. He began saving money. He even cut down on playing arcade games. John was out of high school by then, enrolled in a local college in electrical engineering, and working at a bank's data processing center. One of his friends owned the hottest hacker home computer around, the Apple, but John did not like the machine's editing capabilities or its quirky graphics.

With money in hand he went computer shopping, for a PET. The salesmen sneered at him. "The only person who buys a PET is a person down to his last penny," they told him. "A person who can't afford an Apple II." But John Harris did not want Wozniak's creation. He had seen more of his friend's Apple and was convinced more than ever that the Apple was severely brain-damaged. His contempt for the Apple grew beyond all bounds. "Even the sight of that computer drives me up the wall," he would later say. At the very mention of the machine, Harris would recoil and make the sign of the cross, as if warding off a vampire. He could explain at length just why he felt this way—no full-screen editor, the necessity of loading the machine up with more hardware before it really cooked, the limited keyboard . . . but this loathing went beyond reason. Somehow Harris felt the Apple stopped you from doing what you wanted to do. Whereas other hackers considered the Apple's limitations as challenging hurdles to leap over or as a seductive whisper saying, "Take me further," Harris deemed them ridiculous. So he asked the salesman at one of the stores about this other machine, the Atari computer.

Atari had just come out with its 800 (and its lower-powered companion, the 400), its competitor to the Apple. On first sight, it appeared to be some sort of jazzed-up game machine with a keyboard. In fact, it had a slot to put cartridges inside, a mark that the machine was geared at least in part for novices too befuddled to handle even a tape cassette, let alone a floppy disk. There wasn't even a decent manual. John Harris played with an 800 in the store, and discovered that, like the PET and unlike the Apple, it had full-screen editing. But he wanted to know what was inside it, so he went to another store, where a salesman slipped him a piece of paper with some commands for this new computer. Like some secret code for use by the French Resistance. No code-breaker devoured a message as avidly as John Harris did these papers. He discovered that the Atari had a set of keystroke graphic symbols, a high-resolution mode, and a separate chip for sound effects. In short, exciting new features, every feature Harris liked on the PET, and even the things he grudgingly considered worthwhile on the Apple. He bought an 800.

He began programming in BASIC, but very soon realized that he would have to learn assembly language to do the games he wanted to do. He quit working at the bank and got a job at a company called Gamma Scientific, which had needed a programmer to do assembly-language work on its system, and was willing to train someone.

Transferring his new assembly-language skills to the Atari was difficult. The Atari was a "closed" machine. This meant that Atari sequestered the information concerning the specific results you got by using microprocessor assembly-language commands. It was as if Atari did not want you to be able to write on it. It was the antithesis to the Hacker Ethic. John would write Atari's people and even call them on the telephone with questions; the voices on the phone would be cold, bearing no help. John figured Atari was acting that way to suppress any competition to its own software division. This was not a good reason at all to close your machine. (Say what you would about Apple, the machine was "open," its secrets available to all and sundry.) So John was left to ponder the Atari's mysteries, wondering why Atari technicians told him that the 800 gave you only four colors in the graphics mode, while on the software they released for it, games like "Basketball" and "Super Breakout," there were clearly more than eight colors. He became determined to discover its secrets, the mysteries of its system, the better to extend it and control it.

For the quest, John enlisted a friend who knew assembly language. They got hold of a cassette-tape disassembler written in BASIC, something which broke down programs into their object code, and disassembled the software sold by Atari line by line. Then they would take these weird instructions, which accessed all sorts of oddball memory locations on the 6502 chip inside the Atari, and poke them into the machine to see what happened. They discovered things like "display list interrupts," which enabled you to use a greater number of colors on the display screen; "user definable characters"; and, best of all, something that they would later know as "player-missile graphics," which was no less than an assembly-language method of accessing a special Atari chip called "Antic" that handled graphics on its own, letting you run the rest of the program on the main chip. Since one of the more difficult aspects of programming games was parceling out the activities of the main chip between sound, graphics, and game logic, player-missile graphics gave you a huge advantage. How could a company that did something so neat in its machine be so Scrooge-like in letting you know it existed?

Harris and his friend had cracked the secrets of the Atari. They wanted to use their knowledge to liberate the machine, distribute the technical data, break the Atari marketplace wide open. But around that time some bootleg hardware manuals appeared. It seemed that some pirates inside Atari had procured copies of its internal hardware and reference manual, and were distributing them for high prices to interested parties. The manual, however, was written in such a way that only people who were already the equivalent of Atari design engineers could divine it. As Harris later put it, "It was written in Atari, not in English." So the bootleg manual wasn't much help except to those people who had integrated the workings of the Atari 800 into their own mental cosmology. People like John Harris.

Eighteen-year-old John Harris used this knowledge to write games. He wrote games that he would like to play, and his desire to make the games flashy enough and exciting enough to please him as a player incited him to learn more about the Atari system. As a science-fiction fan who often attended the "Cons"—the conclaves of sci-fi nuts, where people lost in technological fantasy were considered normal—he naturally gravitated to space warfare games. He would create spaceships, space stations, asteroids, and other extraterrestrial phenomena. From his imagination he would make these shapes appear on his display screen, and then he would control them. Putting them up on the screen and controlling them was much more important than the eventual fate of the game itself: John Harris could be careless, and he often lost entire programs by saving files on the wrong side of the cassette tape, or expanding the code so the program would crash—finding out only then that he had failed to make a backup tape. He would feel bad about it, but keep hacking.

Hacking was the best thing in his life. He had started working full-time at Gamma Scientific to support himself. The pay was less than ten thousand dollars a year. He liked the job insofar as it allowed him to work on the computer. At home, he had his 800, now equipped with a disk drive for fancy assembly-language programming. But without a tightly knit community like the one the MIT hackers had, he found that hacking was not enough. He yearned for more social contact. His relationship to his family was shaky. He later claimed he was "kicked out" of his home because his father had expectations John could not quite match. He describes his father as less than enthusiastic about his mania for programming games on an Atari 800 computer. So Harris moved into a house with a few fellow sci-fi fans. He would attend the Cons with them, wild affairs where they could stay up for days at a stretch, prowling the hotel halls with plastic dartguns. But it often seemed to John that his friends were planning some neat excursion without inviting him. John Harris was a friendly, loping, puppy-dog youngster, and very sensitive to these apparent rejections.

He wanted a girlfriend. The isolated times when he'd been out with members of this desirable yet elusive gender always seemed to end in some kind of disappointment. His housemates were often involved in romantic intrigue—they jokingly called the house "Peyton Place of Outer Space"—but John was rarely involved. There was one girl he saw for a couple of weeks, and had even made a New Year's Eve date with. But she'd called him just before New Year's. "I don't know how to tell you this," she said, "but I met a guy and I'm going to marry him." That was typical.

So he kept hacking games. Just like the MIT hackers, or the Homebrewers, his reward was the satisfaction of doing it. He joined a local Atari users' group and borrowed programs from their library to make them run faster and do neat things. He took, for instance, a version of the arcade game "Missile Command" and sped it up, jazzed up the explosions when one of your ICBMs stopped the enemy nuke from destroying your city. He'd show his work to others and they'd get a kick out of it. All his hacking automatically reverted to the public domain; ownership was a concept he never dealt with. When someone in the users' group told John Harris that he had a little company that sold computer games and he'd like to market a game of John's, Harris' reaction was Sure, why not? It was like giving a game away and getting money for it, too.

He gave the man a game called "Battle Warp," which was remarkably like the old MIT Spacewar, a two-player game where ships "fly around and shoot at each other," as John was later to describe it. Harris made around two hundred dollars from Battle Warp, but it was enough to get him thinking about having his stuff distributed more widely than through the users' group network.

In March of 1981, Harris went to the Computer Faire in San Francisco, primarily to attend a seminar on programming the

Atari, given by one of Atari's best programmers, Chris Crawford. John was extremely impressed with Crawford, a mousy fellow who bounced around when he talked and was skillful at explaining things. John Harris was on a high after that, wandering around the densely packed aisles of Brooks Hall, looking at all the hot new machines, and checking out the dozens of new software companies that had taken booths that year.

John had gotten the courage by then to ask a few companies whether they needed any programs on the Atari. They generally said no. Then he reached the booth rented by On-Line Systems. Someone introduced him to Ken Williams, who seemed nice, and John told Ken that he was an assembly-language business programmer, but he was kind of fed up with it.

Ken Williams at that time had been discovering that people who could write good assembly-language games were rare finds. He wanted to lure these assembly-language programmers to Coarsegold, California. On-Line Systems had seen explosive growth—at the last Computer Faire, Ken had been testing the waters for Mystery House, and one year later he was an established game publisher, in need of products. He had placed an ad in *Softalk* headlined "Authors Wanted," promising "highest royalties in the industry . . . No need to ever work anyone else's hours again." The ad mentioned another benefit: a chance to work with Apple guru Ken Williams, who would "be personally available at any time for technical discussions, helping to debug, brainstorming . . ." Ken was smart enough to realize that the programmers to create these products were not necessarily veteran computer workers. They might well be awkward teen-agers. Like John Harris.

"Well," Ken said to John Harris, not missing a beat, "how would you like to program amongst the trees?"

As appealing as that sounded, it meant working for On-Line Systems, which John Harris knew a little about. He knew they sold mostly Apple software. "I don't know the Apple system," he said, tactfully omitting that as far as he did know the Apple system he wanted to flush it down a toilet.

Ken said the magic words. "We want to expand to the Atari system. We just haven't found anyone who can program it."

John was almost speechless.

"Can you program it?" Ken asked.

Within a month, Ken Williams had bought John Harris a plane ticket to Fresno, where he was picked up at the airport and driven up Route 41 to Oakhurst. Ken promised Harris a place to live, and then they started talking salary. John had just gotten a raise at Gamma, so the one thousand dollars a month Ken offered him would actually have been a pay cut. John found the courage to say that he was getting more than that now. Did Ken think he could pay twelve hundred a month, and throw in the free place to live? Ken looked over at Roberta (at that time any employee in the tiny On-Line office could at any time look over at anyone else working there) and she said she didn't think they could afford that.

Williams said, "I tell you what. How about if I put you on a 30 percent royalty basis and you won't have to work with the company? You work out of your house and I'll give you seven hundred dollars a month to live off of until you finish your first game, in two or three months. If you don't have a game finished by that time, you won't make it in this business anyway."

John thought that sounded great. When he got home, though, his father told him he was being taken advantage of. Why not get a bigger salary and a lower percentage of royalties? What security did John have? John, who had been intimidated by the blustery Ken, did not want to jeopardize his chance to live in an atmosphere built around hacking games. He really wanted to get out of San Diego, hack games, and be happy. Even though it might mean less money, he'd hold on to the 30 percent royalty.

It was the most lucrative decision he ever made.

•

Ken Williams had purchased several houses around Oakhurst for the benefit of his programmers. John Harris moved into the one called Hexagon House, named after the shape of the upper floor, which was the only part visible from the road: it jutted above the rest of the house like a large solid gazebo. From the front door, the living room and kitchen were visible; the bedrooms were downstairs. Living there with John was Ken's twenty-year-old brother, John Williams, who ran On-Line's advertising and marketing division. Though John Williams liked Harris, he considered him a nerd.

The first project that John Harris had mentioned to Ken was inspired by the arcade game Pac-Man. This was the hottest coin-operated game in 1981, and would soon be known as the most popular coin-op of all time. John Harris saw nothing wrong with going to the arcade, learning the game in and out, and writing his own version to run on the Atari 800. To a hacker, translating a useful, or fun, program from one machine to another was inherently good. The idea that someone could *own* Pac-Man, that clever little game where ghosts chase the dot-munching yellow Pac-Man, apparently was not a relevant consideration for John Harris. What was relevant was that the Pac-Man game seemed a natural fit to the Atari's features. So even though he personally preferred games with space scenarios and lots of shooting, John suggested to Ken that he do an Atari 800 Pac-Man.

Ken had already been marketing a Pac-Man look-alike for the Apple under the name of "Gobbler." The program had been written by a professional scientific programmer named Olaf Lubeck, who had sent Williams the game, unsolicited, after seeing the "Authors Wanted" ad. The program was selling around eight hundred copies a month, and Ken had arranged with Lubeck to duplicate it for the Atari home computer.

John Harris, though, was appalled at the Apple game. "It didn't look spectacular, no animation," he later explained. "The collision detection is very unforgiving." Harris did not want Olaf to compound the error on his beloved Atari by translating the Apple game bit by bit on the 6502 chip, which the Apple and Atari shared. This would mean that none of what John considered the superior Atari features, most of which were housed on separate chips, would be utilized. The thought was horrifying.

John insisted that he could do a better-looking game within a month, and Ken Williams took Lubeck off the project. John Harris embarked on a period of intense hacking, often wrapping around till morning. John's style was freewheeling. He improvised. "Whatever my mind is doing, I just let it flow with it . . . things come out pretty creative," he later explained. Sometimes John could be sensitive about this, particularly at times when a more traditional programmer, armed with flowcharts and ideas about standard structure and clear documentation, examined his code. When John left Gamma Scientific to move to Coarsegold, for example, he worried that his replacement would be someone like that, who would throw away all his clever code, replacing it with something structured, concise . . . and worse. As it turned out, Gamma considered six programmers, five of whom "had degrees coming out of their ears," John later said. The sixth was a hacker with no degrees; John begged his bosses to hire the hacker.

"But he wants as much money as the people who have degrees," the boss told John.

John said, "He's worth *more.*" His boss listened. When John broke this new employee in and explained his system, the new hacker became very emotional over John's code. "You program like I do!" he said. "I didn't think there was anyone in the world that does this!"

Working with large conceptual blocks and keeping focused, John had a Pac-Man-style game running on the Atari in a month. He was able to use some of the subroutines he had developed in earlier efforts. This was a fairly good example of the kind of growth that creative copying could encourage: a sort of subroutine reincarnation in which a programmer developed tools that far transcended derivative functions. One day, John's subroutines would be modified and used in even more spectacular form. This was a natural, healthy outgrowth of the application of hacker principles. It was only too bad that this third generation of hackers had to write their own software tool kits, supplementing them only by haphazard additions from users' groups and friends.

The Pac-Man game looked remarkably like the arcade version. It might well have been one of the best assembly-language programs written so far for the Atari Home Computer. But when Harris took his work to Ken Williams, there was a problem. Lately, some companies were insisting that the copyrights they owned on coin-operated games made unauthorized home computer translations illegal. One of the biggest owners of copyrights was Atari, and it had sent the following letter to small publishers like Brøderbund, Sirius, and On-Line:

ATARI SOFTWARE
PIRACY
THIS GAME IS OVER

Atari is a leader in the development of games such as Asteroids™ and MISSILE COMMAND™ . . . We appreciate the response we have received from videophiles of the world who have made our games so popular. Unfortunately, however, there are companies and individuals who have copied ATARI's games in an attempt to reap undeserved profits from games they did not develop. ATARI must protect our investment so that we can continue to invest in the development of new and better games. Accordingly, ATARI gives warning to both the intentional pirates and to the individuals simply unaware of the copyright laws that ATARI registers the audiovisual works associated with its games with the Library of Congress and considers its games proprietary. ATARI will protect its rights by vigorously enforcing these copyrights and taking the appropriate action against unauthorized entities who reproduce or adapt substantial copies of ATARI games regardless of what computer or other apparatus is used in their performance . . .

Ken Williams knew that Atari had spent millions of dollars for the rights to Pac-Man. After looking at John Harris' brightly colored, fast-moving, non-flickering duplication of the arcade game, he realized it was such a faithful copy that it was unmarketable. "It looks too much like Pac-Man," he said. "You've wasted your time, John Harris." He suggested that John alter the game. Harris took the game home and reprogrammed the graphics. This new version was virtually the same; the difference was that the ghosts, those goofy little shapes that chased the Pac-Man, were wearing tiny moustaches and sunglasses. Incognito ghosts! Perfect ironic commentary on the stupidity of the situation.

It wasn't exactly what Ken Williams had in mind. For the next two weeks, John and Ken consulted with lawyers. How could they keep the essence of Pac-Man and still keep Atari at bay? The lawyers said that the only thing Atari really owned was the image of the character, what the game looked like.

So a new scenario was developed, with the unlikely theme of preventive dentistry. Ken's brother John Williams suggested the ghosts be replaced with "happy faces." They would spin and flip around. John Harris replaced the yellow Pac-Man with a set of clicking false teeth. Instead of dots, John drew "lifesavers," and programmed a routine that would occur when the player cleared the dots—a toothbrush would appear and brush the teeth. None of this was difficult to program. John Harris simply drew the new images on shape tables and wrote them into his existing machine. One of the wonderful things about the computer was that you could change the world on impulse.

The lawyers assured Ken that this new "Jawbreaker" scenario presented no problem with Atari. They did not know Atari. It was a company owned by the Warner Entertainment Conglomerate; it was ruled by a former textile executive who saw little distinction between computer software and any other consumer item. Since engineers no longer ran Atari, the company had been characterized by a bureaucracy which stifled hacker impulses. Programmers at Atari were paid far less than the astronomical sales figures of their games would seem to call for, and convincing the marketing "experts" to release an innovative game was a formidable task. Atari would not include the name of the game programmer on the package; it even refused to give this artist credit when the press requested an author's name. When some of the company's top programmers complained, the textile alumnus who ran Atari reportedly called the hackers "towel designers." Those hackers were among many who quit to form companies which would decimate Atari's market share of game cartridges.

Atari did not seem to address this loss outright, but instead focused its creative efforts on litigation and high-rolling licensing of seemingly failure-proof properties from other media, from coin-operated games to movies. A prominent example was Pac-Man, for which Atari spent millions. The idea was to first convert the game to the VCS game machine, then to the Atari home computers, the 400 and 800. The two divisions were separate and competitive, but both shared the problem of disappearing programmers. So imagine the joy of the executives in Atari's Home Computer Division when one day, out of the blue, some random person sent Atari a copy of a program that had been circulating around the users' groups that summer of 1981. It was a brilliant version of Pac-Man which ran beautifully on the Atari 800.

It was the result of a classic John Harris Real World goof-up. When John had been working on the "Jawbreaker" revision, some people at a computer store in Fresno heard rumors of a brilliant Pac-Man hacked by the skinny, nervous kid who would often drop by and check out peripherals and software. They asked John Harris to show them the game. Without a thought to such non-hacker restrictions as corporate secrecy, John Harris drove down and proudly watched them play the version in progress, and saw nothing unusual about their request to borrow a copy of the disk. He left a copy there, went back to the Hexagon House, and continued writing his revision.

Copies of the game began circulating through users' groups across America. When it reached Atari, people there called all the software companies they could think of to find its author. Eventually, they spoke to Ken Williams, who later recalled an Atari executive telling him that he was in possession of a Pac-Man game of obviously superior quality and was looking for its creator.

"Tell me about the game," said Ken, and the Atari man described it as having happy faces. "That's John Harris!" said Ken. The Atari man said he wanted to buy the program from John Harris. Ken had John Harris return the call to Atari's head of acquisitions, Fred Thorlin—from Ken's office. According to Ken, Thorlin was wild about John Harris' game. He promised Harris a large royalty, mentioned a contest Atari was running for best software program, with a twenty-five-thousand-dollar prize, and said none of the entries so far had come close to Harris' game.

But John Harris remembered how mean Atari had been when he had been trying to learn assembly language. He knew that it had been Atari's letter to On-Line that was forcing him to do all this revision in the first place. Atari had acted, John later said, like "a bunch of babies," holding on to information like a selfish kid protecting a toy from his playmates. John Harris told Ken that he would not consider having his name on anything published by Atari (not that Atari had mentioned putting his name on the program), and that he would finish Jawbreaker for Ken.

Jawbreaker was an instant bestseller. Almost everyone who saw it considered it a landmark for the Atari Home Computer. Except Atari. The men who ran Atari thought John's program infringed on their right, as owners of Pac-Man, to make as much money as they could from the game, by marketing it in any way they saw fit. If Ken Williams released a game that gave a player the feeling he was playing Pac-Man, especially if John Harris' version was better than the one Atari's programmer might come up with, that player would not be likely to buy Atari's version of Pac-Man. And Atari felt that its purchase of the Pac-Man license entitled it to every penny to be earned from home computer games that played like Pac-Man.

It was a challenge to the Hacker Ethic. Why shouldn't Atari be happy with a royalty paid by people who wanted to hack Pac-Man code and eventually improve the game? Did the public benefit from one company "owning" a piece of software and preventing others from making it more useful?

Atari did not see merit in that argument. This was the Real World. So after Jawbreaker's release, Atari began pressuring On-Line Systems. On one hand, it wanted Ken Williams to stop marketing the game. On the other hand, it wanted to buy John Harris' program.

•

Ken had no desire to fight Atari. He was not an unconditional supporter of the Hacker Ethic, so he had no political problem, as John Harris did, with selling the program to Atari. When Atari's

Fred Thorlin invited Ken and John Harris to come up to Sunnyvale, Ken agreed.

John Harris, who seemed only rarely to handle the simple mechanics of living as masterfully as he evoked magic from the guts of the Atari 800, missed his flight, and got to Atari's complex of low-lying glass-and-concrete buildings in Sunnyvale after the meeting ended. He had been lucky.

Ken later recounted the experience under oath. Fred Thorlin had ushered him into an office where some of Atari's in-house lawyers were waiting. Atari's associate general counsel, Ken Nussbacher (who was not at the meeting), later described his company's approach to publishers like On-Line as "carrot-and-stick," and this might have been a classic example. According to Ken Williams, one attorney told them that he would like to see On-Line agree to produce a Pac-Man game for Atari so that they could quietly resolve the problem of infringement which Jawbreaker had created (the carrot). Ken said he would be happy to deal with Atari and he hoped to hear a proposal.

A second attorney delivered the stick. According to Ken, this attorney began shouting and cursing. Ken recalled him saying "he had been hired by Atari to find companies infringing on Atari's copyrights and put them out of business . . . he said [Atari] would be able to afford much, much more legal support than I would and that if I did not play ball with them, they were going to put me out of business."

Ken was so scared he was shaking. But he told the attorneys that a judge might be better qualified to see if Jawbreaker was a copyright infringement.

About that time, Fred Thorlin asked the attorney to calm down and consider the prospect of the two companies working together (the carrot). They discussed how long it would take John Harris, the nineteen-year-old hacker who loved Atari computers but despised Atari and was lost somewhere between Coarsegold and Sunnyvale, to finish a new Pac-Man game for Atari. But Thorlin's offer of a 5 percent royalty was insultingly low. After Thorlin told him "You have no choice," Ken's fear began to turn to anger. He decided he would rather let Atari sue him than give in to blackmail. To signify his distaste, he threw the specifications for converting Pac-Man on Thorlin's desk, and returned to Coarsegold without a deal.

For a while it looked like Atari would close down On-Line. Ken's brother John later recalled that one day someone let him know that Atari had gotten an injunction to confiscate any machinery that might copy disks of Jawbreaker—every computer and disk drive in the company. The marshal from Fresno was on the way. John Williams, twenty years old and running the company that day, could not get hold of Ken and Roberta, so he ordered everyone to carry out the computers before the marshal arrived. Otherwise, the company couldn't have run for another day.

Al Tommervik, who drove a wheezing Toyota all night to get to court to be by Ken during the injunction hearing, suggested that Roberta mail down all the masters to him for safekeeping. He said he'd find a place for On-Line if Atari closed down its offices. It never came to that, but there were some very tense times in the fall of 1981.

John Harris was particularly shaken. He had been getting enough in royalties to buy himself a house outside of Oakhurst, a big, orange-colored wood structure. He also bought himself a four-wheel-drive pickup. He was working on a new game for On-Line, another maze game called "Mouskattack." Despite this upswing in his fortunes, it was a very nervous John Harris who appeared for deposition in early December.

It made an odd picture. John Harris, a nineteen-year-old hacker in jeans and T-shirt, facing the best pin-striped legal talent of one of the biggest entertainment conglomerates in America. On-Line's legal team was headed by one Vic Sepulveda, a flip-talking Fresno lawyer with short gray hair, large, aviator-style black glasses, and a laid-back confidence. His previous experience in copyright law was in a case in which some printers had insisted that the text to the homily "Desiderata" was in the public domain.

During the deposition, John Harris was so nervous he could not keep still. Atari's lawyer began by asking him about his early programming efforts, his job in San Diego, how he met Ken, how he wrote Jawbreaker . . . all questions John could easily answer, but because of his tenseness he kept getting entangled and correcting himself—at one point cutting himself off and saying, "Oh God, that sounded awkward." John was usually a person who liked to talk about his work, but this was different. He was aware that this lawyer's goal was to make him say something he didn't mean, to trip him up. Supposedly a deposition is a search for truth, where the most effective questions are asked to get the most accurate responses. It should work like a smooth program in assembly language, where you have given the fewest instructions to access the 6502 chip, direct information in and out of memory, keep the proper flags on the registers, and, out of thousands of operations taking place each second, get your result on the screen. In the Real World it did not work that way. The truth that you found in a computer was worthless here. It was as if the lawyer were feeding John Harris bogus data in hopes of a system crash.

While the hacker in John Harris was appalled at the adversarial nature of the legal system, the legal system had its difficulties adjusting to him. The rules of evidence were somewhat more rigorous than John's own archival standards. Ken Williams, in his own deposition, had warned Atari's lawyers of this when they had asked him about the status of Harris' source code for the program and he had replied: "I know John Harris and I'm positive there's nothing written down. He doesn't work like that."

Doesn't work like that? Impossible! A programmer at Atari, like any "professional" programmer, probably had to submit code regularly, allow for proper supervision. What Atari's lawyers did not realize was that Ed Roberts, Steve Wozniak, and even the designers of their own Atari 800 had wrought a Third Generation of hackers, idiot savants of the microprocessor, kids who didn't know a flowchart from Shinola, yet could use a keyboard like a palette and hack their way to Picasso-esque peaks.

ATARI LAWYER (to Ken): Isn't it a fact that typically the programmer who's designing these games at least produces a flow chart and then writes out the source code manually prior to punching it in?

KEN WILLIAMS: No.

ATARI LAWYER: Do they simply sit down at the keyboard and punch in the program?

KEN WILLIAMS: My programmers are typically too lazy to make up any sort of a flow chart. In most cases they don't even know where they're going when they start a program. They try to get a routine working to put in a background, and from that move toward some game.

It couldn't have been too much of a surprise to Atari's lawyers, on the second day of John Harris' deposition, that he was unable to find the copy of the pre-Jawbreaker Pac-Man game he'd written. On-Line's Atari machines were in use copying Wizard and The Princess, and John's equipment was broken, so he couldn't even find the disk it was on. "It's not labeled on the front," John explained, saying, "As far as I know it should be somewhere in my library."

So Atari's lawyers continued with John Harris, probing the difference between the versions of his game. And as the examination continued, the line between creative freedom and plagiarism got fuzzier and fuzzier. Yes, John Harris consciously copied from Pac-Man in programming his game. But some of the routines he used were written before he'd ever seen Pac-Man. Since the Atari 800 was radically different from the Pac-Man arcade machine, using different chips and requiring different programming techniques, John Harris' code bore no resemblance at all to the Atari code. It was completely original.

Still, his first game had looked like Pac-Man, using the characters protected by copyright. But Ken had refused to market that version, and John had changed the characters. Atari insisted that this change was insufficient. Atari had its marketing chief come in to explain "the magic of Pac-Man" to the judge, calling it "a game with a little guy, a little Pac-Man" who gobbles dots and power pills, which enable him to "turn the tables" and go after the goblins who have been devouring him. The marketing man went on to say that the "magic of Atari" rested in its commitment to buying the rights to popular arcade games.

Vic Sepulveda insisted that John Harris had simply taken the *idea* of Pac-Man from Atari, and cited law which stated that ideas are not copyrightable. Vic's brief listed side by side the differences between Pac-Man and Jawbreaker. Atari's reply was that despite the differences the game was Pac-Man. Of all the mazes John Harris could have chosen, Atari's lawyers noted, he chose the Pac-Man maze. By On-Line's own admission, they had simply performed cosmetic surgery on a virtual copy of Pac-Man!

But the judge refused to grant Atari a preliminary injunction to force On-Line to stop marketing Jawbreaker. He looked at the two games, figured he could tell the difference, and ruled that, pending a full trial, On-Line should be allowed to keep marketing Jawbreaker. Atari's lawyers seemed stunned.

David had temporarily smitten Goliath. Still, Ken Williams was not as thrilled with the decision as one might have expected. Because On-Line had its own games, and its own copyrights. It was becoming clear to Ken Williams that in the bottom of his heart he identified with Atari's point of view much more than he cared about the Hacker Ethic. "If this opens the door to other programmers ripping off my software," he told Al Tommervik immediately after the decision, "what happened here was a bad thing." He would settle the lawsuit before it came to trial.

17

SUMMER CAMP

KEN Williams came to rely on people like John Harris, Third
Generation hackers influenced not so much by Robert Heinlein or
Doc Smith as by Galaxian, Dungeons and Dragons, and *Star Wars*.
A whole subculture of creative, game-designing hacker-program-
mers was blooming, beyond the reach of executive headhunters.
They were mostly still in high school.

To lure young programmers to Coarsegold, Williams took out
ads in the Los Angeles *Times* tempting programmers to "Boot into
Yosemite." Typical of the replies was a man who told Ken, "My
son's a great Apple programmer and would like working with
you." "Why don't you let me talk to your son?" Ken asked. The
man told him that his son didn't come across well on the phone. At
the job interview at Oakhurst, the man insisted on answering all
the questions for his son, a small, round-eyed, sixteen-year-old
blond who had peach-fuzz on his cheeks and seemed intimidated
by the entire situation. None of this mattered when Ken discovered
the kid was capable of grasping the intricacies of Apple assembly
language. Ken hired him for three dollars an hour.

Slowly, Ken Williams began to fill up the house he bought in the
Sierra Sky Ranch area, just beyond Oakhurst where Route 41
starts climbing to elevations of over five thousand feet. Besides free
rent, there were Ken's impromptu graphics tutorials. Ken was now
known as a certified Apple wizard. He could turn on his hacker
inquisitiveness almost on whim. He refused to accept what others

considered generic limitations on the Apple. He would use page-flipping, exclusive-or-ing, masking technique . . . anything to get something up on the screen. When looking at someone else's program, he could smell a problem, circle around it, get to the heart of the matter, and come up with a solution.

On-Line's corporate headquarters in 1981 was the second floor of a dark brown wood-frame structure on Route 41 whose ground floor housed a stationery store and a little print shop. You entered the office after climbing a flight of stairs on the outside of the building; you had to go outside past the staircase to go to the bathroom. Inside the office were a group of desks, fewer desks than there were employees. People played a continuous game of musical chairs to claim desk space and use of one of the several Apples. Boxes of disks, discarded computer monitors, and stacks of correspondence were piled on the floor. The disarray was mind-boggling. The noise level, routinely intolerable. The dress code, nonexistent. It was productive anarchy, reminiscent of the nonstructured atmosphere of the AI lab or the Homebrew Club. But since it was also a prosperous business, and the participants so young, the On-Line office resembled a weird combination of *Animal House* and *The Millionaire*.

It was indicative of Ken Williams' priorities. He was involved in a new type of business in a brand-new industry, and was not about to establish the same hateful, claustrophobic, secretive, bureaucratic environment that he despised so much at almost every company he had worked for. He was the boss, but he would not be the kind of boss Dick Sunderland at Informatics was, obsessed with detail. He was in control of the bigger picture. Besides getting rich, something that seemed to be falling neatly into place as his programs regularly placed in the top ten or fifteen of the "Top 30 Bestsellers" list published by *Softalk* each month, Ken felt that he had a dual mission to fulfill at On-Line.

The first was to have fun, an element he felt had been lamentably lacking in the decorum-bound establishments of the Old Age. Ken Williams became, in effect, the head counselor in a high-tech Summer Camp. There was Summer Camp fun and rowdiness and drinking and dope-smoking. Stoned or not, everyone was on a high, working in a field that felt good, politically and morally. The extended party was fueled regularly by an influx of envelopes of money.

Packages would also arrive containing new games—whether games from friendly competitors like Sirius or Brøderbund, games from would-be software superstars looking to get published, or games from one of On-Line's outside authors working under Ken's supervision. No matter. Everything stopped for new games. Someone would run off copies and everyone would take to the Apples, playing the game, making fun of its bugs, admiring its features, and seeing who could get the highest score. As long as the money kept coming in, and it certainly did, who cared about a little disorganization, or an excessive tendency to shift into party mode?

Outsiders would visit the office and not believe what they saw. Jeff Stephenson, for instance. At thirty, he was an experienced programmer who had recently worked for Software Arts, the Cambridge, Massachusetts, company that had written the bestselling Apple program of all time, the financial "spreadsheet" VisiCalc. That company was also headed by programmers—Jeff could recall the two presidents, one of them a former MIT hacker and the other a meticulous young Orthodox Jew, arguing for half an hour about where a comma should go on some report. Jeff, a quiet, unassuming vegetarian who held a black belt in Korean sword-fighting, had moved to the mountains with his wife recently, and called On-Line to see if the closest company to his new home needed a programmer. He put on cord jeans and a sport shirt for the interview; his wife suggested he dress up more. "This is the mountains," Jeff reminded her, and drove down Deadwood Mountain to On-Line Systems. When he arrived, Ken told him, "I don't know if you're going to fit in here—you look kind of conservative." He hired Jeff anyway, for eighteen thousand dollars a year—eleven thousand less than he'd been making at Software Arts.

At the time, the most ambitious project On-Line had ever attempted was bogged down in an organizational disaster. "Time Zone," the adventure game Roberta had been working on for almost a year, was a program out of control, gripped by a literary equivalent to the Creeping Feature Creature. Almost drunk with the giddy ambition of creating on the computer, Roberta was hatching a scenario which not only would re-create scenes from all over the world but would take in the breadth of recorded history, from the dawn of man to the year 4081. When Roberta played a good adventure game she always wished it would never end—this game, she decided, would have so many plots and rooms that it would take even an experienced adventurer a year to solve. You would see the fall of Caesar, suffer the Napoleonic wars, fight Samurai warriors, rap with prehistoric Australian aborigines, sail with Columbus, visit hundreds of places, and witness the entire panorama of the human experience, eventually winding up on the planet Neburon, where the evil leader Ramadu is planning to destroy Earth. A microcomputer epic, conceived by a housewife in central California.

Programming this monster was grinding the business of On-Line to a halt. One staff programmer was working on a routine to triple the speed with which the program would fill in colors for the hi-res pictures. The young programmer whose father had arranged his employment tried to cope with the game logic, while a former alcoholic who had bootstrapped his way to the title of programmer keyed in the Adventure Development Language messages. A local teen-ager was painstakingly drawing the fourteen hundred pictures, first on graph paper, then retracing on an Apple graphics tablet.

Jeff Stephenson was asked to somehow tie the program together. He was dismayed at the disorganization, and appalled at the deadline: autumn, so the game would be on sale for Christmas. (He was later to conclude that any deadline Ken gave was usually overoptimistic by a factor of three.)

Despite the project being so far behind schedule, the company was still run like Summer Camp. Tuesday night was "Men's Night," with Ken out on a drinking excursion. Every Wednesday, most of the staff would take the day off to go skiing at Badger Pass in Yosemite. On Fridays at noon, On-Line would enact a ritual entitled "Breaking Out the Steel." "Steel" was the clear but potent Steel's peppermint schnapps which was On-Line Systems' beverage of choice. In the company vernacular, a lot of steel would get you "sledged." Once they broke out the steel on Fridays, it could be reasonably assumed that work on Time Zone would be halted while the staff, Ken leading the way, would explore the hazy, timeless zone of sledgedom.

Christmas came and went, and Time Zone did not ship until February. Twelve times the size of Wizard and the Princess, filling both sides of six floppy disks, it retailed for one hundred dollars. The first person to solve it, a jovial, adventure-game fanatic named Roe Adams (who was also the chief reviewer for *Softalk*), went virtually without sleep for a week until he vanquished Ramadu and declared Roberta's creation one of the greatest gaming feats in history.

Time Zone, though, did not earn nearly the notoriety of another On-Line adventure which was well in keeping with the spirit of the company. The game was called "Softporn." In the Spring of 1981,

Ken had met a programmer who had been talking to publishers about an adventure game he had written and was trying, with little success, to market himself. This game was not your usual adventure where you quest for jewels, or try to solve a murder, or try to overthrow some evil Emperor Nyquill from the Planet Yvonne. In this game, you were a bachelor whose quest was to find and seduce three women. The programmer had written the program as a training exercise to help teach himself about data bases, using the sexual theme to make it interesting. It was the kind of thing that hackers, at least the ones who were aware that a thing called sex existed, had been doing for years, and it was rare to find a computer center without its own particular sexual specialty, be it an obscene-joke generator or a program to print out a display of a naked woman. The difference was that in 1981, all sorts of things that hackers had been doing as cosmic technical goofs had a sudden market value in home computer translations.

The program in question was a cleaned-up variation of the original. It would get vile only if you used obscenity in your command. Still, in order to win the game you needed to have sex with a prostitute, buy a condom to avoid venereal disease, and engage in sadomasochism with a blonde who insisted on marrying you before you could bed her. If you wanted to do well in this adventure, the replies you typed into the computer had to be imaginatively seductive. But there were perils: if you came across the "voluptuous blonde" and typed in EAT BLONDE, the computer would type out a passage intimating that the blonde was leaning over and performing oral sex on you. But then she'd flash her gleaming choppers and *bite it off!*

To those with a sense of humor about that sort of thing, Softporn was a uniquely desirable Apple game. Most software publishers wanted nothing to do with the game; they considered themselves "family" businesses. But Ken Williams thought the game was a riot: he had a great time solving the adventure in three or four hours. He thought the controversy would be fun. He agreed to market Softporn.

One day not long afterward, Ken walked into the office and said, "Who wants to come over my house and take pictures in the hot tub naked?"

The idea was to get three women to pose topless in Ken's hot tub for the Softporn advertisement. Somewhere in the picture would be an Apple computer, and in the tub with the three naked women would be a male waiter serving them drinks. They borrowed a waiter from The Broken Bit, a Coarsegold steak house which was about the only decent place to eat in town. The three women, all On-Liners, who took their blouses off were the company bookkeeper, the wife of Ken's assistant, and Roberta Williams.

The full-color ad, with the women holding wineglasses (the water in the hot tub tactfully covering their nipples), the fully clothed male waiter holding a tray of more wineglasses, and an Apple computer standing rather forlornly in the background, caused a sensation. On-Line got its share of hate mail, some of it full of Bible scripture and prophecy of the damnation ahead. The story of the game and the ad caught the imagination of the news services, and the picture ran in *Time* and over the UPI wire.

Ken Williams loved the free publicity. Softporn became one of On-Line's biggest sellers. Computer stores that wanted it would be reluctant to order just that one program. So, like the teenager who goes to the drugstore and says, "I'd like a comb, toothpaste, aspirin, suntan oil, stationery, and, oh, while I'm here I might as well pick up this *Playboy,*" the store owners would order a whole sampling of On-Line products . . . and some Softporn too. Ken guessed that Softporn and its ripple effect just about doubled his revenue.

Having fun, getting rich, becoming famous, and hosting a neverending party were only part of Ken's mission; there was a more serious component as well. He was developing a philosophy about the personal computer and its ability to transform people's lives. The Apple, and the group of computers like it, were amazing not only for what they did, but also for their accessibility. Ken had seen people totally ignorant about computers work with them and gain in confidence, so that their whole outlook in life had changed. By manipulating a world inside a computer, people realized that they were capable of making things happen by their own creativity. Once you had that power, you could do anything.

Ken Williams realized that he was able to expose people to that sort of transformation, and he set about using the company he and Roberta had founded as a sort of rehabilitation project on some of the underutilized people around Oakhurst and Coarsegold.

The area had been suffering from the recession, especially in the industrial-mining realm which once supported it. There hadn't been any boom since the Gold Rush. On-Line Systems quickly became the largest employer around. Despite Ken's unorthodox management style, the appearance of a high-tech firm in town was a godsend—they were, like it or not, part of a community. Ken enjoyed his role as nouveau riche town father, dispatching his civic responsibilities with his usual bent for excess—huge donations to the local fire department, for example. But the close friends Ken and Roberta would make did not seem to come from the upper reaches of Oakhurst society. They were, instead, the people Ken lifted from obscurity by the power of the computer.

Rick Davidson's job was sanding boats, and his wife Sharon was working as a motel maid. Ken hired them both; Rick eventually became vice-president in charge of product development, and Sharon headed the accounting department. Larry Bain was an unemployed plumber who became Ken's head of product acquisition.

A particularly dramatic transformation occurred in the person of Bob Davis. He was the prime specimen in Ken's On-Line Systems human laboratory, a missionary venture using computers to transmogrify life's has-beens and never-weres into masters of technology. At twenty-seven, Davis was a former musician and short-order cook with long red hair and an unkempt beard. In 1981, he was working in a liquor store. He was delighted at the chance to reform his life by computers, and Ken was even more delighted at the transformation. Also, the wild streak in Bob Davis seemed to match a similar kink in Ken's personality.

Whenever Ken Williams went into the liquor store to buy his booze, Bob Davis would beg him for a job. Davis had heard of this new kind of company and was curious about computers. Ken finally gave him work—copying disks at night. Davis began coming in during the day to learn programming. Though he was a high school dropout, he seemed to have an affinity for BASIC and he sought extra help from Ken's crew of young hackers. Street-smart Davis saw that a hell of a lot of money was coming in to On-Line from those games, and vowed to write one himself.

Bob and his wife began hanging out with the Williamses. On-Line Systems was a loose enough company to accommodate an arrangement that flouted traditional taboos between owners and employees. They went on trips together, to places like Lake Tahoe. Bob's status at the company rose. He got appointed to programmer, and was project director of the Time Zone venture. Mostly, he typed in ADL code, not knowing much about assembly language. It bothered a few people—even amiable Jeff Stephenson, who liked Bob a lot—that Bob Davis was going around calling himself a programmer, when a *real* programmer, anyone with hacker credentials, should have been able to perform a lot more concentrated wizardry than Davis had.

Once Davis learned Ken's ADL tools, though, he had the key to writing a professional-level Adventure game. He'd always been interested in mythology, and he read up on some Greek classics, particularly those dealing with Jason, and worked the ancient tales into an adventure game. He programmed the game, he claimed, in his spare time (though some at On-Line thought that he neglected his Time Zone duties for his own project) and with some help from Ken, he finished it. Less than a year after being rescued from clerkdom in a liquor store he was a software star. On-Line's lawyer guessed there might be a problem in calling the game "Jason and the Golden Fleece" because that was a movie title which might be copyrighted, so On-Line released the game as "Ulysses and the Golden Fleece."

It was an instant hit, placing comfortably in *Softalk*'s Top Thirty. *Videogame Illustrated* magazine called it "one of the most important and challenging videogames ever created," though it really did not represent any significant advance over previous hi-res adventures except that it was longer and its graphics looked considerably more artful than the Mystery House pictures with their stick-figure look. The magazine also interviewed Davis, who sounded quite the pundit, talking about what gaming consumers might expect in the next five years ("computers hooked up to every phone and every television . . . voice synthesis . . . voice recognition . . . special effects generated by videodisks . . ."). A utopian scenario, and why not? Look what computers had done for Bob Davis.

•

The changes that personal computers were making in people's lives were by no means limited to California. All over the country, the computer was opening up new areas of creativity. Part of the hacker dream was that people who had unfulfilled creative tendencies would be liberated by the computer. They might even ascend to a level of wizardry where they might earn the appellation of hacker. Ken Williams now could see this happening. Almost as if predestined, some of his programmers, once immersed in communion with the machine, had confidently blossomed. No transformation was more dramatic than that of Warren Schwader.

Perhaps the most significant event in Warren Schwader's life occurred in 1977, when Warren was eighteen: his brother purchased one of the first Apple II computers. His brother had been paralyzed in a car accident, and wanted the Apple to relieve his boredom. It was up to tall, blond, thick-featured and slow-talking Warren to help his brother key commands into the Apple. And it was Warren who became the hacker.

At that time Warren was working at the Parker Pen Company in his hometown in rural Wisconsin. Though Warren had a talent for math, he stopped his schooling after high school. His job at Parker was running an injection molding machine, which consisted of a big mold and a tube where plastic was heated. The hot plastic would be injected into the mold, and after twenty seconds of cooling Warren would open the door and take out the newly formed pen parts. Then he would shut the door again. Warren Schwader considered the job a challenge. He wanted the pen parts to be perfect. He would constantly be adjusting the loader, or twisting the key, or tightening the nuts and bolts on the molder. He loved that machine. Years after leaving Parker, he said with pride that the pen parts from his molder were indeed perfect.

He approached programming with the same meticulous compulsiveness. Every day he would try a different graphics demo. In the morning he would decide what he wanted to try. During the twenty-second intervals that his molding machine allowed him, he would use pencil and paper to flowchart a program for the demo. At night, he would sit down at the Apple and debug the program until his intended effect filled the screen. He was particularly fond of kaleidoscopic, multicolored displays.

One of the graphics demos Warren tried appealed to him so much that he decided to try to expand it into a game. Ever since he first played Pong in arcades, Warren had been a videogame fan. He tried to copy a game he'd seen in an arcade: it had a paddle on the bottom of the screen and little bricks at the top of the screen. You would hit a blip with the paddle and it would bounce like a pinball machine. That took Warren a month of twenty-second intervals and nighttime debugging, and though it was written in lo-res graphics, which weren't as sharp as the things you could do in assembly language and hi-res, the game he turned out was good, too.

Up until this time Warren had been working on the Apple solely to discover what he could do on it. He had been absorbed in pure process. But seeing these games on the screen, games he had created from thin air, games which might have been the most creative things that he had ever accomplished, Warren Schwader began to realize that his computing could actually yield a tangible result. Like a game that others might enjoy.

This epiphany drove Warren deeper into the machine. He resolved to do an assembly-language game, even if it took him months. There were no books on the subject, and certainly no one Warren knew in Wisconsin could tell him anything about it. Also, the only assembler Warren had was the simple and slow mini-assembler that was built into the Apple. None of this stopped Warren Schwader, who in personality and outlook is much like the fabled turtle who eventually outraces the rabbit.

Warren did an assembly-language game called "Smash-Up," in which the player, controlling a little car, tries to avoid head-on collisions with other cars. He considered it good enough to sell. Warren didn't have enough money for a magazine ad, so he just made as many copies as he could on cassette tapes, and sent them to computer stores. This was 1980, when the newly minted Apple game market was switching from cassette to the faster and more versatile floppy disks. Warren sold only about two thousand dollars' worth of Smash-Up games, spending out almost twice that in expenses.

Parker Pen company closed down the factory, so Warren had a lot more time to work on his next game. "I had just learned [the card game] Cribbage and I really loved it," Schwader would later recall. "There was nobody that knew how to play it [with me] so I said, 'Why don't I write a program that plays Cribbage?'" He worked perhaps a total of eight hundred hours on it, often wrapping around until the Wisconsin dawn. He was attempting graphics tricks he didn't quite understand, things he would later know as indirect addressing, and zero-page graphics. He worked so hard at the game that "the whole time I felt that I was inside the computer. People would talk to me, but I couldn't interact," he later said. His native tongue was no longer English, but the hexadecimal hieroglyphics of LDX #$0, LDA STRING,X, JSR $FDF0, BYT $0, BNE LOOP.

The finished program was superb. Warren had developed some inspired algorithms that allowed the computer to evaluate its hand by twelve major rules. He considered the program flawless in its choosing of cards to throw in the crib. It was only because Warren was familiar with the program's traits—he knew it like an old-time card partner—that he could beat it around 60 percent of the time.

Warren Schwader sent the game to Ken Williams, who was impressed with the logic and with the graphics, which gave a clear, sharp picture of each card dealt. What was even more amazing was that Schwader had done this on the limited Apple mini-assembler.

It was as if someone had sent Ken a beautifully crafted rocking chair, and then had told him that the craftsman had used no saw, lathe, or other conventional tools, but had built the chair with a penknife. Ken asked Warren if he wanted to work for On-Line. Live in the woods. Boot into Yosemite. Join the wild, crazy Summer Camp of a new-age company.

Warren had been subsisting on the couple-hundred dollars a month he received from the state for taking care of his brother. Warren was worried about leaving him to day nurses, but his brother told Warren that this On-Line thing was a big opportunity and he should take it. And it appealed to Warren, this idea of going off and making money programming games and living in the woods. So he decided to do it. But there was one part of the package that did not appeal to him. The Summer Camp fun and rowdiness and drinking and dope-smoking that were common practices at On-Line Systems.

Warren was a Jehovah's Witness.

Around the time Warren was working on Cribbage, his mother had died. Warren got to thinking about where he was headed, and what his purpose was in life. He found that computers were the main thing he was living for. He felt there had to be more, and turned to his late mother's religion. He began intense study of the Bible. And he vowed that his new life in California would be characterized by adherence to the precepts of Jehovah.

At first this did not interfere much with his life at On-Line. Warren Schwader did not criticize *la dolce vita* at On-Line Systems. But because of the godless habits of his colleagues, he generally limited his transactions with them to business or technical discussions. He preferred to stick with people of his faith so he would be protected from temptation.

He was living alone, free of charge, in one of Ken's houses, a small two-bedroom. His social life was confined to a hall of the Kingdom of Jehovah's Witnesses in Ahwahnee, five miles west of Oakhurst. The very first time he went to a service there, he felt he had made more friends than he ever had before. They approved of computers, telling him that they could do much good for man, though one must beware that much can be done through computers to do harm. Warren became aware that the love he had for hacking was a threat to his devotion to God, and though he still loved programming he tried to moderate his hacking sessions so that he was not diverted from his true purpose. So while he kept programming at night, he would also maintain his Bible studies, and during afternoons and weekends he would travel through the area, knocking on doors and going into people's houses, bearing copies of *Awake!* and *The Watchtower,* and preaching the faith of Jehovah.

Meanwhile, he was working on a game based on some of Ken's fastest, most spectacular assembly-language subroutines yet. It was a game like Space Invaders, where you had a rocketship and had to fight off waves of invaders. But the waves were full of weird shapes, and moved in all kinds of directions, and if the player tried to send a constant stream of bullets off to fight them, his "laser gun" would overheat and he would face almost certain death. It was the kind of game designed to spur cardiac arrest in the feeble-hearted, so fierce were the attackers and so violent were the explosions. It was not exactly a landmark in Apple gaming, since it was so derivative of the Space Invaders school of shoot-'em-ups, but it did represent an escalation in graphic pyrotechnics and game-playing intensity. The name of this computer program was "Threshold," and it made Warren Schwader almost one hundred thousand dollars in royalties, a significant percentage of which was tithed to the Kingdom Hall in Ahwahnee.

But as Warren drew closer to the community of the Kingdom, he began to question deeply the kinds of things he had been doing for On-Line. He wondered if his very joy in programming wasn't some kind of sin. The act of programming the game had been carnal—Warren had worked through the night with his stereo blaring Led Zeppelin (Satan's rock band). Worse, the shooting nature of the game left no doubt that it glorified war. Warren's study of scripture convinced him one should not learn war any more. He felt ashamed that a war game he had programmed would be played by kids.

So he was not surprised to see an *Awake!* article about videogames which compared them to drugs, and said that the warlike games "promote aggression without mercy." Warren decided to stop programming violent games, and he vowed that if *Watchtower* were to come out strongly against all games, he would have to stop programming and find something else to do with his life.

He began work on a nonviolent game with a circus theme. The work went slowly because he tried not to lose himself in programming to the point that he would be a zombie who had lost contact with God. He got rid of all his hard rock albums and played music like Cat Stevens, Toto, and the Beatles. He even began to like music he once would have considered sappy, like Olivia Newton-

John (though when he played her record he always had to remember to lift the needle when the sinful song "Physical" played).

Still, when Warren talked about his new game, how he was using dual-page animation with twelve different patterns to control the rolling barrels that the character must leap over, or how it would have zero-flicker and be "100 percent playable," it was clear that despite his asetic efforts he took a sensual pride in the hack. Programming meant a lot to him. It had changed his life, giving him power, made him someone.

•

As much as John Harris loved living away from San Diego in the Sierra foothills, as much as he appreciated the footloose Summer Camp atmosphere, and as happy as he was that his programs were recognized as colorful, creative efforts, one crucial part of his life was totally unsatisfactory. It was a common disease of Third Generation hackers, to whom hacking was important, but not everything, as it was to the MIT hackers. John Harris hungered for a girlfriend.

Ken Williams took the concerns of his young programmers seriously. A happy John Harris would be a John Harris writing hit games. Roberta Williams also felt affection for the ingenuous twenty-year-old, and was touched by what she believed was a secret crush he harbored for her. "He would look at me with those puppy-dog eyes," she later recalled. The Williamses resolved to clear up John's problem, and for a considerable length of time an unofficial corporate goal of On-Line Systems was Getting John Harris Laid. It was not so easy. Though John Harris could conceivably be called "cute" by women his age, though he could be verbally clever and was certainly making enough money to please all but the most exacting of gold diggers, women did not seem to react to him sexually.

Around Oakhurst, of course, even *finding* women was a problem. John Harris had taken a part-time job in the local arcade, figuring that any girl who liked games would have something in common with him; he made it a point to stay around almost all the hours the arcade was open. But the girls who spent time at the arcade were still in high school. Any local girl with much in the way of brains would go away to college; the ones that stayed were into motorcycle types, and didn't relate to gentle guys who were nervous around women, as John Harris was. John asked a lot of girls out, and they usually said no, probably making him feel as he did when people would choose sides for basketball games and he'd be standing there unchosen.

Ken vowed to change all that. "I'm going to get you laid, John Harris," he would always say, and though John was embarrassed and urged Ken to stop saying those things, he secretly hoped that Ken would keep his promise. But the mishaps continued.

Every time John went out, there were calamities. First the teenage girl he met in a fast-food restaurant who accompanied him for pizza and would not go out with him again. Then a woman who packaged disks for On-Line, a date arranged by Ken. John embarrassed himself by locking his keys in his new four-wheel-drive, had trouble getting into the saloon where they all went, and was mortified when Ken, in front of the woman, began making crude remarks about how horny John was—"That really embarrassed me," John Harris later said. When everybody went back to the Williamses' house to get in the hot tub, John's four-wheel-drive got stuck in the snow; and finally, the girl met up with her old boyfriend and left with him. That was the end of a typical John Harris date.

Ken Williams did not give up that easily. The Williamses took John Harris to the Club Med in Haiti. How can a guy not get laid at Club Med? When a woman wearing no bikini top—*you could see her breasts right there in front of you*—asked John if he'd like to go snorkeling, Ken just laughed. Pay dirt! The woman was around ten years older, but perhaps an experienced woman was what John Harris needed. The snorkeling trip was lots of fun, and on the way back all the girls were fooling around, putting their tops on the guys. Roberta grabbed John's arm and whispered, "If you don't do something with this girl, I'll never talk to you again!"

John Harris suppressed his shyness at that point. "I finally put my arm around the girl," he later recalled. "She said—'Can I talk to you?' We sat down and she brought up our age difference." It was clear that there was no romance in the offing. "I'd planned to take her sailing, but I was too embarrassed after that," John later said.

Ken got even bolder after Haiti. "He did quite a few things [to find me a woman]," John Harris later said. At one point, Williams asked a waitress at Lake Tahoe, "How would you like to sleep with a rich twenty-year-old?"

Probably the worst of all happened at a bachelor party they threw for an On-Line employee. Ken had hired two strippers. The party was held at the office, and it was indicative of the freewheel-

ing, anything-goes spirit in Ken's company. People imbibed heavily; somebody started a game where you would try to look the
other way and throw beer bottles into a far cubicle. The office
became covered with broken glass, and the next day almost everyone at the party woke up with cuts and bruises.

John liked the looks of one of the strippers. "She was unbeliev-
ably gorgeous," he recalled. She seemed shy to John, and confessed
to him that until a couple of weeks back she'd been a secretary, and
was doing this because the money was so good. She danced right
around John Harris, at one point taking her bra off and draping it
around his head.

"I want to talk to you," Ken said, taking John aside. "I'm being
perfectly honest. This is what she said—'He's really cute.' "

John just listened.

"I told her you make three hundred thousand dollars a year. She
asked if you were married."

Ken was not being totally forthright. He had made a deal with
the woman to have sex with John Harris. Ken arranged it all,
telling John she would be at the Chez Paree in Fresno, and John
got all dressed up to see her. Ken went along. John and the woman
retreated to a rear table. Ken told John he'd buy them drinks, but
all she wanted was Seven-Up. Ken bought the couple a bottle of
Seven-Up. "The bottles were expensive," John later recalled.
"Twenty dollars a bottle." It was the first of many bottles of
twenty-dollar Seven-Ups. "I was totally entranced by this girl. She
was really easy to talk to. We talked about things she did before,
why she decided to be a stripper. She didn't seem like the stripper
type." By then Ken was gone and John was buying the twenty-
dollar bottles of Seven-Up. The place was closing down. It was the
moment of truth. The girl was acting like it was natural for her to
go her way, and John to go his. So John went home. When Ken
called later and asked if he'd "scored," John later recalled, "I
didn't have much to say in my defense."

It looked like a permanent plight. Success on the Atari, but no
luck with women.

•

Despite John Harris' female troubles, he was a new role model
for a new age: the hacker superstar. He would sit for magazine
interviews and gab about the virtues of the Atari 800. The articles
would often mention his six-figure income from his 30 percent
royalty deal. It was an enviable, suddenly hip position. All over

America, young, self-described hackers were working on their masterpieces: it was the new-age equivalent to all those young men in the forties trying to write the Great American Novel. The chances that a bestselling game might come in over On-Line's transom, while not great, were somewhat better than those of an unsolicited bestselling novel.

Ken realized that he was in competition with other companies of the Brotherhood for these programmers. As more people learned the Apple and Atari assembly-language wizardry that was unique when Ken Williams started out, the home computer consumer was becoming more discerning about what he or she bought. Companies besides On-Line were now publishing graphic adventures, having figured out their own tricks to put dozens of pictures with text on Apple disks. Also, a new company in Cambridge called Infocom, using text only, had developed an advanced interpreter that would accept large vocabularies of words—in complete sentences. The company was begun by MIT hackers. Their first microcomputer game, lifted straight from the game they'd written for fun on one of the Tech Square computers, was "Zork," a supercharged elaboration on the original Adventure dungeon tale written by Crowther and Woods at Stanford. It was selling like crazy.

It was indicative of how fast the computer game market was moving. What was brilliant one year looked dated the next. The Apple and Atari hackers had taken the machines far beyond their limits. It had only been a few months, for example, since its introduction that On-Line's "Skeet Shoot" program looked so crude it was embarrassing, and Ken dropped it from the product line. Threshold, for instance, blew that previous standard away. And a hacker named Bill Budge wrote a program that simulated a pinball machine, "Raster Blaster," that blew away almost anything On-Line had to offer on the Apple.

Ken Williams knew On-Line had to present itself as a desirable place to work. He and his staff put together a printed package full of promises and dreams to prospective software superstars. Oddly, the enticements that On-Line offered had little to do with the Hacker Ethic. The package did not emphasize the happy Summer Camp community around On-Line. Instead, it seemed almost a paean to Mammon.

One part of the package was titled "Questions and Answers."

QUESTION: Why Should I Publish With On-Line (and not someone else)?

ANSWER: One very good reason is money. ON-LINE pays the highest and most regular royalties in the business . . . Our job is to make your life easier!

QUESTION: Why Not Publish Myself?

ANSWER: With ON-LINE your product will receive support from a highly trained technical staff. This frees you for more important things like Caribbean Cruises, skiing at Aspen, and all of life's other "rough" activities." To put it simply, we do all the work . . . The only thing we do ask of you is to remain available to us in case any bugs occur. Other than that, just sit back and watch the money roll in!

Also in the package was a letter from Ken Williams ("Chairman of the Board") explaining why On-Line Systems was the most professional and effective marketing operation around. He cited the ace programming staff of Schwader, Davis, and Stephenson, and trumpeted his own technical expertise. There was also a letter from On-Line's sales manager: "We are the best and want only the best to be on our team. If you fit this simple description, come breathe the rarified air with us at the top. Success is heady. Can you stand it?" A note from the Software Acquisitions Department summed up the message to prospective programmers: "We're interested in you because you are the life blood of our business. Programming has become a premium commodity."

It was quite a transformation from the days when a hacker would be more than satisfied to see someone appreciate the artistry in his software. Now that there was a marketplace, the Real World had changed hackerism. It was perhaps a necessary trade-off for the benefits of widespread computer availability. Look at all the wonderful transformations computers had made in the lives of the people in the On-Line community.

Ken was hugely proud of these transformations. They seemed to bear out the brilliant promise of the hacker dream. Not only was he prospering, but he and the other companies in the Brotherhood were doing it in an unselfish, new-age mind-frame . . . they were the pioneers of the New America! And what was more, as the months rolled by it became clearer and clearer that computers were a boom industry the likes of which no one had seen since the auto industry. *Everybody wanted a piece of it.* Apple Computer, which seemed like some questionable venture when Ken first saw the Apple II, was on its way to becoming a Fortune 500 company, more quickly than any company in history had ever done. Venture capitalists were focusing on the computer field, and seemed to identify software—things to make these computers work—as the hottest speculative investment in the land. Since games were, by sheer volume of floppy disks sold, the bestselling computer applications, and the Brotherhood companies between them had a sizable percentage of the computer game market, offers for investment and buy-outs came in as often as packages of new games. Though Ken loved to talk to these wealthy suitors, whose names often appeared in *The Wall Street Journal,* he held on to his company. The phones of the Brotherhood would often ring with the last report of a buy-out offer—"He said he would pay ten million!" "Well, I just got offered ten for *half* the company!" "Oh, and I turned down so-and-so for *that* much!" Ken would meet these suitors at airport breakfast meetings, but the respective executives would jet off to their final destinations without buy-out agreements. Ken Williams was having too much fun changing people's lives and driving to work in his new, fire-engine-red Porsche 928 to consider giving it up.

18

FROGGER

As 1982 progressed and the second anniversary of his company rolled around, Ken Williams was beginning to lose patience with John Harris, and with young hackers in general. He no longer had the time, nor the inclination, to give hours of technical assistance to his hackers. He began to regard the questions his programmers would ask him (How can I put this on the screen without flicker? How can I scroll objects horizontally? How do I get rid of this bug?) as distractions from what was becoming his main activity: hacking On-Line Systems as it grew in logarithmic leaps and bounds. Until now, when a programmer would call Ken and frantically howl that he was stuck in some subroutine, Ken would go over, cry with him, and fiddle with the program, doing whatever it took to make his hacker happy. Those days were ending.

Ken did not see the shift in attitude as making his company any less idealistic. He still believed that On-Line was changing lives through the computer, both the lives of its workers and the lives of its customers. It was the beginning of a computer millennium. But Ken Williams was not sure that the hacker would be the central figure in this golden age. Especially a hacker like John Harris.

The split between Ken Williams and John Harris symbolized something occurring all over the home computer software industry. At first, the artistic goals of the hacker coincided neatly with the marketplace, because the marketplace had no expectations, and the hackers could blithely create the games *they* wanted to play, and adorn business programs with the nifty features that displayed their artistry.

But as more nontechnical people bought computers, the things that impressed hackers were not as essential. While the programs themselves had to maintain a certain standard of quality, it was quite possible that the most exacting standards—those applied by a hacker who wanted to add *one more feature,* or wouldn't let go of a project until it was demonstrably faster than anything else around —were probably counterproductive. What seemed more important was marketing. There were plenty of brilliant programs which no one knew about. Sometimes hackers would write programs and put them in the public domain, give them away as easily as John Harris had lent his early copy of Jawbreaker to the guys at the Fresno computer store. But rarely would people ask for public domain programs by name: they wanted the ones they saw advertised and discussed in magazines, demonstrated in computer stores. It was not so important to have amazingly clever algorithms. Users would put up with more commonplace ones.

The Hacker Ethic, of course, held that every program should be as good as you could make it (or better), infinitely flexible, admired for its brilliance of concept and execution, and designed to extend the user's powers. Selling computer programs like toothpaste was heresy. But it was happening. Consider the prescription for success offered by one of a panel of high-tech venture capitalists, gathered at a 1982 software show: "I can summarize what it takes in three words: marketing, marketing, marketing." When computers are sold like toasters, programs will be sold like toothpaste. The Hacker Ethic notwithstanding.

Ken Williams yearned for the bestsellers, games whose very names had the impact of brand names. So when his star programmer, John Harris, mentioned that he would like to try converting a popular coin-op arcade game called "Frogger" to the Atari Home Computer, Ken liked the idea. Frogger was a simple yet bewitching game in which the player tried to manipulate a cute little frog over a heavily trafficked highway and across a stream by making it hop on the backs of logs and turtles; the game was popular, and, if well hacked, might well be a bestselling computer game. "John Harris saw it and said it was really neat. He told me he could program it in a week. I agreed—it looked trivial," Ken later recalled.

Instead of having Harris copy the program and give it another name, Ken Williams played by corporation rules. He called the owner of the game's rights, the Sega division of the Gulf & Western conglomerate. Sega did not seem to understand the value of their property, and Ken managed to acquire computer-disk and cassette rights for a paltry 10 percent royalty fee. (Sega licensed cartridge rights to the Parker Brothers game company; the marketers of "Monopoly" were breaking into the videogame market.) He set John Harris to work immediately on the conversion of the game to the Atari computer. He also assigned a programmer to do an Apple version, but since the Apple graphics were not well suited to the game, it would be the Atari which would showcase the excellence of Ken's company.

John Harris guessed that it would be a quick and dirty three-week project (his original one-week boast had been an idle one) to do a perfectly admirable Atari version of Frogger. This was the kind of illusion with which hackers often begin projects. Working in the office he had set up in the smallest of three bedrooms in his rambling orange-wood house—a room cluttered with papers, discarded hardware, and potato-chip bags—John put the graphics on the screen in short order; during that period, he later recalled, "I glued my hands to the keyboard. One time I started programming at three in the afternoon. After cranking out code for a while, I looked out and it was still light outside and I thought, 'It seems like I've been typing for more than a few hours.' And of course it had already been through the night and that was the next morning."

The work went swiftly, and the program was shaping up beautifully. A friend of John's in San Diego had written some routines to generate continuous music, using the three-voice sound synthesizer chip in the Atari to mingle the strains of the original Frogger theme with "Camptown Races," all with the gay contrapuntal upbeat of a calliope. Harris' graphic shapes were never better—the leaping frog, the little hot rods and trucks on the highway, the diving turtles and the goofy-looking alligators in the water . . . every detail lovingly defined on shape tables, worked into assembly-language subroutines, and expertly integrated into game play. It was the kind of game, Harris believed, that only a person in love with gaming could implement. No one but a true hacker would approach it with the lunatic intensity and finicky artistic exactitude of John Harris.

It did not turn out to be a quick and dirty three-week project, but no one had really expected it to. Software always takes longer than you expect. Almost two months into the project, though, John was well over the hump. He decided to take off work for a couple of days to go back to San Diego for Software Expo, a charity benefit for muscular distrophy. As a leading software artist, John was going to display his work, including the nearly completed Frogger. So John Harris packed the pre-release Frogger into his software collection, and took the whole box with him to Southern California.

When traveling with a cargo as valuable as that, extreme care was called for. Besides including the only version of Frogger, the most important program John Harris had ever written (John had a backup copy, of course, but he brought that along in case the primary disk didn't boot), John's library included almost every disk he owned, disks loaded with software utilities—self-modified assemblers, routines for modifying files, music generators, animation routines, shape tables . . . a young lifetime of tools, the equivalent to him of the entire drawer of paper-tape programs for the PDP-1 at MIT. One could not turn one's back on a priceless collection like that; one held it in one's hand almost every moment. Otherwise, in the single moment that one forgot to hold it in one's hand and turned one's back on it—for instance, during a moment of rapt conversation with an admirer—well, as Murphy's Law holds ("Whatever can go wrong, will"), one's valuable software library could be tragically gone.

That was precisely what happened to John Harris at the Software Expo.

The instant that John Harris ended his interesting conversation and saw that his software collection was gone, he knew his soul had been wounded. Nothing was more important to John than the floppy disks in that box, and he felt the void deeply. It was not as if the computer had chomped up one disk and he could go into marathon mode for a few days to restore what he had lost onto the screen. This was a full-blown masterpiece totally wiped. And even worse, the tools with which he had created the masterpiece were gone as well. There was no worse disaster imaginable.

John Harris went into a deep depression.

He was much too upset to boot up his Atari and begin the laborious task of rewriting Frogger when he returned to Oakhurst. For the next two months, he wrote no more than ten lines of source code. It was hard to even sit in front of the computer. He spent almost all day, every day, at Oakhurst's single arcade, a small storefront in a tiny shopping center across the street from the two-story office building that On-Line was moving into. As arcades went, this was a hole, with dark walls and nothing for decoration but the videogame machines themselves, and not even the latest models. But it was home to John. He took a part-time job as cashier. He would exchange game tokens for quarters, and when he wasn't on duty he would play Starpath and Robotron and Berzerk and Tempest. It seemed to help. Other times he would get in his four-wheel-drive truck, go off-road, look for the biggest hill he could find, and try to drive to its crest. He would do anything, in fact, but program.

"I spent almost every hour of every day down at the arcade waiting for some girl to walk in there," he later recalled. "I'd go home and play a game on my computer and then try to slip in the program disk and try to start programming as if I were playing the game." None of it worked. "I could not motivate myself to write two lines of source code."

Ken Williams' heart was unmoved by John Harris' loss. It was hard for Ken to have sympathy for a twenty-year-old boy to whom he was paying several thousand dollars a month in royalties. Ken felt a sense of friendship toward John, but Ken had also developed a theory about friends and business. "Everything is personal and good friends up to about ten thousand dollars," Ken later explained. "Once past ten thousand dollars, friendship doesn't matter." The possible earnings of Frogger were worth many times that five-figure threshold.

Even before John had once again proved his idiocy to Ken Williams by his carelessness at the Software Expo, Ken had been impatient with his ace programmer. Ken thought John should have written Frogger in less than a month to begin with. "John Harris is a perfectionist," Ken Williams later said. "A hacker. He will keep working on a project for two months after anyone else would have stopped. He likes the ego satisfaction of having something out that's better than anything else in the marketplace." Bad enough, but the fact that John was not working at all now, just because he suffered a setback, drove Ken wild. "He would say his heart wasn't in it," Ken recalled. "Then I would find him in the arcade, working for tokens!"

In front of John's friends, Ken would make nasty remarks about how late Frogger was. Ken made John too nervous to think of pithy rejoinders right on the spot. Only away from Ken could John Harris realize he should have said that he was not Ken's employee, he was a free-lance programmer. He had not guaranteed Ken any delivery date. John could do whatever he wanted. *That* was what he should have said. Instead, John Harris felt bad.

It was torture, but finally John dragged himself to the Atari and began to rewrite the program. Eventually he re-created his earlier work, with a few extra embellishments as well. Forty-four colors, the player-missile graphic routines fully redefined, and a couple of neat tricks that managed to make the eight bits of the Atari 6502 chip emulate ten bits. John's friend in San Diego had even made some improvement on the three-voice concurrent sound track. All in all, John Harris' version looked even better than the arcade game, an astounding feat since arcade games used custom-designed chips for high speed and solid-color graphics, and were almost never approximated by the less powerful (though more versatile) home computers. Even experienced programmers like Jeff Stephenson were impressed.

The dark period was over, but something had changed in the relationship between Ken and John. It was emblematic of the way that On-Line was changing, into more of a bureaucracy than a hacker Summer Camp. Whereas the procedure for releasing John's previous games had been impromptu testing on-site ("Hey! We got a game to play today! If everyone likes it, let's ship it!"), now Ken had a separate department to test games before release. To John, it seemed that it now took about fifty exchanges of interoffice memos before anyone got around to saying that he liked a game. There were also logjams in packaging, marketing, and copy protection. No one quite knew how, but it took over two more months—two months after John had turned in his fully completed Frogger—for the game to be released.

When it was finally on the market, everyone recognized that Frogger was a terrific conversion from arcade to home computer. John's check for the first month's royalties was for thirty-six thousand dollars, and the program went to number one on Softsel Distributors' new "Hot List" of programs (which was compiled weekly and patterned after *Billboard*'s record chart), staying there for months.

Ken Williams never forgot, though, the troubles that John Harris had given him during the depressed stage, when it looked like John would never deliver a working Frogger. And by the summer of 1982, Ken began to plan for the day that he would be free of all the John Harrises of the world. As far as Ken Williams was concerned, the age of the hacker had ended. And its end had come not a moment too soon.

•

Like his early role model, Jonas Cord of *The Carpetbaggers,* Ken Williams loved making deals. He would call a prospective programmer on the telephone and say, without any shame and only a slight sense of parody, "Why don't you let me make you rich?" He also liked dealing with executives from giant corporations on a peer basis. In 1982, one of the early boom years of the computer revolution, Ken Williams talked to many people, and the kinds of deals he made indicated what kind of business home computer software was becoming, and what place, if any, hackers, or the Hacker Ethic, would have in the business.

"On-Line's crazy," Williams said that summer. "I have this philosophy that I either want to pretend to be IBM or not be here."

He dreamed of making a national impact on the mass marketplace. In the summer of 1982, that meant the Atari VCS machine, the dedicated game machine for which bestselling games were not counted in tens of thousands, as Apple software was, but in millions.

Atari regarded the workings of its VCS machine as a secret guarded somewhat more closely than the formula for Coca-Cola. Had it been a formula for a soft drink, the schematic plan of the VCS—which memory location on the chip triggered color on the screen, and which hot spot would ignite sound—might well have remained within Atari's vaults. But this was the computer industry, where code-breaking had been a hobby ever since the lock-hacking days at MIT. With the added incentive of heady profits obtainable by anyone who topped the rather mundane software offerings that complacent Atari sold for its machine, it was only a matter of time before the VCS secrets were broken (as were the Atari 800 secrets).

The first companies to challenge Atari on the VCS, in fact, were start-ups formed by the former Atari programmers who had been called "towel designers" by Atari's president. Almost all of Atari's VCS wizards jumped ship in the early 1980s. This was no small loss, because the VCS machine was hopelessly limited in memory, and writing games on it required skills honed as finely as those required in haiku composition. Yet the Atari programmers who left knew how to extend the machine far beyond its limitations; the games they wrote for their own companies made Atari's look silly. The improved quality of the games extended the market life of the VCS for years. It was a stunning justification of the hacker insistence that when manuals and other "secrets" are freely disseminated the creators have more fun, the challenge is greater, the industry benefits, and the users get rewarded by much better products.

Meanwhile, other companies were "reverse engineering" the VCS, dissecting it with oscilloscopes and unspeakably high-tech devices until they understood its secrets. One such company was Tiger Toys, a Chicago-based company which contacted Ken Williams to set up an arrangement to share his programming talent.

Williams flew three hackers to Chicago, where Tiger Toys taught them what a bitch the VCS was to program. You had to be penurious with your code, you had to count cycles of the machine to space out the movements of things. John Harris in particular hated it, even though he and Roberta Williams had sat down one night and figured out a nifty new VCS layout for Jawbreaker which looked less like Pac-Man. John Harris was used to the much faster routines on the Atari 800 computer, and was indignant that this other machine refused to accept similar routines. He considered the VCS ridiculous. But John really wanted to do a program that would blow Atari's VCS version of Pac-Man out of the water, and with the new Jawbreaker scheme he was able, in his opinion, to accomplish that task. Atari's VCS Pac-Man was full of flicker, a big loser; John's VCS program had no flicker, was colorful, and was blindingly fast.

Ken Williams' dealings did not stop with the VCS market. Since computer games were becoming as successful as the movies, he was able to pursue ties to that industry. The world-famous creator of the Muppets, Jim Henson, was coming out that Christmas with a $20 million movie called *Dark Crystal* that had the earmarks of a blockbuster. Ken and Henson made a deal.

While Ken guessed that the idea of tying a computer game to an unreleased movie was risky—what if the movie bombed?—Roberta Williams loved the idea of writing an adventure game based on *Dark Crystal* characters. She considered computer games as much a facet of the entertainment world as movies and television, and thought it natural that her genre should merge with those glamorous counterparts. Indeed, other videogame and computer companies were working on projects with movie tie-ins. There was Atari's "E.T.," Fox Videogames' "M.A.S.H.," and Parker Brothers' "The Empire Strikes Back." A computer game company named DataSoft was even working on an adventure game based on the television show "Dallas." This was quite a step from the early days, when all a programmer had to work with was creativity. Now he could work with a bankable property.

If *Dark Crystal* was not quite the big leagues, the next deal was. For this one, Ken Williams was dealing with the biggest company of all.

IBM.

International Business Machines, toe-to-toe with the Coarsegold, California, company that did not exist two years ago. Whiteshirted, dark-tied, batch-processed IBM'ers coming to Ken's new corporate headquarters, which consisted of a series of offices in the same building that housed the little office where Oakhursters and Coarsegoldians paid their electric bills, a little furniture store on the ground floor, and a beauty parlor next to the office where Ken ran marketing and advertising.

To On-Liners, hackers, and Oakhurst natives dressed in Summer Camp shorts and T-shirts, IBM's cloak-and-dagger behavior was absurd. Everything was so solemnly top secret. Before IBM would divulge even an inkling of its intentions, its poker-faced personnel insisted that everyone who might possibly know about the deal—and this was to be kept to the smallest number of people possible—sign lengthy and binding nondisclosure forms which mandated severe tortures and complete frontal lobotomies, almost, to anyone leaking the name of the three-initial company or its plans.

The predictions of *Computer Lib* author Ted Nelson and others that the personal computer revolution would put IBM "in disarray" had proven a pathetic underestimation of the monolithic firm. The Hulking Giant of computer companies had proven to be more nimble than anyone had expected. In 1981, it had announced its own computer, the IBM "PC," and the very specter of this entry led many in the small computer industry to make preparations for rolling over and dropping dead for IBM, which they promptly did when the IBM's PC machine was put on the marketplace. Even people who *hated* IBM and its batch-processed philosophy rolled over and dropped dead, because IBM had done something which represented a virtual turnaround from everything they had previously stood for: they opened their machine up. They encouraged outsiders to write software. They even enlisted outside firms to help *design* the thing, firms like MicroSoft, headed by Bill Gates (the author of the original software piracy letter, directed at the Homebrew Altair BASIC copiers). Gates wrote the IBM operating system which almost instantly became a new industry standard. It was almost as if IBM had studied the Hacker Ethic and decided that, in this case, it was good business sense to apply it.

IBM did not plan to apply the Hacker Ethic *too* much, though.

It still valued secrecy as a way of life. So IBM waited until all the nondisclosure forms were signed before its men in the white shirts told Ken Williams what they had in mind. IBM was planning a new machine for the home, cheaper and better at playing games than the PC. It was code-named Peanut, but would eventually be known as PCjr. Would On-Line like to do a new kind of adventure interpreter, more sophisticated than anything that came before it? And also write an easy-to-use word processing program for the PCjr? Ken thought they could, no problem, and while Roberta began charting yet another adventure plot, Ken set about hiring a top secret team of wizards to hack code for the project.

It would cost On-Line a lot of money to participate in some of these high-rolling ventures. But Ken Williams had taken care of that by the most significant deal of all. Venture capital. "I had never even *heard* of venture capital," Ken Williams later said. "I had to be convinced to take it." Still, On-Line was spending money very quickly, and the $1.2 million the company received from the Boston firm called TA Associates (plus two hundred thousand dollars for Ken and Roberta personally) was essential to maintain cash flow. In return, TA got 24 percent of the company and consultation rights on various aspects of the business.

The woman at TA who made the deal was vibrant, gray-haired Jacky Morby, with precise features, a studied intensity, and the ability to insinuate herself as a distant godmother to the company. Jacky Morby was very experienced in situations where brilliant entrepreneurs begin companies that grow so fast they threaten to get out of hand, and she immediately advised Ken Williams, in such a way that he knew this was not merely casual advice, to get some professional management. She recognized that Ken was not an MBA type—not one who would properly nurture his company to take its place in the traditional line of companies that make this country great and venture capital firms like TA very rich. If On-Line Systems were to go public and shift everybody into Croesus Mode, there would have to be a firm rudder to guide it in the waters ahead. Ken's rudder was bent. He kept veering to wild schemes, crazy deals, and hacker Summer Camp blowouts. Someone would have to come in and supply a new rudder.

The idea was not unappealing to Ken, who had announced to *Softalk* as early as March 1981 that he was "firing himself from the On-Line staff in hopes that [he'd] be able to get some programming done." And surely it was clear that something had to be done about the managerial mess that was thickening as the company sold more software, took on more deals, tried to get hold of more programmers, and shuffled more paper, even if a lot of the paper was in the form of data handled in Apple computers.

The problem came from Ken's hacking On-Line as if it were a computer system, tweaking a marketing plan here, debugging the accounting there. Like his computer hacking, which was characterized by explosive bursts of innovation and inattention to detail, his business style was punctuated by flashes of insight and failures to follow through on ideas. He was among the first to recognize the value of a low-cost word processing package for the Apple (a culmination of the idea MIT's Model Railroad Club hackers had when they wrote "Expensive Typewriter" on the TX-0), and had the patience to support the program through innumerable revisions —the program, eventually called "Screenwriter II," would gross over a million dollars in sales. But his friendly competitors would laugh at his habit of writing huge royalty checks for programmers on the same checkbook he used for his supermarket accounts. He would help develop a program called "The Dictionary," which corrects an Apple user's spelling, but then would place a magazine advertisement for the product which contained ten spelling errors, including a misspelling of the word "misspell."

Ken's new office was just about buried in junk. One new employee later reported that on first seeing the room, he assumed that someone had neglected to take out a huge, grungy pile of trash. Then he saw Ken at work, and understood. The twenty-eight-year-old executive, wearing his usual faded blue Apple Computer T-shirt and weatherbeaten jeans with a hole in the knee, would sit behind the desk and carry on a conversation with employees or people on the phone while going through papers. The T-shirt would ride over Ken's protruding belly, which was experiencing growth almost as dramatic as his company's sales figures. Proceeding at lightning pace, he would glance at important contracts and casually throw them in the pile. Authors and suppliers would be on the phone constantly, wondering what had happened to their contracts. Major projects were in motion at On-Line for which contracts hadn't been signed at all. No one seemed to know which programmer was doing what; in one case two programmers in different parts of the country were working on identical game conversions. Master disks, some without backups, some of them top secret IBM disks, were piled on the floor of Ken's house, where one of his kids might pick it up or his dog piss on it. No, Ken Williams was not a detail person.

He knew it, too. Ken Williams came to believe that his company had grown so big it had to be run in a more traditional manner by someone without hacker tendencies. Finally, he came up with a candidate. His former boss, Dick Sunderland.

Ken knew Dick Sunderland as a representative of the vague qualities that a respectable business should have, qualities that On-Line conspicuously lacked: predictability, order, control, careful planning, uniform outlook, decorum, adherence to guidelines, and a structured hierarchy. It was no accident that these missing qualities were things that hackers loathed. If Ken had set out to find someone who best represented the antithesis of the Hacker Ethic, he would have been hard-pressed to top his former boss. The act was akin to someone acknowledging that he was sick, and perversely choosing the worst-tasting medicine as a restorative.

There was something more insidious in the choice as well. One reason why Ken had left Informatics several years earlier was that Dick Sunderland had told him, "Ken, you have no management potential." The idea of being Dick Sunderland's boss, therefore, appealed greatly to Ken's affection for toppling the established order.

For Dick Sunderland, the prospect of working for Ken Williams initially struck him as absurd. "Come up and run my company!" Ken had chirped to him over the phone from this mountain complex near Yosemite. This was no way to recruit *executives,* thought Dick. There is no way, he told himself, I am going to get mixed up in a deal like this. Dick was completing an MBA program, a move which he felt would put him in line for the very top positions at Informatics. But by the time Ken called him a second time, Sunderland had been worrying about his future at Informatics, and had been thinking of the booming microcomputer field. In early June, Dick drove up, and had lunch at the Broken Bit with the motley crew of Oakhurst retreads and college dropouts that made up Ken's upper management. He looked at the venture capital deal and was impressed. Eventually, he came to think that On-Line, as he later put it, "had a hell of a potential, something I could work with. I could bring what was missing—cohesive leadership to make things jell." Dick realized the home software industry was "new, like clay . . . you could mold it and make it happen, make a winner . . . BOOM! It was the opportunity of a lifetime for me."

On the other hand, he would be working for Ken Williams. For over a month, Dick and his wife April would spend hours sitting in the backyard of the Los Angeles house they had carefully decorated over the years, kicking around this fantasy that would mandate their evacuation from the house, and it would be clear that the number one risk was the personality of this wild programmer-turned-software-czar. Dick consulted professionals to discuss what it would be like, a careful manager working for this reckless entrepreneur; he spoke to management experts, even a psychiatrist. Sunderland became convinced he could handle the Ken Problem.

On September 1, 1982, Dick Sunderland began as the president of On-Line Systems, which coincidentally was also changing its name. Reflecting the proximity of Yosemite, the company would now be called Sierra On-Line, and the new logo had a drawing of Half-Dome Mountain in a circle. A change to accommodate the new age.

A week before Dick arrived, Ken was feeling expansive. It was the day that he drifted over to give his blessing to the hacker who had "auditioned" with his Wall Wars game. After that encounter, he talked to a visitor about the potential stardom of his charges. He admitted that some of his authors had become brand names, almost like rock stars. "If I release a game and put the John Harris name on it, it will sell a ton more copies than if I don't," he said. "John Harris is a household name in [Atari] households. Among Atari computer owners, probably a higher percentage have heard of John Harris than [of] most rock stars."

But now that Dick Sunderland's approach was imminent, Ken was hoping that the programmers' power would be lessened. He was now a hacker who was convinced that hackers should be stifled. He was counting on Dick to get the standard programmer royalty down from 30 percent to 20. "I don't think you need a genius of programming" to make a hit game, said Ken. "The days of needing an A-student programmer to write an acceptable game aren't over, but within a year of being over. Programmers, they're not a dime a dozen, but they're 50K a dozen. Moving the spaceship [on the video display] isn't a problem anymore. What's needed is to guess what the marketplace wants, access to the distribution channels, money, gimmicks, marketing promotion."

Sitting in his office that day, speaking in his startlingly candid what-the-hell tone, guessing that his company would "either be $200 million in sales by 1985 or bankrupt," adding "I'm not real hung up on which," Ken Williams promised to retreat to the mountain, like some high-tech pilgrim, and contemplate the next step in bringing about the computer millennium.

But to the surprise of almost no one, Ken Williams did not keep his promise to "fire himself." It would have been as out of character as a hacker abandoning a hot game program before all the proper features were written into it. Ken Williams had presented the company to Dick as if his goal—getting a company to a point where it was big enough to be left to a manager—were accomplished. But like a hacker, Ken Williams did not see things in terms of goals. He was still enamored of the *process* of running On-Line, and the clash of cultures between hacker informalism and bureaucratic rigidity threw the company into turmoil.

It was almost as if a fight were being waged for the soul of the industry. Among the first things Dick Sunderland tried to impose at Sierra On-Line was a rigid corporate structure, a hierarchy in which employees and authors would only be permitted to take up problems with immediate superiors. Dick requested the secretaries to distribute copies of the organization chart, with a box at the top for Ken, one underneath for Dick, and a series of boxes underneath, all connected by lines which represented the only authorized channels of communication. That this approach was antithetical to hackerism did not disturb Dick, who felt that hacker attitudes had almost brought the company to bankruptcy and ruin.

Dick particularly wanted an end to Summer Camp. He had heard stories about the rowdy goings-on, the drugs, the impromptu parties, the pranks during working hours . . . he'd even heard from the janitorial staff that there'd been actual fucking in the office at night! Those kinds of things had to stop. He particularly wanted Ken to maintain a more executive-like relationship with his employees, and to promote more orderly, rational lines of communication. How can you maintain a hierarchical structure when the chief executive gets in his hot tub with low-level employees?

To Dick's mind, the flow of information should be channeled with discretion, with an unambiguous interpretation controlled by the people at the top. People who don't have the broad view of things should not be upset by getting dribs and drabs of information. What Dick had to contend with at On-Line, though, was an incredible rumor mill, fed by the unfettered flow of information that company had been accustomed to. And Ken Williams, Dick said, "nurtures [the rumor mill] rather than quells it. He has no sense of discretion!" Everything was public record with Ken, from his personal life to his bank account.

Dick was convinced, though, that Ken knew On-Line needed responsible management, or it would die. But Ken was so reluctant to step back. Sunderland could settle the personnel situation, bring

in carefully considered candidates, keep the payroll under control
. . . and then Ken would tell him, bang, that he just hired somebody to be his administrative assistant, a job opening that did not
exist until that very minute. "And who did he hire?" Dick would
say. "Some guy driving a Pepsi truck in L.A.!"

"This is casebook stuff," Dick said. He recalled reading about it
in business school: entrepreneur who gets going on a brilliant idea,
but can't handle it when the business gets big. It all came from the
hacker origins of the company. Ken was saying that the time for
hackers was over; he wanted to limit programmers' power in the
company. But he wasn't making it easy for Dick.

It was particularly tough trying to negotiate the royalty down
from 30 to 20 percent when the programmers had the impression
that the company was rolling in money. It really wasn't, but no one
believed that when they saw green just about falling from the windows. Everyone knew about the house Ken was building outside of
town. It would be four hundred feet long. A party room that would
be the biggest in the area. A crew of over a dozen were working
full-time on it . . . they had constructed an entire office on the
work site, with phone hookups and everything. The house was not
even half finished, and already Ken had invited the whole company
to come to the site on weekends to play in the built-in racquetball
court. It was not the best way to convince programmers to opt for
austerity.

Ken Williams' point of view was somewhat different. He had
hired Dick, and would often defend him. But he thought it necessary to keep his hand in. Ken felt responsible to the people he had
hired, and to the vision of the company itself. He knew the industry as well as anyone; Dick was a newcomer to the family. Also,
Ken Williams was having too much fun: leaving now would be like
walking away from a crap table when you're on the hottest roll of
your life. Or, more to the point, it was like telling a hacker that he
could no longer play with the machine. Those words did not register with hackers. Once you had control, the godlike power that
comes from programming mastery, you did not want to let go of it.

Roberta Williams would agree. Just as Ken treated On-Line like
a complex computer program to be hacked, Roberta thought of the
company as a creative project which should be lovingly embel-
lished and elegantly structured, like an adventure game. Like authors of an adventure game, she and Ken had enjoyed ultimate
control over the company; turning it over was difficult. She compared the situation to hiring a governess: "You would think,

wouldn't it be great to have someone come in and watch the kids every day while I'm doing this thing I want to do. I can design adventure games. But then she starts telling the kids everything they can do—'Oh yes, you can have a peanut butter and jelly sandwich.' And I may not believe in peanut butter and jelly. I might prefer them to have beef. That person says, 'Peanut butter is good, there's a lot of protein in peanut butter. You hired me, let me do my job.' That's what we're running into with Dick. He said, 'You gave me the power to do this, you wanted to go off and program.' Now we are saying, 'Yeah, that's what we thought we wanted, but it turns out we don't want to give up control.' "

•

While the management of Sierra On-Line struggled to find itself, the Third Generation hackers there were glum over the changes in their company. They would talk over frozen dinners at the Hexagon House before playing Dungeons and Dragons. Or they would discuss the deteriorating moral state of the company over pizza and Cokes at Danny's, a bleak roadhouse on Route 41 with picnic-style tables covered with plastic checkered tablecloths. Most of the customers were local families who didn't seem to like the On-Line people much, but it was almost the only place in town where you could get a pizza and play videogames, which the hackers played compulsively, with no visible sense of involvement or even interest, while they waited for their food.

They were proud of their positions, and almost puzzled at their good fortune in getting paid for work they loved. In the early 1980s, hacking games was about the only form of commercially viable artistry where, with almost no capital, you could truly be an auteur: single-handedly you could conceive, script, direct, execute, and polish a work, completing an objet d'art which was every bit as good as the bestselling game on the market. This Third Generation found itself in an artistically privileged position. The fact that publishers competed for their wares made things pleasant on the one hand, but confusing on the other. There were no rules for this kind of thing. It was a rare twenty-year-old hacker who had the business acumen and intestinal fortitude to cope with a negotiator as forceful as Ken Williams, or as formally intimidating as Dick Sunderland. Since money wasn't the main issue for the hackers, they'd agree to almost anything if they thought it was fair. Business wasn't as much fun as hacking was.

Still, in the fall of 1982, it was the most creative programmers who drove the industry. Brøderbund was riding high on "Choplifter," written by a twenty-eight-year-old former artificial-intelligence hacker named Dan Gorlin. The game was based on the Iran hostage crisis: a chopper crossed enemy lines and tried to rescue sixty-four hostages—little animated figures who waved when they saw the helicopter. It was the big game of the year, and consistent with the Carlstons' classy approach to the business. They loved their hackers. They talked all the time about what great artists their "game designers" were.

Sirius had been developing its own superstars, but Gebelli, the designer who had done almost all their games in the first year of Sirius' existence, was not one of them. According to Jerry Jewell, Gebelli thought that Sirius was not the best agency for display and sale of his artworks—this after receiving a quarter of a million dollars in his first year, noted Jewell incredulously—and, along with a defecting Sirius executive, began his own company, modestly named Gebelli Software. It did not join the top ranks of the industry.

Sirius survived the loss by importing teen-age hackers from other parts of the country, and they delivered some hit games called "Beer Run," "Twerps," and "The Earth Dies Screaming." Jerry Jewell acted as a sometimes rowdy big brother to his young programmers. What Jewell really lusted after was the mass VCS market, and after signing a major deal to develop games for Twentieth-Century Fox's new videogame division he was afire with visions of his products as household words, not just in the Apple or Atari world, but everywhere. He figured that some of his programmers might make as much as a million dollars a year.

At On-Line, where the VCS had been a mere flirtation, Ken Williams and Dick Sunderland were not talking about a million dollars a year for their programmers. They were trying to cut the royalty down from 30 to 20 percent. And when On-Line hackers gathered at places like Danny's, they would compare notes and find that they were in agreement: 30 percent was fair, and 20 percent was not. Brøderbund and Sirius were still offering higher royalties. Some of the hackers had been approached by an exciting new company called Electronic Arts. It consisted of ex-Apple people who promised to treat hackers as culture heroes, like rock stars.

Ken and Dick had tried to convince them that 20 percent was a fair figure in light of the drastically increased costs of promoting and testing and distributing a game in this new, more professional stage of the industry. On-Line was increasing its advertising, hiring more support people, boosting its promotional staff. But the programmers saw Sunderland and his regime as bureaucracy, to which, as hackers, they had a generic allergy. They missed the days of Summer Camp and handshakes for contracts. John Harris, for instance, chafed at the idea of paying a lawyer to help him negotiate a six-figure contract ("They charge one hundred dollars just to *read* it!" he howled). Harris and the other On-Line hackers would see all these managers and support people being hired, just to do the same thing that the company did before—release the games that the hackers wrote. From their point of view, it seemed to indicate another hacker sin—inefficiency. Along with an emphasis on the sizzle of marketing rather than the substance of hacking.

For instance, On-Line spent a lot of money for colorful new boxes in which to package their games—but did not see fit to include the name of the programmer on the package. Ken had thought it sufficient to give that credit only in the instruction manual stuffed inside the box. "The authors should realize that this will give us more money for advertising and royalties," he said. It was indicative of a new "professionalism" in dealing with authors.

But to listen to the conversations at Danny's during the fall of 1982, it was clear that an atmosphere conducive to hacking was far more important to those programmers than a mantle of "professionalism." And the consensus was that almost every programmer was thinking of leaving.

Even if Ken Williams was aware of a potential programmer exodus, the problem seemed of little concern to the founder of the company. Williams was busy hiring a staff of programmers quite different from the potential defectors. Impatient with the hackers who had come to him with their assembly-language skills and uneven work habits fully formed, Ken decided to try an alternate source: he would utilize the messianic power of the computer to create programming gurus where none existed. After all, the now testy hackers who were complaining about the royalty cuts had come to him with, at most, the experience of a game or two. Now they felt he owed them the world. Why not find people *before* that first game, people who had some programming skills but were not yet assembly-language wizards, and let them develop under him? Surely they would not be so ungrateful as to leave him for some random offer from another firm. But more important, this daring kind of recruitment would be in keeping with the vision that Ken had for his company: the place where the computer future comes to the people, improving their lives.

He set up On-Line's old office above the TV sales shop on Route 41 as an office especially for in-house programmers. Some of the people working there were royalty-basis programmers whom Ken had offered free living space to, like Chuck Bueche, a twenty-one-year-old programmer who drove to the Sierras from Texas in an old Jaguar XKE and who wrote under the *nom de computer* of "Chuckles." Dick liked one specific part of Chuckles' first game, a maze-chase called "Creepy Corridors": the piercing, hideous scream heard when the little man you were moving through the maze got caught by the monster who chased him. Considering the relatively brain-damaged sound capabilities of the Apple, the scream was quite an achievement. Chuckles had screamed the most hideous scream he could into a tape recorder, and used a digital analyzer to print out five long pages of data that, when fed into the Apple, would exactingly POKE the memory location to duplicate the scream. It took almost a fifth of the available memory of the machine, but to Chuck it was worth it. The purer programmers at On-Line were appalled at the inefficiency.

A few of the newer programmers, though, were so far behind Chuck that issues like that were almost incomprehensible to them. The qualifications of these newcomers ranged from college degrees in computer science to a passion for getting stoned and playing videogames. Two were students of Japanese extraction whom Ken had hired because someone had told him that Orientals were fantastically devoted workers. Some were attracted because of the excellent skiing at nearby Badger Pass. Others hoped to convert On-Line games from one machine to another by day, and hack The Great American Computer Game by night. All in all, in the space of a few months Ken had hired almost a dozen inexperienced, non-hacker programmers for bargain-basement wages, in hopes that they would grow as quickly as the industry was growing.

Of all Ken's new programmers, none exemplified his zeal for reforming lives by computer power as much as did Bob and Carolyn Box. Bob Box was in his fifties: they had lived in the area for well over a decade and worked at their ranch-style home five miles from Oakhurst, in the almost undetectable hamlet of Ahwahnee. Bob, who had dark hair, soulful eyes, and a nose of basset-hound proportions, was approximately four feet in height. He was a former New Yorker, a former engineer, a former race car driver, a former jockey, and a former Guinness Book of World Records champion in gold panning. Carolyn Box was slightly over five feet tall, had long brown hair and a world-weary attractiveness, and was the *current* Guinness Book of World Records champion in gold panning. They'd married twenty-six years ago, when Carolyn was fifteen. For the past few years, they'd been running a gold-prospecting supply business and searching for gold in the Fresno River, which ran in their backyard. The Oakhurst-Coarsegold area was on the southern rim of the California mother lode, and the gold the Boxes dredged up from the river—one morning they came up with two thousand dollars' worth in a half hour—financed their programming courses at a Fresno trade school.

They had realized that the gold of the 1980s would be software, and their goal was to work at On-Line. Though Carolyn Box had been apprehensive about dealing with a computer, she instantly understood the required concept, as if computers were a language she'd always been talking. It was almost supernatural. She was the first one in the history of the school to get a 4.0 average in her courses. Bob did well, too: programming was like gold panning, he realized—you proceeded in logical steps, and concentrated while you did it.

But when they presented themselves to Ken, he was skeptical. He told them that programmers usually peaked at nineteen and were over the hill at twenty—even Ken, at twenty-eight, was just about washed up. (Not that he believed it.) Ken wanted to give the Boxes a chance, though, because they fit right in with the dream he had about On-Line and the great computer future. So he told them to put up something on the screen using assembly language, in thirty days. The Boxes' school had taught them programming in high-level languages on mainframe computers; they knew nothing about Apple assembly language. But working day and night, they came up with an 82-line program only five days later. It moved a dot around the screen. Ken asked them to try something else, and, again working almost every waking hour, the Boxes created a 282-line program with a little airplane moving around the high-resolution screen. Ken hired them, and set them to work programming a pet project of his, an educational game.

Soon the Boxes were hard at work getting a little dog, whom they named Dusty after their own dog, to walk across the screen. They would proudly explain to visitors that their hack used a so-phisticated technique called exclusive-or-ing, which allowed for zero-flicker animation. They felt they'd given life to Dusty Dog. "This dog is like our pet," Carolyn Box would say. When Ken first saw Dusty Dog move across the screen, the little basset legs moving with steady, non-flickering fluidity, he almost burst. "It's days like this that make you proud to be in this business," he told them. Even these middle-aged gold prospectors could be software superstars . . . and Ken was the Moses who led them to the promised Computer Land.

•

To Roberta Williams, it all represented something: the rehabilitation of the Boxes, Ken's community-minded efforts, her own ascension to the rank of bestselling game designer, the big Dark Crystal collaboration with Henson Associates, the artistic efforts of their software superstars, and above all the fantastic way that computers had nurtured what was a mom-and-pop bedroom operation to a $10-million-a-year company that would soon be employing over one hundred people. She considered their story inspiring. It said a lot about the power of the computer, and the different, better lives that people would be leading with the computer. In the two years of On-Line's growth, Roberta had shed some of her shyness, exchanging a bit of it for a fierce pride in their accomplishments. "Look at us!" she'd sometimes say in conversation, partially in disbelief and partially as an all-purpose trump card. "People ask me," she said that fall of 1982, " 'Don't you just sit around and say "Wow"? Doesn't it do something for you?' The answer is that we're just so constantly amazed all the time that it's almost a state of mind."

Roberta wanted the message of On-Line spread to the world. She insisted that On-Line hire a New York public relations firm to promote not only the programs, but the people behind them. "Programmers, authors, are going to be the future new entertainers," she explained. "It might be presumptuous to say they might be new Robert Redfords . . . but to a certain extent [they will be] idolized. Tomorrow's heroes."

Dick Sunderland did not share Roberta's enthusiasm for the New York public relations firm. He had come out of an industry where programmers were anonymous. He was worried about On-Line's programmers getting big heads from all that attention. It's tough enough to deal with a twenty-year-old who's making a hundred thousand a year—can you imagine how tough it will be after he's profiled in *People* magazine, as John Harris would be that winter?

The spotlight was beginning to find its way to the mysterious software company whose letterhead still carried the address of the Williamses' A-frame wooden house from which they had run the company when it was a two-person operation. Mudge Ranch Road, Coarsegold, California. The world wanted to know: What kind of computer madness had taken hold out there in the sticks, and what sorts of millions were being made, there on Mudge Ranch Road? There was no subject in the media hotter than computers in the early 1980s, and with the New York public relations firm helping channel the dazzled inquisitors, a steady stream of long-distance phone calls and even long-distance visitors began to arrive in Oakhurst that autumn.

This included an "NBC Magazine" camera crew which flew to Oakhurst from New York City to document this thriving computer-age company for its video magazine show. NBC shot the requisite footage of Roberta mapping a new adventure game at her home, Ken going over his phone messages, Ken and Roberta touring the building site of their new home. But the NBC producer was particularly anxious to speak to the heart of the company: the young programmers. Whiz kids writing games and getting rich. The programmers, those in-house and those working for royalties, were duly assembled at the programming office.

The NBC producer, with his gray hair, bushy moustache, and twinkling eyes, resembled a carnival barker who knows the gruesome ropes, yet has maintained compassion. He urged the programmers to play at the terminals so his crew could shoot an establishing shot of a thriving factory that measured production by lines of computer code. One of the hackers immediately began concocting a program to create a twenty-one-sided flower on the screen—a program involving the retention of the value of pi to the sixth decimal place. Even after the NBC crew finished the establishing shot, the teen-age programmer felt compelled to finish the display hack.

The producer by then was interviewing one of Ken's twenty-one-year-old whiz kids.

"Where is the industry going?" he asked him solemnly.

The whiz kid stared at the producer. "I have no idea," he said.

19

APPLEFEST

THE Third Generation lived with compromises in the Hacker Ethic that would have caused the likes of Greenblatt and Gosper to recoil in horror. It all stemmed from money. The bottom line of programming was ineluctably tied to the bottom line on a publisher's ledger sheet. Elegance, innovation, and coding pyrotechnics were much admired, but a new criterion for hacker stardom had crept into the equation: awesome sales figures. Early hackers might have regarded this as heresy: all software—all information—should be free, they'd argue, and pride should be invested in how many people *use* your program and how much they are impressed with it. But the Third Generation hackers never had the sense of community of their predecessors, and early on they came to see healthy sales figures as essential to becoming winners.

One of the more onerous of the compromises in the Ethic grew out of publishers' desire to protect their sales figures. It involved intentional tampering with computer programs to prevent a program from being easily copied by users, perhaps for distribution without further payment to the publisher or author. The software publishers called this process "copy protection," but a substantial percentage of true hackers called it war.

Crucial to the Hacker Ethic was the fact that computers, by nature, do not consider information proprietary. The architecture of a computer benefited from the easiest, most logical flow of information possible. Someone had to substantially alter a computer process to make data inaccessible to certain users. Using one short command, a user could duplicate an "unprotected" floppy disk down to the last byte in approximately thirty seconds. This ease was appalling to software publishers, who dealt with it by "copy-protecting" disks: altering the programs by special routines which prevented the computer from acting naturally when someone tried to copy a disk. A digital roadblock which did not enhance the program's value to the user, but benefited the seller of the program.

The publishers had legitimate reason to resort to such unesthetic measures. Their livelihood was invested in software. This was not MIT, where software was subsidized by some institution. There was no ARPA footing the bill. Nor was this the Homebrew Computer Club, where everyone was trying to get his hardware built and where software was written by hobbyists, then freely swapped. This was an industry, and companies would go broke if no one bought software. If hackers wanted to write games free and hand them out to friends, that was their business. But the games published by On-Line and Brøderbund and Sirius were not merely paper airplanes of truth released into the wind to spread computer gospel. They were products. And if a person coveted a product of any sort in the United States of America, he or she had to reach into a pocket for folding green bills or a plastic credit card in order to own it.

It drove publishers crazy, but some people refused to recognize this simple fact. They found ways to copy the disks, and did. These people were most commonly hackers.

Users also benefited from breaking disks. Some of them could rattle off a list of rationalizations, and you would hear them recited like a litany in meetings of users' groups, in computer stores, even in the letters column of *Softalk*. *Software is too expensive. We only copy software we wouldn't buy anyway. We only do it to try out programs.* Some of the rationalizations were compelling—if a disk was copy-protected, a legitimate owner would be unable to make a backup copy in case the disk became damaged. Most software publishers offered a replacement disk if you sent them a mangled original, but that usually cost extra, and besides, who wanted to wait four weeks for something you already paid for?

But to hackers, breaking copy protection was as natural as breathing. Hackers hated the fact that copy-protected disks could not be altered. You couldn't even look at the code, admire tricks and learn from them, modify a subroutine that offended you, insert your own subroutine . . . *You couldn't keep working on a pro-*

gram until it was perfect. This was unconscionable. To hackers, a program was an organic entity that had a life independent from that of its author. Anyone who could contribute to the betterment of that machine-language organism should be welcome to try. If you felt that the missiles in Threshold were too slow, you should be welcome to peruse the code, and go deep into the system to improve on it. Copy protection was like some authority figure telling you not to go into a safe which contains machine-language goodies . . . things you absolutely need to improve your programs, your life, and the world at large. Copy-protect was a fascist goon saying Hands Off. As a matter of principle, if nothing else, copy-protected disks must therefore be "broken." Just as the MIT hackers felt compelled to compromise "security" on the CTSS machine, or engaged in lock hacking to liberate tools. Obviously, defeating the fascist goon copy-protect was a sacred calling, and would be lots of fun.

Early varieties of copy-protect involved "bit-shifting" routines that slightly changed the way the computer read information from the disk drive. Those were fairly simple to beat. The companies tried more complicated schemes, each one broken by hackers. One renegade software publisher began selling a program called "Locksmith," specifically designed to allow users to duplicate copy-protected disks. You didn't have to be a hacker, or even a programmer, to break copy protection anymore! The publisher of Locksmith assured the Apple World that his intent, of course, was only to allow users to make backup copies of programs they'd legally purchased. He insisted that users were not necessarily abusing his program in such a way that publishers were losing sales. And Buckminster Fuller announced he was becoming a placekicker for the New York Jets.

With most publishers guessing that they lost more than half their business to software pirates (Ken Williams, with characteristic hyperbole, estimated that for every disk he sold, five or six were pirated from it), the copy-protection stakes were high. Oddly, most companies hired as copy-protect specialists the same kind of young hacker who commonly spent hours figuring out countermeasures to bust someone else's protection routine. This was the case with Sierra On-Line. Its copy-protect person was Mark Duchaineau. He was twenty years old, and for some time during the big 1982 San Francisco Applefest, he single-handedly held this ten-million-dollar-a-year company hostage.

Mark Duchaineau was yet another Third Generation hacker

who had been seduced by computers. He had brown hair which flowed magnificently down his back. His blue eyes blazed with an intensity which hinted of raging fires beneath his almost orientally calm demeanor, fires which could easily lead him to inexplicable acts. He had merged his sensibilities with the computer at Castro Valley (California) Junior High School. "They had a teletype," he would later explain. "After school I would stay many hours. They let me program away. I was never popular, just a loner. [Other] kids would get into baseball or whatever, I was into science and math. [I didn't have] really close friends; I didn't mind. It was really interesting being able to teach a machine how to do things. You communicate with the machine . . . it's like dealing with another person. There's this whole other universe you almost live in when you're programming. And when you get into it young like I did, you feel a oneness with the computer, almost as if it's an extension of yourself. When I print comments in my code, I say things like 'We do this, we do that . . .' It's like Us."

Without computer access, Mark Duchaineau later said, "there would have been this big void . . . it would be like you didn't have your sight, or hearing. The computer is like another sense or part of your being."

Coming to this discovery in the late seventies, Mark was able to get access to computers for his personal use, and become a hacker of the Third Generation. While still in high school, he landed a job at the Byte Shop in Hayward. He loved working at the computer shop. He'd do some of everything—repairs, sales, and programming for the store owner as well as the customers who needed custom programs. The fact that he was getting no more than three dollars an hour didn't bother him: working with computers was pay enough. He kept working at the shop while he attended Cal State at Hayward, where he zipped effortlessly through math and computer courses. He transferred to Berkeley, and was shocked at the rigorousness of the computer science curriculum there. He had developed a hacker attitude: he could work intensely for long periods of time on things that interested him, but had little patience for the things that didn't. In fact, he found it virtually impossible to retain what he called "the little nitpicking things that I knew I'd never need" that were unfortunately essential for success in Berkeley's computer science department. So like many Third Generation hackers, he did not get the benefit of the high-level hacking that took place in universities. He dropped out for the freedom that personal computers would provide, and went back to the Byte Shop.

An intense circle of pirates hung out at the shop. Some of them had even been interviewed in an article about software piracy in *Esquire* that made them seem like heroes. Actually, Mark considered them kind of random hackers. Mark, however, was interested in the kinds of discoveries that it took to break down copy protection, and was fairly proficient at breaking copy-protected disks, though he really had no need for the programs on the disks. A student of the Hacker Ethic, he didn't think too much of the idea of being a person who writes copy-protection schemes.

But one day Mark was playing around with the Apple operating system. He often did this—the common hacker pursuit of wandering around within a system. "My big thing is discovery," he explained later. Working with computers, he could always unearth something new, and got incredible satisfaction from these finds. Mark was trying to figure out what turned the disk drive on and off in the operating system, and soon knew what triggered it, spun it, worked the head, moved the motor. As he experimented with variations on the usual ways to work the disk drive, he realized that he was on to a very big discovery: a new way to put information on a disk.

Mark's scheme involved arranging data in spiraling paths on the disk, so information could not be accessed concentrically, like a needle following a record, but in several spiraling paths. That was why Mark called the scheme "Spiradisk." The different arrangement would thwart programs which broke copy protection and allowed pirates to copy disks. While not being totally pirate-proof (nothing is), Mark's scheme would defy Locksmith, and any other commercial scheme. And would take a hell of a long time for even a devoted hacker to crack.

Through a friend who was working on a game for On-Line, Mark met Ken Williams. Ken expressed only vague interest in Mark's scheme, and over the next few months they talked about it over the phone. Ken always seemed to pick out faults in Mark's system. For one thing, Mark's scheme consumed too much space on a floppy disk. Spiradisk only allowed you to put in half the information you could normally fit on a disk.

While fixing that, Duchaineau came up with another revelation, which allowed him not only to store the full amount of information on a disk but also to speed up the process by which the computer and the disk drive swapped information. At first, Duchaineau doubted it could be done. But like any good hacker, he tried, and after some intense hours of hacking he looked up, flabbergasted, and said, "Gee, this works."

According to Duchaineau's calculations, the Spiradisk process worked twenty times faster than the normal Apple operating system. That meant that you could load the information from a disk into the computer memory in a fraction of the time. It was revolutionary, truly amazing. Mark Duchaineau did not understand why Ken Williams was so reluctant to use it.

Ken saw some value in Duchaineau's system but did not want to risk his whole company on an untried scheme concocted by some random kid genius. In his two years as head of On-Line, Ken had seen plenty of them by now—true wizards who were brilliant conceptualists, but hackers in the worst sense, people who couldn't finish. What insurance did he have that Duchaineau could—or would—fix any dire bugs that would inevitably appear in such a revolutionary scheme? He was impressed enough with Duchaineau, though, to ask him to come to Oakhurst to do more conventional copy protection. Mark, miffed at Ken's rejection of Spiradisk, said he didn't think so.

"What do you want to get paid?" Ken asked him.

Mark Duchaineau had been living at home and working in the computer store for three dollars an hour. He took a shot and said, "Ten bucks an hour," mainly because, he later said, "that sounded like a neat number to me."

"Well," said Ken, "what if I let you live in one of my houses and give you $8.65 an hour?"

Deal.

Ken basically wanted a fairly reliable copy-protect system to work with the Form Master, a big disk-copying machine On-Line had bought to churn out products. Could Mark come up with a program that could do that? Yes. In half an hour, Duchaineau conceived of a plan, and set about writing code for the next twenty-four hours, finishing with a complete protection scheme that he says "wasn't incredibly reliable, wasn't very high-quality, but it did work, if you [had] clean disk drives and normal disk speeds." Over the next few months, Mark used it to protect about twenty-five products.

He also became the official Dungeonmaster for a running Dungeons and Dragons game at Hexagon House. Built as a traditional suburban family home, the house was beginning to show some wear from neglect by a shifting roster of hacker-boarders. The walls, the wooden banisters, and the kitchen cabinets all had a battered, war-pocked look. No one had bothered to get furniture, and the main room had only a Formica dining table and cheap kitchen chairs, a six-foot-tall sword-dueling arcade game, and a large color TV without a stand, connected to a Betamax that seemed to constantly play *Conan the Barbarian*. On D&D nights, a few of the programmers would gather around the table, while Mark sat cross-legged on the soiled wall-to-wall carpet surrounded by hardbound D&D guides for running games. He would roll dice, ominously predicting that this person . . . or troll, as the case might be . . . had a 40 percent chance of getting hit by a lightning bolt cast by a wizard named Zwernif. He'd roll an eighteen-sided die, peer down at it, and look up with those disconcertingly intense eyes and say, already eager for the next crisis, "You're still alive." Then he'd thumb through the book for another life-and-death confrontation for the role players. Running a D&D game was a great exercise in control, just as computers were.

Mark kept lobbying for Spiradisk. His eagerness to implement the hard-to-crack scheme was not due to a desire to thwart would-be pirates; Duchaineau considered it a sacrifice to bring about his more altruistic master plan. He hoped Spiradisk would generate enough royalties for him to begin his own company, one which would be guided not by the unproductive standards of commercialism, but by the forward-thinking goals of research and development. Duchaineau's company would be a hacker paradise, with programmers having every conceivable tool at their disposal to create awesome software. If a programmer felt the company needed a piece of equipment, say some supercalibrated oscilloscope, he would not have to get permission from unconnected management channels . . . he and his fellow hackers would have a large say in the process. Initially, Mark's company would write state-of-the-art software—Mark himself dreamed of writing the ultimate computer version of Dungeons and Dragons.

But software was only the beginning. Once revenues could support it, Mark's company would get into hardware. The ultimate goal would be to create a computer good enough to handle an arcade game as good as the most sophisticated coin-operated games. It would have a built-in music synthesizer better than the most advanced current models; it would have more than enough power to run Mark's dream software "environment" called SORDMASTER (*S*creen *O*riented *D*ata *M*anipulation *S*ystem), which would be like taking the best program running today and extending its value to the tenth power . . . a computer, in Mark's words, that would "do anything you want."

Finally, Ken Williams agreed to allow the Dungeonmaster to copy-protect On-Line's programs with Spiradisk. Mark would get forty dollars an hour for setting things up, five thousand dollars a month to maintain the system, and a 1 percent royalty on all disks which used his system. Mark also fixed it so that the first thing a user would see when he booted up a Spiradisk was the name of Mark's "company," Bit Works.

As Ken suspected, there were problems with the scheme. The disks often had to be rebooted once or twice before the program would properly load. Williams began to get disenchanted with Duchaineau. In Ken's view, Mark was one of those brilliant but unfocused hacker prima donnas. Ken believed that Mark was capable of pulling off a coup that could prove critical for the whole industry: creating a disk format that would support Apple, Atari, and IBM on the same disk, instead of the current system, which required a separate disk to run on each machine. "Mark knows how to do it," Ken complained. "He could do it in six weeks. He doesn't want to make the effort. It's work. He sat down, worked for a week, lost interest in the project. He can do it, but it doesn't *excite* him. It's not fun." According to Ken Williams, "You'd have to be suicidal to let your company depend on a guy like Duchaineau." When it was pointed out to Ken that his company *did* depend on that Third Generation hacker, Ken Williams admitted that that was the case.

This came into sharp focus at the annual Applefest in San Francisco. One of the highlights of that big weekend event, a bazaar in which all the companies selling products for the Apple would display and sell their wares, was to be the introduction of a long-awaited and ornately augmented sequel to one of the best-loved Apple games of all time, "Ultima." In a tremendous coup, On-Line Systems had landed the game and its mercurial author, who wrote under the pseudonym of Lord British.

The original Ultima was a fantasy role-playing game where the player created a character, assigned certain "attribute points" in areas of durability, wisdom, intelligence, dexterity, and strength, and, traveling about a mysterious planet, searched dungeons and towers, went to villages for supplies and helpful gossip, and fought elves, warriors, and wizards. Even though the game was written in BASIC and ran rather slowly, it was a masterful feat of imagination, and was an Apple bestseller. But when Lord British prepared his sequel, he let it be known that he wished to leave his current publisher—who, he said, was not paying him all his royalties.

He was deluged with offers from software houses. Though he was only twenty at the time, Lord British was no stranger to pressure situations: his real name was Richard Garriott, and he was the son of Skylab astronaut Owen K. Garriott. He'd known and enjoyed the reflected limelight of his father's fame, especially when his Skylab 2 was aloft and the family seemed the focus of the world's attention. Richard had grown up in the engineering-intensive Nassau Bay area of Houston, and had gotten into computers in high school, where he convinced his teachers to allow him to take private classes in programming. His curriculum was writing games.

In many respects, he was a well-adjusted all-American boy. On the other hand, he would stay up all night on the Apple Computer in his bedroom. "Once the sun came up I'd realize how late it was and crash right there on the spot," he later explained. He had long held an interest in fantasy role-playing games, and was particularly fascinated by medieval culture, belonging to a club called the Society of Creative Anachronisms. While a freshman at the University of Texas, he joined the fencing team, but was really much more into swashbuckling—free-swinging, climbing-on-table, Errol Flynn–style sword-fighting. He wanted to merge his two interests, and attempted to make a computer game that would do it. After writing for months, he completed his twenty-eighth game and named it "Alkabeth," and was astounded when a publisher who happened to see one of the copies that Richard sent to friends for free offered to publish it and send him money. Why not? He requested the pseudonym Lord British because some kids at a computer camp once teased him that he sounded as if he'd come from England (he didn't).

Alkabeth made enough money for several college educations. His next game, Ultima, was more ambitious, and with his six-figure royalties he bought a car, established fat Keogh and IRA accounts, and invested in a Houston restaurant. Now he was considering real estate.

Garriott saw his follow-up as something special. He had learned machine language especially to write it, and was dizzy with the new power it gave him: he felt that it enabled him to *see* the memory, the microprocessor, the video circuitry . . . you understood what each bit did and where the data lines went. And the speed it gave you was incredible. Only with this power could he bring Ultima 2 to fruition. Because, in Ultima 2, Richard Garriott was writing a true epic, one that enabled the player to do more than any player of a computer game had ever done before. He insisted that some of these abilities be listed in the box in which the program was sold:

- Seize Ships
- Hijack Airplanes
- Travel Throughout the Solar System
- Clash with Innocent Bystanders
- Be Pursued by KGB Agents
- Get Accosted in Dark Alleys
- Battle Pirates on the Open Sea
- Be Seduced in a Bar
- Dine at Your Favorite Restaurant
- Meet Prominent People Within the Computer Industry
- Cast Magical Spells at Evil Creatures
- Visit the Castle of Lord British
- Explore Deep Dark Deadly Dungeons
- Burglarize Merchants
- Slay Vicious Creatures
- Charge Through Impenetrable Forces
        and
- Grow to Wield the Most Powerful Magic Known to Man

Garriott had embodied the metaphor of the computer—creating and populating a private universe—into a game which allowed the player to live in the world of Lord British's imagination. Moving the character that you created by designating personality traits, you gained powers, tools, transportation craft, weapons . . . and among the murderous Orcs and evil wizards, you might also chance upon characters based on real people, many of them friends of Richard Garriott's—characters who, in keeping with their real personalities, would give you cryptic information that helped to solve the riddle.

Richard Garriott might have displayed Joycean ambition and intricacy, but he admittedly lacked literary skills: "I can't spell, have no grammar techniques, and have read less than twenty-five books in my life." This embarrassed him at first, but now he told himself that the computer was a viable artistic form. And in peddling Ultima 2 to a new publisher, his prime concern, besides a nonnegotiable 30 percent royalty rate, was that the package and marketing be artistically consistent with the virtuoso computer program contained therein. This would require a large, professionally illustrated box, a cloth map of the universe with lines designating time warps, special cardboard cards holding the dozens of commands available to players, and an elaborate, oversized manual in which each of the sixteen pages resembled a faded sheepskin document.

None of these demands discouraged software publishers from attempting to sign this most bankable of hackers. Ken Williams pursued him relentlessly, smelling bestseller. After flying the young author to Oakhurst, he agreed to all of Lord British's demands, even the 30 percent royalty. Ken Williams wanted him to sign then and there, and, Garriott later said, "got all huffy at the fact that I wasn't going to sign anything [that day]." But after he returned to Texas, Garriott did sign. "I couldn't see a reason not to."

Now, after months of delay, some due to an unexpectedly long debugging period (there has never been an unexpectedly short debugging period in the history of computers), some due to the fact that the cloth maps were ordered from a firm in Iran, which was suddenly closed off to American commerce after the hostage crisis, the program was complete.

Garriott had the game in hand at Applefest; festooned in gold chains and a suede-and-leather tunic, the tall, brown-haired, angular-featured Texan drew crowds to the On-Line booth as he unveiled his masterpiece. The people could not believe their good fortune as they gathered around the twenty-one-year-old Garriott, who was casually demonstrating how they might find occasion in Ultima 2 to travel to Pluto. *This is the guy who wrote Ultima!* Back orders for the $59.95 program numbered in the tens of thousands; Richard Garriott expected the first royalty check for Ultima 2 to be bigger than the sum of checks he had previously collected for game authorship. He would have been a very happy young man, except for this one problem that was preventing Ultima 2 from being released that very weekend. The problem was Mark Duchaineau. He had not copy-protected the program, and it was not clear that he would.

The Dungeonmaster had insisted to Dick Sunderland that his Spiradisk system would work perfectly on Ultima 2, speeding up the loading time, and substantially slowing down the pirate network eagerly awaiting the challenge of breaking it. He dismissed On-Line's previous Spiradisk problems as insignificant. He hinted that there might be some problems copy-protecting the program *without* Spiradisk. Dick suspected that Mark's arguments were motivated by his eagerness to promote Spiradisk and to collect the royalty—which would be worth over ten thousand dollars on a best-seller like Ultima 2.

Richard Garriott, his friend and fellow programmer Chuck Bueche, and On-Line's product manager jointly concluded that Spiradisk would be too risky. Dick Sunderland called Duchaineau to tell him to copy-protect the old way. But Mark was still evasive.

Dick was furious. This odd-looking creature, this twenty-one-year-old megalomanic Dungeonmaster, living in one of Ken's houses, taking advantage of On-Line's reputation to promote his system . . . now had the gall to hint to Dick that the most lucrative program of the season would not ship—because he wanted to copy-protect *his* way! As frightening as his threat sounded, Mark, as the sole copy-protect person, had the power to back it up—it would take weeks to bring in a replacement. What was even more frightening was that Mark Duchaineau, if he chose, could withhold his services for On-Line's entire product line! The company could not release *any* products without him.

Sunderland was at a loss. Ken had not arrived at the Fest. He was still on his way back from Chicago, where he had attended the convention of pinball and coin-op videogame manufacturers. Dick did not even have the technical wherewithal to judge the validity of Duchaineau's claims. So he recruited one of On-Line's young programmers, Chuck Bueche, to go to the long bank of pay phones by the entrance to Applefest and call Duchaineau—not letting on that it was at Dick's behest, of course—and get a grasp of the technicalities involved. It wouldn't hurt, either, if the programmer softened the Dungeonmaster's hard line.

Indeed, though Bueche was an uneasy double agent, the call seemed to break the logjam. Perhaps what made Duchaineau relent was that the call reminded him he was slowing down a process that would eventually allow users to benefit from a fellow programmer's triumph—Mark Duchaineau was in the awkward role of a hacker trying to stop another hacker's worthy program from *getting out*. In any case, he agreed to copy-protect the product, though when Ken Williams found out about the incident, his regard for the hacker Mark Duchaineau sank even lower. He later vowed to run Duchaineau out of Oakhurst in tar and feathers—as soon as On-Line could figure out how to replace him.

•

For two years, the Applefest show had been the prime gathering of the Apple World companies like On-Line, Sirius, Brøderbund, and dozens of suppliers of software, add-on boards, and peripherals that ran on the Apple. It was a time to celebrate the machine that had given the Brotherhood its livelihood and inspiration, and the companies were more than happy to entertain the thousands of Apple owners eagerly immersing themselves in a sea of arcade games, printer buffers, disk drives, programming guides, joysticks, RAM cards, RGB monitors, war simulations, and hard-shell computer carrying cases. It was a time to renew the bonds within the Brotherhood, to seek new programmers, to write up orders, to let people see who you were and how you were running your own show.

But the 1982 San Francisco Applefest would turn out to be the last of the important Applefests. For one thing, On-Line and its competitors were now releasing programs for several machines; the Apple was no longer dominant. Also, the companies were beginning to see the open-to-users shows as drains on time, energy, and money—resources which could be spent on what were becoming the essential shows: the big, trade-only Consumer Electronics Shows in Las Vegas and Chicago. Where the hero was not the hacker, but the man who wrote up sales.

Still, the show was packed, one more indication of the economic explosion that had come to computers. Amid Applefest's din of shuffling feet, voices, and electronic game noises, what emerged was a melody of unprecedented prosperity. Almost everywhere you turned there were millionaires manning booths, millionaires who only two years ago were mired in obscure and unprofitable activities. Then there were the start-ups, with smaller booths or with no booths at all, dreamers drawn by the thrilling, aphrodisiac scent emanating from the Apple World and the related world of home computers.

That smell of success was driving people batty.

People idly swapped unbelievable stories, with even the most startling high-tech Horatio Alger saga effortlessly topped by a more startling example of the boom. It was a gold rush, but it was also true that the minimum buy-in for serious prospectors was a more formidable sum than it had been when Ken Williams began. Venture capital was a necessity, obtained from the men in pinstripe suits who dined at the mediocre French restaurants in the Valley, uttered In-Pursuit-Of-Excellence koans at industry seminars ("Marketing, Marketing, Marketing"), and solemnly referred to themselves as "risk-takers." These were intolerable people, carpet-baggers of the hacker dream, but if you could get them to wink at you, the rewards could be endless. No one knew this better than the people at the Applefest who were working to start a company called Electronic Arts. Their idea was to bypass what they regarded as the already old-fashioned practices of the companies in the Brotherhood, and establish a firm that was even newer than New Age. A company that took software into another realm entirely.

Electronic Arts had defined its mission in a little booklet directed to "software artists" they were trying to lure away from their current publishers. This prospectus sounded like something penned by an ad copywriter who had successfully merged the sensibilities of three-piece suits and top-grade Hawaiian dope. It was loaded with one-sentence paragraphs which contained words like "excitement," "vision," and "nontraditional." Its true brilliance lay in the focus of its appeal—aimed directly at the hacker heart of its readers. Electronic Arts knew better than to whip up the greed factor by promising hackers enough royalties to buy cherry-red Trans-Ams and Caribbean trysts with hot-blooded software groupies. It confided instead: "We believe that innovative authors are more likely to come from people who are independent and won't work in a software 'factory' or 'bureaucracy.' " It promised to develop fantastic and powerful tools and utilities that would be available to EA authors. It vowed to maintain the kind of personal values that hackers appreciate more than money. What this would result in was "a great software company." The implication was that as far as creative, honest, foward-thinking programmers with hacker values were concerned, there was at present no such company.

Electronic Arts was the brainchild of Trip Hawkins, who had quit his job as Apple's director of marketing for the LISA project to do this. He started the company out of an extra room in the office of a venture capital firm. Hawkins brought together a team from Apple, Atari, Xerox PARC, and VisiCorp, and, in a coup sure to charm the heart of any hacker, got Steve Wozniak to agree to sit on the board of directors.

Electronic Arts had no booth at the Applefest, but its presence was felt. It hosted a big party on opening night, and its people worked the show floor like politicians. One of them, a former Apple executive named Pat Mariott, a tall, thin, blond woman with huge round glasses and a deep tan, was enthusiastically explaining the company to a reporter. Trip started Electronic Arts, she said, because he saw how fast the business was starting to happen and he "didn't want to miss the window." Pat went with him because she saw it as an opportunity to have fun and, not incidentally, make money.

"I want to get rich, by the way," she said, explaining how, in Silicon Valley, wealth was omnipresent. Everywhere you looked you saw its artifacts: BMWs, stock options, and, though she didn't mention it, cocaine in snowdrift quantities. This was not your garden-variety, hundred-thousand-dollar-a-year wealth, either—this was Croesus Mode, where floating-point arithmetic was barely sufficient to count the millions. When you saw your friends come into it, you thought, *Why not me?* So when a window into wealth opened, you naturally leapt through it. There has never been a window as inviting as that of the software industry. Pat Mariott summed it up in a whisper, quoting gonzo journalist Hunter S. Thompson: "When the going gets weird, the weird turn pro."

Pat Mariott hoped to kick into Croesus Mode without compromising her sixties-shaped personal values. She would never, for instance, work for a cutthroat company. Pat had been a programmer herself, experiencing hacker culture at Berkeley and the professional milieu at evil IBM. "Berkeley was truth and beauty. IBM was power and money. I wanted both," she said. Electronic Arts seemed the way. The products and philosophy of the company would be truth and beauty, and the company founders would all be powerful and rich. And the programmers, who would be treated with the respect they deserved as the artists of the computer age, would be elevated to the status of rock or movie stars.

This message managed to find its way around the Applefest, enough so knots of programmers began gathering outside the Convention Hall for the buses that supposedly would take them to the Stanford Court Hotel, where Electronic Arts was throwing its big party. One odd group included, among others, several On-Line programmers and John "Captain Crunch" Draper.

John Draper, whose dark stringy hair was flying out in all directions, had done well by himself. During his stint in prison after he was caught using the Apple phone interface as a blue box, he had written a word-processing program called "Easy Writer," which made him a considerable sum. Amazingly, when IBM sought a program to issue as its official word processor, it chose Easy Writer; the company that published Draper's program had the good sense to act as intermediary with IBM, not letting on that the program's author was the notorious Captain Crunch. Reputedly, Draper had made a million dollars from the transaction. You wouldn't have known it from his faded jeans, his old polo shirt, and his apparent need for dental work. Mark Duchaineau regarded him with a mixture of awe and repulsion as the former phone hacker harangued him about some technical aspect of the IBM PC.

Soon, they gave up on the bus and hailed a cab. The cab driver made the mistake of smoking. John Draper almost ripped the cigarette out the driver's mouth, demanding at the top of his lungs that all the cab windows be opened in the chilly, damp November night of San Francisco.

The hotel was quite fancy, and the hackers, in jeans and sneakers, seemed intimidated. Electronic Arts had prepared for them, though: along with a rock band playing dance music, the company had rented over a dozen stand-up, coin-operated videogames, adjusted to give unlimited free games. This was where the hackers immediately headed. As the party heated up, it was apparent that many of the industry's biggest authors had appeared, some to check things out, others genuinely interested in this newer-than-new-age venture.

The center of attention, though, was EA board member Steve Wozniak, cited in a series of speeches as "the man who started it all." It was an epithet that would have haunted some young genius eager to shake the past and get on to newer things, but Wozniak seemed to revel in it; for over a year now he had been traveling around the country to industry gatherings, accepting the same accolades. He had spent a considerable portion of his Croesus Mode bankroll on presenting massive rock festivals. He still fervently believed in the Hacker Ethic, and wherever he went he not only preached that gospel but set himself as an example of it. Tonight, for instance, he preached to a small group on the evils of secrecy, using Apple's current policy as a prime example. The secrecy and the stifling bureaucracy there were such that he was not sure if he would ever return to the company built on his brainchild, the Apple II.

All in all, the party was a success, crackling with the sweet feeling that everybody was riding on the crest of a tidal wave. Were things like this in the early days of Hollywood? In the record industry in the sixties? The future stood at their feet, a blend of hackerism and untold wealth, and the aggregate impression was that history was being made right there.

The On-Line hackers left impressed. Some would sign with Electronic Arts in the following months. And one of the hackers left with a particularly satisfied grin—he had scored the high totals on Pac-Man, Robotron, *and* Donkey Kong. For a bestselling author, a night to remember.

•

Ken Williams arrived at Applefest in a bad mood. The pinball manufacturers' convention in Chicago had been frustrating; giant companies, particularly Atari, had thrown truckloads of money at the coin-op manufacturers to nail down first rights of refusal for the home computer version of any game that was even vaguely playable. A repeat of Frogger, which Ken had procured for a mere 10 percent royalty fee, was out of the question.

Ken, traveling with Roberta, went straight to his company's Applefest display. On-Line had taken a huge booth, situated right at the entrance, by the escalators which would carry the masses down into the underground Brooks Hall complex. The booth featured a giant photo mural of a Sierra waterfall, emphasizing the name change from On-Line Systems. The booth also had plenty of computer-joystick-monitor combinations embedded within panels so that the hordes of computer-freak youngsters could play the latest Sierra On-Line games. The monitors were set into the panels well above eye level, so spectators could easily appreciate how deftly crafted the games were. And to draw customers to the booth, a huge projection-screen color television was hooked up to a computer which continuously played the best-selling On-Line game, Frogger. Since the Apple version did not have the continuous music and arcade-level graphics of John Harris' Atari version, On-Line employees discreetly hid an Atari 800 computer underneath a drape, and was running that version at the Applefest: the equivalent of displaying a Japanese car at a General Motors exhibition. With all those crowds, all that hoopla, who would notice?

Two people who noticed were Al and Margot Tommervik, publishers of *Softalk*. They noticed right away because Frogger was not just another On-Line program to them. It represented a depressing turn of events. Like everyone who had seen John Harris' brilliant conversion, they had been awed and delighted when they saw it earlier that year. But when they viewed the Apple counterpart soon after, they were shocked. It was awful. To Al and Margot, the miserable graphics in this version of Frogger represented at best an error, and at worst an absolute betrayal of the Apple market, which had nurtured On-Line in the first place.

The Apple World was a spiritual preserve to the Tommerviks, and it seemed that by making an inferior Apple Frogger, On-Line had contemptuously spit on the floor of this exalted preserve. Obviously, Al and Margot owed it to the rest of the Apple World to do something they rarely did in their magazine: give a game a negative review. The reviewer they assigned agreed with the Tommerviks, and wrote a scathing description of the game: "It has about as much soul as month-old lettuce in the Sahara," he wrote. "Your frog resembles a chess pawn with vestigial wings . . . the logs on the river look like they just escaped from an Oscar Meyer factory . . ."

The reviewer did not stop there. He asked what had become of the company which once stood as a "bastion of quality in a sea of mediocrity." While giving Atari owners a great program, On-Line was giving Apple owners "a slap in the face." Serious stuff, cutting to the heart of the Hacker Ethic, which instructs you to keep working until your hack tops previous efforts. "Have they forsaken us?" the review asked of On-Line.

Since Margot and Al had been so close to Ken and Roberta, they tried to explain the review to their friends before it appeared in the December *Softalk*. But they had difficulty reaching Ken or Roberta. The lines of bureaucracy were hardening at On-Line; no longer would one of the Williamses be picking up the phone. You'd get a receptionist, who would connect you to a secretary, who would take your name and your company's number and tell you someone would return your call. If you were lucky. Finally, Al reached Ken's brother John, who said there were reasons the game looked the way it did . . . but these reasons were never presented to the Tommerviks. People at On-Line were too swept up in management battles to explain.

Al and Margot had carried early copies of the magazine to Applefest with them. Seeing On-Line's devious trick with the Atari Frogger only confirmed their belief that the review was a righteous one. They figured that after talking to Ken and Roberta, things would be amicably settled. Weren't they all in this for the same thing? To maintain the fantastic humanistic momentum of Apple World? You couldn't let a disagreement like Frogger affect an important mission like that.

When someone at On-Line's booth gave Ken a copy of the new *Softalk*, he turned immediately to the Frogger review. Roberta read over his shoulder. They had known the review would be negative, and more or less expected some criticism of the game's graphics, though not in such scathing language. But they had no idea that the review would go on to question whether the company, by releasing such a great Atari version of Frogger and such a pitiful Apple version, had sold out the Apple World. "Either Frogger is a mistake or a betrayal," the review concluded. "You'll have to make up your own mind."

"This goes way beyond what's fair," Ken said. For one thing, he said, *Softalk* did not realize how difficult it was to do the game on the Apple as compared to the Atari. The Tommervicks had apparently chosen to attack the company—all after the Williamses had helped get the magazine off the ground when the Brotherhood was just forming. Roberta thought that this confrontation had been brewing for a while: for some reason *Softalk* seemed always to give On-Line short shrift. But every time Roberta asked the Tommervicks if anything was wrong, they said things were fine.

"They don't want us in that magazine," Roberta told Ken. "We should pull our ads."

It was another sign that the Brotherhood was not inviolate. Things were bigger now than personal friendships. Now that the companies of the Brotherhood were more like Real World businesses, they were competing among themselves. The Williamses rarely spoke to people at Brøderbund or Sirius, and never swapped secrets anymore. Jerry Jewell later summed it up: "We used to socialize a lot with Brøderbund and On-Line . . . now the attitude is that if you invite competitors to parties, all they're going to do is dig up as much dirt about you as they can and try to hire your programmers away. [Socializing] gets less and less possible as the business gets more and more cutthroat. You want your competitors to know less and less what you're doing." It was something you had to accept.

Ken touched on this briefly when he ran into Doug Carlston on the show floor. Doug seemed to have changed the least—he was as sincere and open as he always was, the sanest in the Brotherhood. Both agreed that they should get together more, as they had in the old days, one year ago. They discussed new competition, including one new company which was entering the market with $8 million in capital. "That makes us look like toys," said Carlston. "We got a million [in venture capital]. You got . . ."

"A million two," said Ken.

"You gave up more. We gave up 25 percent."

"No, we gave up 24."

They talked about Sirius Software's no-show at the Applefest—another indication that the action was switching to trade-only shows. Ken thought that Jerry Jewell's push to mass-market cartridges was a good one. "He'll be richer than all of us," he predicted.

Doug smiled. "I don't care if everybody else gets rich . . . as long as I do."

"I don't care if anybody gets rich," said Ken, "as long as I get richer."

Ken tried to throw himself into the spirit of the show, and took Roberta, looking chic in designer jeans, high boots, and a black beret, on a quick tour of the displays. Ken was a natural schmoozer, and at almost every booth he was recognized and greeted warmly. He asked about half a dozen young programmers to come up to Oakhurst and get rich hacking for On-Line.

Though they took pains to avoid the *Softalk* booth, the Williamses did run into Margot Tommervik. After an awkward greeting, she asked Ken if he'd seen the "Dark Crystal" cover.

"All I saw was the Frogger review," he said. Pause. "I thought it was kinda nasty."

Margot hugged him to show no hard feelings. "Oh Ken, the game was crummy," she said. "We did it because we love you. Because your stuff is so much better than that. We expect more of you."

"Well," said Ken, smiling through his teeth, "didn't you think it went beyond the game? It said all kinds of things about our company."

Margot would not hear about it. The Williamses, though, did not consider that matter closed. To them, it was one more case of how people changed when things got big.

That night On-Line hosted a dinner at an Italian restaurant at North Beach. Ken had been talking for weeks about the potential for a good, old-fashioned night of On-Line rowdiness, but though everybody was in a celebratory mood, the affair never took off. Maybe because only two programmers were invited—Richard Garriott and Chuck Bueche—and the rest of the people were older, many of them mired in the mind-frame of sales, accounting, and marketing. There were the usual repeated toasts, and of course there was the Steel—peppermint schnapps—large swigs of it from a bottle with a metal drink-pourer attached. Many of the toasts were directed to the guest of honor, Steve Wozniak. Ken had run into him that afternoon, and to Ken's delight the legendary hacker had accepted the belated invitation to dinner. Ken Williams made a point of telling Woz about his prize possession, the most cherished tie he had to the spirit of the liberating age of the home computer: an original Apple I motherboard. Ken loved that hunk of epoxy and silicon; it meant something to him that Woz himself had hand-wired it in a garage, back in the Pleistocene era of 1976. Woz never tired of hearing about Homebrew days, and he appreciated Ken's compliment. Wozniak smiled widely as he was toasted, this time by Dick Sunderland. The Steel went around once more.

For Woz, though, the highlight of the evening was meeting Lord British. Months afterward, he was still talking about how excited he'd been to talk to such a genius.

Dinner was followed by a hectic trip to a disco in the Transamerica building. After all that reveling, Ken and Roberta were exhausted by the time they returned to their hotel. An emergency call awaited them. There had been a fire in the A-frame wooden home on Mudge Ranch Road. Only the heroism of a baby-sitter had saved their two sons. The house, though, was severely damaged. Ken and Roberta demanded to speak to their children to make sure they were safe, and immediately drove home.

It was daylight by the time they arrived at the site where their house once stood. The children were safe, everything seemed covered by insurance, and the Williamses had planned to move anyway the following year, to the palatial home currently under construction. The fire was not the catastrophe it might have been. Ken Williams had only one lingering sorrow: the loss of a certain irreplaceable material item in the home, an artifact that meant something to him far beyond its raw utility. The fire had consumed Ken's Apple I motherboard, his link to the idealistic beginning of the humanistic era of computers. It was somewhere in the rubble, damaged beyond repair, never to be found.

20

WIZARD vs. WIZARDS

In December of 1982, Tom Tatum, lanky, dark-haired, moustached, and as cool as his lazy Southern drawl implied, stood at the ballroom podium of the Las Vegas Sands. Behind him, sitting uncomfortably on a row of chairs, were ten hackers. Tom Tatum, former lawyer, lobbyist, and Carter campaign aide, now a leading purveyor of video "docusports" programming, thought he had serendipitously latched on to a jackpot bigger than that of any slot machine in the casino only yards away from where he stood.

"This is the event where Hollywood meets the Computer Age," said Tom Tatum to the crowd of reporters and computer tradespeople in town for the Comdex show. "The ultra-contest of the eighties."

Tom Tatum's creation was called "Wizard vs. Wizards." It was to be a television contest where game designers play each other's games for a set of prizes. Tatum had gathered programmers from companies like On-Line and Sirius because he sensed the arrival of a new kind of hero, one who fought with brains instead of muscle, one who represented America's bold willingness to stay ahead of the rest of the world in the technological battle of supremacy: the hacker.

Unlike Tom Tatum's previous sports productions, which included the 1981 Maui Windsurfing Grand Prix and the Telluride Aerobatics Invitational, this "Wizard vs. Wizards" had the potential to draw a new audience to the docusports genre. "Only a small percentage of the population will own a Super Cross bike," he later explained. "But when you look at people computing at home, it's awesome."

Obviously, the contests people cared about were now occurring in arcades and in front of Apple computers. Imagine how many would tune in to see *pros* compete. What's more, as Tatum put it, "the sizzle in this show is the double whammy" of the authors themselves—those weird, sci-fi computer guys—competing against each other.

"These are the new stars!" said Tom Tatum in Las Vegas, but the new stars seemed ill at ease being paraded on a Las Vegas stage like so many misshapen Miss Universe contenders. The beauty in hackerism was Taoistic and internal, blindingly impressive when one could perceive the daring blend of idealism and cerebration, but less than compelling when presented as a chorus line in a Las Vegas ballroom. The hacker smiles were wooden, their suits ill-fitting (though a few were wearing specially made—though still ill-fitting—athletic warm-up suits). Even the most obtuse observer could divine that most of them would rather be home hacking. But with mixed motivations of curiosity, pressure from their publishers, a desire to spend a few days in Vegas, and, yes, vanity, they had come to the Sands to compete in the hottest thing Tom Tatum had ever done, with the possible exception, he later conceded, of the Miller High Life Super Cross Finals.

The contest would include hackers from seven companies. Jerry Jewell was on the scene with Sirius' two most awesome arcaders. On-Line would arrive tomorrow. After the presentation, Jewell bragged to one of the competitors that one of his men might well be the world's best videogamer. "I've seen him play Robotron for four hours," he said.

The hacker was not intimidated. "You see this?" he replied in a shrieky voice, holding his hand out. "This is my Robotron blister. I usually stop after an hour because my hands are so sensitive."

Later, in his hotel room, Jewell watched as his hackers practiced the games scheduled for the competition. Jewell was exultant about his company's deal with Twentieth-Century Fox Games. The VCS cartridges his programmers now designed were widely distributed and heavily marketed by Fox; his was the first company of the Brotherhood to have its games advertised on television, and distributed in mass-market outlets. "It's one thing to see your Apple product on the wall of a computer store," Jerry Jewell was saying, "but when you see a rack of your stuff in K-Mart, you know you've arrived."

Ken Williams arrived in Las Vegas in time for a pre-contest meeting that Tatum held for the twelve contestants and their sponsors. Having bounced back quickly from the fire, Williams was ready to be the only competitor in the show who was actually a publisher. He and the others drew chairs in a semicircle to hear Tatum describe the rules.

"This is a new kind of contest," Tom Tatum addressed the group. "It wouldn't happen except for television. It is created for television. The rules have been developed for television." He explained that two sets of conflicting values were involved in this new kind of contest: Value One was the urge for an honest, fair competition, and Value Two was the need to do everything possible to make things look good on television. Tatum said that both values were important, but whenever the two values conflicted he would choose Value Two.

Then Tatum described the image with which the show would begin: a shot of the nighttime Las Vegas neon strip with a wizard—symbol of the hacker—looming over it, bolts of lightning streaming from his fingertips. An omnipotent New Age icon. This image seemed to impress the computer people, as did the picture Tom Tatum drew of the benefits of competing in a television event. It might boost them, Tatum said, to the status of household names. "Once this show hits and other shows start to happen, things will start to happen," Tatum said. "You can earn income from other sources, like advertising products."

On the morning of the television show, before the cameras were turned on, the meager audience in the Sands Ballroom was able to witness something that ten or twenty years before would have been considered beyond the imagination of Heinlein, Bradbury, or even MIT's resident visionary Ed Fredkin. Makeup specialists casually were applying pancake makeup to the faces of antsy young computer programmers. The age of the media hacker had begun.

Tom Tatum had hired a soap opera actress, coiffed to kill and armed with a tooth-polish smile, to host the show. She had trouble with her opening line about how this was the first time in intergalactic history that the world's computer wizards and techno-geniuses had gathered to compete; it took fifteen iterations before a take. Only then did the competition begin, and only then was it woefully clear how boring it was to watch a bunch of hackers sitting at long tables, joysticks between their legs, each with one sneakered foot curled under the chair and the other foot extended under the table, jaw slightly slack, and eyes dully planted on the screen.

Unlike more compelling forms of video competition, the programmers were undemonstrative when clearing a screen of aliens or getting wiped out by an avenging pulsar ray. Discerning spectators had to watch very carefully for grimaces or for squinty frustration to tell when a wrong move ended in a video explosion. When players were confonted with the despised GAME OVER signal before the five-minute time limit was reached, they would sadly raise a hand so one of the judges would take note of the score. A lackluster agony of defeat.

Tatum figured that this videogenic deficiency would be remedied by quick cutting, shots of the computer screens, and pithy interviews with the silicon gladiators. The interviews generally went like the one that the soap opera star conducted with Sirius' nineteen-year-old Dan Thompson, who quickly established himself as a front-runner.

SOAP OPERA STAR: How does it feel to have such a commanding lead going into the semi-finals?

THOMPSON (shrugs): Great, I guess.

Cut! Can we do this one again? The second time, Dan did not shrug. Once more, please? By now, Dan Thompson's digital logic and problem-solving technique had been applied to the puzzle. As soon as the question left the soap opera star's mouth, he leaned to the mike, eyes to the camera.

"Well, it feels wonderful. I just hope I can continue this . . ." He had synthesized the superficialities of jockspeak.

Thompson, beneficiary of hours of joysticking at a Chuck E. Cheese Pizza Time Theatre in Sacramento, won the contest. Ken Williams had performed admirably, considering he barely had a chance to look at some of the games before he played them; the fact that he placed sixth overall was testament to his ability to instantly get to the heart of a computer game, and the fact that at twenty-eight he still had some reflexes left.

In Tatum's suite that night, the video impresario was beside himself. "I think we've seen the most revolutionary television event in years," he said. He predicted that these hackers would capture the imagination of America—athletes who don't take a physical beating, but emanate a transfixing intensity. He raised his liquor glass to the future of the hacker as the new American hero.

•

One On-Line programmer who had shown signs of becoming a media hero was Bob Davis, the former alcoholic whom Ken Williams had elevated to the status of game author and considered a best friend. Williams had co-written with Davis the adventure game Ulysses and the Golden Fleece, and the closing lines of Margot Tommervik's *Softalk* review read like a triumphal justification of Ken Williams' decision to go into partnership with the computer to change the world:

> On-Line Systems has two new winners in "Ulysses": The adventure, which is the best from On-Line since "Wizard and the Princess"; and Bob Davis, a new author from whom we hope we'll be seeing many new adventures.

The package Sierra On-Line sent to entice prospective authors included an open letter from Bob Davis, who told of his experience of being "bitten by the computer bug," seeing his game go through a painless production process, and receiving royalties, "more than ample and always on time." Davis concluded by writing: "So now I just spend my time skiing the slopes of Lake Tahoe, watching my video recorder, driving my new car and living quite comfortably in my new three-bedroom house. I strongly suggest you do the same."

Yet not long after Ken's return from Las Vegas, Bob Davis could not be reached at the ski slopes, behind the wheel of his car, or in his new home. He was receiving visitors only at the Fresno County jail. Davis wore a scuffed red prison jumpsuit and a haunted look. He had long, bright red hair, an unkempt red beard, and worry lines in his face that made him seem older than his twenty-eight years. Since the glass between prisoner and visitor was thick, his discussions were conducted through telephone receivers at either side of the glass.

Bob Davis had not received many visitors in his few weeks in jail. He had been trying to get Ken Williams to bail him out, so far unsuccessfully. He had gone from alcoholic to software superstar to drug-addicted convict, all in months. He had thought the computer would deliver him. But the computer had not been enough.

For a high school dropout turned boozer who secretly liked logic puzzles, programming had been a revelation. Davis found that he could get so deeply into it that he didn't need to drink any more. His fortunes in the company rose as he headed the Time Zone project, co-wrote his adventure game, and began to learn assembly language for the confounding VCS machine. But just as suddenly as his life had changed for the better, it began to fall apart.

"I have a little bit of trouble handling success," he said. The heady feeling he got from a being a bestselling software author made him think he could handle the kinds of drugs that had previously made his life miserable.

There had been drugs around On-Line, but Bob Davis could not indulge with the moderation that others managed. It affected his work. Trying to learn VCS code was hard enough. But Davis' quick success with Ulysses, written in Ken Williams' relatively simple Adventure Development Language, had geared him to instant programming gratification, and he became frustrated. "I tried to make up excuses," Davis later said. "[I said] On-Line was becoming too corporate for me." He quit, figuring he'd write games on his own and live on royalties.

He had been working on a VCS game, but despite hours of trying to get some movement on the screen, he couldn't. Though Ken Williams realized that Bob was the kind of person who got his breakthroughs only when someone guided him—"If someone's there, he'll be there [working] till 4 A.M.," Ken once commented—Ken could not take the time to help his friend. Davis would try to reach Ken and tell him how unhappy he was, but Ken was often out of town. Bob would take more coke, shooting it directly into his veins. At odds with his wife, he would leave the house when shot up, all the time yearning to be home, back in the new, computer-centered life he had begun: the kind of software superstar life he had talked about in that first-person testimonial that On-Line was still including in the package sent to prospective authors.

Bob Davis would return home late at night, find his wife gone, and begin calling everyone he knew at On-Line, all the programmers' houses, places where he knew she couldn't possibly be, in hopes someone might know where she was. Even strangers who answered the phone would hear his plaintive voice, scraped to bare bones of panic. "Have you seen my wife?" No, Bob. "Do you know where she might be?" I haven't seen her, Bob. "It's very late, and she isn't home, and I'm very worried." I'm sure she'll come home. "I hope she's all right," Bob would say, choking back sobs. "No one will tell me where she is."

Everyone felt horrible about Bob Davis. It was one of the first

things that tipped off Dick Sunderland that On-Line was not just
another company in just another industry: the very night Dick was
hired, Davis was out on one of his Oakhurst crawls. Here was this
ghost, this haunting blight of the computer dream, this golden
opportunity missed. Like an unrelenting conscience, Bob Davis
would plague his former friends with calls, often begging for
money. Programmer and Jehovah's Witness Warren Schwader,
who had liked Bob despite his frequent swearing and smoking,
once offered to pay his mortgage bill directly, and Bob, wanting
cash instead, slammed down the phone . . . but later convinced
Warren to lend him a thousand dollars.

Like everybody else, Schwader wanted to believe that Bob Davis
could come back to the computer and program his way out of his
drug-ridden whirlpool. Eventually they all gave up. People like
steady programmer Jeff Stephenson, who tried to enroll Bob in an
AA program, got disgusted when Bob began passing bad checks.
"My habit ran from three hundred to nine hundred dollars a day,"
Davis later explained. "I wound up driving my wife out. I tried to
kick the habit twice." But couldn't. He asked Dick Sunderland for
advances on his royalties, and when Dick refused, he offered to sell
his future royalties "for a pittance," Sunderland later said. But
soon Davis' royalties were going straight to the bank to pay off past
debts. He was selling the furniture to get more money for drugs.
Finally, he sold his Apple computer, the instrument of magic that
had made him into somebody.

It was a relief to the people at On-Line when Bob Davis wound
up in jail. Arrested at a motel. People assumed the charge was
passing bad checks, but Davis himself said it was for cocaine, and
that he'd pled guilty. He wanted to get into a drug rehabilitation
program to start over again. He'd been trying to get a message to
Ken, but Ken figured that Bob Davis was better off in jail, where
he might shake the habit.

The author of the twelfth bestselling computer game in the
country, according to Softsel's Hot List, spoke into the prison telephone and explained how he'd blown it, how he'd seen the dazzling
light the computer gave, basked in it, but could not live up to it. He
was in mid-sentence when the phone went dead and visitors to
Fresno Jail had to go back into the night. The visitor could make
out his words as he screamed them into the glass before he was led
off: "Have Ken call me."

•

Bob Davis' plight exemplified the disarray at Sierra On-Line that winter. On the surface it seemed a company approaching respect-ability—conglomerates still tendered buy-out offers, the most recent for $12.5 million plus a $200,000-a-year contract for Williams. But underneath the veneer of a growing, thriving enterprise was nagging doubt. This was heightened by a December 1982 announcement that Atari's sales figures of videogames had plummeted. People at On-Line and other computer game companies refused to see this as indication that the field was a fading fad.

Disorganization had only increased with Sierra On-Line's new, unwieldy size. For instance, one game which Dick had thought compelling, a multilevel game with a mining scenario, had been languishing in the acquisitions department for weeks. The programmer called to make a deal, and by the time Dick managed to trace its path through the company, the college student who had programmed the game had given up on On-Line and sold the program to Brøderbund. Under the name "Lode Runner," the game became a bestseller, named "1983 Game of the Year" by many critics. The story was an eerie parallel to what had occurred when Ken Williams had tried to sell Mystery House to Apple less than three years before—the young computer company, too muddled in management to move with the lightning-quick responses that the computer industry demanded, did not get around to expressing interest until too late. Was Sierra On-Line, still an infant company, already a dinosaur?

The conflict for control beween Ken Williams and Dick Sunder-land had grown worse. The newer, sales-oriented people supported Dick; most of the early employees and the programmers, though, disliked the president and his secretive management techniques. Feelings toward Ken were mixed. He would speak of On-Line spirit; but then, he would speak of the company "growing up," as if computer software was something that required a traditionally run company, replete with business plans and rigid bureaucracy. If this were true, what did this say about the hacker dream of relying on the computer as a model of behavior that would improve and enrich our lives? It was a moral crisis that haunted all of the industry pioneers who had begun their businesses thinking that the magic technology they had to offer would make their businesses special. Mass marketing loomed in front of them like some omnipotent Tolkienesque ring: could they grab the ring and not be corrupted? Could whatever idealism existed in their mission be preserved?

Could the spirit of hackerism survive the success of the software industry?

Ken worried about this: "When I used to work for Dick, I used to bitch about working eight to five [and not in the freewheeling, hacker mode]. Now I want a programming staff that works from eight to five. It's like going from being a hippie to being a capitalist or something. I think there's a lot of programmers [here] who feel betrayed. Like John Harris. When he came up, it was open house, my door was open anytime. He could come in, we could talk programming techniques. I'd take him places. We never did business with a contract. Didn't need it. If we didn't trust each other, we shouldn't do business together. [Now] that's changed. I don't know what my goals are anymore. I'm not sure which is the way to run the company. Somehow, by hiring Dick, I copped out. It's the uncertainty that bothers me—I don't know if I'm right or wrong."

Inexplicable events kept occurring. Like the incident in the programming office. A young man working overtime drawing computer pictures for the overdue Dark Crystal adventure game, an On-Line employee from nearly the beginning, put down his graphics tablet one day and began screaming, pounding the walls, pulling down posters, and waving a long knife at the terrified young woman who had been tracing pictures beside him. Then he grabbed a stuffed toy dog and furiously stabbed it, tearing it to shreds, its stuffing flying around the tiny workroom. The programmers in the next room had to stop him, and the young man waited quietly until he was calmly led away. Explanation: he just lost it, was all.

Hacker Jeff Stephenson, working on the secret IBM project (also behind schedule), expressed the overall frustration: "I don't know who the company is being run for, but it's not the authors, who strike me as the bread and butter of the company. The attitude is 'So you're John Harris, who needs you?' We do. He'd made a lot of bucks for this company. But they seem to think that as long as you can get fancy packing and nice labels, it's going to sell."

Indeed, John Harris had noticed this trend. The talkative game designer who had written two of the most popular programs in microcomputer history was torn between loyalty and disgust at the way the Hacker Ethic was being ignored. Harris hadn't liked the fact that authors' names weren't on the new boxes, and he certainly hadn't liked it when, after he mentioned this to Dick, Dick replied, "Hold on—before we do anything, when is your next game for us done?" Quite a change from the Summer Camp days. Harris believed that the times everybody would stop working and pull pranks—like going to Hexagon House and turning everything in the house, even the furniture, *upside down*—were the best times for On-Line; everybody worked better and harder for a company that was fun to work for.

John Harris was also upset by what he considered the company's retreat from high artistic standards. John took it as a personal offense if the company released a game he felt was brain-damaged in some way. He was absolutely horrified at the Atari and Apple versions of Jawbreaker 2. The fact that the games were official sequels to his original game design was nettling, but John wouldn't have minded if he'd felt the games were superbly executed. But they weren't—the smiley faces were too big and the ends of the chutes in which the faces moved back and forth were closed. John resented the drop in quality. He felt, in fact, that On-Line's newer games in general weren't very good.

Perhaps the worst thing of all about On-Line as far as John was concerned was the fact that Ken Williams and his company had never sufficiently genuflected to what, in John Harris' mind was the undeniable greatness of the Atari 800. He had a savage identification with that machine. John sadly concluded that at On-Line, Atari would always have second billing to the Apple. Even after the Frogger debacle, when John's Atari version was state-of-the-art and the Apple version was relatively a mess, Ken did not seem to take the Atari seriously. This depressed John Harris so much that he decided he would have to leave On-Line for a company which shared his views on the Atari.

It was not easy. On-Line had been good to John Harris. He now had a house, respect, reporters from *People* magazine coming to interview him, a four-wheel-drive truck, a projection television, a hefty bank account, and, after all those travails from Fresno to Club Med, John Harris now had a girlfriend.

At a science-fiction convention, he'd run into a girl he'd known casually in San Diego. She had changed since then—"She looked great," John would later recall. "She lost weight and had got a nose job." She was now an actress and a belly dancer in Los Angeles. She had even been asked to dance, John explained, at the most prestigious belly dancing location in Hollywood. "In San Diego, she'd always seemed to be with someone else; this time she wasn't. She paid more attention to me than [to] anyone else. We spent nineteen out of the next twenty-four hours together." He saw her often after the sci-fi convention; she would stay at his house for weeks, and he would go to L.A. to see her. They began to talk of marriage. It was a happiness that John Harris had never known.

He knew that his mentor Ken Williams had been instrumental in bringing about the change in his life. It would seem logical, then, that John Harris, harboring these deep doubts about the company with which he was so closely identified, would have taken his objections directly to Ken Williams. But John Harris could not bring himself to talk to Ken about how close he was to leaving On-Line. He no longer trusted Ken. When John would try to explain why he felt cheated by On-Line, Ken would talk about all the money John was making. At one point, Ken told a reporter from *People* that John was making $300,000 a year, and when Harris had tried to correct that figure, Ken had embarrassed him by giving John his most recent royalty check. The four-month check (Harris was paid monthly, but sometimes would not get around to picking it up for a while) was for $160,000. But that wasn't the point; Ken never talked about the money On-Line was making from John Harris' work. Instead of telling Ken this, though, John would just agree with whatever Ken proposed. He didn't know if it was shyness or insecurity or what.

So he did not talk to Ken Williams. He visited his new girlfriend and he worked on a new assembler for the Atari and visited the local arcade (setting a high score on the Stargate machine) and thought up ideas for his next game. And talked to the people at Synapse Software, a company which took the Atari 800 seriously.

In fact, Synapse was almost exclusively an Atari Home Computer software company, though it was planning to do conversions to other systems. The games Synapse produced were full of action, explosions, shooting, and brilliantly conceived graphics. John Harris considered them awesome. When he went to visit them in Berkeley, he was impressed that the programmers were catered to, that they swapped utilities and communicated by a company-run computer bulletin board. When John Harris found out from a Synapse programmer that part of a sound routine on one Synapse game had been literally lifted out of the object code from a copy of the Frogger disk stolen from John at the Software Expo—that theft which had plunged John into his deep and painful depression—he was less angry at the violation than he was delighted that a Synapse hacker had gone through his code and found something worth appropriating. Synapse promised John that he would get all the technical support he needed; he could join their community of programmers. And they offered a straight 25 percent royalty. In

short, Synapse offered everything to an Atari hacker that On-Line
did not.

John agreed to do his next project for Synapse. On-Line's software superstar was gone.

John was sitting in his house wondering how to tell Ken Williams when the phone rang. "Earth," John answered, as usual. It
was Ken. John was flustered. "I'm programming for Synapse
now," he blurted out, in a tone that Ken took to be insufferably
cocky. Ken asked why, and John told him because they were offering 25 percent royalty instead of Ken's 20 percent. "That was kind
of stupid," Ken said. But John had many things to say. In a rush,
he began to finally say all the things to Ken about On-Line that
he'd been too intimidated to say before. Even more things than
he'd previously thought of: John later would shudder at the memory of it—telling the president of the company which had done so
much for him that the company's products were garbage.

John Harris, with all his lost programs, quirky source codes,
perfectionist delays, and Atari 800 chauvinism, had been the
hacker soul of Sierra On-Line. He had been both the bane of Ken
Williams' existence and the symbol of Ken's accomplishments. His
closeness with Ken had been representative of the new benevolence
which companies like On-Line would substitute for the usual
chasms between boss and worker. Now John Harris was gone,
having delivered a jeremiad on the way On-Line had abandoned its
original mission. What he left behind was Frogger—for weeks now
the bestselling program on the Softsel Hot List.

•

Far from being shaken by the loss of John Harris, Ken seemed
ebullient in the aftermath. It was as if he had not been crowing
several months back that John Harris' name on an Atari program
would sell games. Ken was certain that the age of the independent
game-hacking auteur was over: "I think I have a view of authors
which is different from authors' views of authors, and I pray I'm
right. Which is, the [hackers] I'm dealing with now just happen to
be in the right spot at the right time. John Harris was. He's a
mediocre programmer who's not creative at all who happened to
be programming Atari at the right time."

Instead of a hacker wasting time trying to make a product perfect, Ken preferred less polished programs that shipped on schedule, so he could start building an ad campaign around them. Not
like Frogger, which was held up because one day John Harris de-

cided he just didn't want to work. "You can't run a business on
people who get depressed when their stuff gets stolen. You need
people who will deliver when they say they will, at the price they
say they will, and are able to work their problems out by themselves. John Harris wants you to go drinking with him, get on the
phone, go to Club Med, get him laid. I'm a real expert on John
Harris and his emotional problems. I wouldn't want to be basing
my 1983 game plan and placing orders for $300,000 in ROM car-
tridges based on a game John Harris is supposed to deliver. If his
girlfriend didn't like him, or said he was bad in bed, he'd be gone.

"If you can do [Frogger] with the silly talent we have in place,
imagine what'll happen when we have a real company in place.
We'll be unstoppable. If I go on depending on guys who could leave
me at any minute because somebody's offering more, or could suddenly quit working one day because their girlfriends are seeing
somebody else, then the company's doomed ultimately. It's just a
matter of time. I have to get rid of the crybabies."

To Ken, software, the magic, messianic, transmogrifying, new-
age tool, had come to that. Business. Cut off from his own hacker
roots, he no longer seemed to understand that the hackers did not
make decisions based on traditional business terms, that some
hackers would not consider working for companies where they did
not get a warm feeling, that some hackers were reluctant to work
for companies at all.

But then, Ken did not care very much at all what hackers
thought. Because he was through with them. Ken was seeking
professional programmers, the kind of goal-oriented people who
approached a task as responsible engineers, not prima donna ar-
tistes hung up on getting things perfect and impressing their
friends. "Good, solid guys who will deliver," was the way Ken put
it. "We'll lose our dependence on programmers. It's silly to think
programmers are creative. Instead of waiting for the mail to come,
for guys like John Harris to design something, we're going to get
some damn good implementers who aren't creative, but *good.*"

Ken felt he had already found some latent game wizards who'd
been buried in corporate programming jobs. One of these goal-
oriented pros Ken recruited was a local programmer for the phone
company. Another was a Southern California family man in his
forties who had worked for years doing government contracts using digital imagery, he said, "with obvious military implications."
Another was a rural Idaho vegetarian who lived with his family in
a wooden geodesic dome.

On Ken went, trying to replace the hackers with professionals. He already deemed the great experiment taking place in the old office on Route 41, where he attempted to turn novices into assembly-language programmers, an overall loser. It took too long to train people, and there was really no one around who had both the time and the technical virtuosity to be a guru. Finding enough assembly-language programmers was tough, and even a dragnet of headhunters and classified ads could not guarantee the winners Ken needed in the next year. He would need many, since his 1983 game plan was to release over one hundred products. Few would involve original creative efforts. On-Line's programming energy instead would go into converting its current games to other machines, especially the low-cost, mass-market, ROM-cartridge-based computers, like the VIC-20, or Texas Instruments. On-Line's expectations were stated in its "strategy outline": "We believe the home computer market to be so explosive that 'title saturation' is impossible. The number of new machines competing for the Apple/Atari segment in 1983 will create a perpetually new market hungry for the winning 1982 titles. We will exploit this opportunity . . ."

The company's energy became focused into converting product into other product. It was an approach which stifled the hacker joy of creating new worlds. Rather than building on past successes in a quest for brilliant programs, On-Line was trying to maximize sales by duplicating even moderate successes, often on relatively limited machines on which the games looked worse than the originals. Nowhere in the flurry to convert was there provision for rewarding an effort like Harris' Frogger, which was so artistically accomplished that it hit the market with the force of an original work.

Back at his unkempt electronic split-level, John Harris was philosophizing that "professional" programmers—any programmers who didn't have a love for gaming in their hearts and hacker perfectionism in their souls—were destined to make soulless, imperfect games. But Ken Williams was not talking to John Harris, who after all was programming for Synapse now. Ken Williams was about to hold a meeting that would put On-Line in contact with a new enterprise—one that would deliver an entire *assembly line* of professional programmers to do conversions. At dirt-cheap prices!

It sounded too good to be true, and Ken entered into the meeting with suspicion. His contact in this new venture was a shoulder-length-haired, Peter Lorre–eyed businessman named Barry Fried-

man. Friedman's fortunes had risen along with the crazily swelling
tide of the home computer industry. Originally, he had represented
artists who did illustrations for the advertisements and packaging
of On-Line products, then had branched out to eventually handle
all the art work for a few computer companies. From there, he
began to service software companies with all sorts of needs. If you
wanted to know where to find the best price for ROM cartridges,
he could act as middleman to get you cheap ROMs, perhaps from
some obscure Hong Kong supplier.

Lately, he had been hinting of access to tremendous sums of
capital to those who needed it. The other day, Ken said, Barry had
called him up and asked how much an outsider would need to buy
On-Line. Ken pulled a $20 million figure out of the air and hung
up. Barry called back that day saying $20 million was fine. Ken,
still not taking it too seriously, said, "Well, I'd need control, too."
Barry called back not long after, saying *that* was OK, too. The
crazy thing about it was that as dubious as Ken was about Barry
Friedman and his growing stable of companies (you never could be
sure which corporate name would be on the business card Barry or
his colleagues handed you), he always seemed to deliver on his
promises. It was as if Barry Friedman were the beneficiary of some
Faustian bargain, Silicon Valley–style.

This new deal sounded the most astonishing of all. Friedman
was escorting to the meeting with Ken Williams the two founders
of a start-up company he was representing. A company that did
nothing but conversions. The rates seemed bargain-basement—a
ten-thousand-dollar fee and a 5 percent royalty. The company was
called "Rich and Rich Synergistic Enterprises," Rich being the
first name of both the founders.

Barry Friedman, wearing a yellow polo shirt, unbuttoned to reveal a gold chain that complemented his silver-and-diamond bracelet and gold watch, led both Riches and one of his partners, a
short, blond, button-nosed man dressed in a somewhat punk suit.
This was Tracy Coats, a former rock music manager who represented backers from "a very wealthy family." This piece of information was conveyed sotto voce, with a knowing raise of the eye-
brow.

With little further fanfare, they took seats around the long,
wooden conference table in the boardroom which adjoined Ken's
office: a perfectly nondescript carpeted and white-walled room
with wooden bookcases and a blackboard; a random, anonymous

room that might exist in any small office complex in any kind of company.

"Rich and Rich . . ." said Ken, looking over the résumés of the two programmers. "I hope you'll make *me* rich."

Neither Rich laughed, and if their unwrinkled visages were any indication, laughing was not something in which the Riches indulged to excess. They were all business, and their résumés were even more no-nonsense than their appearance. Both had held responsible positions in the digital-intensive area of the recently completed Tokyo Disneyland ("The whole place is based on silicon," said Rich One), but that authoritarian fun factory was the closest thing to frivolity in their résumés, which were crammed with phrases like snake circuit analysis, Jet Propulsion Lab, nuclear control, missile systems analyst, Hound Dog Missile flight internal guidance and control system. Both Riches wore sports jackets without ties, and the clothes had the well-maintained air that clothes take on when draped over compulsively maintained bodies. Both looked in their thirties, with well-cropped hair and attentive eyes, constantly scanning the room for indiscretions.

Rich Two spoke. "Our people are from more of a professional arena than others in the home computer field. People who have been in a more controlled environment than home computer types. People who know how to document and write code *correctly.*" Rich Two paused. "Not hacker types," he added.

Their company would develop a set of tools and techniques for game conversion. The techniques, algorithms, and cross-assemblers would, of course, be proprietary. Because of that, Rich and Rich would routinely keep their source code. It would be sequestered at Rich and Rich's offices in Southern California. No matter how brilliant the tricks were, no matter how elegant the bum, it would not be available for hacker reading pleasure. Only the product would be available. Opacity. People buying programs as product, with the programming deeply hidden, as unimportant as the machinery which makes grooves in records that play music. Likewise, the programmers at Rich and Rich would be anonymous. No hacker egos to cope with. Just submit a wish list of games and the assembly line would churn them out.

Ken loved the idea. "It will make them rich and make me money," he said afterward. If the two trial projects he gave to Rich and Rich worked out, he said, "I could do all my conversions with them! This is much better than John Harris!"

Ken was feeling at the top of his game. Besides Rich and Rich, a reporter for *The Wall Street Journal* was in town, talking to him and Roberta for a piece about the company. As he often did in the middle of the day, he rewarded himself by leaving the office and heading out to the site of his new house. Today, they were lowering the seven twenty-five-foot-long roof beams which would go over the mammoth game room in the house, not far from the indoor racquetball court. He put a flannel shirt over his ragged, blue Apple T-shirt and he drove over to the muddy site and watched the hydraulic crane lift the beams, and the twelve-man work crew settle each one into its niche. It went smoothly, like a well-written subroutine that worked the first time the code was assembled, and Ken stared with a dazed pride at what he was building. "Isn't it weird?" he kept asking. "Isn't it weird?"

The house went on and on, rambling down the hill for a hundred and forty feet; the frame finally filling out, with stairs you could climb and doorways to peep through. Right now the house was open to the elements, for wind to blow through and rain to fall through, and no doors or walls prevented free movement. A perfect, endless hacker house. But the builders would soon put walls to keep the world from peering in the house, and doors to keep the people in the house from bursting in and violating a person's privacy. No one in his right mind would want it any different.

The same with hackerism, perhaps . . . no one running a business could want it *really* run by the Hacker Ethic. Sooner or later you had to cope with reality; you would yearn for those old, familiar walls and doors which were always considered so natural that only madmen would eliminate them. Only in a computer simulation maybe, using the computer to hack Utopia, could you preserve that sort of idealism. Maybe that was the only place you could preserve a dream. In a computer.

Ken walked around the house a few times, talked to the builder, and then was reminded that he had to get back. He had to speak to the reporter from *The Wall Street Journal* about the strange little mom-and-pop software company that had started with an adventure game.

•

Ken and Roberta Williams held the housewarming party on Labor Day weekend, 1983. Over two hundred people wandered through the ten-thousand-square-foot cedarwood house, admired the stained-glass pictures, marveled at the fireplace of river rock, participated in a tournament on the racquetball court (which had a full-color Apple Computer logo embedded in the gleaming wood), sweated in the sauna, relaxed in the hot tub, played tug-of-war in the backyard Fresno River, spiked volleyballs on the court, watched video piped in from the satellite dish outside, laughed at the comedy troupe flown in from San Francisco, and played the six coin-op arcade games in the giant game room with the full-length wet bar.

It was a bittersweet occasion. Between the competition from big-money newcomers, the slump in the economy, the huge capital outlay for ROM cartridges fitting low-end machines like the VIC-20 (outlays which would never be recouped), and Sierra On-Line's lack of a new, innovative, Third Generation hacker-coded hit, the company was headed for a year with revenues *lower* than the previous year. Ken had been forced to seek more venture capital, three million dollars of it. A half million had gone directly to him, considerably less than the cost of the new house.

Earlier that summer, Ken had asked Dick Sunderland to meet him at the Broken Bit. Before they exchanged a word, Ken handed his former boss a note which read, "You are hereby terminated as president of Sierra On-Line." Dick Sunderland was furious, and eventually filed a lawsuit against Ken and On-Line. "I'm mad," he would explain. "I have my reputation. I've built him a company that can be run, and *he* wants to run it." Other On-Liners, especially those who fondly remembered the Summer Camp days, rejoiced. They took Sunderland's name plate from his parking space and stuck it on the door to the women's lavatory. They took a pile of memos dating from the Sunderland regime, which was dubbed "The Age of Oppression," and tossed them into an impromptu bonfire. For a fleeting moment it was as if the employees of a company could reduce the bureaucracy to ashes.

There were other optimistic notes. Ken had hopes that his new, low-cost word-processing program would bring in money, and that he would do well with a million-dollar deal to license the cartoon characters from "B.C." and "The Wizard of Id." He was negotiating with John Travolta for use of the actor's name in a body fitness program. But despite these projects, the software business had turned out to be more precarious than it had first appeared.

One only had to talk to Jerry Jewell to find out why: Jewell of Sirius did come down from Sacramento, and he was lamenting the disastrous end to his Twentieth-Century Fox Games deal—the cartridge games that his company had written had been lost in the 1983 videogame glut, and he had received almost no money in exchange for focusing his entire market thrust on the Atari VCS machine. His company was hanging by a thread, and he doubted whether any of the Brotherhood would be able to survive in the next few years. His top programmers had left him, days before he was about to lay them off.

Ken Williams was still having programmer problems, too. There was the hacker who was running the IBM project, far behind schedule. There were some of the "professional" programmers who, not familiar with the pleasures of immersion into a computer-game universe, were unable to synthesize those pleasures themselves. There was even a dispute with Bob and Carolyn Box: the two gold-panners-turned-programmers had rejected Ken's criticisms of the game they showed him, and had left the company to be independent software authors.

And then there was John Harris. Lately, he and Ken had been feuding over a royalty disagreement on Frogger, still On-Line's bestselling program. Parker Brothers wanted to buy the program to convert to cartridge, and Ken offered John 20 percent of the two-hundred-thousand-dollar buy-out. To John that was not enough. They discussed it in Ken's office. It had ended with Ken Williams looking at his former software superstar and saying, "Get out of my office, John Harris. You're wasting my time."

That was the last time they had spoken before the housewarming, to which Ken had not invited John. Nonetheless, Harris had showed up with his girlfriend, who was wearing a large diamond engagement ring he had given her. Ken greeted the hacker cordially. It was not a day for animosity, it was a day for celebration. Ken and Roberta Williams had their new, eight-hundred-thousand-dollar house, and no dark clouds hung over the Sierras, at least. The computer had delivered them all to riches and fame they had never dared dream of, and as dusk peeked over Mount Deadwood, Ken Williams, dressed in shorts and a T-shirt, danced happily to the tunes of a bluegrass band he had shipped in from Southern California. Later on, just as he always dreamed, he sat in the hot tub with friends, a millionaire in his twenties with a hot tub in the mountains. As the friends sat in the hot tub, their arms ringing the side, they could hear the faint electronic sounds of the arcade games in the nearby game room, mingling incongruously with the rustling Sierra forest.

EPILOGUE

THE LAST
OF THE
TRUE HACKERS

CAMBRIDGE:
1983

THE LAST
OF THE TRUE HACKERS

AROUND the time of Ken Williams' housewarming party, twenty-five years after the MIT Tech Model Railroad Club discovered the TX-0, a man who called himself the last true hacker sat in a room on the ninth floor of Tech Square—a room cluttered with printouts, manuals, a bedroll, and a blinking computer terminal connected to a direct descendant of the PDP-6, a DEC-20 computer. His name was Richard Stallman, and he spoke in a tense, high-pitched voice that did not attempt to veil the emotion with which he described, in his words, "the rape of the artificial intelligence lab." He was thirty years old. His pale complexion and scraggly dark hair contrasted vividly with the intense luminescence of his deep green eyes. The eyes moistened as he described the decay of the Hacker Ethic at Tech Square.

Richard Stallman had come to MIT twelve years before, in 1971, and had experienced the epiphany that others had enjoyed when they discovered that pure hacker paradise, the Tech Square monastery where one lived to hack, and hacked to live. Stallman had been entranced with computers since high school. At camp one summer, he had amused himself with computer manuals borrowed from his counselors. In his native Manhattan, he found a computing center to exercise his new passion. By the time he entered Harvard he was an expert at assembly languages, operating systems, and text editors. He had also found that he had a deep affinity for the Hacker Ethic, and was militant in his execution of its principles. It was a search for an atmosphere more compatible with hacking that brought him from Harvard's relatively authoritarian computing center, down Massachusetts Avenue, to MIT.

The thing he liked about the AI lab at Tech Square was that "there were no artificial obstacles, things that are insisted upon that make it hard for people to get any work done—things like bureaucracy, security, refusals to share with other people." He also loved being with people for whom hacking was a way of life. He recognized that his personality was unyielding to the give-and-take of common human interaction. On the ninth floor he could be appreciated for his hacking, and be part of a community built around that magical pursuit.

His wizardry soon became apparent, and Russ Noftsker, the administrator of the AI lab who had taken the tough security measures during the Vietnam protests, hired Stallman as a systems programmer. Richard was often in night phase, and when the people in the lab discovered after the fact that he was simultaneously earning a magna cum laude degree in physics at Harvard, even those master hackers were astonished.

As he sat at the feet of such as Richard Greenblatt and Bill Gosper, whom he considered his mentor, Stallman's view of the Hacker Ethic solidified. He came to see the lab as the embodiment of that philosophy, a constructive anarchism which, as Stallman wrote into a computer file once, "does not mean advocating a dog-eat-dog jungle. American society is already a dog-eat-dog jungle, and its rules maintain it that way. We [hackers] wish to replace those rules with a concern for constructive cooperation."

Stallman, who liked to be called by his initials, RMS, in tribute to the way he logged on to the computer, used the Hacker Ethic as a guiding principle for his best-known work, an editing program called EMACS which allowed users to limitlessly customize it—its wide-open architecture encouraged people to add to it, improve it endlessly. He distributed the program free to anyone who agreed to his one condition: "that they give back all extensions they made, so as to help EMACS improve. I called this arrangement 'the EMACS commune,'" RMS wrote. "As I shared, it was their duty to share; to work with each other rather than against." EMACS became almost a standard text editor in university computer science departments. It was a shining example of what hacking could produce.

But as the seventies progressed, Richard Stallman began to see changes in his beloved preserve. The first incursion was when passwords were assigned to Officially Sanctioned Users, and unauthorized users were kept off the system. As a true hacker, RMS despised passwords, and was proud of the fact that the computers he was paid to maintain did not use them. But the MIT computer science department (run by different people than the AI lab) decided to install security on its machine.

Stallman campaigned to eliminate the practice. He encouraged people to use the "Empty String" password—a carriage return instead of a word. So when the machine asked for your password, you would hit the RETURN key and be logged on. Stallman also broke the computer's encryption code and was able to get to the protected file which held people's passwords. He started sending people messages which would appear on screen when they logged onto the system:

> I see you chose the password [such and such]. I suggest that you switch to the password "carriage return." It's much easier to type, and also it stands up to the principle that there should be no passwords.

"Eventually I got to a point where a fifth of all the users on the machine had the Empty String password," RMS later boasted.

Then the computer science laboratory installed a more sophisticated password system on its other computer. This one was not so easy for Stallman to crack. But Stallman was able to study the encryption program, and, as he later said, "I discovered that changing one word in that program would cause it to print out your password on the system console as part of the message that you were logging in." Since the "system console" was visible to anyone walking by, and its messages could easily be accessed by any terminal, or even printed out in hard copy, Stallman's change allowed any password to be routinely disseminated by anyone who cared to know it. He thought the result "amusing."

Still, the password juggernaut rolled on. The outside world, with its affection for security and bureaucracy, was closing in. The security mania even infected the holy AI computer. The Department of Defense was threatening to take the AI machine off the ARPAnet network—to separate the MIT people from the highly active electronic community of hackers, users, and plain old computer scientists around the country—all because the AI lab steadfastly refused to limit access to its computers. DOD bureaucrats were apoplectic: anyone could walk in off the street and use the AI machine, and connect to other locations in the Defense Department network! Stallman and others felt that was the way it should be. But he came to understand that the number of people who stood with him was dwindling. More and more of the hard-core hackers were leaving MIT, and many of the hackers who had formed the culture and given it a backbone by their behavior were long gone.

What had happened to the hackers of yesteryear? Many had gone to work for businesses, implicitly accepting the compromises that such work entailed. Peter Samson, the TMRC hacker who was among the first to discover the TX-0, was in San Francisco, still with the Systems Concepts company co-founded by master phone hacker Stew Nelson. Samson could explain what had happened: "[Hacking] now competes for one's attention with real responsibilities—working for a living, marrying, having a child. What I had then that I don't have now is time, and a certain amount of physical stamina." It was a common conclusion, more or less shared by people like Samson's TMRC colleague Bob Saunders (working for Hewlett-Packard, two children in high school), David Silver (after growing up in the AI lab, he now headed a small robotics firm in Cambridge), Slug Russell (the author of Spacewar was programming for a firm outside of Boston and playing with his Radio Shack home computer), and even Stew Nelson, who despite remaining in Bachelor Mode complained that in 1983 he wasn't able to hack as much as he'd like. "It's almost all business these days, and we don't have that much time for the technical stuff we'd like to do," said the man who over two decades ago had instinctively used the PDP-1 to explore the universe that was the phone system.

There would never be another generation like them; Stallman realized this every time he saw the behavior of the new "tourists" taking advantage of the freedom of the AI computer. They did not seem as well intentioned, or as eager to immerse themselves into the culture, as their predecessors. In previous times, people seemed to recognize that the open system was an invitation to do good work, and improve yourself to the point where you might one day be considered a real hacker. Now, some of these new users could not handle the freedom to poke around a system, with everyone's files open to them. "The outside world is pushing in," Stallman admitted. "More and more people come in having used other computer systems. Elsewhere it's taken for granted that if anybody else can modify your files you'll be unable to do anything, you'll be sabotaged every five minutes. Fewer and fewer people are around who grew up here the old way, and know that it's possible, and it's a reasonable way to live."

Stallman kept fighting, trying, he said, "to delay the fascist advances with every method I could." Though his official systems programming duties were equally divided between the computer science department and the AI lab, he went "on strike" against the Lab for Computer Science because of their security policy. When he came out with a new version of his EMACS editor, he refused to let the computer science lab use it. He realized that, in a sense, he was punishing users of that machine rather than the people who made policy. "But what could I do?" he later said. "People who used that machine went along with the policy. They weren't fighting. A lot of people were angry with me, saying I was trying to hold them hostage or blackmail them, which in a sense I was. I was engaging in violence against them because I thought they were engaging in violence to everyone at large."

Passwords were not the only problem Richard Stallman had to face in what was becoming more and more a solitary defense of the pure Hacker Ethic at MIT. Many of the new people around the lab had learned computing on small machines and were untutored in hacker principles. Like Third Generation hackers, they saw nothing wrong with the concept of ownership of programs. These new people would write exciting new programs just as their predecessors did, but something new would come along with them—as the programs appeared on the screen, so would copyright notices. Copyright notices! To RMS, who still believed that all information should flow freely, this was blasphemy. "I don't believe that software should be owned," he said in 1983, years too late. "Because [the practice] sabotages humanity as a whole. It prevents people from getting the maximum benefit out of the program's existence."

It was this kind of commercialism, in Richard Stallman's view, that delivered the fatal blow to what was left of the idealistic community he had loved. It was a situation that embodied the evil, and immersed the remaining hackers into bitter conflict. It all began with Greenblatt's LISP machine.

•

With the passing of years, Richard Greenblatt had remained perhaps the prime link to the days of ninth-floor hacker glory. In his mid-thirties now, the single-minded hacker of the Chess Machine and MacLISP was moderating some of his more extreme personal habits, grooming his short hair more often, varying his wardrobe more, and even tentatively thinking about the opposite sex. But he still could hack like a demon. And now he was beginning to see the realization of a dream he had formed long ago—a total, all-out hacker computer.

He had come to realize that the LISP language was extensible and powerful enough to give people the control to build and explore the kind of systems that could satisfy the hungriest hacker mentality. The problem was that no computer could easily handle the considerable demands that LISP put on a machine. So in the early seventies Greenblatt started to design a computer which would run LISP faster and more efficiently than any machine had done before. It would be a single-user machine—finally a solution to the esthetic problem of time-sharing, where the hacker is psychologically frustrated by a lack of ultimate control over the machine. By running LISP, the language of artificial intelligence, the machine would be a pioneering workhorse of the next generation of computers, machines with the ability to learn, to carry on intelligent dialogues with the user on everything from circuit design to advanced mathematics.

So with a small grant, he and some other hackers—notably Tom Knight, who had been instrumental in designing (and naming) the Incompatible Time-sharing System—began work. It was slow going, but by 1975 they had what they called a "Cons" machine (named for the complicated "constructor operator" function that the machine performed in LISP). The Cons machine did not stand alone, and had to be connected to the PDP-10 to work. It was two bays wide, with the circuit boards and the tangle of wires exposed, and they built it right there on the ninth floor of Tech Square, on the uplifted floor with air-conditioning underneath.

It worked as Greenblatt hoped it would. "LISP is a very easy language to implement," Greenblatt later explained. "Any number of times, some hacker goes off to some machine and works hard for a couple of weeks and writes a LISP. 'See, I've got LISP.' But there's a hell of a difference between that and a really usable system." The Cons machine, and later the stand-alone LISP machine, was a usable system. It had something called "virtual address space," which assured that the space programs consumed wouldn't routinely overwhelm the machine, as was the case in other LISP systems. The world you built with LISP could be much more intricate. A hacker working at the machine would be like a mental rocket pilot traveling in a constantly expanding LISP universe.

For the next few years they worked to get the machine to be a stand-alone. MIT was paying their salaries, and of course they were all doing systems work on ITS and random AI hacking, too. The break came when ARPA kicked in money for the group to build six machines for about fifty thousand dollars each. Then some other money came to build more machines.

Eventually the hackers at MIT would build thirty-two LISP machines. From the outside, the LISP computer looked like a central air-conditioning unit. The visual action all occurred in a remote terminal, with a sleek, long keyboard loaded with function keys and an ultra-high-resolution bit-mapped display. At MIT the idea was to connect several LISP machines in a network, so while each user had full control he could also be hacking as part of a community, and the values arising from a free flow of information would be maintained.

The LISP machine was a significant achievement. But Greenblatt realized that something beyond making a few machines and hacking on them would be necessary. This LISP machine was an ultimately flexible world-builder, an embodiment of the hacker dream . . . but its virtues as a "thinking machine" also made it a tool for America to maintain its technological lead in the artificial intelligence race with the Japanese. The LISP machine had implications bigger than the AI lab, certainly, and technology like this would be best disseminated through the commercial sector. Greenblatt: "I generally realized during this whole process that we [were] probably gonna start a company some day and eventually make these LISP machines commercially. [It was a] sooner-or-later-it's-gonna-happen kind of thing. So as the machine got to be more complete we started poking around."

That was how Russell Noftsker got into the situation. The former AI lab administrator had left his post under duress in 1973 and gone to California to go into business. Every so often he would come back to Cambridge and stop by the lab, see what the AI workers were up to. He liked the idea of LISP machines and expressed interest in helping the hackers form a company.

"Initially pretty much everyone was against him," Greenblatt later recalled. "At the time that Noftsker left the lab I was on considerably better terms with him than anyone else. Most of the people really hated this guy. He had done a bunch of things that were really very paranoid. But I said, 'Well, give him a chance.'"

People did, but it soon became clear that Noftsker and Greenblatt had different ideas of what a company should be. Greenblatt was too much a hacker to accept a traditional business construct.

What he wanted was something "towards the AI pattern." He did not want a load of venture capital. He preferred a bootstrap approach, where the company would get an order for a machine, build it, then keep a percentage of the money and put it back into the company. He hoped that his firm could maintain a steady tie to MIT; he even envisioned a way where they could all remain affiliated with the AI lab. Greenblatt himself was loath to leave; he had firmly set out the parameters for his universe. While his imagination had free rein inside a computer, his physical world was still largely bounded by his cluttered office with terminal on the ninth floor and the room he had rented since the mid-sixties from a retired dentist (now deceased) and the dentist's wife. He would travel all over the world to go to artificial intelligence conferences, but the discussions in these remote places would be continuations of the same technical issues he would debate in the lab, or in ARPAnet computer mail. He was very much defined by the hacker community, and though he knew that commercialization to some extent was necessary to spread the gospel of the LISP machine, he wanted to avoid any unnecessary compromise of the Hacker Ethic: like lines of code in a systems program, compromise should be bummed to the minimum.

Noftsker considered this unrealistic, and his point of view filtered down to the other hackers involved in the project. Besides Tom Knight, these included some young wizards who had not been around in the golden age of the ninth floor, and had a more pragmatic approach to what was called for. "My perception [of Greenblatt's idea] was to start a company which made LISP machines in sort of a garage shop. It was clear that it was impractical," Tom Knight later said. "The world just isn't that way. There's only one way in which a company works and that is to have people who are motivated to make money."

Knight and the others perceived that Greenblatt's model for a company was something like Systems Concepts in San Francisco, which included former MIT hackers Stewart Nelson and Peter Samson. Systems Concepts was a small-scale company, guided by a firm resolve not to have to answer to anyone holding purse strings. "Our initial goal was not necessarily to get infinitely rich," explained co-founder Mike Levitt in 1983, "but to control our own destiny. We don't owe anybody anything." The MIT hackers, though, asked what the impact of Systems Concepts had been—after over a decade, they concluded, it was still small and not terribly influential. Knight looked at Systems Concepts—"Low-risk, don't take any external funding, don't hire anybody you don't know, that mode," he said. "Not going very far." He and the others had a larger vision for a LISP machine company.

Russ Noftsker also saw, and exploited, the fact that many of the hackers were reluctant to work in a company led by Greenblatt. Greenblatt was so focused on making LISP machines, on the mission of hacking, on the work that *had to be done,* that he often neglected to acknowledge people's humanity. And as old-time hackers got older, this was more and more an issue. "Everyone tolerated him for his brilliance and productivity," Noftsker later explained, "[but] finally he started using the bludgeon or cat-o'-nine-tails to try to whip people into shape. He'd berate people who weren't used to it. He'd treat them like they were some kind of production mule team. It finally got to the point where communications had broken down and they even took the extreme measure of moving off the ninth floor in order to get away from Richard."

Things came to a head in a meeting in February 1979, when it was clear that Greenblatt wanted a hacker-style company, and power to insure that it remain so. It was an awkward demand, since for so long the lab had, as Knight put it, "been run on anarchistic principles, based on the ideal of mutual trust and mutual respect for the technical confidence of the people involved built up over many years." But anarchism did not seem to be The Right Thing in this case. Nor, for many, was Greenblatt's demand. "I couldn't see, frankly, having him fulfilling a presidential role in a company that I was involved in," said Knight.

Noftsker: "We were all trying to talk him out of it. We begged him to accept a structure where he would be equal to the rest of us and where we would have professional management. And he refused to do it. So we went around the room and asked every single person in the technical group if they would accept an organization that had any of the elements [that Greenblatt wanted]. And everyone said they would not participate in [such a] venture."

It was a standoff. Most of the hackers would not go with Greenblatt, the father of the LISP machine. Noftsker and the rest said they would give Greenblatt a year to form his own company, but in somewhat less than a year they concluded that Greenblatt and the backers he managed to find for his LISP Machine Incorporated (LMI) were not "winning," so they formed a heavily capitalized company called Symbolics. They were sorry to be making and selling the machines to which Greenblatt had contributed so much, but felt it had to be done. LMI people felt betrayed; whenever

Greenblatt spoke of the split, his speech crawled to a slow mumble, and he sought ways to change the uncomfortable subject. The bitter schism was the kind of thing that might happen in business, or when people invested emotion in relationships and human interaction, but it was not the kind of thing you saw in the hacking life.

The AI lab became a virtual battleground between two sides, and the two firms, especially Symbolics, hired away many of the lab's remaining hackers. Even Bill Gosper, who had been working at Stanford and Xerox during that time, eventually joined the new research center Symbolics had formed in Palo Alto. When Symbolics complained about the possible conflict of interest of LMI people working for the AI lab (it felt that MIT, by paying salaries to those LMI part-timers, was funding their competitor), the hackers still affiliated with the lab, including Greenblatt, had to resign.

It was painful for everybody, and when both companies came out with similar versions of LISP machines in the early 1980s it was clear that the problem would be there for a long time. Greenblatt had made some compromises in his business plan—making, for example, a deal whereby LMI got money and support from Texas Instruments in exchange for a fourth of the stock—and his company was surviving. The more lavish Symbolics had hired the cream of hackerism and had even signed a contract to sell its machines to MIT. The worst part was that the ideal community of hackers, those people who, in the words of Ed Fredkin, "kind of loved each other," were no longer on speaking terms. "I'd really like to talk to [Greenblatt]," said Gosper, speaking for many Symbolics hackers who had virtually grown up with the most canonical of hackers and now were cut off from his flow of information. "I don't know how happy or unhappy he is with me for having thrown in with the bad guys here. But I'm sorry, I'm afraid they were right this time."

But even if people in the companies were speaking to each other, they could not talk about what mattered most—the magic they had discovered and forged inside the computer systems. The magic was now a trade secret, not for examination by competing firms. By working for companies, the members of the purist hacker society had discarded the key element in the Hacker Ethic: the free flow of information. The outside world was inside.

•

The one person who was most affected by the schism, and its effect on the AI lab, was Richard Stallman. He grieved at the lab's

failure to uphold the Hacker Ethic. RMS would tell strangers he
met that his wife had died, and it would not be until later in the
conversation that the stranger would realize that this thin, plaintive youngster was talking about an institution rather than a tragically lost bride.

Stallman later wrote his thoughts into the computer:

> It is painful for me to bring back the memories of this time.
> The people remaining at the lab were the professors, students,
> and non-hacker researchers, who did not know how to main-
> tain the system, or the hardware, or want to know. Machines
> began to break and never be fixed; sometimes they just got
> thrown out. Needed changes in software could not be made.
> The non-hackers reacted to this by turning to commercial
> systems, bringing with them fascism and license agreements. I
> used to wander through the lab, through the rooms so empty
> at night where they used to be full and think, "Oh my poor AI
> lab! You are dying and I can't save you." Everyone expected
> that if more hackers were trained, Symbolics would hire them
> away, so it didn't even seem worth trying . . . the whole cul-
> ture was wiped out . . .

Stallman bemoaned the fact that it was no longer easy to drop in or
call around dinnertime and find a group eager for a Chinese dinner. He would call the lab's number, which ended in 6765
("Fibonacci of 20," people used to note, pointing out a numerical
trait established early on by some random math hacker), and find
no one to eat with, no one to talk with.

Richard Stallman felt he had identified the villain who destroyed
the lab: Symbolics. He took an oath: "I will never use a Symbolic
LISP machine or help anybody else to do so . . . I don't want to
speak to anyone who works for Symbolics or the people who deal
with them." While he also disapproved of Greenblatt's LMI company, because as a business it sold computer programs which Stallman believed the world should have for free, he felt that LMI had
attempted to avoid hurting the AI lab. But Symbolics, in
Stallman's view, had purposely stripped the lab of its hackers in
order to prevent them from donating competing technology to the
public domain.

Stallman wanted to fight back. His field of battle was the LISP
operating system, which originally was shared by MIT, LMI, and
Symbolics. This changed when Symbolics decided that the fruits of

its labor would be proprietary; why should LMI benefit from improvements made by Symbolics hackers? So there would be no sharing. Instead of two companies pooling energy toward an ultimately featureful operating system, they would have to work independently, expending energy to duplicate improvements.

This was RMS's opportunity for revenge. He set aside his qualms about LMI and began cooperating with that firm. Since he was still officially at MIT, and Symbolics installed its improvements on the MIT machines, Stallman was able to carefully reconstruct each new feature or fix of a bug. He then would ponder how the change was made, match it, and present his work to LMI. It was not easy work, since he could not merely duplicate the changes —he had to figure out innovatively different ways to implement them. "I don't think there's anything *immoral* about copying code," he explained. "But they would sue LMI if I copied their code, therefore I have to do a lot of work." A virtual John Henry of computer code, RMS had single-handedly attempted to match the work of over a dozen world-class hackers, and managed to keep doing it during most of 1982 and almost all of 1983. "In a fairly real sense," Greenblatt noted at the time, "he's been out-hacking the whole bunch of them."

Some Symbolics hackers complained not so much because of what Stallman was doing, but because they disagreed with some of the technical choices Stallman made in implementation. "I really wonder if those people aren't kidding themselves," said Bill Gosper, himself torn between loyalty to Symbolics and admiration for Stallman's master hack. "Or if they're being fair. I can see something Stallman wrote, and I might decide it was bad (probably not, but someone could convince me it was bad), and I would still say, 'But wait a minute—Stallman doesn't have anybody to argue with all night over there. He's working alone! It's *incredible* anyone could do this alone!' "

Russ Noftsker, president of Symbolics, did not share Greenblatt's or Gosper's admiration. He would sit in Symbolics' offices, relatively plush and well decorated compared to LMI's ramshackle headquarters a mile away, his boyish face knotting with concern when he spoke of Stallman. "We develop a program or an advancement to our operating system and make it work, and that may take three months, and then under our agreement with MIT, we give that to them. And then [Stallman] compares it with the old ones and looks at that and sees how it works and reimplements it [for the LMI machines]. He calls it reverse engineering. We call it theft of trade secrets. It does not serve any purpose at MIT for him to do that because we've already given that function out [to MIT]. The only purpose it serves is to give that to Greenblatt's people."

Which was exactly the point. Stallman had no illusions that his act would significantly improve the world at large. He had come to accept that the domain around the AI lab had been permanently polluted. He was out to cause as much damage to the culprit as he could. He knew he could not keep it up indefinitely. He set a deadline to his work: the end of 1983. After that he was uncertain of his next step.

He considered himself the last true hacker left on earth. "The AI lab used to be the one example that showed it was possible to have an institution that was anarchistic and very great," he would explain. "If I told people it's possible to have no security on a computer without people deleting your files all the time, and no bosses stopping you from doing things, at least I could point to the AI lab and say, 'Look, we are doing it. Come use our machine! See!' I can't do that anymore. Without this example, nobody will believe me. For a while we were setting an example for the rest of the world. Now that this is gone, where am I going to begin from? I read a book the other day. It's called *Ishi, the Last Yahi*. It's a book about the last survivor of a tribe of Indians, initially with his family, and then gradually they died out one by one."

That was the way Richard Stallman felt. Like Ishi.

"I'm the last survivor of a dead culture," said RMS. "And I don't really belong in the world anymore. And in some ways I feel I ought to be dead."

Richard Stallman did leave MIT, but he left with a plan: to write a version of the popular proprietary computer operating system called UNIX and give it away to anyone who wanted it. Working on this GNU (which stood for "Gnu's Not Unix") program meant that he could "continue to use computers without violating [his] principles." Having seen that the Hacker Ethic could not survive in the unadulterated form in which it had formerly thrived at MIT, he realized that numerous small acts like his would keep the Ethic alive in the outside world.

•

What Stallman did was to join a mass movement of Real World hackerism set in motion at the very institution which he was so painfully leaving. The emergence of hackerism at MIT twenty-five years before was a concentrated attempt to fully ingest the magic of the computer; to absorb, explore, and expand the intricacies of those bewitching systems; to use those perfectly logical systems as an inspiration for a culture and a way of life. It was these goals which motivated the behavior of Lee Felsenstein and the hardware hackers from Albuquerque to the Bay Area. The happy by-product of their actions was the personal computer industry, which exposed the magic to millions of people. Only the tiniest percentage of these new computer users would experience that magic with the all-encompassing fury of the MIT hackers, but everyone had the chance to . . . and many would get glimpses of the miraculous possibilities of the machine. It would extend their powers, spur their creativity, and teach them something, perhaps, of the Hacker Ethic, if they listened.

As the computer revolution grew in a dizzying upward spiral of silicon, money, hype, and idealism, the Hacker Ethic became perhaps less pure, an inevitable result of its conflict with the values of the outside world. But its ideas spread throughout the culture each time some user flicked the machine on, and the screen came alive with words, thoughts, pictures, and sometimes elaborate worlds built out of air—those computer programs which could make any man (or woman) a god.

Sometimes the purer pioneers were astounded at their progeny. Bill Gosper, for instance, was startled by an encounter in the spring of 1983. Though Gosper worked for the Symbolics company and realized that he had sold out, in a sense, by hacking in the commercial sector, he was still very much the Bill Gosper who once sat at the ninth-floor PDP-6 like some gregarious alchemist of code. You could find him in the wee hours in a second-floor room near El Camino Real in Palo Alto, his beat-up Volvo the only car in the small lot outside the nondescript two-story building which housed Symbolics' West Coast research center. Gosper, now forty, his sharp features hidden behind large wire-frame glasses and his hair knotted in a ponytail which came halfway down his back, still hacked LIFE, watching with rollicking amusement as the terminal of his LISP machine cranked through billions of generations of LIFE colonies.

"I had the most amazing experience when I went to see *Return of the Jedi,*" Gosper said. "I sat down next to this kid of fifteen or sixteen. I asked him what he did, and he said, 'Oh, I'm basically a hacker.' I almost fell over. I didn't say anything. I was completely unprepared for that. It sounded like the most arrogant thing I ever heard."

The youngster had not been boasting, of course, but describing who he was. Third Generation hacker. With many more generations to follow.

To the pioneers like Lee Felsenstein, that continuation represented a goal fulfilled. The designer of the Sol and the Osborne 1, the co-founder of Community Memory, the hero of the pseudo-Heinlein novel of his own imagination often would boast that he had been "present at the creation," and he saw the effects of the boom that followed at a close enough range to see its limitations and its subtle, significant influence. After he made his paper fortune at Osborne, he saw it flutter away just as quickly, as poor management and arrogant ideas about the marketplace caused Osborne Computer to collapse within a period of a few months in 1983. He refused to mourn his financial loss. Instead he took pride in celebrating that "the myth of the mega-machine bigger than all of us [the evil Hulking Giant, approachable only by the Priesthood] has been laid to rest. We're able to come back down off worship of the machine."

Lee Felsenstein had learned to wear a suit with ease, to court women, to charm audiences. But what mattered was still the machine, and its impact on people. He had plans for the next step. "There's more to be done," he said not long after Osborne Computer went down. "We have to find a relationship between man and machine which is much more symbiotic. It's one thing to come down from one myth, but you have to replace it with another. I think you start with the tool: the tool is the embodiment of the myth. I'm trying to see how you can explain the future that way, create the future."

He was proud that his first battle—to bring computers to the people—had been won. Even as he spoke, the Third Generation of hackers was making news, not only as superstar game designers, but as types of culture heroes who defied boundaries and explored computer systems. A blockbuster movie called *WarGames* had as its protagonist a Third Generation hacker who, having no knowledge of the groundbreaking feats of Stew Nelson or Captain Crunch, broke into computer systems with the innocent wonder of their Hands-On Imperative. It was one more example of how the computer could spread the Ethic.

"The technology has to be considered as larger than just the inanimate pieces of hardware," said Felsenstein. "The technology represents inanimate ways of *thinking,* objectified ways of thinking. The myth we see in *WarGames* and things like that is definitely the triumph of the individual over the collective dis-spirit. [The myth is] attempting to say that the conventional wisdom and common understandings must always be open to question. It's not just an academic point. It's a very fundamental point of, you might say, the survival of humanity, in a sense that you can have people [merely] survive, but *humanity* is something that's a little more precious, a little more fragile. So that to be able to defy a culture which states that 'Thou shalt not touch this,' and to defy that with one's own creative powers is . . . the essence."

The essence, of course, of the Hacker Ethic.

AFTERWORD: TEN YEARS AFTER

"I think that hackers—dedicated, innovative, irreverent computer programmers—are the most interesting and effective body of intellectuals since the framers of the U.S. Constitution . . . No other group that I know of has set out to liberate a technology and succeeded. They not only did so against the active disinterest of corporate America, their success forced corporate America to adopt their style in the end. In reorganizing the Information Age around the individual, via personal computers, the hackers may well have saved the American economy. . . . The quietest of all the '60s sub-subcultures has emerged as the most innovative and powerful . . ."

—Stewart Brand
Founder, *Whole Earth Catalog*

IN November 1984, on the damp, windswept headlands north of San Francisco, one hundred fifty canonical programmers and techno-ninjas gathered for the first Hacker Conference. Originally conceived by *Whole Earth Catalog* founder Stewart Brand, this event transformed an abandoned Army camp into temporary world headquarters for the Hacker Ethic. Not at all coincidentally, the event dovetailed with the publication of this book, and a good number of the characters in its pages turned up, in many cases to meet for the first time. First-generation MIT hackers like Richard Greenblatt hung out with Homebrew luminaries like Lee Felsenstein and Stephen Wozniak and game czars Ken Williams, Jerry Jewell, and Doug Carlston. The brash wizards of the new Macintosh computer met up with people who hacked Spacewar. Everybody slept in bunk beds, washed dishes and bussed tables, and slept minimally. For a few hours the electricity went out, and people gabbed by lantern light. When the power was restored, the rush to the computer room—where one could show off his hacks—was something probably not seen in this country since the last buffalo stampede.

I remember thinking, "These be the *real* hackers."

I was in a state of high anxiety, perched among one hundred fifty potential nit-picking critics who had been issued copies of my first book. Those included in the text immediately found their names in the index and proceeded to vet passages for accuracy and technological correctness. Those not in the index sulked, and to this day whenever they encounter me, in person or in the ether of cyberspace, they complain. Ultimately, the experience was exhilarating. The Hacker Conference, which would become an annual event, turned out to be the kickoff for a spirited and public debate, continued to this day, about the future of hacking and the Hacker Ethic as defined in this book.

The term "hacker" has always been bedeviled by discussion. When I was writing this book, the term was still fairly obscure. In fact, some months before publication, my editor told me that people in Doubleday's sales force requested a title change—"Who knows what a hacker is?" they asked. Fortunately, we stuck with the original, and by the mideighties the term had become rooted in the vernacular.

Unfortunately for many true hackers, however, the popularization of the term was a disaster. Why? The word hacker had acquired a specific and negative connotation. The trouble began with some well-publicized arrests of teenagers who electronically ventured into forbidden digital grounds, like government computer systems. It was understandable that the journalists covering these stories would refer to the young perps as hackers—after all, that's what the kids called *themselves*. But the word quickly became synonymous with "digital trespasser."

In the pages of national magazines, in television dramas and movies, in novels both pulp and prestige, a stereotype emerged: the hacker, an antisocial geek whose identifying attribute is the ability to sit in front of a keyboard and conjure up a criminal kind of magic. In these depictions, anything connected to a machine of any sort, from a nuclear missile to a garage door, is easily controlled by the hacker's bony fingers, tapping away on the keyboard of a cheap PC or a workstation. According to this definition a hacker is at best benign, an innocent who doesn't realize his true powers. At worst, he is a terrorist. In the past few years, with the emergence of computer viruses, the hacker has been literally transformed into a virulent force.

True, some of the most righteous hackers in history have been known to sneer at details such as property rights or the legal code in order to pursue the Hands-On Imperative. And pranks have always been part of hacking. But the inference that such high jinks were the essence of hacking was not just wrong, it was offensive to true hackers, whose work had changed the world, and whose methods could change the way one viewed the world. To read of talentless junior high school students logging on to computer bulletin boards, downloading system passwords or credit bureau codes, and using them to promote digital mayhem—*and have the media call them hackers . . .* well, it was just too much for people who considered themselves the real thing. They went apoplectic. The hacker community still seethes at the public burning it received in 1988 at Hacker Conference 5.0, when a reporting crew from CBS News showed up ostensibly to do a story on the glory of canonical hackers—but instead ran a piece loaded with security specialists warning of the Hacker Menace. To this day, I think that Dan Rather would be well advised to avoid attending future Hacker Conferences.

But in the past few years, I think the tide has turned. More and more people have learned about the spirit of true hacking as described in these pages. Not only are the technically literate aware of hacker ideas and ideals, but they appreciate them and realize, as Brand implied, that they are something to nurture.

Several things have contributed to this transformation. First was the computer revolution itself. As the number of people using computers grew from hundreds of thousands to hundreds of millions, the protean magic of the machine spread its implicit message, and those inclined to explore its powers, naturally sought out their antecedents.

Second was the Net. Millions of people are linked together on computer networks, with the bulk of serious hackers joining the ten million people on the confederation called the Internet. It's a pipeline connecting people to each other, facilitating collaborative projects. And it's also a hotbed of conferencing and conversation, a surprising amount of it dealing with issues arising from the Hacker Ethic and its conflicts with finances and the Real World.

Finally, true hackers became cool. Under the rubric of "cyberpunk," a term appropriated from the futuristic noir novels of smart new science fiction writers like William Gibson, Bruce Sterling, and Rudy Rucker, a new cultural movement emerged in the early 1990s. When the flagship publication of the movement, *Mondo 2000* (a name change from *Reality Hackers*) began to elucidate cyberpunk principles, it turned out that the majority of them originated in the Hacker Ethic. The implicit beliefs of MIT's Tech Model Railroad Club (Information Should Be Free, Access

to Computers Should Be Unlimited and Total, Mistrust Authority . . .)
have been shuffled to the top of the stack.

By the time cyberpunk hit the zeitgeist, the media was ready to
embrace a broader, more positive view of hacking. There were entire
publications whose point of view ran parallel to hacker principles:
Mondo 2000, and *Wired*, and loads of fanzines with names like *Intertek*
and *Boing Boing*. There was an active computer trade press written by
journalists who knew that their industry owed its existence to hackers.
Even more significant, the concepts of hackerism were embraced by
journalists at the same traditional publications whose cluelessness had
tainted hackerism to begin with.

Once people understood what motivated hackers, it was possible to
use those ideas as a measure to examine the values of Silicon Valley. At
Apple Computer in particular the hacker ideals were considered crucial
to the company's well-being . . . its very soul. Even more straitlaced
companies came to realize that if they were to lead in their fields, the
energy, vision, and problem-solving perseverance of hackers were
required. In turn, it would be required of the companies to loosen their
rules, to accommodate the freewheeling hacker style.

Best of all, these ideas began to flow beyond the computer industry
and into the culture at large. As I learned while writing *Hackers*, the
ideals of my subject could apply to almost any activity one pursued with
passion. Burrell Smith, the designer of the Macintosh computer, said it
as well as anyone in one of the sessions at the first Hacker Conference:
"Hackers can do almost anything and be a hacker. You can be a hacker
carpenter. It's not necessarily high tech. I think it has to do with
craftsmanship and caring about what you're doing."

Finally, an update of a few principal characters in *Hackers*, a decade
later.

Bill Gosper is a consultant living in Silicon Valley. He still hacks,
pursuing the secrets of mathematics, fractals, and the game of Life,
while making a living as a consultant. He is also still a bachelor,
explaining to an interviewer in the book *More Mathematical People* that
having children, or even a mate, would be problematic in that "no
matter how conscious an effort I made to give kids the attention that they
deserve, they would sense the computer was winning out."

Richard Greenblatt's Lisp Machines company got swallowed in the
corporate maw. After working as a consultant, he now runs his own
small company, devoted to making medical devices that combine voice
information and data over telephone lines. He thinks a lot about the
future of hacking, and rues the day when commercialization overwhelmed the kind of projects routinely undertaken (with government

funding) at MIT in the golden days. But, he says, "the good news is that the cost of this stuff is falling so rapidly that it's possible to do things as a quote-unquote hobby. It's possible to do serious work on your own."

Unlike some of his fellow personal computer pioneers from the Homebrew era, Lee Felsenstein never became wealthy. Though he enjoyed fame within the techno-culture, his own enterprises, conducted through his struggling Golemics company, remained marginal. Recently, however, he landed a dream job as a leading engineer at Interval, a well-funded new Silicon Valley company devoted to concocting the next generation of technical wizardry. As he approaches fifty, Lee's personal life is more settled—he's had several serious relationships and is currently living with a woman he met through the Whole Earth 'Lectronic Link computer network. He remains passionately committed to social change through computers. He has long been circulating the idea of forming a sort of digital Boy Scouts (though not gender specific) called the Hacker's League. And he still believes that Community Memory, once it gets on the network, will have an impact on the world.

Ken Williams is still chairman of Sierra On-Line. The company has had its highs and lows, but like its successful competitor Broderbund and unlike the defunct Sirius, it is bigger than ever, employing around 700 people at its Oakhurst headquarters. Sierra went public in 1992; Ken's holdings make him many times a millionaire. Sierra also has invested millions of dollars in an interactive computer-game-playing network; AT&T has purchased twenty percent of the venture. Roberta Williams is Sierra's most popular game designer, acclaimed for her King's Quest series of 3-D graphic adventure games.

Ken Williams thinks that there's little room for the old hacker spirit at Sierra. "In the early days, one person, John Harris, could do a project," Ken says. "Now, our games have fifty or more names in the credit. We don't do any products without at least a million development budget. In *King's Quest VI*, there is a seven-hundred-page script, read by over fifty professional actors. It was the single largest voice-recording project ever done in Hollywood."

Ken Williams tells me that John Harris still lives in the Oakhurst area, operating a small business selling software to generate display screens for cable television operators. According to Williams, John Harris is still writing his software for the long discontinued Atari 800 computer.

As one might expect of the last true hacker, Richard Stallman has most emphatically remained true to the ideals of the MIT Artificial Intelligence lab. His company, the Free Software Foundation, is, according to *Wired*, "the world's only charitable organization with the mission of developing free software." Stallman has also been an instrumental force in the League for Software Freedom, a group reflecting his belief that proprietary software is a pox upon the digital landscape. In 1991, his efforts came to the attention of those in charge of parceling out the coveted McArthur Fellowship "genius grants." The last time I saw him, Stallman was organizing a demonstration against the Lotus Development Corporation. His protest regarded their software patents. He believed, and still does, that information should be free.

Steven Levy
August 1993

ACKNOWLEDGMENTS

I'M indebted to many people who assisted me in various ways while I was working on *Hackers*. First, to the people who agreed to be interviewed for the book. Some were veterans of this sort of journalistic exchange; others had only spoken to interviewers on technical matters, and hadn't spoken of the personal or philosophical nature of hacking before; others just hadn't spoken to people like me. Almost all spoke freely and candidly; I think it not coincidental that hackers are as free in conversation, once they get started, as they are with sharing computer code. Many of the following consented to multiple interviews, and often follow-up calls to verify facts or clarify technical details.

My conversations with them were the backbone of the book, and I would like to thank, in alphabetical order, Arthur Abraham, Roe Adams, Bob Albrecht, Dennis Allison, Larry Bain, Alan Baum, Mike Beeler, Dorothy Bender, Bill Bennett, Chuck Benton, Bob and Carolyn Box, Keith Britton, Lois Britton, Bill Budge, Chuck Bueche, David Bunnell, Doug Carlston, Gary Carlston, Marie Cavin, Mary Ann Cleary, Bob Clements, Tracy Coats, David Crane, Edward Currie, Rick Davidson, Bob Davis, Jack Dennis, Peter Deutsch, Steve Dompier, John Draper, Dan Drew, Mark Duchaineau, Les Earnest, Don Eastlake, Doug Englebart, Chris Espinosa, Lee Felsenstein, LeRoy Finkel, Howard Franklin, Bob Frankston, Ed Fredkin, Gordon French, Martin Garetz, Harry Garland, Richard Garriott, Lou Gary, Bill Gates, Bill Godbout, Vincent Golden, Dave Gordon, Ralph Gorin, Dan Gorlin, Bill

Gosper, Richard Greenblatt, Margaret Hamilton, Eric Hammond, John Harris, Brian Harvey, Ted Hoff, Kevin Hunt, Chris Iden, Jerry Jewell, Robert Kahn, David Kidwell, Gary Kildall, Tom Knight, Joanne Koltnow, Alan Kotok, Marc LeBrun, Bob Leff, Mike Levitt, Efrem Lipkin, David Lubar, Olaf Lubeck, John McCarthy, John McKenzie, Robert Maas, Patricia Mariott, Bob Marsh, Roger Melen, Jude Milhon, Marvin Minsky, Fred Moore, Stewart Nelson, Ted Nelson, Jim Nitchals, Russ Noftsker, Kenneth Nussbacher, Rob O'Neal, Peter Olyphant, Adam Osborne, Bill Pearson, Tom Pittman, Larry Press, Malcolm Rayfield, Robert Reiling, Randy Rissman, Ed Roberts, Steve Russell, Peter Samson, Bob Saunders, Warren Schwader, Gil Segal, Vic Sepulveda, David Silver, Dan Sokol, Les Solomon, Marty Spergel, Richard Stallman, Jeff Stephenson, Ivan Strand, Jay Sullivan, Dick Sunderland, Gerry Sussman, Tom Tatum, Dick Taylor, Robert Taylor, Dan Thompson, Al Tommervik, Margot Tommervik, Mark Turmell, Robert Wagner, Jim Warren, Howard Warshaw, Joseph Weizenbaum, Randy Wigginton, John Williams, Ken Williams, Roberta Williams, Terry Winograd, Donald Woods, Steve Wozniak, and Fred Wright.

I would like to particularly thank those of the above who gave me extraordinary amounts of attention, people who include (but are not limited to) Lee Felsenstein, Bill Gosper, Richard Greenblatt, Peter Samson, Ken Williams, and Roberta Williams.

During the course of my research I was benefited by the hospitality of institutions that included the MIT Computer Science Library, the Stanford Library, the Computer Museum, the Lawrence Hall of Science, and the University of California Library.

On my travels to California and Cambridge, I benefited from the hospitality of Phyllis Coven, Art Kleiner, Bill Mandel, and John Williams. Lori Carney and others typed up thousands of pages of transcripts. Viera Morse's exacting copy editing kept me linguistically honest. Magazine editors David Rosenthal and Rich Friedman gave me work that kept me going. Good advice was given by fellow computer scribes Doug Garr, John Markoff, Deborah Wise, and members of the Lunch Group. Support and cheerleading came from my parents, my sister Diane Levy, friends Larry Barth, Bruce Buschel, Ed Kaplan, William Mooney, Randall Rothenberg, David Weinberg, and many others—they know who they are—who will have to accept this insufficient mention.

The book was also a product of the enthusiasm and patience of my agent, Pat Berens, and my editor, James Raimes, who encouraged me mightily. Those terms also apply to Teresa Carpenter, who coped magnificently with the book and its author through the long process of research and writing.

Finally, thanks to Steve Wozniak for designing that Apple II on which I wrote the book. Had it not been for the revolution which I address in *Hackers,* my labors might have continued for another year, just to get a clean draft out of my typewriter.

NOTES

The main source of information for *Hackers* was over a hundred personal interviews conducted in 1982 and 1983. Besides these, I refer to a number of written sources.

Part One

P. 23 Some of the TMRC jargon was codified by Peter Samson in the unpublished "An Abridged Dictionary of the TMRC Language," circa 1959. This was apparently the core of a hacker dictionary, kept on-line at MIT for years, which eventually was expanded to *The Hacker Dictionary* by Gus Steele et al. (New York: Harper & Row, 1983).

P. 24 Samson's poem printed in *F.O.B.*, the TMRC newsletter, Vol. VI, No. 1 (Sept. 1960).

P. 24 ". . . stories abounded . . ." See Philip J. Hilts' *Scientific Temperaments: Three Lives in Contemporary Science* (New York: Simon & Schuster, 1982).

P. 41 For IBM background, see Katharine Davis Fishman's *The Computer Establishment* (New York: Harper & Row, 1981).

P. 59 In addition to personal interviews, some information on Spacewar was gleaned from J. M. Garetz' article, "The Origin of Spacewar!" in *Creative Computing Video and Arcade Games,* as well as the same author's paper, "Spacewar: Real-time Capability of the PDP-1," presented in 1962 before the Digital Equipment Computer Users' Society, and Stewart Brand's "Spacewar: Fanatic Life and Symbolic Death Among the Computer Bums," in *Rolling Stone,* Dec. 7, 1972.

P. 67 "What the user wants . . ." McCarthy quoted from his *Time Sharing Computer Systems* (Cambridge, Mass.: MIT Press, 1962).

P. 76 How the Peg Solitaire game works is described in "Hakmem," by M. Beeler et al. (Massachusetts Institute of Technology, A.I. Lab Memo No. 239, Feb. 1972).

P. 78 Gosper's memo is part of "Hakmem," above.

P. 89 Simon is quoted from Pamela McCorduck's *Machines Who Think: A Personal Inquiry into the History and Prospects of Artificial Intelligence* (San Francisco: W. H. Freeman & Co., 1979), a book I found extremely helpful for background on the planners of the AI lab.

P. 127 Donald Eastlake's report was "ITS Status Report" (Massachusetts Institute of Technology, A.I. Lab Memo No. 238, Apr. 1972).

P. 133 Joseph Weizenbaum, *Computer Power and Human Reason* (San Francisco: W. H. Freeman & Co., 1976).

P. 142 Bruce Buchanan quoted in the "Introduction to the Memo Series of the Stanford Artificial Intelligence Laboratory" (Stanford University Heuristic Programming Project, Report No. HPP-83-25).

P. 145 Besides the "Mathematical Games" column in the October 1970 and November 1970 *Scientific American,* Martin Gardner writes at length on Conway's LIFE in his *Wheels, Life, and Other Mathematical Amusements* (New York: W. H. Freeman & Co., 1983), which mentions Gosper prominently.

Part Two

P. 157 Benway's message and other electronic missives on the system were found in Community Memory's extensive scrapbooks kept on the project.

P. 159 Felsenstein's quote from his four-page "Biographical Background Information," dated Jan. 29, 1983.

P. 160 Robert A. Heinlein, *Revolt in 2100* (New York: Signet, 1954).

P. 168 A first-person account of Albrecht's activities in the early 1960s is found in "A Modern-Day Medicine Show," *Datamation,* July 1963.

P. 170 ". . . the possibility of millions . . ." See John Kemeny, *Man and the Computer* (New York: Scribners, 1972), quoted in Robert A. Kahn, "Creative Play with the Computer: A

Course for Children," unpublished paper written for the Lawrence Hall of Science, Berkeley, California.

P. 170 ". . . dymaxion . . ." See Hugh Kenner, *Bucky: A Guided Tour of Buckminster Fuller* (New York: Morrow, 1973).

P. 172 Back issues of *PCC,* generously provided by Bob Albrecht, were particularly helpful for information about early seventies Bay Area hacking.

P. 174 Ted Nelson, *Computer Lib/Dream Machines* (self-published, distributed by The Distributors, South Bend, Ind., 1974).

P. 176 Brautigan's poem is in *The Pill Versus the Springhill Mine Disaster* (New York: Dell, Laurel, 1973). Reprinted by permission.

P. 178 ". . . a manipulator . . ." William Burroughs in *Naked Lunch* (New York: Grove Press, 1959).

P. 181 Ivan Illich, *Tools for Conviviality* (New York: Harper Colophon Books, 1973).

P. 182 ". . . in honor of the American folk hero . . ." See Felsenstein's paper, "The Tom Swift Terminal, A Convivial Cybernetic Device," *Journal of Community Communications,* June 1975.

P. 183 For background on the evolution of the microchip and its effect on the Silicon Valley, see Dirk Hansen's *The New Alchemists* (Boston: Little, Brown, 1982).

P. 198 "Moore seemed to get the money . . ." See Thomas Albright and Charles Moore, "The Last Twelve Hours of the Whole Earth," *Rolling Stone,* July 8, 1971. Maureen Orth followed up the story for *Rolling Stone* in "Whole Earth $$$ Demise Continues" (March 16, 1972).

P. 200 The leaflet was reprinted in the first issue of *Homebrew Computer Club Newsletter* (HBCCN), which I found invaluable for research in this section.

P. 236 Pittman's article was published in *The Second West Coast Computer Faire Proceedings* Jim Warren, ed., (Palo Alto: Computer Faire, 1978).

P. 240 "When [Marsh] had little else . . ." Felsenstein's article, "Sol: The Inside Story," appeared in the first issue (July 1977) of the short-lived *ROM* magazine.

P. 246 The *Esquire* article, "Secrets of the Black Box," by Ron Rosenbaum, is reprinted in his *Rebirth of the Salesman: Tales of the Song and Dance 70's* (New York: Delta, 1979).

P. 246 "The winning isn't as important . . ." An unpublished interview with journalist Doug Garr.

P. 248 Some of the Draper information was drawn from Donn Parker's *Fighting Computer Crime* (New York: Scribners, 1983).

P. 252 "Fidel Castro beard . . ." See Paul Ciotti, "Revenge of the Nerds," *California,* July 1982.

P. 266 "Prepare for blastoff . . ." See Elizabeth Fairchild, "The First West Coast Computer Faire," *ROM,* July 1977.

P. 267 Nelson's speech is reprinted in *The First West Coast Computer Faire Proceedings,* Jim Warren, ed. (Palo Alto: Computer Faire, 1977).

Part Three

P. 286 *The Carpetbaggers* (New York: Pocket Books, 1961).

P. 302 The letter was printed in *Purser's Magazine,* Winter 1981.

P. 312 "One participant later explained to a reporter . . ." The reporter was from *Softline,* another Tommervick publication, this one started with funds from the Williamses. Both *Softline* and *Softalk* provided considerable background information on the Brotherhood.

P. 325 ". . . towel designers . . ." See John F. Hubner and William F. Kistner, "What Went Wrong at Atari?"—an article reprinted in *InfoWorld,* Nov. 28, 1983, and Dec. 5, 1983. Other background on Atari from Steve Bloom's *Video Invaders* (New York: Arco, 1982).

P. 376 ". . . interviewed in an article . . ." See Lee Gnomes, "Secrets of the Software Pirates," *Esquire,* January 1982.

P. 416 "does not mean . . ." Stallman stored several "flames" (impassioned writings) on the MIT computer system, including "Essay," "Gnuz," and "Wiezenbomb." The quote is from his autobiographical "Essay."

P. 416 "that they give back all extensions . . ." From Stallman's "Essay."

P. 425 "It is painful for me . . ." "Essay."

INDEX